Debra Heller

Life-Span Development and Behavior

VOLUME 8

Life-Span Development and Behavior

VOLUME 8

Edited by

Paul B. Baltes

Max Planck Institute for
Human Development and Education
Berlin, Federal Republic of Germany

David L. Featherman

University of Wisconsin
at Madison
Madison, Wisconsin

Richard M. Lerner

The Pennsylvania State University
University Park, Pennsylvania

LAWRENCE ERLBAUM ASSOCIATES, PUBLISHERS
1988 Hillsdale, New Jersey London

Lawrence Erlbaum Associates, Inc., Publishers
365 Broadway
Hillsdale, New Jersey 07642

The Library of Congress has cataloged this work as follows:

Life-span development and behavior.
v. 1–

1978–
v. 24 cm. annual.
Key title: Life-span development and behavior, ISSN 0161-9454

1. Developmental psychology—Periodicals.
BF712.L535 155'.05 78-643797
ISBN 0-89859-950-4
Printed in the United States of America
10 9 8 7 6 5 4 3 2 1

Contents

Expression through Affect and Words in the Transition from Infancy to Language

Lois Bloom, Richard Beckwith, Joanne Bitetti Capatides and Jeremie Hafitz

Stability of Type A Behavior from Early Childhood to Young Adulthood

Laurence Steinberg

Some Implications of the Trait-State Distinction for the Study of Development over the Life-Span: The Case of Personality

John R. Nesselroade

Stability and Change in Self over the Life Course

L. Edward Wells and Sheldon Stryker

The Role of Family Experience in Career Exploration: A Life-Span Perspective

Harold D. Grotevant and Catherine R. Cooper

The Demography of Kinship and the Life Course

Susan De Vos and Steven Ruggles

Reconstruction in Cognitive Development: A Post-Structuralist Agenda

Daniel P. Keating and Darla J. MacLean

Contributors

Numbers in parentheses indicate pages on which author's contribution begins.

Richard Beckwith (99), Department of Human Development, Cognition, and Learning, Teachers College, Columbia University, New York, NY 10027

Lois Bloom (99), Department of Human Development, Cognition, and Learning, Teachers College, Columbia University, New York, NY 10027

Jochen Brandtstädter (61), Department of Psychology, University of Trier, PO Box 3825, 5500 Trier, West Germany

Joanne Bitetti Capatides (99), Department of Human Development, Cognition, and Learning, Teachers College, Columbia University, New York, NY 10027

Catherine R. Cooper (231), Department of Home Economics, University of Texas, Austin, TX 78712

Susan De Vos (259), Center for Demography and Ecology, University of Wisconsin-Madison, 1180 Observatory Drive, Madison, WI 53706

Alexander von Eye (61), S-106 College of Human Development, Pennsylvania State University, University Park, PA 16802

Harold D. Grotevant (231), Department of Home Economics, University of Texas, Austin, TX 18712

Jeremie Hafitz (99), Department of Human Development, Cognition, and Learning, Teachers College, Columbia University, New York, NY 10027

Daniel P. Keating (283), Department of Psychology, University of Maryland, Baltimore County, Catonsville, MD 21228

Darla J. MacLean (283), Department of Psychology, University of Maryland, Baltimore County, Catonsville, MD 21228

John R. Nesselroade (163), S-106 College of Human Development, Pennsylvania State University, University Park, PA 16802

Robert Plomin (1), S-110 College of Human Development, Pennsylvania State University, University Park, PA 16802

Steven Ruggles (259), Department of History, University of Minnesota, Minneapolis, MN 55455

Laurence Steinberg (129), Child and Family Studies, University of Wisconsin-Madison, 1430 Linden Drive, Madison, WI 53706

Sheldon Stryker (191), Department of Sociology, Indiana University, Bloomington, IN 47504

Lee Thompson (1), Institute for Behavioral Genetics, University of Colorado, Boulder, CO 80309

Maris A. Vinovskis (33), Department of History, University of Michigan, Ann Arbor, MI 48109-1045

L. Edward Wells (191), Department of Sociology, Indiana University, Bloomington, IN 47504

Preface

The serial publication *Life-Span Development and Behavior* is aimed at reviewing life-span research and theory in the behavioral and social sciences, with a particular focus on contributions by psychologists and sociologists. As co-editors we do not attempt to organize each volume around a particular topic or theme. Rather, we solicit manuscripts from investigators who are conducting programmatic research on current problems or who are interested in refining particular theoretical positions. Occasionally, authors are invited to identify new areas of concern worthy of theoretical articulation or exploration. The lack of a single substantive focus for any given volume resulting from our editorial policy is somewhat compensated by listing the contents of previous volumes of the series in each new volume. Thus, it is possible to link articles from the entire series along substantive or theoretical dimensions of particular interest.

The prefaces to the seven preceding volumes stated the purposes of introducing more empirical research into the field of life-span development and of increasing its interdisciplinary character. These two purposes are reaffirmed in the current volume. Life-span research on human development contributes to a variety of intellectual positions, some of which deserve particular elaboration at this time.

First, in the past few years research and theory in life-span development have given increased attention to the issue of constancy and change in human development and to the issue of opportunities for and constraints on plasticity in structure and function across life. For example, the assumption that the experiences of infancy and early childhood have a lasting and generalized effect on adulthood and personality is under increasing challenge by careful studies of the effects of early experiences, the results of which have not been entirely supportive of the simple view of continuity. In turn, research involving biological and cognitive processes has shown, at several portions of life (e.g., infancy, adolescence, the aged years), that the directions and outcomes of development are more open than believed on the basis of previous available evidence. A life-span approach, then, acknowledges the need for and existence of interconnection between age and developmental periods. It also focuses on conditions for possibly discontinuous development that emerge at later periods and exhibit less generality in terms of sequencing and occurrence than is true for many facets of child development such as physical and cognitive growth. A concern with nonnormative and atypical life events as major contributing factors to life-span change are cases in point.

Second, life-span development scholars are sensitive to the restrictive consequences of studying only specific age periods such as old age, infancy, or adolescence. A life-span development view encourages each scholar to relate the facts about one age group to similar facts about other age groups, and to move toward the study of transformation of characteristics and processes over the life span. A third issue of high salience in current life-span research is the relationship between individual development, the social context, and historical change. Particular social institutions and the course of history influence life patterns of different birth cohorts, and we see that each birth cohort has features of uniqueness because it shares the experience of certain events and conditions at the same age as it moves through its lifetime. These perspectives and others are evident in the articles in this volume and others of the Series (see listing of content of previous volumes).

The co-editors also wish to acknowledge with gratitude and respect the contributions of many colleagues who assisted as consultants in making Volume 8 what it is. In addition to our regular roster of advisory editors, a number of ad hoc reviewers provided valuable comments and suggestions to the contributors before final chapters were prepared. They are:

Gerald R. Adams
Diana Baumrind
Doug Behrend
Vern L. Bengtson
Avshalom Caspi
Clifford C. Clogg
Steven W. Cornelius
Alexander von Eye
Lynne Feagans
Terryl T. Foch
Nancy Howell
Denise Kandel
David I. Kertzer
Margie Lachman
Jacqueline V. Lerner
David Magnusson
Gerald Marwell
Robert McCrae
Suzanne Miller
John Modell
John R. Nesselroade
Adam Niemczynski
Willis F. Overton
David S. Palermo
Sally I. Powers
Morris Rosenberg
Sandra Scarr
Roberta Simmons
M. Brewster Smith
Laurence D. Steinberg
Ralph Turner
Peter Uhlenberg
Susan Watkins
Alan S. Waterman
Ronald S. Wilson
Christopher Winship

Our special thanks go to Silvia Sörensen and Amy Michèle for their outstanding editorial assistance, and to Val Kelley, Jackie English, and Teri Charmbury for their splendid secretarial work.

Paul B. Baltes
David L. Featherman
Richard M. Lerner

Contents of Previous Volumes

VOLUME 1

VOLUME 2

VOLUME 3

VOLUME 6

VOLUME 7

Life-Span Development and Behavior

VOLUME 8

Life-Span Developmental Behavioral Genetics

Robert Plomin[1] *and Lee Thompson*
INSTITUTE FOR BEHAVIORAL GENETICS
UNIVERSITY OF COLORADO
BOULDER, COLORADO

Abstract

The exciting possibilities of combining developmental behavioral genetics and life-span developmental psychology are explored in this chapter. Behavioral genetics focuses on genetic and environmental origins of individual differences; developmental behavioral genetics combines behavioral genetics with a developmental orientation that considers change as well as continuity during development. The first half of the chapter consists of a description of quantitative genetic theory and methods that underlie developmental behavioral genetics. In the second half of the chapter, mutual interests of developmental behavioral genetics and life-span developmental psychology are discussed and relevant research is summarized in terms of broad principles of life-span developmental behavioral genetics.

In the first *Annual Review of Psychology* chapter on life-span developmental psychology, Baltes, Reese, and Lipsitt (1980) concluded: "The speed and intensity of the growth of the field during the last decade has been impressive. Yet it is also obvious that much of the work has been conceptual and methodological rather than empirical. Although this is perhaps a natural stage in any rapidly developing field, we believe that a stronger infusion of empirical life-span work

[1]Currently in the Department of Individual and Family Studies, Pennsylvania State University

is now imperative.'' (p. 101) The purpose of this chapter is to suggest that the field of behavioral genetics is likely to make important empirical contributions to life-span developmental psychology and that behavioral genetics has much to gain from the conceptual advances of life-span developmental psychology. The two fields differ in important ways; however, these differences add to the exciting possibilities for hybrids produced by cross-fertilization between the two fields.

The chapter is divided into three parts: (1) a review of quantitative genetic theory and methods that provide the foundation of behavioral genetics, (2) a brief description of two approaches to the study of genetic change and continuity, which is the focus of the new interdiscipline of developmental behavioral genetics; and (3) speculations concerning the interface between developmental behavioral genetics and life-span developmental psychology.

I. Behavioral Genetics

It is necessary to consider the theory and methods underlying behavioral genetics in order to understand possible points of contact between behavioral genetics and life-span developmental psychology. The single most important issue is that behavioral genetics focuses on variance among individuals in a population.

A. VARIANCE

Behavioral genetics does not address the causes of universal or species-typical behavior, the causes of average differences between groups within a population, or average (normative) developmental trends. Its goal is to describe inter-individual variability in a population and to ascribe this variance to genetic and environmental influences. *Genetic influence* refers to variance that arises because of DNA variation and *environmental influence* refers to all other sources of variance, including an immense range of influences from variations in the cytoplasm of the primordial zygote cell and prenatal influences to life events such as entering school, starting one's own family, and retirement. Before this century has ended, it is likely that we will be able to make direct assessments of genetic variation among individuals by studying the 3.5 billion nucleotide bases of DNA. Until then, we must resort to the indirect methods of quantitative genetics that compare pairs of relatives who differ in their genetic or environmental relatedness in order to assess genetic influence, as described later.

The normative and individual-differences perspectives can be thought of in terms of the distinction between means and variances. The well-known evolutionary biologist, Ernst Mayr (1982), considers these two approaches as different world views. The former view, which Mayr calls essentialism, sees things in terms of their essence, as physicists view atomic particles. In biology, an essentialist looks at members of a species as representatives of a common type. In contrast, Mayr argues that biology must recognize the uniqueness of individuals within a species; without variation among individual members of the species, evolution cannot occur.

It usually is difficult to disagree with suggestions for rapprochement between different approaches; McCall (1979) has made this argument specifically for the instance of individual differences and normative approaches in development. McCall is certainly correct in saying that developmentalists must eventually understand both means and variances. However, at this time, we would argue that it is important to maintain the distinction between these approaches and that more theory and research on individual differences are needed. In terms of applying developmental research to the world outside our laboratories, it is individual-differences research that is needed because it is to individuals that such research must be applied.

It is important to maintain the distinction between means and variances in order to avoid confusion in description and explanation. Descriptions of means and variances are independent. For example, from 12 to 24 months, infants increase in height by 15% and in weight by 25% on the average. However, these dramatic average changes in height and weight are accompanied by stable rank orders of individuals' height and weight: The correlation for height and weight is about .70 from 12 to 24 months. In this example, group averages show substantial change across age, whereas rank orders of individuals' differences show substantial age-to-age stability. Examples of the reverse situation—means that do not change across age and substantial change in the rank order of individual differences—also occur (for example, for some aspects of personality) because the description of means and variances are independent. Similarly, explanations of means bear no necessary relationship to explanations of individual differences. For example, the rapid average increase in cognitive capabilities during infancy seems likely to be due to maturational events highly canalized at the species level, yet individual differences in infant mental development appear to be largely attributable to differential environmental experiences (Scarr, 1976). Another example is that mean performance on cognitive tests can be improved by training (Baltes & Willis, 1982), although the rank order of individuals may remain largely unchanged and substantially due to genetic differences among individuals.

Confusion between the normative and individual-differences perspectives has led to errors of interpretation in research. For example, language researchers have mistakenly used individual differences data on the relationship between language-learning environments and language acquisition to address the question of the innateness of language use in the human species (see the discussion by

Hardy–Brown, 1983). Some aspect of differences among language-learning environments, such as contingent vocal responsiveness, may be shown to relate to individual differences in language acquisition; however, this individual-differences analysis has no bearing on the question of why the human species is a natural language user. In other words, the causes of individual differences within a population have no necessary relationship to the causes of typical performance of the population as a whole. Moreover, confusion between the two approaches is responsible for some misguided antipathy toward behavioral genetics; for example, heritability (the relationship between genetic differences among individuals and observed individual differences in a population) has been mistakenly assumed to imply innateness (hard-wired, species-wide genetic determination that is impervious to environmental influence).

The major conceptual leap that needs to be made in order to appreciate behavioral genetics is from a normative to an individual-differences perspective, consideration of "the very standard deviation." However, this leap involves some hurdles. Compared with the study of means, the study of variance is more demanding psychometrically; for example, reliability of measurement is a paramount concern. It also employs different statistics—the statistics of individual differences, which focus on variance rather than treating individual differences as "error variance" in analyses of mean differences among groups. Once the leap to an individual-differences perspective is accomplished, it is a small step to recognize the usefulness of behavioral genetics.

B. QUANTITATIVE GENETIC THEORY

Although life-span theory considers both means and variances (Baltes & Nesselroade, 1984), empirical work has tended to be normative in the sense that researchers describe and attempt to explain the average developmental sequence of our species. Life-span studies of individual differences tend to be rare and atheoretical, with the exception of sociological contributions involving gender, class, and ethnicity. However, the quantitative genetic theory that underlies the methods of behavioral genetics provides one important theoretical approach to individual differences. Ignoring the philosophical intricacies of the word *theory,* from the pragmatic view of a researcher, theories should clarify our thinking by describing, predicting, and explaining behavior. At a minimum, a theory should be descriptive—organizing and condensing already-existing facts in a reasonable, internally consistent manner. It should also make predictions concerning phenomena not yet investigated and permit clear tests of these predictions. At their best, theories explain phenomena as well as describe and predict them. We suggest that quantitative genetic theory provides an individual-differences theory of scope and power rarely seen in the behavioral sciences.

Quantitative genetic theory emerged in the early 1900s from disagreements between Mendelians who rediscovered Mendel's laws of inheritance and so-called biometricians. The biometricians felt that Mendel's laws, derived from experiments with qualitative characteristics in pea plants, were not applicable to complex characteristics in higher organisms that are nearly always distributed quantitatively on a normal, bell-shaped curve. When Ronald Fisher (1918) put the finishing touches on the resolution to the dispute, quantitative genetic theory was born. The essence of quantitative genetic theory is that Mendel's mechanisms of discrete inheritance also apply to normally distributed complex characteristics if we assume that many genes, each with a small effect, add up to produce observable differences among individuals in a population. If more than three or four genes affect a trait, the observed distribution cannot be distinguished from a normal curve. For example, a trait influenced by two alleles at each of three loci yields 27 different genotypes. Even if the alleles at the different loci equally affect the trait and there is no environmental variation, seven different phenotypes will be observed and the resulting distribution will be very difficult to distinguish from a normal curve. Each of the alleles is transmitted according to the laws of inheritance established by Mendel, and each allele codes and controls the production of polypeptides according to the central dogma of molecular genetics. Quantitative genetic theory speaks to the "bottom line" of genetic variability as it affects phenotypic variability regardless of the molecular complexity of the genetic or physiological processes that intervene between DNA and development.

Although molecular genetics, single-gene analyses, and chromosomal analyses also are important genetic approaches, we limit this chapter to quantitative genetics because it is most appropriate for the study of normal variation in the development of complex behaviors likely to show the influence of environmental as well as genetic factors. In fact, significant variation in complex characters is very seldom attributable to a single gene. This statement is not contradicted by the existence of many single-gene mutations and chromosomal anomalies that seriously disrupt normal development: These simple genetic effects rarely account for a significant portion of variance in a population. For example, children with a double dose of the recessive allele for phenylketonuria (PKU) are unable to metabolize phenylalanine so that it builds up to amounts that are damaging to the developing brain, causing severe retardation unless the child is given a diet low in phenylalanine. However, only about 1 in 20,000 children has a double dose of the PKU allele. Carriers for the recessive allele are much more common, approximately 1 in 50 individuals, and some evidence suggests that these carriers may have slightly lower IQs than individuals who do not have the PKU allele (Bessman, Williamson, & Koch, 1978); even so, the PKU gene does not contribute a detectable amount of variability to the distribution of IQ scores in the general population.

Any one of many genes can disrupt development, but the normal range of behavioral variation is likely to be orchestrated by a system of many genes, each with small effect, as well as by environmental influences, as seen in mutation analyses of bacteria, paramecia, nematodes, and *Drosophila*. For example, at least 40 genes are involved in normal swimming in bacteria, yet any one of these genes can seriously alter their swimming (Parkinson, 1977). An example closer to home is the human brain. It has been estimated that the adult brain contains 100 billion neurons, each with approximately 1500 synapses, and that at each synapse there are a million receptor molecules, including more than 30 classical neurotransmitters and 200 other neuropeptides (Cowan, 1979; Snyder, 1980). Even though these neurotransmitters and neuropeptides are directly coded by DNA, how likely is it that the activity of any neuron or group of neurons (let alone the effect of neuronal activity on behavior) is significantly determined by a single major gene?

The fundamental point of quantitative genetic theory is that genetic differences among individuals can lead to phenotypic (observed) differences even when many genes and many environmental factors are involved. The essence of quantitative genetic theory is the specification of genetic and environmental sources of phenotypic resemblance expected for different types of family relationships (Falconer, 1981). These differential expectations for the covariance of relatives lead directly to methods that can be used to estimate the relative contributions of genetic and environmental influences to variance of a trait in a population. These methods are discussed in the following section.

C. QUANTITATIVE GENETIC METHODS

As in all experimentation, when two factors potentially influence a dependent variable, the effects of one factor are studied while the other factor is randomized or controlled in some way.

Twin Method. The classical twin design comparing phenotypic resemblances of identical and fraternal twin pairs is based on the assumption that both types of twins, because members of a pair are reared in the same family, share family environmental influences that potentially make the twin partners similar. However, the two types of twins differ dramatically in terms of genetic components of covariance. Identical twin partners are genetically identical to each other, whereas fraternal twins are about 50% similar, on the average, for segregating genes; assortative mating could increase this similarity a bit, and nonadditive genetic variance could lower it somewhat. Thus, if heredity affects a trait, the essentially twofold greater genetic similarity of identical twins will make them more similar phenotypically than are fraternal twins. If identical and fraternal twin correlations do not differ, then heredity does not have important effects on the trait. All experiments have possible confounds; for example, in the twin method, it is possible that identical twins experience more similar family environments than do fraternal twins. If this were the case, some of the greater observed similarity of identical twins might be due to greater similarity of their experiences. Results of research on this possible confounding effect suggest that it is not a problem for the twin design (Plomin, DeFries, & McClearn, 1980).

Adoption Method. Adoption designs are particularly powerful. In nonadoptive families, quantitative genetic theory predicts resemblance among relatives to the extent that heredity is important; however, the fact that these family members also share the same family environment makes it possible that observed familial resemblance is due to shared environmental experiences as well as genetic influences. Adoption designs separate these two types of influence on familial resemblance. Genetic background can be randomized while the effects of family environment are evaluated by studying pairs of genetically unrelated individuals in the same adoptive family. Similarly, family environment can be randomized while the effects of heredity are assessed by studying pairs of genetically related individuals reared in different families. The resemblance found in the adoptive families in which family environment is shared and the resemblance found for adopted-apart relatives for whom heredity is shared should sum to the resemblance observed in nonadoptive families in which both family environment and heredity are shared.

A possible confound in the adoption design is selective placement, matching the adoptive and biological backgrounds of adoptees. Selective placement complicates the separation of genetic and environmental influences: Because the phenotypes of the biological and adoptive relatives of adoptees are correlated in the presence of selective placement, some of the apparent genetic resemblance between individuals and their adopted-away relatives could be mediated environmentally. In the same way, some of the ostensibly environmental similarity between adoptive relatives could be mediated genetically. Fortunately, the extent of selective placement can be assessed and its effects on genetic and environmental estimates can be taken into account.

Effect Size. In addition to providing means of estimating the statistical significance of genetic and environmental influences on observed variance in a population, quantitative genetic methods can also be used to estimate the size of genetic and environmental effects in producing variation among individuals (not means). *Heritability* is the extent to which genetic influence accounts for phenotypic variance, and *environmentality* is the proportion of phenotypic variance that is due to environmental variance. For example, a significant correlation between identical twins reared apart in uncorrelated environments implies significant genetic influence on a trait because identical twins reared apart resemble each other solely for genetic reasons, not because they shared the same family environment. The twin correlation represents the proportion of variance that covaries between the twins. Twin covariance for identical twins represent total genetic variance because identical twins are identical genetically. Thus, the correlation for identical twins reared apart directly estimates heritability, the proportion of phenotypic variance that is due to genetic variance. For example, if a trait yielded a correlation of .50 for identical twins reared apart, heritability would be estimated as 50%. Familial correlations are not squared—the issue is the extent to which family members covary, not the extent to which one family member's score can be predicted from another family member's score, in which case correlations would be squared to determine variance explained (Ozer, 1985).

Correlations for first-degree relatives adopted apart are doubled to estimate heritability because first-degree relatives only covary 50% genetically. For example, if the correlation between first-degree relatives adopted apart is .25, heritability would be estimated to be 50%. The twin method estimates genetic influence by comparing identical and fraternal twin correlations for twins reared together. Significant genetic influence is suggested when identical twin correlations significantly exceed fraternal twin correlations. Heritability is estimated by doubling the difference between the identical and fraternal twin correlations because this difference estimates the proportion of phenotypic variance due to half of the additive genetic variance—identical twins share all of the additive genetic variance, whereas fraternal twins share only half. For example, if the correlation for identical twins is .50 and the correlation for fraternal twins is .25, heritability would be estimated to be 50%. All of these estimates of 50% heritability imply that the remaining half of the phenotypic variance is due to environmental factors. It should be emphasized that heritability and environmentality are descriptive statistics and thus will change as the relative contributions of genetic and environmental influences change over time or in different populations. These statistics imply no more precision than do other descriptive statistics; as for all descriptive statistics, standard errors of estimate need to be consulted to evaluate precision. Again, heritability implies neither immutability nor level of possible outcome. It simply refers to the proportion of observed interindividual variance in a population that is due to genetic differences among individuals within the population's particular genetic and environmental context.

A more powerful analytical strategy uses model-fitting approaches that analyze data from different kinships simultaneously, make assumptions explicit, and permit tests of the relative fit of different models. Path models were developed by Sewall Wright (1931) to address quantitative genetic issues; subsequent applications of models incorporate assortative mating and selective placement parameters and employ procedures that explicitly evaluate the fit between the model and the observed data (see Loehlin, 1978, 1979).

II. Developmental Behavioral Genetics

The new interdiscipline, developmental behavioral genetics, moves the field of behavioral genetics closer to a life-span orientation. The fundamental tenet of developmental behavioral genetics is that genes produce change as well as continuity during development (Plomin, 1983; 1986a). Similarly, the environmental contexts within which genetic effects are studied also change with age. One reason why developmental behavioral genetics has a promising future is that it will inherit the effort, energy, and excitement of molecular geneticists' recent focus on development (Scarr & Kidd, 1983). The key issue in molecular genetics today is genetic regulation of short-term changes and, especially, of long-term changes that are responsible for developmental differentiation. How does an individual begin life as a single cell and, in a few months' time, become a complex differentiated organism with trillions of specialized cells, each containing the same DNA? All that is known with confidence is that development is complex: Recent advances in research with eukaryotes (organisms with nuclei in their cells) have led to the discovery of regulatory processes far more complicated than the classic operon model of gene regulation (Jacob & Monod, 1961) that is based on studies of bacteria.

One conceptual advance in understanding genetic change during development is the realization that there are no genes that code for development in the literal sense—there is no separate set of genes to code for development in childhood, adolescence, or adulthood, even though certain genes may exert their effects during specific phases of the life span. In other words, DNA has no explicit representation of each developmental phase in the life span of an organism. Rather, a series of genetic changes eventuates in developmental steps that culminate in a reproducing adult. Sydney Brenner, who initiated developmental genetic research in the roundworm, put it bluntly in a recent interview (Lewin, 1984):

> At the beginning it was said that the answer to the understanding of development was going to come from a knowledge of the molecular mechanisms of gene control. . . . I doubt whether anyone believes that anymore. The molecular mechanisms look boringly simple, and they don't tell us what we want to know. We have to try to discover the principles of organization, how lots of things are put together in the same place. I don't think these principles will be embodied in a simple chemical device, as it is for the genetic code. (p. 1327)

For example, a thousand complex molecules must be synthesized in a specific sequence during the half-hour life cycle of bacteria. It used to be assumed that this sequential synthesis was programmed genetically, perhaps by assembling the proper sequence of enzymes as a single coordinated unit so that component enzymes would pass efficiently from one step to another. However, the developmental system is not efficient in this hard-wired sense; the sequence of steps is probabilistic, not programmed. In other words, there is no code for the specific sequence of enzymes needed for development in bacteria; rather, it seems to be a case of "this leads to that." Development is the jerry-built result of millions of small evolutionary experiments throughout the life span in an attempt to sculpt an efficient and effective reproducing organism in its age-graded and history-graded context.

Although quantitative genetic theory is usually phrased in terms of structural genes (DNA that codes for enzymes and proteins), quantitative genetics is just as relevant to the study of genetic variability that arises from gene regulation (primarily DNA that codes for products that regulate expression of structural genes or DNA such as promoters that affect gene expression in other ways). In this sense, behavioral genetics will remain one major step ahead of molecular genetics. Behavioral genetic research detects trait-relevant genetic variability which arises from any of the DNA factors, regardless of whether these factors have been discovered or understood by molecular geneticists. Even when the function of genetic phenomena, such as transposable genes and repetitive DNA sequences, is understood, we will be a long way from understanding the relationship between individual differences in these genetic systems and individual differences in behavior. In contrast, behavioral genetics begins at the "bottom line" by assessing the total impact of genetic variability on behavioral traits. Developmental molecular genetics makes it clear that many opportunities exist for genetic change during development; developmental behavioral genetics charts changes in the impact of such genetic influences during the course of development. The relationship between molecular genetics and developmental behavioral genetics has been discussed in greater detail elsewhere (Plomin, 1986a).

From the perspective of developmental behavioral genetics, genetic change can be viewed in two major ways: as changes across age in the relative magnitude of genetic and environmental contributions to variance in a particular characteristic, and as age-to-age changes in genetic covariance during development.

A. DEVELOPMENTAL CHANGES IN HERITABILITY

When we say that heritability can change during development, we mean that the relative magnitudes of genetic and environmental influences on interindividual variability can change. As emphasized earlier, heritability estimates only address individual differences, not group differences. With regard to the twin method, a change in heritability is implied by a change in the difference between identical and fraternal twin correlations. A larger difference between identical and fraternal twin correlations implies greater heritability. Developmental changes in heritability do not implicate molecular mechanisms of change. For example, heritability could increase from one age to another even if the same genes were actively transcribed at both ages: If environmental variance declines during development, genetic variance accounts for a relatively larger portion of the phenotypic variance. Conversely, heritability could remain the same for a particular trait at two ages, yet completely different sets of genes could be transcribed, for reasons described in the next section.

Although developmental changes in heritability are not especially informative for molecular geneticists, it could be useful for psychologists to know, for example, that—for a particular population with that population's blend of environmental and genetic influences at that point in history—variance in a trait of interest is entirely due to environmental variance early in development and then becomes increasingly affected by genetic variance as development proceeds. Although few developmentalists have considered the issue of developmental change in heritability, most would probably guess the reverse to be closer to the truth: As children develop, they experience more diverse environments and thus environmental variance will increasingly account for phenotypic variance. In other words, heritability will decrease during development. This is the explicit position of Soviet developmentalists (Mangan, 1982). However, when developmental changes in heritability have been found, they have so far occurred in the opposite direction: Heritability increases during development (Plomin, 1986a).

The earliest twin studies (Galton, 1875; Merriman, 1924; Thorndike, 1905) considered developmental change in twin resemblance by dividing their twin samples into younger and older pairs; differential change in twin resemblance for identical and fraternal twins was not assessed. However, a far more powerful method for analyzing changes in heritability during development is hierarchical multiple regression, a method that can be used to determine whether twin resemblance differs as a function of both age and twin zygosity (Ho, Foch, & Plomin, 1980).

B. AGE-TO-AGE GENETIC CORRELATIONS

Developmental change in heritability, as described in the previous section, is a cross-sectional concept. The second concept of genetic change addresses the genetic contribution to longitudinal, age-to-age change and continuity. Age-to-age genetic correlations indicate the extent to which genetic effects at one age are correlated with genetic effects at another age (Plomin & DeFries, 1981). A genetic correlation of 1.0 means that genetic effects correlate completely between the two ages. In other words, whatever effects genetic differences among individuals have on a particular trait at one age, they have the same effects at another age. This does not necessarily mean that the same genes are actively expressed at both ages—it may be, for example, that the relevant genes have an irreversible effect early in development which continues to affect the trait throughout life. A genetic correlation of zero implies that completely different sets of genetic factors affect individual differences on the trait at the two ages. Age-to-age environmental correlations can be conceptualized in a similar manner. Genetic and environmental correlations are critical concepts in developmental behavioral genetics because they indicate the extent to which developmental change and continuity for particular traits are mediated genetically or environmentally. Space does not permit a detailed description of these important concepts; what follows is a brief overview of material that is discussed in detail elsewhere (Plomin, 1986a).

The concept of developmental genetic and environmental correlations involves a simple extension of multivariate analysis to the longitudinal case. Basically, any behavioral genetic design that can be employed to estimate genetic and environmental components of the variance of a single trait can also be used to estimate genetic and environmental components of the covariance between two traits (Plomin & DeFries, 1979) and between two ages (Plomin & DeFries, 1981; see Fig. 1). Using the twin method as an example, suppose longitudinal data were obtained for a large sample of twins. Instead of correlations between one twin's score at one age and the twin partner's score at the same age, age-to-age cross-correlations can be calculated. A cross-correlation is the correlation between one twin's score at one age and the other twin's score at the other age. In the usual univariate analysis, doubling the difference between identical and fraternal twin correlations estimates heritability, the proportion of phenotypic variance that can be accounted for by genetic variance, as explained earlier. In longitudinal analyses of age-to-age twin cross-correlations, doubling the difference between identical and fraternal twin cross-correlations estimates the genetic contribution to phenotypic stability, the heritability of stability (Plomin, 1986b). As illustrated in the path diagram in Fig. 1, this genetic contribution to phenotypic stability is the product of the genetic correlation between the two ages and the square roots of the heritabilities at the two ages, which standardizes the genetic covariance in terms of its contribution to phenotypic variance. Thus, the genetic correlation itself can be estimated by dividing the genetic contribution by the product of the square roots of the heritabilities at the two ages.

The genetic correlation answers some questions and the heritability of stability answers others. If one's goal is to assess the extent to which phenotypic stability of interindividual differences across ages is mediated genetically, the appropriate term is the heritability of stability. The genetic correlation itself is also of considerable interest in developmental behavioral genetics. The genetic correlation indicates the extent to which genetic effects on individual differences overlap at

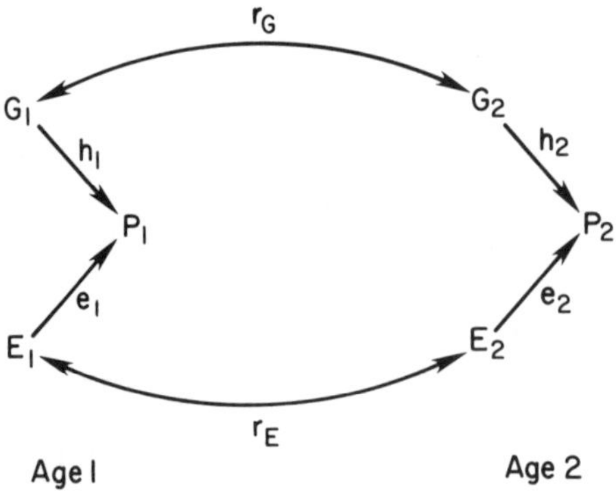

Fig. 1. The phenotypic correlation between longitudinal measurements of a trait can be mediated genetically and environmentally. Adapted from Plomin and DeFries (1981).

two ages, regardless of their relative contribution to phenotypic variance. The genetic correlation can be substantial even though heritabilities are low.

For example, suppose phenotypic stability is a moderate .50, and the identical and fraternal twin correlations for the trait at both ages are .75 and .50, respectively. This pattern of twin correlations suggests a heritability of 50% at each age. However, this does not imply that phenotypic stability between the two ages is mediated genetically to any extent—that depends on the genetic correlation. If the identical twin cross-correlation is .40 and the fraternal twin cross-correlation is .275, heredity is responsible for only half of the phenotypic stability and the genetic correlation between the two ages is .50. This example implies genetic change as well as continuity of individual differences from Age 1 to Age 2. The remaining half of the phenotypic stability of individual differences can be attributed to environmental factors, and the environmental correlation between the two ages is .50. (For details of these calculations, see Plomin, 1986a).

A recent longitudinal twin study of height and weight in adulthood provides an example of these concepts. Albert Stunkard and his colleagues (Stunkard, Foch, & Hrubec, 1985) obtained height and weight data on 1975 pairs of male identical twins and 2097 pairs of male fraternal twins when they were inducted into the U.S. military at the average age of 20. The twins reported their height and weight 25 years later. The twin correlations for height were quite similar at 20 and 45 years and suggest heritabilities of individual differences of about 80% at both ages. Considerable confidence can be attached to these estimates of heritability because in samples of this size and with twin correlations of this magnitude, standard errors of heritability estimates are only about .04. Heritabilities of individual differences of about 80% were also found for weight at both ages. Twin cross-correlations from 20 to 45 years were calculated and the differences in cross-correlations for identical and fraternal twins were used to estimate genetic correlations between 20 and 45 years. For height, the genetic correlation between 20 and 45 years was .97, indicating that genetic effects on individual differences in height at 20 years covary completely with genetic effects on height at 45 years. The environmental correlation between 20 and 45 years was also high (.60). However, environmental variance scarcely affects height; thus, the phenotypic stablity of individual differences between 20 and 45 years for height ($r = .89$) is mediated almost entirely by genetic continuity. Phenotypic stability was lower for weight ($r = .65$), and the genetic correlation between 20 and 45 was also lower (.74). This finding suggests that heredity exerts somewhat different effects on individual differences in weight at 20 and 45. The environmental correlation between the two ages also was low for weight ($r = .27$).

Although analyses of genetic and environmental correlations will become a hallmark of developmental behavioral genetic analyses in the future, few longitudinal behavioral genetic studies have been conducted and little is known as yet about the extent to which genetic factors mediate change and continuity of individual differences in development. In fact, in addition to the Skodak and Skeels (1949) adoption study of IQ, there are only two long-term longitudinal genetic studies. One is the Louisville Twin Study (Wilson, 1983); the other is the Colorado Adoption Project (Plomin & DeFries, 1985). They complement each other: The twin design provides estimates of genetic parameters for the same-aged sibling relationship of twins, whereas the parent–offspring adoption design, from a genetic perspective, is an ''instant'' longitudinal study from infancy to adulthood. Together, data from the two studies point to a surprising model of developmental genetics based on the concept of genetic correlation and discussed later as the ''amplification'' model.

III. Life-Span Behavioral Genetics

In the last half of this chapter, possible nodes of contact between life-span developmental psychology and developmental behavioral genetics will be considered. However, because the territory of life-span developmental behavioral genetics has just begun to be explored, we cannot offer a detailed map of the terrain.

Three general examples of benefits that will accrue to behavioral genetics from continued impact of life-span concepts include: (1) collection of data during adulthood and senescence, (2) consideration of cohort effects, and (3) concern with life events. A major theme of life-span developmental psychology is its insistence that development continues beyond adolescence; development is a lifelong process. This proposition is especially relevant to developmental behavioral genetics because so little is known about individual differences in adults, at least beyond early adulthood, and next to nothing is known about the etiology of differences among elderly individuals. The second example involves the long-term perspective of life-span developmentalists that extends beyond the life span of the individual to consider historical change, such as cohort effects. As discussed later, the possibility of historical change has rarely been considered in behavioral genetics. Samples in behavioral genetic research usually include such narrow ranges of cohorts that history-graded variance is essentially excluded from the phenotypic variance in these analyses. A third example is that a life-span orientation attenuates the hegemony of chronological age in studies of development. For instance, the rapid changes of early adolescence might be better understood if studied in the context of stages of physical maturation rather than chronological age. The relationship between development and chronological age becomes weaker as life goes on; in gerontology, chronological age bears only a weak relationship to biological aging. However, the few extant developmental behavioral genetic studies have focused on chronological age. Furthermore, behavioral geneticists tend to assess the same cognitive and personality traits throughout the life span, rather than studying behaviors important in the context of life events.

A. HYPOTHETICAL LIFE-SPAN PROFILE OF INFLUENCES

Another needed emphasis of life-span developmental psychology is its pluralistic conception of development. For many developmental psychologists, development has been viewed as growth—unidirectional and cumulative changes such as the unfolding of Piagetian stages of cognitive development. In contrast, life-span adherents suggest that developmental processes differ in terms of onset, duration, termination, and directionality.

At the level of explanation, researchers with a life-span perspective also attempt to be pluralistic in terms of considering normative and nonnormative influences as well as biological and environmental influences (e.g., Baltes, 1979). Two types of normative factors have been emphasized. *Normative age-graded* influences are those environmental and biological influences that are strongly related to chronological age. The novel addition of the approach is consideration of *normative history-graded* influences such as cohort effects that are associated with historical time rather than chronological age. *Nonnormative* influence refers to ''biological and environmental determinants that do not occur in any normative age-graded or history-graded manner for most individuals'' (Baltes, Reese, & Lipsitt, 1980, p. 76). Although ''biological'' is included in the definition of nonnormative life events, the examples used most often to describe such influences are environmental life events such as career changes, divorce, and accidents (Callahan & McCluskey, 1983).

Although life-span research ''has explicitly and consistently demonstrated concern for interindividual variation within each of the components of influence'' and assumes that ''genes and environments are part and parcel of all three systems'' (Baltes & Nesselroade, 1984, pp. 843–844), behavioral genetic analyses of genetic and environmental influences on interindividual differences appear to be relevant primarily to the nonnormative component. Most behavioral genetic studies, by necessity, focus on individuals from a narrow cohort. Furthermore, variance due to age is controlled statistically or by subject selection because average age effects cannot be assigned to either genetic or environmental components of variance. In other words, variance due to age and cohort exist in the population but not in most behavioral genetic samples. For example, if a sample represents only a narrow cohort, variance due to cohort will be negligible. One implication for life-span research is that the results of behavioral genetic analyses cannot be generalized beyond the age and historical context of their samples.

In this sense, the results of behavioral genetic studies of individual differences do not bear on normative issues of cohort and age. For this reason, in the following discussion, we use the phrase *nonnormative* as a synonym for individual differences, although life-span researchers would disagree with this restricted use of the word (P. Baltes, personal communication). Fortunately, the value of the following discussion does not rest on the validity of this interpretation of the words "normative" and "nonnormative."

Baltes (1979) has suggested a prototypical pattern of the roles played by age-graded, history-graded, and nonnormative life events, as shown in Fig. 2. Normative age-graded influences are thought to peak in childhood and show a second lesser peak in advanced old age. The hypothesized peak in childhood is predicted by the view that species-typical canalization weakens as children develop (McCall, 1979). The hypothesized secondary peak of normative, age-graded influence in advanced old age is quite speculative, emerging from notions of "a genetically based program of dying" (Baltes et al., 1980, p. 78).

The role of history-graded influences is thought to be strongest in adolescence and early adulthood when societal and intergenerational factors have their greatest impact. Nonnormative life events are thought to increase throughout the life span as "significant life events take on a more and more important role in determining the course of human development" (Baltes et al., 1980, p. 78).

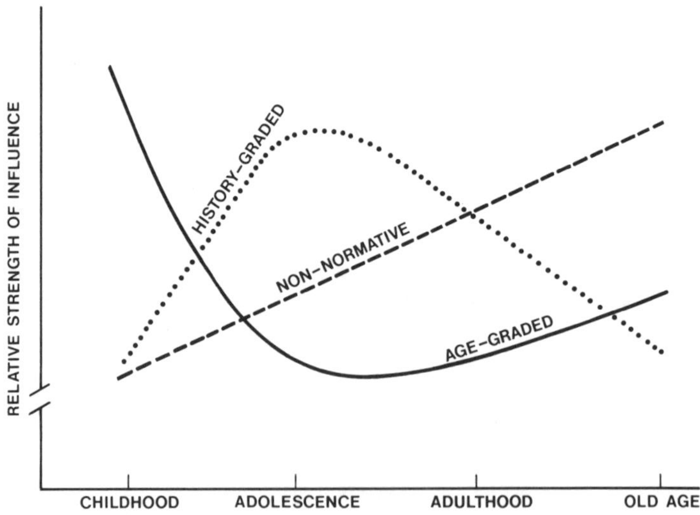

Fig. 2. Hypothetical life-course profiles representing the relative impact of normative age-graded, normative history-graded, and nonnormative influences on life-span development. (Reproduced, with permission, from the *Annual Review of Psychology,* Vol. 31. © 1980 by Annual Reviews Inc.)

B. BEHAVIORAL GENETICS AND NORMATIVE INFLUENCES

Because behavioral genetics addresses issues of individual differences rather than species-typical development, its major contribution lies not in accounting for normative effects. However, average age-graded and history-graded effects on variance analyses in the field of behavioral genetics need more careful attention. In terms of age-graded influences, the theme of developmental behavioral genetics is that we cannot assume that behavioral genetic results based on subjects of a certain age will generalize to subjects of another age—we need to explore developmental changes in the relative contribution of genetic and environmental influences on individual differences and, especially, to study genetic and environmental sources of change and continuity in development.

History-graded effects also need to be considered in behavioral genetic research, particularly because behavioral genetic studies have a longer history than nearly any other area of psychology. Although it is a standard caveat that behavioral genetic analyses are sample-specific, cohort effects have not been systematically examined. Nonetheless, it would be surprising if the dramatic changes in our society during the past three decades did not have some effect on the genetic and environmental influences underlying variance in psychological measures. The introduction of radio and television and the greater availability of education are obvious examples of environmental change. Possible genetic changes in the population should also be considered. For example, the United States is not just a cultural melting pot, it is also a genetic melting pot in which genetically diverse populations are blended.

Behavioral genetic data on IQ from the past 50 years suggest possible cohort effects on heritability estimates (Plomin & DeFries, 1980). IQ data collected prior to 1960 are compatible with a very high heritability, perhaps .70, whereas the newer data suggest a heritability closer to .50. Possible explanations other than cohort effects include differences in sample size and representativeness, in the tests employed, and in methods of test administration and analysis such as age adjustment. However, the difference could be a real cohort effect attributable to environmental or genetic change in the population. One attempt to examine these possibilities suggested that newer studies show less variance than older studies (Caruso, 1983). However, restriction of range could be a cohort effect rather than a statistical artifact. For example, the increasing normalization of society could reduce the range of environmental influences. Similarly, genetic variance would be decreased if assortative mating declined or if genetic differences among ethnic groups were broken down through intermarriage.

Schaie (1975) has proposed that quantitative genetic designs and analyses be extended to include combinations of cross-sectional and longitudinal data in order to assess cohort effects separately from age effects. The cohort-sequential method is the best design for this purpose; this method basically replicates the traditional longitudinal design over a succession of cohorts by sampling two or more cohorts at two or more times of measurement. One ongoing behavioral genetic study, the La Trobe Twin Study, has been designed along these lines as a mixed longitudinal study of 1356 twins and their siblings and cousins, who are studied several times between the ages of 3 and 15 (Hay & O'Brien, 1983).

C. BEHAVIORAL GENETICS AND NONNORMATIVE INFLUENCES

Behavioral genetics is especially relevant for the exploration of the etiology of nonnormative influences. Research from this field has led to some interesting hypotheses concerning the roles of nature and nurture on interindividual variability throughout the life span.

Genetic Sources of Nonnormative Influence. It is necessary to consider genetic sources of nonnormative influences, not just idiosyncratic life events. For most domains of development, genetic variance accounts for significant and sometimes substantial variance. For mental development, genetic influence increases dramatically from infancy to childhood and there is some evidence for continuing increases during adolescence (Plomin, 1986a). Figure 3 depicts these developmental changes in terms of variance explained rather than "relative strength" as in Fig. 2, which illustrates the hypothetical influences of normative as well as nonnormative life events. The components of variance are summarized from studies of particular samples in which variance due to age-graded effects is usually removed and cohorts are so narrow that variance due to cohorts is negligible. Genetic effects account for about 15% of the variance in infant mental test scores and increase in importance to explain about 50% of the variance during adolescence. Even for IQ, the most studied trait in behavioral genetics, the variance accounted for in adulthood and especially in old age is estimated on the basis of considerable guesswork.

Not enough is known about specific cognitive abilities even to begin such a summary illustration. The best guess is that verbal and spatial abilities follow a developmental profile roughly similar to that of general mental development, although some variations are apparent. For example, individual differences in verbal ability show greater genetic influence early in life than does spatial ability or even general mental development. Genetic influence on individual differences in verbal ability remains high throughout adolescence and early adulthood. There is some suggestion in the literature that genetic influence on spatial ability increases during adulthood (Plomin, 1986a).

The developmental profile for personality is even less clear. For individual differences in the EAS temperaments of emotionality, activity, and sociability

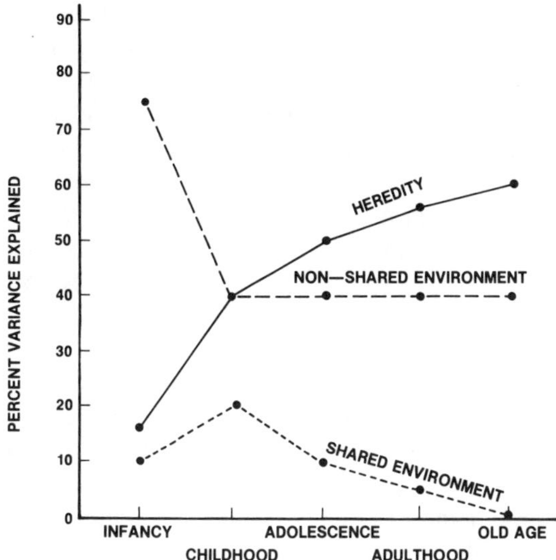

Fig. 3. A life-span profile of nonnormative genetic and environmental influences on individual differences in mental development. (Reproduced, with permission, from R. Plomin (1986), *Development, genetics and psychology,* Lawrence Erlbaum Associates.)

(Buss & Plomin, 1984), genetic influence appears to be substantial and relatively unchanging from infancy through childhood. Data from self-report questionnaires in adolescence and adulthood show substantial genetic involvement for these three traits—perhaps accounting for as much as 50% of the variance—and a hint of increasing genetic influence in adulthood. For the myriad other personality traits, much less is known, although it is reasonable to suppose that they will show varied patterns of genetic influence and perhaps developmental changes in its magnitude.

Even when the relative proportion of genetic variance shows no developmental change, as in the case of the EAS temperaments, this does not imply that the same genetic mechanisms are involved at each age. The same heritability at different ages could mask drastically different genetic effects. As explained earlier, the critical issue for developmental behavioral genetics is the study of genetic sources of change and continuity in individual differences. This requires longitudinal behavioral genetic studies, and such studies are rare.

Shared and Nonshared Environmental Influences. Another nonnormative distinction made in developmental behavioral genetics is shared versus nonshared environmental influences (Rowe & Plomin, 1981). The environmental variance for a particular trait in a particular population can be divided into two components. One component makes members of a family similar to one another and the other is the remainder of the environmental variance, that is, environmental influences that do not make family members similar. These two components of environmental variance are referred to as shared and nonshared environmental variance, respectively. The distinction came about because, normally, relatives can resemble each other for reasons of shared family environment or heredity; thus, the primary goal of behavioral genetics is to disentangle shared family environment from heredity in terms of their effect on familial resemblance. Again, we refer only to differential experiences that happen to be shared or not shared by members of a family, not constants that are nonvarying for members of a culture or species.

How can environmental variance be decomposed into these two components? The most direct method employs unrelated children adopted into the same family. Their correlation for a particular trait directly estimates the proportion of phenotypic variance in the trait that is due to shared family environment. Unlike the correlation for biological siblings, the correlation for pairs of adoptees in the same family cannot be due to heredity. Nonshared environmental variance denotes the remainder of the environmental variance, that is, trait-relevant environmental influences that do not make members of a family similar. Traditionally, the nonshared environmental component of variance includes variance due to error of measurement, although error variance could be deducted from the nonshared environmental component of variance if good estimates of reliability were available.

One of the most important findings to emerge from human behavioral genetic research is that individual differences due to environmental factors in development are primarily of the nonshared type, especially for personality and psychopathology and perhaps for cognition as well. This conclusion has far-reaching implications for the study of environmental influences on development. It implies that the unit of environmental transmission is not the family but rather micro-environments within families. Previous studies of the environment have begun with the assumption that the family is the level at which environments are experienced by children. This assumption has usually been implicit in that one environmental assessment is made and one child's development is studied per family, and then covariance between the environmental measure and children's development is analyzed across families. These studies have yielded few significant and no substantial relationships (Maccoby & Martin, 1983). However, the behavioral genetic data are telling us that the environmental action producing individual differences lies within families, not between them. The question that needs to be asked is why children in the same family are so different from one another. To answer this question, we need to study more than one child per family. Categories of nonshared environmental influence include unsystematic influences, such as accidents, illnesses, and other idiosyncratic experiences;

systematic, differential sibling experiences within the family, such as their differential treatment of each other or differences in treatment by their parents; and differential extrafamilial influences, such as interactions with different peer groups.

Evidence suggesting the importance of nonshared environmental influence has been reviewed elsewhere (Rowe & Plomin, 1981). More recent data continue to support this conclusion (Plomin & Daniels, in press). For example, three recently reported adoption studies of personality have found that familial resemblance due to shared family environment is negligible—the average adoptive sibling correlation is .04, and the average adoptive parent/adopted child correlation is .05 (Loehlin, Horn, & Willerman, 1981; Scarr et al., 1981; Scarr & Weinberg, 1978a). In the area of psychopathology, a recent review of familial concordance rates for schizophrenia in a dozen studies reported about 10% concordance for first-degree relatives (Gottesman & Shields, 1982). Recent adoption studies in Denmark yield the same concordance of about 10% for individuals adopted away from a first-degree schizophrenic relative (Gottesman & Shields, 1982). This suggests that sharing the same family environment with a schizophrenic relative does not increase concordance. Environmental influences on manic-depressive psychosis yields similar results and less severe forms of psychopathology, such as neuroses and alcoholism, also appear to be predominantly nonshared. Sibling concordances are generally less than 20% and, when twin and adoption studies have been conducted, most of this familial resemblance is found to be genetic in origin (Fuller & Thompson, 1978). Thus, a consistent pattern of results emerges from research on personality and psychopathology: Heredity is a significant source of individual differences and environmental variance is substantial; however, nearly all of the environmental variance is of the nonshared variety, making members of the same family as different as individuals chosen randomly from the population.

Until recently, environmental variance that affects individual differences in IQ was thought to be primarily of the shared type. In 11 studies, the average IQ correlation for adoptive siblings was .30, suggesting that 30% of the variance in IQ scores is due to shared family environmental influences (Bouchard & McGue, 1981), although some of this variance is due to selective placement. Adoptive-parent/adopted-child IQ correlations were lower (about .20), but still suggest substantial influence of shared family environment. Twin studies agree: The average IQ correlations in more than 30 studies were .85 for identical twins and .58 for fraternal twins (Bouchard & McGue, 1981), which suggests that about 30% of the variance of IQ scores can be accounted for by family environment shared by twins.

Although these data appear to converge on the reasonable conclusion that shared family environment accounts for a substantial portion of environmental variance relevant to IQ, doubts have begun to arise. Twins share family environment to a greater extent than do nontwin siblings—the IQ correlation for fraternal twins is about .60 and the correlation for nontwin siblings is about .40, which means that the twin method overestimates the importance of shared family environment. The crucial piece of evidence in support of substantial shared environmental variance is the correlation of .30 for pairs of adopted children reared together. However, these studies have included preadolescent adoptive siblings still living at home. One exception is a study of postadolescent adoptee pairs from 16 to 22 years of age by Scarr and Weinberg (1978b) that found a correlation of −.03 for IQ. This suggests the important possibility that shared family environment is important for IQ while children live at home, then fades in importance to negligible levels later. A recent study suggests that the importance of shared family environment fades even earlier: For 52 pairs of adoptive siblings whose average age was 13 years, their IQ correlation was −.16 (Kent, 1985).

Fig. 3 summarizes these results (for details, see Plomin, 1986a) and suggests that shared family environmental influences relevant to IQ differences increase in importance during infancy and early childhood and then decline sharply during adolescence. By adolescence, the influence of shared family environment wanes to negligible levels. Although twin data suggest substantial shared family environmental influence from birth through the first 2 or 3 years, this is a perinatal effect peculiar to twins.

Fig. 3 also indicates that nonshared environmental influences are responsible for the variance not accounted for by heredity or shared family environment. Variance due to error of measurement, as mentioned earlier, is included in the nonshared environmental component of variance. Because genetic and shared family environmental influences account for so little variance in infancy, nonshared environmental influence is credited with the bulk of the variance. During adolescence and throughout adulthood, nonshared environmental influence (and error of measurement) accounts for about 40% of the variance, as the influence of heredity increases and shared family environment fades in importance.

In terms of specific cognitive abilities, individual differences in verbal ability—especially vocabulary—continue to show some influence of shared family environment, even in adulthood. Perhaps the most surprising finding in human behavioral genetics is that, for most aspects of personality and psychopathology, nonshared environmental influence accounts for all of the relevant environmental variance: Growing up in the same family contributes nothing to siblings' similarity.

D. PRINCIPLES OF LIFE-SPAN BEHAVIORAL GENETICS

Developmental behavioral genetic findings have recently been reviewed from a life-span perspective (Plomin, 1986a), and there is not nearly enough space to include such a review in this chapter. Furthermore, it may be more useful for the present purpose to step back from the welter of research findings to consider general principles that can be drawn from this research. These principles might more appropriately be considered as hypotheses to be tested by future research because the data base is spotty, especially as we proceed down the list. We have attempted to phrase these principles as broadly as possible rather then enumerating a lengthy list of specific statements.

As indicated earlier, the two main questions of developmental behavioral genetics involve the etiology of behavioral variance at each age and covariance between ages. The first question involves the relative contributions of genetic and environmental factors to variance at each age, not assuming that the findings at one age will generalize to any other age. The second question addresses the extent to which genetic and environmental factors at one age covary with those at another age. More is known about the first question because it can be answered with cross-sectional data, whereas the second question requires longitudinal data. In addition to these two major questions, behavioral genetic studies have led to two novel discoveries about environmental influences on development that are included in our list.

Heredity is Influential Throughout the Life Span. The influence of heredity on individual differences in development is nearly ubiquitous. So far, only a handful of traits appear not to be influenced by heredity. For example, measures of creativity show little genetic influence; in the domain of personality, a few traits, such as conservatism and religiosity, appear to be only slightly influenced by heredity. However. for the vast majority of psychological traits, heredity is not only a significant force but is also substantial in its impact. Genetic influence sometimes accounts for as much as 50% of the observed variance—as in the case of IQ from adolescence through senesence. This relationship between individual differences in genes and individual differences in behavior is remarkably strong, perhaps unparalleled in the behavioral sciences, where relationships often account for only 1% of the variance and rarely more than 10%.

When heritability changes in development, it increases. One surprising principle that emerges from research in developmental behavioral genetics is that when developmental changes in the magnitude of genetic influence have been observed, the changes are in the direction of increased influence. This can be seen most clearly for mental development: As illustrated in Fig. 3, heritability is less than 20% in infancy, increases to 40% in childhood and about 50% in adolescence, and continues to increase slightly through adulthood, although the evidence becomes less clear later in the life span. It should be emphasized that this finding refers to phenotypic variance in IQ measures and does not speak to the processes that lead to these outcomes. For example, increasing genetic variance for IQ could be due to measurement artifacts rather than to additional genetic variance in the cognitive processes assessed by IQ tests. Nonetheless, it is noteworthy that IQ, as we measure it, shows sharply increasing genetic influence from infancy through adolescence.

For many characteristics, heritability does not appear to change much during development; at least, sufficient data are not available to detect change. For example, the EAS temperaments do not show striking changes in heritability during development; however, when change is seen, it is in the direction of increasing heritability. For instance, activity level appears to show an increase in heritability during infancy and the heritabilities of extraversion and neuroticism also appear to increase slightly during adulthood (Plomin, 1986a).

It would be incredible if this principle of increasing heritability were literally true for all domains—exceptions are bound to be observed. However, it is interesting that extant data point so consistently in this direction and that no one seems to have anticipated this finding. Indeed, as mentioned earlier, most developmentalists would probably guess that the reverse would be true: As children develop and experience more diverse environments, environmental variance would increasingly account for phenotypic variance and heritability would decrease. It should be emphasized that developmental increases in heritability mean that genetic variance comes to account for larger portions of phenotypic variance in the population. This could occur because genetic variance increases or because environmental variance decreases.

Environment is influential throughout the life span. Behavioral genetic results indicate that genetic influence is significant and often substantial; however, these same analyses also provide evidence for the importance of the environment in generating individual differences. There is not a single psychological characteristic nor a period of development for which genetic variance accounts for all of the phenotypic variance. In fact, heritability rarely exceeds 50%. The rest of the variance is nongenetic in origin, although the specific environmental factors responsible for this major portion of phenotypic variance have rarely been isolated.

Most environmental influence is of the nonshared type. One important lead for finding specific environmental influences is that, whatever these influences may be, they operate in such a way as to make two children in the same family as different as are children reared in different families. Throughout the life span, shared family environment has little effect on personality and psychopathology. IQ shows an interesting developmental trend: Shared family environment accounts for a substantial amount of IQ variance in childhood, but its influence wanes to negligible levels by late adolescence. Thus, even for cognition, nonshared environmental influences are of major importance.

Nature is involved in nurture. An important direction for future research in developmental behavioral genetics is the study of the developmental interface between nature and nurture. So far, research indicates no striking genotype–environment interactions within the normal range of genotypes and environments. Genotype–environment correlation is more promising: Although it is not yet possible to abstract any general principles from this work, Scarr and McCartney's (1983) theory that the passive form of genotype–environment correlation diminishes in importance during childhood and that reactive and active forms become more important should serve to guide research on this important topic.

A recent advance in understanding the interface between nature and nurture is the demonstration that heredity affects measures of the environment and that it mediates relationships between measures of the environment and measures of development (Plomin, Loehlin, & DeFries, 1985). For example, the adoption design can be used to estimate genetic mediation of ostensibly environmental influences on individual differences in children's development. In nonadoptive homes, parents share heredity as well as family environment with their children. Thus, relationships between environmental measures and measures of children's development could be mediated genetically via parental characteristics. However, in adoptive homes, correlations between measures of the environment and of children's development cannot be mediated genetically because adoptive parents share only family environment with their adopted children. Thus, if genes underlie relationships between environmental differences and children's differential development, environment/development correlations in nonadoptive homes will be greater than those in adoptive homes. Following a path model based upon this approach, data suggest that more than half of the relationship between environmental measures and developmental measures in nonadoptive families is mediated genetically. As always, these behavioral genetic results are limited to individual differences within the genetic and environmental context of the particular sample at a certain point in history.

Genetic correlations across the life span are substantial. The previous statements are based on analyses of cross-sectional data that assess genetic and environmental components of variance. However, the most interesting issues involve age-to-age genetic and environmental covariance. As discussed earlier, low genetic correlations from age to age indicate genetic change and high age-to-age genetic correlations imply genetic continuity. Genetic correlations can be high even though heritability is low; that is, even if genetic deviations at two ages make only a small contribution to phenotypic variance at each age, genetic deviations at the two ages could correlate perfectly.

Questions of continuity and change must be addressed by analyses of longitudinal behavioral genetic data, and these are quite rare. However, data from the Colorado Adoption Project using the parent–offspring adoption design suggest that genetic correlations from infancy to adulthood are substantial for individual differences in mental development, temperament, height, and weight (Plomin & DeFries, 1985). In other words, when genetic effects on individual differences are observed in infancy, these genetic factors are highly correlated with those that affect behavior in adulthood as seen in correlations between adopted-away infants and their biological parents which, as mentioned earlier, is like an instant longitudinal study from infancy to adulthood. It should be emphasized that substantial genetic correlations from age to age do not necessarily imply substantial phenotypic continuity from age to age: Phenotypic stability of individual differences depends on the heritability at each age as well as on the genetic correlation between the ages.

It is with some hesitation that we include genetic continuity in development as a general principle. Even though extant research findings are consistent with the hypothesis, there are not many relevant data. Nonetheless, this statement is potentially so important for thinking about genetic influence throughout the life span that it seems worthwhile to include it in a list of hypotheses about life-span developmental behavioral genetics that are intended to stimulate research in the area.

Genetic effects are amplified during development. Combining two of the previous principles leads to an intriguing hypothesis. If genetic covariance from age to age is very high and yet heritability increases, this implies that genetic effects on individual differences are amplified during development (DeFries, 1983; Plomin & DeFries, 1985). In other words, slight genetic effects early in development are magnified as development proceeds, creating increased genetic variance while genetic covariance from age to age remains high. For example, slight differences in neuroanatomy or neurophysiology early in life could culminate in increasingly larger behavioral differences among children as life goes on.

This principle concerning age-to-age covariance is based on a small amount of data. However, the novelty of the model of genetic amplification and its import for understanding the processes by which heredity affects individual differences in development make this a worthy heuristic for future research. The amplification model makes some strong and testable predictions. For example, the model predicts that longitudinal twin data will show a similar pattern of high age-to-age genetic correlations despite increasing heritability during childhood—data from the longitudinal Louisville Twin Study (Wilson, 1983) could be used to test this hypothesis; however, the relevant analyses have not yet been conducted. A related prediction from the amplification model is that increasing stability of IQ during childhood comes about because the high age-to-age genetic correlation begins to account for more of the phenotypic variance. That is, heritability increases and the high genetic correlation from age to age results in increasing phenotypic stability. This could explain the apparent relationship between heritability and stability in development.

Genes produce change as well as continuity in development. An age-to-age genetic correlation less than 1.0 implies genetic change in that genetic influences at one age do not correlate perfectly with genetic influences at the other age. In other words, a genetic correlation of less than 1.0 implies that genes have different effects at the two ages. Although the magnitude of genetic continuity is surprisingly high, the age-to-age genetic correlations throughout the life span are certainly less than 1.0. Genetic change, even in the midst of considerable genetic continuity, is likely to be interesting and important. Furthermore, genetic change is suggested by the principle that heritability increases during development, even though the amplification model suggests that increased genetic variance later in development might be attributable to the amplification of genetic differences earlier in life.

IV. Summary

The purpose of this chapter has been to explore the synergistic possibilities of an interdiscipline of life-span developmental behavior genetics that are, for now, primarily a promissory note because so little relevant work has been done. However, it is our hope that this chapter conveys an idea of the substantial collateral that backs up this promissory note.

At both descriptive and explanatory levels of analysis, it is critical that individual differences (variance) and normative (means) perspectives be distinguished. Quantitative genetics is a powerful theory of individual differences and provides methods, such as the twin and adoption designs, that can be used to assess the significance of genetic and family environmental differences as influences on behavioral variability and to estimate the magnitude of the effects of genetic and environmental parameters. These effects, however, are always related to individual differences. They do not estimate normative genetic and environmental influences on means of groups or species; they are also limited to particular samples with the genetic and environmental influences of those samples at a particular point in history.

Developmental behavioral genetics focuses on change and continuity on individual differences in development. Genetic change during development is the target of much current research in molecular genetics; the relationship between developmental molecular genetics and developmental behavioral genetics is briefly considered. Two ways of thinking about genetic change during behavioral development involve developmental changes in heritability and age-to-age genetic correlations. Heritability is a descriptive statistic that refers to the proportion of phenotypic (observed) variance that can be accounted for by genetic variance among individuals. Age-to-age genetic correlations, which require longitudinal behavioral genetic data, indicate the extent to which genetic effects on individual differences at one age are correlated with genetic effects on individual differences at another age.

Research relevant to life-span developmental behavioral genetics is discussed in the context of Baltes's (1979) hypothetical life-span profile of normative and nonnormative influences. Because behavioral genetics is concerned with individual differences, life-span developmental behavioral genetics focuses on those aspects of Baltes's life-span scheme that involve interindividual differentation. This could include individual differences in age- and history-graded influences but is most relevant to nonnormative influences.

An empirical life-span profile is presented for IQ, by far the most studied trait in behavioral genetics. Heritability of IQ scores increases from about 20% in infancy to 40% in childhood and 50% during adolescence and perhaps increases slightly during adulthood. The amount of variance explained by shared family environmental influences—environmental factors that cause family members to resemble one another—increases during infancy to about 20% and then decreases to negligible levels by early adulthood. Nonshared family environment accounts for approximately 40% of the variance of IQ scores during childhood, adolescence, and adulthood. Not enough is known about traits other than mental development to begin to construct similar life-span profiles.

The chapter ends with a summary of behavioral genetic research in terms of principles (or, more modestly, hypotheses) of life-span developmental behavioral genetics. Three of the most solid principles are these: Heredity is influential on individual differences throughout the life span; environment is influential on individual differences throughout the life span; and most environmental influence is of the nonshared type.

Acknowledgments

Preparation of this chapter and the research described in this chapter on the Colorado Adoption Project has been supported by the National Institute of Child Health and Human Development (HD-10333 and HD-18426) and the National Science Foundation (BNS-8200310). We are grateful for helpful criticism from an extremely thorough review by an anonymous reviewer, and for excellent editorial advice from Rebecca Miles at the Institute for Behavioral Genetics.

References

Baltes, P. B. (1979). Life-span developmental psychology: Some converging observations on history and theory. In P. B. Baltes & O. G. Brim, Jr. (Eds.), *Life-span development and behavior* (pp. 256–281). New York: Academic Press.

Baltes, P. B., & Nesselroade, J. R. (1984). Paradigm lost and paradigm regained: Critique of Dannefer's portrayal of life-span developmental psychology. *American Sociological Review, 49,* 841–847.

Baltes, P. B., Reese, H. W., & Lipsitt, L. P. (1980). Life-span developmental psychology. *Annual Review of Psychology, 31,* 65–110.

Baltes, P. B., & Willis, S. L. (1982). Plasticity and enhancement of intellectual functioning in old age. In F. I. M. Craik & S. Trehub (Eds.), *Aging and cognitive processes* (pp. 352–389). New York: Plenum.

Bessman, S. P., Williamson, M. L., & Koch, R. (1978). Diet, genetics, and mental retardation interaction between phenylketonuric heterozygous mother and fetus to produce nonspecific diminution of IQ: Evidence in support of the justification hypothesis. *Proceedings of the National Academy of Sciences U.S.A., 78,* 1562–1566.

Bouchard, T. J., Jr., & McGue, M. (1981). Familial studies of intelligence: A review. *Science, 212,* 1055–1059.

Buss, A. H., & Plomin, R. (1984). *Temperament: Early-developing personality traits.* Hillsdale, NJ: Lawrence Erlbaum Associates.

Callahan, E. J., & McCluskey, K. A. (1983). *Life-span developmental psychology: Nonnormative life events.* New York: Academic Press.

Caruso, D. (1983). Sample differences in genetics and intelligence data: Sibling and parent–offspring results. *Behavior Genetics, 13,* 453–458.

Cowan, W. M. (1979). The development of the brain. *Scientific American, 241,* 121–133.

DeFries, J. C. (1983). *Amplification model of developmental genetics.* Unpublished manuscript.

Falconer, D. S. (1981). *Introduction to quantitative genetics.* London: Longman.

Fisher, R. A. (1918). The correlation between relatives on the supposition of Mendelian inheritance. *Transactions of the Royal Society of Edinburgh, 52,* 399–433.

Fuller, J. L., & Thompson, W. R. (1978). *Foundations of behavior genetics.* St. Louis: Mosby.

Galton, F. (1875). The history of twins as a criterion of the relative powers of nature and nurture. *Journal of the Anthropological Institute, 6,* 391–406.

Gottesman, I. I., & Shields, J. (1982). *Schizophrenia: The epigenetic puzzle.* Cambridge, England: Cambridge University Press.

Hardy–Brown, K. (1983). Universals and individual differences: Disentangling two approaches to the study of language acquisition. *Developmental Psychology, 19,* 610–624.

Hay, D. A., & O'Brien, P. J. (1983). The La Trobe Twin Study: A genetic approach to the structure and development of cognition in twin children. *Child Development, 54,* 317–330.

Ho, H. Z., Foch, T. T., & Plomin, R. (1980). Developmental stability of the relative influence of genes and environment on specific cognitive abilities in childhood. *Developmental Psychology, 16,* 340–346.

Jacob, F., & Monod, J. (1961). On the regulation of gene activity. *Cold Spring Harbor Symposia on Quantitative Biology, 26,* 193–209.

Kent, J. (1985). *Genetic and environmental contributions to cognitive abilities as assessed by a telephone test battery.* Unpublished doctoral dissertation, University of Colorado, Boulder.

Lewin, R. (1984). Why is development so illogical? *Science, 224,* 1327–1329.

Loehlin, J. C. (1978). Heredity–environment analyses of Jencks's IQ correlations. *Behavior Genetics, 8,* 415–436.

Loehlin, J. C. (1979). Combining data from different groups in human behavior genetics. In J. R. Royce & L. P. Mos (Eds.), *Theoretical advances in behavior genetics* (pp. 303–334). The Netherlands: Sijthoff & Noordhoff.

Loehlin, J. C., Horn, J. M., & Willerman, L. (1981). Personality resemblance in adoptive families. *Behavior Genetics, 11,* 309–330.

Maccoby, E. E., & Martin, J. A. (1983). Socialization in the context of the family: Parent–child interaction. In P. H. Mussen (Ed.), *Handbook of child psychology (4th ed.): Vol. IV. Socialization, personality, and social development* (pp. 1–101). New York: John Wiley.

Mangan, G. (1982). *The biology of human conduct: East/West models of temperament and personality.* Oxford, England: Pergamon Press.

Mayr, E. (1982). *The growth of biological thought.* Cambridge, MA: Harvard University Press.

McCall, R. B. (1979). The development of intellectual functioning in infancy and the prediction of later IQ. In J. D. Osofsky (Ed.), *Handbook of infant development* (pp. 707–741). New York: Wiley–Interscience.

Merriman, C. (1924). The intellectual resemblance of twins. *Psychological Monographs, 33,* Whole No. 152.

Ozer, D. J. (1985). Correlation and the coefficient of determination. *Psychological Bulletin, 97,* 307–315.

Parkinson, J. S. (1977). Behavioral genetics in bacteria. *Annual Review of Genetics, 11,* 397–414.

Plomin, R. (1983). Developmental behavioral genetics. *Child Development, 54,* 253–259.

Plomin, R. (1986a). *Development, genetics, and psychology.* Hillsdale, NJ: Lawrence Erlbaum Associates.

Plomin, R. (1986b). Developmental behavioral genetics and multivariate analysis: Change as well as continuity. *Behavior Genetics, 16,* 25–43.

Plomin, R., & Daniels, D. (in press). Why are children in the same family so different from each other? *The Behavioral and Brain Sciences.*

Plomin, R., & DeFries, J. C. (1979). Multivariate behavioral genetic analysis of twin data on scholastic abilities. *Behavior Genetics, 9,* 505–517.

Plomin, R., & DeFries, J. C. (1980). Genetics and intelligence: Recent data. *Intelligence, 4,* 15–24.

Plomin, R., & DeFries, J. C. (1981). Multivariate behavioral genetics and development: Twin studies. In L. Gedda, P. Parisi, & W. E. Nance (Eds.), *Twin Research 3, Part B: Intelligence, personality and development* (pp. 25–33). New York: Liss.

Plomin, R., & DeFries, J. C. (1985). *Origins of individual differences in infancy: The Colorado Adoption Project.* New York: Academic Press.

Plomin, R., DeFries, J. C., & McClearn, G. E. (1980). *Behavioral genetics: A primer.* San Francisco: Freeman.

Plomin, R., Loehlin, J. C., & DeFries, J. C. (1985). Genetic and environmental components of "environmental" influences. *Developmental Psychology, 21,* 391–402.

Rowe, D. C., & Plomin, R. (1981). The importance of nonshared (E1) environmental influences in behavioral development. *Developmental Psychology, 17,*517–531.

Scarr, S. (1976). An evolutionary perspective on infant intelligence: Species patterns and individual variations. In M. Lewis (Ed.), *Origins of intelligence* (pp. 165–197). New York: Plenum.

Scarr, S., & Kidd, K. K. (1983). Developmental behavior genetics. In P. H. Mussen (Ed.), *Handbook of child psychology: Vol. 2. Infancy and developmental psychology* (4th ed., pp. 345–433). New York: John Wiley.

Scarr, S., & McCartney, K. (1983). How people make their own environments: A theory of genotype → environment effects. *Child Development, 54,* 424–435.

Scarr, S., Webber, P. I., Weinberg, R. A., & Wittig, M. A. (1981). Personality resemblance among adolescents and their parents in biologically related and adoptive families. *Journal of Personality and Social Psychology, 40,* 885–898.

Scarr, S., & Weinberg, R. A. (1978a). Attitudes, interests, and IQ. *Human Nature,* April, 29–36.

Scarr, S., & Weinberg, R. A. (1978b). The influence of "family background" on intellectual attainment. *American Sociological Review, 43,* 674–692.

Schaie, K. W. (1975). Research strategy in developmental human behavior genetics. In K. W. Schaie, V. E. Anderson, G. E. McClearn, & J. Money (Eds.), *Developmental human behavior genetics: Nature–nurture redefined* (pp. 205–219). Lexington, MA: Lexington Books.

Skodak, M., & Skeels, H. M. (1949). A final follow-up of one hundred adopted children. *Journal of Genetic Psychology, 75,* 85–125.

Snyder, S. H. (1980). Brain peptides as neurotransmitters. *Science, 209,* 976–983.

Stunkard, A. J., Foch, T. T., & Hrubec, Z. (1985). *Genetics and human obesity: Results of a twin study.* Manuscript submitted for publication.

Thorndike, E. L. (1905). Measurement of twins. *Archives of Philosophy, Psychology, and Scientific Methods, 1,* 1–64.

Wilson, R. S. (1983). The Louisville Twin Study: Developmental synchronies in behavior. *Child Development, 54,* 298–316.

Wright, S. (1931). Statistical methods in biology. *Journal of the American Statistical Association, 26,* 155–163.

The Historian and the Life Course: Reflections on Recent Approaches to the Study of American Family Life in the Past

Maris A. Vinovskis
DEPARTMENT OF HISTORY AND CENTER FOR POLITICAL STUDIES
OF THE INSTITUTE FOR SOCIAL RESEARCH
UNIVERSITY OF MICHIGAN, ANN ARBOR

Abstract

The study of American family life in the past is one of the most popular and innovative areas of historical inquiry today. Little attention has been paid to the conceptual and methodological issues involved in selecting a framework of analysis. Historians have used generations or mean household size, but are now moving away from these approaches. Family-cycle models are gaining in popularity among some historians, but these schemes suffer from major conceptual and methodological shortcomings. Life-course analysis seems to be emerging as one of the most useful analytical frameworks for the study of the past. The essay assesses the strengths and weaknesses of a life-course perspective for investigating individuals and their families historically.

I. Introduction

The study of American family life in the past is one of the most popular and innovative areas of historical inquiry today. Initially, investigations (Demos, 1970; Greven, 1970; Lockridge, 1970) concentrated on the New England family in the seventeenth and eighteenth centuries, but recently the focus has shifted to the colonial South (Lewis, 1983; Smith, 1980) or the nineteenth century (Censer, 1984; Hareven, 1982b; Lebsock, 1984). The field of American family history also experienced great variations and changes in methodology. One of the most popular analytical frameworks since the late 1970s is life-course analysis—a widely prescribed but often poorly defined and commonly misunderstood approach.[1]

Although there are several useful reviews of developments in American family history (Degler, 1980; Gordon, 1978; Ryan, 1982), most of them do not pay much attention to the conceptual or methodological issues involved in reconstructing family life from limited historical records. Most of these overviews do not include a comparative perspective by also considering recent developments in European family history. Particularly missing is an evaluation of the strengths and weaknesses of the life-course approach for historical analysis before the availability of longitudinal social-science data originating in the 1920s and 1930s.[2] Therefore, this chapter will review the evolution of the alternative ways of studying American family life in the past. It will also assess the efforts within the past 5 years to use more developmental approaches to the study of families and of individuals such as the family-cycle model or the life-course perspective.

II. Generations and Mean Household Size

The rediscovery of family history by American colonial historians (Demos, 1965, 1968; Greven, 1966; Lockridge, 1966) in the mid-1960s relied heavily upon the use of family reconstitution techniques to estimate rates of births, deaths, and marriages from vital events recorded in the church or town records. Most of these studies analyzed family life among seventeenth-century New England Puritans with an emphasis on deriving demographic rates for events such as marriages. The results of the demographic analyses were then usually incorporated within a more traditional study of New England community life of which family life was only one component.[3]

A few scholars tried to analyze family life by comparing the experiences of different generations of New England settlers. The use of generations as an

[1]One of the more confusing aspects of analyzing family life and households is the lack of agreement among scholars on how to categorize families and households. In part this confusion arises because individuals in the past did not always clearly define or agree upon what constituted a family or household. While some authors see the family as the basic domestic unit, others concentrate on the household. Boarders and lodgers are included within the household in some studies, but excluded in others. As a result, one must be very careful when reading historical work to be aware of the particular definition of family and household being employed. For an overview of the meaning of family and household as well as a modern definition of them that is now widely used by historians, consult the volumes (Laslett, 1972; Wall, Robin, & Laslett, 1983) produced by the Cambridge Group for the History of Populations and Social Structure.

[2]There is considerable work on the use of life-course analysis for the more recent period. Especially helpful, from a historical perspective, are the writings of Glen Elder (1978, 1983).

[3]For an introduction to these studies of American colonial demography, see Lockridge (1977) and Vinovskis (1971, 1978).

analytical framework was useful in that it points to the changes in the lives of settlers over time as well as to the process of the transmission of wealth from one generation to the next. Philip Greven (1970), for example, analyzed the experiences of the first settlers of Andover, Mass., in the seventeenth century and those of their successors in the next three generations. He focused on the transfer of wealth from one generation to the next and how the fathers used their possession of property to control the marital behavior of their sons.

The use of generational analysis for the study of family life can be useful—especially when one is analyzing the transmission of wealth from one generation to another. The concept of generations is limited, however, by the problems involved in defining who belongs to which generation. In the analysis of colonial Andover, the distinction between the initial settlers (first generation) and their children (second generation) is clear and was meaningful to those individuals. But by the third and fourth generations any such distinctions are much less clear since there is considerable overlap in generational designations for those cohorts born at the same time (Vinovskis, 1977). In other words, some of the individuals born in Andover from 1700 to 1709 were members of the third generation of the initial settlers of Andover while others were members of the fourth generation and there is no indication that these two subgroups perceived themselves or were treated any differently because of their generational identity. Thus, while the use of generations to study family life is useful under certain conditions and for specific problems, it loses its analytical rigor and meaning when applied to investigating the experiences of several generations over a long period.[4]

While a few American historians were individually and cautiously exploring family life using demographic analysis in the 1960s, Peter Laslett (1972) and the Cambridge Group for the History of Population and Social Structure initiated a major, collective reappraisal of the Western family and introduced a new measure for the analysis of family history which was to have a far-reaching impact. Sociologists (Parsons & Bales, 1955) in the 1950s argued that industrialization led to the demise of the extended family and the emergence of the nuclear one. Laslett and his colleagues disagreed and tried to demonstrate that the preindustrial West European households usually were nuclear rather than extended, by using mean household size as the index of the limited complexity of those units.

> Mean household size is of importance to social scientists from several points of view. For the demographer, and especially for the historical demographer, it is useful as a multiplier, which makes it possible to calculate total population from numbers of households. For the sociologist and the anthropologist it is a preliminary indicator of household structure. When the mean household is large, they suppose that there are grounds for assuming the presence of the

[4]Scholars often misuse the word "generation" by confusing it with different age-cohorts (Mannheim, 1952) or developmental stages (Eisenstadt, 1956). David Kertzer (1982) provides a good critique of the way scholars have used and misused the concept of generations.

> extended family in the society, and when small, that most familial and household groups may be assumed to consist exclusively of the primary or nuclear family group of man, wife and children. (Laslett, 1969, pp. 199–200)

Based upon a study of 100 parishes from 1574 to 1821, Laslett (1969) found that the size of the households in England remained at about 4.75 (including servants) from the sixteenth century to the early twentieth century and therefore concluded that the proportion of extended households in preindustrial England was never very large.[5] Laslett emphasized that Frederic Le Play's classic stem family (where only one child married while remaining in the household and eventually inheriting the family property) was not prevalent in either England or the rest of Western Europe.

Under the stimulation and sponsorship of the Cambridge Group, historians (Laslett, 1972) measured mean household size in several countries since the only data requirement for such an analysis was the availability of lists of individuals arranged by household. They concluded that at least for Western Europe, mean household size was relatively small and constant during the preindustrial period and that most households were nuclear at any given time. Therefore, industrialization did not destroy the extended family as it never really flourished in Western Europe. During the late 1960s and early 1970s the study of mean household size dominated much of the analysis of family history—especially among those studying the European family.

At first glance, the mean household size is a very attractive and useful index of household structure. Since lists of household members were frequently recorded in the past, one can find roughly comparable data for many different countries and compute the mean household size without expending too much time or energy. In addition, by providing a simple index of family life, the researcher seemingly is able to reduce the complex phenomenon of family life to a single number. Furthermore, the utility of mean household size in disproving the existence of extensive extended households in the past seemed to confirm its analytical usefulness.

While there was considerable initial enthusiaism for measuring mean household size, the limitations of this approach also became increasingly apparent. There was a tendency, for example, to confuse large household size with the complexity of the family. When Laslett first learned of the large households in colonial America, he assumed that they must have been extended in structure (Laslett, 1970). Yet a closer examination of the large American colonial households in Bristol, R.I., in 1689 revealed that only few of them were extended. As

[5]It should be noted, however, that while most households in England were small, the majority of inhabitants lived in households of six or more individuals (Laslett, 1969).

a result, Laslett (1972) reluctantly acknowledged that mean household size by itself is not an accurate or reliable guide to the complexity of family structure:

> Bristol which has by far the largest households, also has the fewest showing any sign of extension, and none at all that is multiple. It would appear that knowledge of the number of households and their sizes would not be a reliable guide to their structure in these communities, and such measures as mean household size of very little use for the purpose. (p. 54)

In other words, while a small mean household size may indicate the absence of complex households, a large household size does not necessarily imply the presence of extended households.

Some scholars accepted Laslett's contention that there were few extended households in the past, but challenged his explanation of this phenomenon. Rather than ascribing the lack of extended households to a preference for couples to live apart from their relatives, they emphasized the high mortality in the preindustrial period as a demographic constraint on the extent of extended households possible. As Marion Levy (1965) has argued, demographic considerations alone would have severely reduced the number of extended households possible since few individuals lived long enough to reside with their married children or grandchildren.

In responding to questions about the demographic constraints on extended households in the past, Laslett joined forces with Kenneth Wachter, a statistician, and Eugene Hammel, an anthropologist, to develop and analyze simulations of English households using different estimates of vital events and incorporating the element of chance. Despite some limitations in their assumptions and models, their work (Wachter, Hammel, & Laslett, 1978) is a convincing demonstration of the usefulness of computer simulations in helping historians assess the impact of demographic factors on household composition. Based upon this analysis, Wachter and his associates (1978) concluded:

> That the population of England in traditional times, at least after the end of the 1500s, was not behaving in such a way as to bring into being nearly as many complex households as they could have engendered whether of the stem-family or, by inference, of other types.
>
> That any given set of household formation principles is likely to be robust to demographic variation. Since the English are found to have been living so predominantly in nuclear family households, we can conclude that they were not prevented from realizing more complicated forms of household composition by the constraints of birth rates, death rates, or even marriage rates. (p. 80)

Perhaps the most direct and damaging attack on the use of mean household size as an index of the structural complexity of the household came from Lutz Berkner (1972). Based upon a study of eighteenth-century Austrian families, Berkner concluded that stem families were much more common than Laslett had suggested—especially if one took into consideration the developmental cycle of the family. Berkner criticized Laslett's use of cross-sectional aggregate data on mean household size as providing an inaccurate and static picture of family life. Instead, Berkner (1972) called for a developmental approach to the study of families:

> Families go through developmental cycles as individuals who compose them go through their life cycles. A census taken at a given point in time takes a cross-section and gives a static picture of households and families that the historian or sociologist can sort out into types. We can count so many extended families, so many nuclear. But rather than being types these may simply be phases in the developmental cycle of the single family organization. There may be a normal series of stages that appear only rarely in a population because they last for only a short period of the family's cycle or in some cases do not appear at all. From this point of view, the extended family is merely a phase through which most families go. (p. 405)

Berkner's finding that stem families were much more prevalent in Western Europe than suggested by Laslett and his associates has been strongly challenged. Serious objections have been raised about the quality of Berkner's data as well as his loose conceptualization of the stem family (Wachter et al., 1978). Based upon a computer simulation of English households which took into account the effects of family cycles on households, Wachter and his colleagues (1978) concluded:

> That the number of extended and multiple forms observed in England are no basis for postulating successive phases of a stem-family cycle occurring in most, some, or even a small proportion of households. Whatever effect the family cycle had on household composition, it does not seem to have been of this character (p. 80).

If Berkner's challenge to those emphasizing the prevalence of nuclear households in Western Europe has not been entirely successful, his plea for the need for a more dynamic view of the family has gained widespread acceptance. Indeed, the growing recognition among scholars (Anderson, 1980; Wrigley, 1977) that mean household size by itself does not necessarily tell us anything about the complexity of the household structure combined with the realization that families and households should be studied from a more dynamic and developmental perspective has greatly eroded the enthusiasm for even compiling data on mean household size. Thus, while Laslett's arguments about the prevalence of nuclear households in England and much of Western Europe seem to have survived, his initial methodology for studying this question has been largely rejected.[6] The analysis of mean household size no longer enjoys the importance in the historical profession today that it held 15 years ago.[7]

[6]While Laslett (1977) is correct in pointing to the prevalence of nuclear households throughout much of Western Europe, he has exaggerated the existence of a clear distinction between Western Europe and other areas (Wall, Robin, & Laslett, 1983). In central Italy and southern France, for example, extended and multiple households were especially common among sharecroppers (Kertzer, 1984).

[7]Despite the strong criticisms of the mean household size approach, a few historians (Morgan & Golden, 1979) continue to use it.

III. Household and Family Cycles

As historians move away from using mean household size as an index of family life, they are looking for a more developmental approach. Unfortunately, it is much easier to criticize the inadequacies of mean household size than to provide an alternative framework. Nonetheless, some historians are now using household or family cycles as a way of portraying the dynamics of family life in the past.

Historians of the European family tend to use household or family cycles that are designed mainly to reflect the changing labor resources of the household or the transmission of property from one generation to the next. Analysts of American family life are more likely to use a family-cycle framework as it relates to childbearing and parenting as well as to the economic functioning of the family. As a result, there is considerable confusion among historians about the definitions of household or family cycle because these concepts are often developed and employed for very different purposes—frequently without any awareness of the multiple meanings and definitions that have been given to these terms by different scholars.

The work of Berkner (1972) illustrates the tendency of European historians to use household and family cycles mainly to analyze economic aspects of family life. Unlike many historians, Berkner clearly distinguishes between household and family cycles.[8] Borrowing from the ideas of the Russian economist A. V. Chayanov (1966), Berkner shows how changes in the ages and number of children in a peasant family can create a labor shortage or surplus in that household. When the children are too young to work or have already left the family, the peasant household is likely to hire servants or lodgers to satisfy the labor requirements of that household. When the children are older and capable of working in the household, there is less need for any servants or lodgers. As a result, although the mean household size may not change very much over time, the labor composition of that household might experience considerable change. To document these stages of the household cycle, Berkner uses the age of the male head of the household (ages 18–27, 28–37, 38–47, 48–57, and 58–90).

Berkner's (1972) stages of the family are also quite simple: Parents retire and their heir marries and operates the farm as an extended family; the parents die and the heir heads a nuclear family; and the heir retires and his son marries and operates the farm as an extended family. Thus, the family cycle alternates between an extended and a nuclear family as the individuals constitute the stem family.

[8]While most historians do not even try to distinguish between family and household cycles, some (Sieder & Mitterauer, 1983) explicitly reject such a division because they question the validity of separating kin and nonkin in such households in the past.

While there are some variations in the ways in which scholars of European families and households conceptualize their developmental cycles (Czap, 1983; Wall, 1983), most of these efforts are quite similar in logic if not identical in detail to Berkner's stages of the household or the family. Almost all of them use the age of the male head of the household to index the stages, but there is little agreement on either the number of such stages or the ages which delineate them. The cycles usually are designed to depict the transfer of the farmstead from one generation to the next with very little attention to the lives of those who will not inherit such property.[9] Unlike historians of the American family, these scholars pay very little attention to the changes in the family as the result of children growing older and entering schools. Indeed, while analysts (Wall, Robin, & Laslett, 1983) of European family life in the past have spent considerable time and energy on defining and analyzing the household structure cross-sectionally, most of them virtually continue to ignore the complex issues involved in trying to develop a household or family-cycle framework of analysis.[10]

If historians of the European family are slow in adopting a developmental approach, those investigating the American family are much more active in this area. Several historians (Hareven, 1974, 1978a, 1978b; Katz, Doucet, & Stern, 1982) of the American family are particularly strong advocates of the family-cycle approach. Many of them have been influenced, directly or indirectly, by the work of family sociologists such as Evelyn Duvall (1967) and Reuben Hill (1964), who pioneered the developmental approach for studying contemporary families.[11]

Perhaps one of the more influential models of the family cycle has been that of Duvall (1967). Her eight-stage model is based upon shifts in the size and composition of the family as well as changes in their social roles (see Table I). The social functioning of the family is largely determined, according to Duvall, by the changes in the lives of the oldest child in the family as he or she enters school, experiences the teen-age years, and finally leaves home. The critical assumption in Duvall's approach is that the changes in the life of the oldest child profoundly affects the entire family as the members adjust themselves to new experiences such as having a child in school or raising a teen-ager.

[9]A few historians of the European family, such as Peter Czap (1983), have a somewhat broader demographic and economic perspective on the family. Czap incorporates M. Fortes's scheme of the domestic group life cycle, which includes three developmental stages: (1) expansion (marriage through childbearing), (2) dispersion or fission (initiated by the marriage of the eldest child), and (3) replacement (begins with marriage of the youngest child who remains with the parents and concludes with the death of the parents).

[10]For a discussion of the efforts of other historians (Anderson, 1971; Tilly, 1979) of the European family to use a family-cycle approach, see the excellent critique by Kertzer and Schiaffino (1983).

[11]On the early efforts to develop a family-cycle approach, see Hill and Rodgers (1964).

TABLE I

Evelyn Duvall's Eight-stage Model of the Family Cycle

Stage I	Beginning families (married couple without children)
Stage II	Childbearing families (oldest child, birth to 30 months)
Stage III	Families with preschool children (oldest child $2\frac{1}{2}$ to 6 years)
Stage IV	Families with schoolchildren (oldest child 6 to 13 years)
Stage V	Families with teen-agers (oldest child 13 to 20 years)
Stage VI	Families as launching centers (first child gone to last child's leaving home)
Stage VII	Families in middle years (empty nest to retirement)
Stage VIII	Aging families (retirement to death of one or both spouses)

Source: Duvall (1967).

One of the obvious limitations of the Duvall model is that it ignores the impact of the presence of any other children in that family. Yet to broaden the family-cycle model to encompass the activities of the other children requires a much more complicated model. Roy Rodgers (1962) modified Duvall's scheme by taking into consideration the youngest as well as the oldest child in these transitions and ended up with a 24-stage family-cycle model. While Rodgers's approach is more satisfactory in that it reflects the complexity of transitions in families with more than one child, it becomes so cumbersome in practice that few scholars have used it analytically.[12]

Probably the most widely used and cited family-cycle model was developed by Reuben Hill (1964). Rejecting Duvall's scheme as too limiting because it focuses narrowly on the impact of the oldest child on the family and dismissing Rodgers's family-cycle model as "unmanageable" in practice, Hill proposed a nine-stage model of the family cycle (see Table II).

Hill's family-cycle model is broader in scope than that of Duvall's and incorporates the presence of children other than just the oldest one in the family. It also recognizes the importance of the retirement of the father from the labor force, but does not take into consideration the possible employment of the mother. Furthermore, as Hill (1964) noted, the scheme "masks the great variation among families in the middle stages of development and gives the illusion of smoothness of family development over time for all families, which empirical observations so far have failed to support" (p. 192).

The sociologists of the family are divided over the advisability of using family cycles. While some continue to employ a family-cycle perspective in their re-

[12]Rodgers (1962) prefers categories rather than stages as names of the phases of the family because he feels that the word categories better reflects the fact that the researcher rather than the family recognizes and designates these analytical constructs.

TABLE II

Robert Hill's Nine-stage Model of the Family Cycle

Stage I	Establishment (newly married, childless)
Stage II	New parents (infant–3 years)
Stage III	Preschool family (child 3–6, and possibly younger siblings)
Stage IV	School-age family (oldest child 6–12, possibly younger siblings)
Stage V	Family with adolescent (oldest 13–19, possible younger siblings)
Stage VI	Family with young adult (oldest 20 until first child leaves home)
Stage VII	Family as launching center (from departure of first to last child)
Stage VIII	Postparental family, the middle years (after children have left home until father retires)
Stage IX	Aging family (after retirement of father)

Source: Hill (1964).

search (Hudson & Murphy, 1980; Velsor & O'Rand, 1984), many others (Elder, 1978; Nock, 1979, 1981; Spanier, Sauer, & Larzelere, 1979) have abandoned it because its focus is too narrow and static to capture the dynamics of family life—especially since other stratification schemes based only on the simple presence of any children or the length of the marriage seem to capture more effectively the empirical variations in certain aspects of family life.[13]

Just as the sociologists of the family are becoming increasingly disenchanted with the family cycle, some historians are enthusiastically advocating it. Although recognizing the inapplicability of the existing contemporary models of the family cycle to the study of the past, Tamara Hareven (1974) was one of the earliest and most articulate proponents of the utility of a family-cycle approach for studying the history of the family:

> The cycle approach to the historical study of the family does not merely substitute a time unit of analysis for the current structural unit. Historians who will substitute longitudinal tracing or record linkage for cross-sectional analysis, without developing a conceptual scheme, will be moving from one mechanical category to another. Family research in the next few years will have to determine what type of family cycles existed and what the significant stages of transition were. Historians of the life cycle (childhood, adolescence, youth) have already demonstrated the fact that stages of psycho-biological development are socially defined, and that it would be impossible, therefore to rely on universal stages. Similarly, stages in the family cycle are not governed simply by biological age grades. In their analysis of contemporary groups, family sociologists are grappling with the classification of stages of the family cycle. Historians will not only need to define such stages for past societies, but to interpret their relationship in the historical contexts. (pp. 326–327)

[13]Despite the extensive criticisms of the family life-cycle approach, many of its original proponents continue to advocate it without any substantial revisions. Thus, Duvall and Miller (1985: 37) conclude that ''the heuristic, conceptual, and empirical utility of the family life cycle continues to be widespread.''

Hareven's enthusiasm for the family cycle has been tempered over time as she is shifting her attention to the life-course approach (Hareven, 1978a) and as other historians (Kertzer, 1984; Vinovskis, 1977) have questioned the practicality of ever devising an adequate overall family-cycle model for the past. Indeed, in her own recent work on Amoskeag (Hareven, 1982b) she mentioned the family cycle only in passing, and does not try to develop or use it analytically.[14] Since Hareven's (1982b) definition of family extends well beyond the immediate members' residing together in a household, it would be even harder to construct a comprehensive model of family stages which takes into account the experiences and involvement of family members living elsewhere. Nevertheless, although Hareven calls for additional refinements in any family cycle used for the analysis of the past, she still believes that "the family cycle continues to serve as a valuable construct" (1978a, p. 100).

While Hareven understands the difficulties involved in adopting any particular family-cycle model, many historians of the American family use the term "family cycle" very casually and loosely. Mary Ryan (1981), for example, refers to a family cycle of religious conversion without any indication of what is her underlying model. Similarly, her appendix (Ryan, 1982, pp. 267–274) is entitled "Family cycles and family strategies, New York State Census," but the accompanying tables merely provide cross-sectional, age-specific data on items such as fertility or occupation, with no attempt to explain what she means by a family cycle. Other historians (Haines, 1981) refer to one or more of the stages of the family cycle, but do not provide any information about the model as a whole. Thus, Chudacoff (1978a, 1978b) analyzes the experiences of newlyweds or couples with first children as two stages of the family cycle while Chudacoff and Hareven (1978) investigate the adult family-cycle stages of older Americans.

Wells (1985) calls for a developmental approach to individuals and families in the past. Trying to incorporate both individual and family cycles into a single scheme, he proposes a model that depicts the lives of the grandparent, the parent, and the first and last child. While his scheme is useful in pointing out the complexities of studying the lives of individuals, it is much too simple as an analytical framework since it focuses only on marriage, childbearing, childrearing, the empty nest, and widowhood. No attempt is made, for example, to distinguish between when the children are at home or in school. Furthermore, while Wells labels family events such as moving west, obtaining a bigger house, and entering a new job and places them on a chronological scale for the parent, the variation in timing and sequencing from one individual to the next could be

[14]For example, Hareven (1982b) states that "migration to Manchester was, therefore, part of the larger historic pattern of rural–urban migration of Quebec sons and daughters at specific stages of the family cycle" (p. 117) but does not provide information about the particular family-cycle model being employed.

so large as to make his model unmanageable analytically if one then tries to translate these location and career changes into part of the family cycle. Thus, although Wells frequently employs the concept of family cycle, what he has actually done is to present an abbreviated but interesting diagram for starting to think about individuals and families; he has not, however, provided us with an operational model for studying family cycles in the past.

The most detailed and ambitious application of a family-cycle model to an analysis of the past is an investigation of family life in Hamilton, Canada, in the second half of the nineteenth century (Katz et al., 1982). Whereas the age of the husband is usually used by historians to demarcate stages of the family cycle, Katz and his colleagues use instead the age of the wife (see Table III). Focusing on the presence of children as an indication of the financial strain on the family, they create a 12-stage, family-cycle model:

> Given the analytical purposes the categories should serve, we felt that it was important to distinguish between phases of the cycle in which families would be under the greatest and the least financial strain. The greatest strain would occur when all children were young. The periods of least strain should be those when no children lived at home or when at least one child was old enough to contribute to the family income. Another significant division separated families all of whose working-age children were female. We suspected that the expectations placed on young women in these families would be different from those placed on girls who had working-age brothers living at home; and this indeed proved to be the case. The application of these principles yielded twelve family-cycle categories. (Katz et al., 1982, p. 288)

Using the 12 stages as their overall framework, Katz and his associates calculate a series of descriptive statistics for 1851, 1861, and 1871 such as the percentage with boarders and percentage with relatives, as well as using multiple classifica-

TABLE III

Katz, Doucet, and Stern's 12-Stage Model of the Family Cycle

Stage I	Young (wife under 25), no children
Stage II	Young (wife under 25), all children aged 1–6
Stage III	Early midcycle (wife 25–34), no children
Stage IV	Early midcycle (wife 25–34), all children aged 1–14
Stage V	Late midcycle (wife 35–44), no children
Stage VI	Late midcycle (wife 35–44), all children aged 1–14
Stage VII	Late midcycle (wife 35–44), at least one male child 15 or over
Stage VIII	Late midcycle (wife 35–44), all children 15 or over female
Stage IX	Late cycle (wife 45 or over), at least one male child 15 or over
Stage X	Late cycle (wife 45 or over), all children 15 or over female
Stage XI	Late cycle (wife 45 or over), no children
Stage XII	Late cycle (wife 45 or over), other

Source: Katz, Doucet, and Stern (1982).

tion analysis to explain the number of relatives and boarders in these households.[15]

The family-cycle model proposed by Katz and his colleagues is an imaginative and original attempt to capture the changes in the well-being of the family overtime, but it has numerous shortcomings that seriously undermine its usefulness. Since their family-cycle model is explicitly concerned with reflecting the economic status of the family, the age of the husband rather than that of the wife might have been a more useful demarcation for the stages. Relatively few married women worked outside the home in the nineteenth century (Mason, Vinovskis, & Hareven, 1978) and therefore the age of the mother is less likely to reflect the levels of the family income. The wages of the husbands who were semiskilled or unskilled workers, however, may have been affected by their age and physical condition and therefore would have been more appropriate than the age of the mothers. It is also disappointing that the model does not include information about the work careers of the parents or their accumulation of assets. As a result, the model provides a very static view of the earnings of a family's primary breadwinners or of its assets.

Using the presence or absence of children of different ages gives us some sense of the financial strains upon the family, but since there is no differentiation between having one or more children in each of the stages, this remains a very crude approximation at best. Furthermore, by not distinguishing between children who are in school or working, the stages only reflect potential rather than actual sources of additional income. Unlike the Duvall (1967) or Rodgers (1962) family-cycle models, this approach also minimizes the importance of the impact on the family of the entry into or the exit from school of the youngest or oldest child.

The model does not take into consideration the fact that some of the families were female-headed and therefore under particularly great financial stress. By seemingly focusing on only intact, two-parent families, the difficulties of children growing up in broken homes in the past are slighted.[16] Furthermore, since being in one of the 12 stages often precludes one from entering another one, this scheme is

[15]Surprisingly, Katz, Doucet, and Stern (1982) seem to be unaware of most of the earlier sociological literature (Duvall, 1967; Hill & Rodgers, 1964) on the family cycle or of the more recent discussions of it by Hareven (1974, 1977, 1978a).

[16]The authors note that "the family cycle ended with dissolution, most often the result of death. In fact widowhood formed a significant part of the life cycle of women." (Katz, Doucet, & Stern, 1982: p. 290) This seems to imply that the family cycle ended with the death of either spouse. Yet later they analyze the percentage of households that are female-headed, using their 12 family-cycle categories. In any case, since nearly one out of six or four of the families in stages 7 through 12 are female-headed, one wonders how accurately their stages portray the economic resources and needs of the family, since their model does not even take into consideration the presence or absence of the husband.

not really a family-cycle model, but one that depicts some possible stages of the family which some individuals may experience during their lifetime.

These are only a few of the many objections that might be raised against this or any other model of family cycles applied to the past. The problem is that the experiences of families in the past as well as in the present are simply too complex to be adequately captured any any single, overall family-cycle model. For more specific and limited questions, perhaps one might use a family-cycle approach as a heuristic device to illuminate the process being investigated, although the particular models applied so far to the study of family life in the past seem limited and deficient.[17] Rather than continuing to hold out the hope for an overall family-cycle model that will be more suitable for historical analysis than those devised by the family sociologists, perhaps our energies might be more profitably devoted to exploring a life-source approach which focuses on individuals and their transitions within the context of their families, the broader social environment, and the historical time period (Kertzer, 1984; Vinovskis, 1977).[18]

IV. Life-Course Analysis

Because of the inherent limitations in any family-cycle model, historians (Hareven, 1977, 1978a, 1982; Mason et al., 1978; Vinovskis, 1977) are increasingly turning to the life course as an alternate framework for studying

[17]One can envision the construction of family-cycle models to analyze, for example, the transmission of property from one generation to the next or the economic stress due to changes in the demographic composition of families. Yet even in these particular situations, it is unlikely that we will develop an overall family-cycle model that will be equally applicable in all periods of the past because of the changing contemporary definitions of what constitutes families and households, patterns of inheritance, and the changes in the economic functioning of the household. Furthermore, it is difficult in practice to follow families or households longitudinally, especially if one identifies them by their residence, because it is not always clear what these groupings mean over time (Kertzer & Schiaffino, 1983).

Even some of the most ardent proponents of the family-cycle approach recognize that any particular scheme may not be applicable or useful in all circumstances. Thus, Rodgers (1973) concedes that "although the set (of stages) developed by one analyst may be used directly by another, it may be preferable to develop a new set which adequately meets the needs of the specific problem" (p. 81). In addition, there seems to be little agreement among scholars using the family-cycle approach on the specific stages of the model (Segalen, 1974).

[18]Whether one tries to study the family as a whole over time, as in family-cycle analysis, or follow individuals, as in life-course analysis, is to some extent an arbitrary decision and influenced by the type of questions one is trying to answer. Because of the conceptual and methodological problems inherent in any American family-cycle approach, most American historians (Vinovskis, 1977; Kertzer, 1984) now seen to prefer following individuals, but some (e.g., Watkins, 1980) argue that "if we are interested in family history, we should explicitly choose the family as the unit of

family life in the past. Unlike the family-cycle approach which follows families, the life course analyzes the lives of individuals and how they are affected not only by their families, but also by larger changes within society as a whole. Life-course analysis is particularly concerned with transitions in an individual's life and tries to understand them within the historical context in which they occurred.

While most family-cycle models consist of fairly simple and clear-cut stages and therefore are relatively easy to comprehend and use, the life-course approach is much more complex and more difficult to employ because it is really more of a perspective than a straightforward prescription for analysis. Perhaps the best summary of the life course is provided by one of its most active and able proponents, Glen Elder (1978):

> The life course refers to pathways through the age-differentiated life span, to social patterns in the timing, duration, spacing, and order of events; the timing of an event may be as consequential for life experience as whether the event occurs and the degree or type of change. Age differentiation is manifested in expectations and options that impinge on decision processes and the course of events that give shape to life stages, transitions, and turning points. Such differentiation is based in part on the social meanings of age and the biological facts of birth, sexual maturity, and death. These meanings have varied through social history and across cultures at points in time, as documented by evidence on socially recognized age categories, grades, and classes. . . . Over the life course, age differentiation also occurs through the interplay of demographic and economic processes, as in the relation between economic swings and the timing of family events. Sociocultural, demographic and material factors are essential elements in a theory of life-course variation. (pp. 21–22)

Life-course analysis is particularly suited for historical analysis because it traces the development of the individual within a broader and more flexible framework than the family-cycle approach. In certain historical periods, for example, the role of the members of the nuclear family may be less significant than that of the larger kinship group (Stone, 1977) and the distinction between members of the household and the family may not be as clear or important as later (Sieder & Mitterauer, 1983). The life-course approach encourages one to look at a larger variety of influences on the individual than just those of other members of his or her family. It also provides a flexible framework for studying the interaction of individuals and institutions such as churches or schools since the nature and importance of these institutions may vary from one period or culture to another. By recognizing that many of the stages of the family-cycle models in the contemporary setting are the product of our particular socioeconomic and cultural historical development, the life-course perspective invites a more flexible approach to the study of individuals and their transitions in the

---

analysis'' (p. 106). Those who advocate the use of the family as the unit of analysis, however, will need to specify exactly how they plan to overcome the methodological problems plaguing the existing family-cycle approaches.

past. Finally, by stressing the importance of timing and sequencing of transitions as well as their occurrence, the life-course approach more aptly captures the complexity of changes and how they are interpreted and treated by society.

There are already several essays (Elder, 1978, 1981a, 1981b; Hareven, 1977, 1978a, 1978b, 1982b; Vinovskis, 1977, 1983a) describing the use of life-course analysis in studying family life in the past. Rather than restating the more general points raised in those discussions, the remainder of this chapter will examine some of the achievements and shortcomings of recent historical applications of the life-course perspective and suggest other ways and areas in which this approach might be profitably employed.[19]

One of the virtues of the life-course approach is that it tries to take into account the biological and psychological development of the individual as he or she ages. This use of life-span development adds a valuable component to the analysis of family life that is neglected by a family-cycle approach. Yet in practice, life-span development is used rarely in historical studies as most of these scholars pay little, if any, attention to biological or psychological factors. Some historians (Demos, 1970) have used the Eriksonian model of the stages of development to analyze children in colonial New England. Others (Moran & Vinovskis, 1982) have probed the implications of different models of child development on how we might interpret the reactions of Puritan children to death and dying. Historians (Fischer, 1978; Vinovskis, 1982) have also speculated on how physical disabilities may have affected aging Protestant ministers in the seventeenth, eighteenth, and nineteenth centuries. Nevertheless, many other potentially important questions, such as the effects of biological aging on the physical ability of laborers to work effectively, still have not been explored.[20]

If historians have neglected the biological and psychological aspects of life-span development, they have been much better in recognizing and addressing the importance of socially defined phases of the life span—though often without reaching any agreement among themselves on the nature or timing of those phases. The existence of adolescence as a stage of the life span, for example, has elicited considerable inquiry. Some (Brumberg, 1984; Demos & Demos, 1969) see adolescence emerging as a distinct stage of development only in the nineteenth century, while others argue that it existed by the mid-seventeenth (Thompson, 1984) or early eighteenth century (Hiner, 1975). Whatever the exact timing of adolescence as a stage (and part of the disagreement stems from the lack of a clear

[19]While most of the examples will be drawn from scholars who have adopted a life-course perspective, a few will include individuals whose work is relevant to this approach but who may not be explicitly operating out of this framework.

[20]There has been a great deal of activity by a small group of psychohistorians (deMause, 1974) to analyze child development in the past, but most of this work is of questionable quality and usefulness (Stannard, 1980). Unfortunately, there is not a good review of the application of more current theories of child development to the past. For some intriguing speculations, see Kagan (1984).

and agreed upon definition of adolescence), almost everyone (Hareven, 1974; Vinovskis, 1983a, in press) agrees that it is a more socially than biologically determined period of life. Furthermore, Modell, Furstenberg, and Hershberg (1976) have demonstrated how the timing and duration of transitional events such as school leaving, entering the labor force, and marrying, have varied in the life course of individuals from the nineteenth to the twentieth centuries.[21]

Most of the attention of historians adopting the life-course approach is on the intersection of individual lives and the demands of their families. The concept of family time (Hareven, 1977) is one of the most frequently used ideas.

> The concept of "family time" designates the timing of events such as marriage, birth of a child, leaving home, and the transition of individuals into different roles as the family moves through its life course. Timing has often been a major source of conflict and pressure in the family, since "individual time" and "family time" are not always in harmony. For example, the decision to leave home, to marry, or to form one's own family could not in the past be timed strictly in accordance with individual preferences, depending instead on the decisions and needs of the family as a collective unit and on institutional supports. Research has only just begun to sketch some of the basic patterns of the timing of family transitions and to link them with "historical time"—that is, with changing social conditions. (p. 59)

Unfortunately, it is not always clear exactly what is meant by family time or how one measures its importance historiccally. Who determines the needs and interests of the family and how arc decisions made and enforced? Are the interests of the family usually commonly agreed upon or are there frequent disagreements among the members? Does the father exercise predominant influence on some issues, such as those relating to the economic well-being of the family, and the mother in other areas, such as the care of the home? Do fathers and mothers have differential authority over their offspring, depending on the children's ages and sex? And does the family consist of closely related kin residing together in the household or does it also include, as Hareven (1982b) suggests, members living elsewhere? In other words, if one of the theroetical strengths of life-course analysis is that it follows the lives of individuals within the context of their families, one of its weaknesses in practice is that there is almost no effort to specify exactly and systematically what is meant by family time and how it operates.

Rather than just speaking of family time in general, we need to specify and operationalize as much as possible the different ways in which family needs and considerations may impact upon the life course of the individual.[22] There have

[21]Although historians have discussed the emergence of different stages or phases of the life cycle, very little effort has been made to develop a more general model of the origins of these stages historically. For a very interesting and useful effort to analyze the emergence of different stages of the life cycle, see Hareven (1982a).

[22]For a critique of the failure of many scholars to define or operationalize their use of the family context in life-course analysis, see Watkins (1980).

been some attempts (Kaestle & Vinovskis, 1978, 1980; Mason et al., 1978), for example, to measure the economic resources and needs of the family as a whole, using information from the lists of family members in the nineteenth-century federal manuscript censuses. Rather than just using the occupation of the head of the household as a reflection of the economic well-being of the family, one can also create an index of the number of workers in that family, weighted by age and sex. Similarly, one can also construct an index of the relative consumption needs of families by using the itemized nineteenth-century household expenditures to approximate the relative needs of individuals (again taking into consideration age and sex). A work/consumption index has been employed in studies of female labor-force participation (Mason et al., 1978) and patterns of school attendance (Kaestle & Vinovskis, 1978, 1980). Along the same lines, Haines (1981) has attempted to estimate the incomes and expenditures of Philadelphia families in 1880, using the federal manuscript census and the 1889/1900 U.S. Commissioner of Labor Survey. While much more work needs to be done on any such work/consumption or income/expenditure index before we have confidence in their accuracy and utility, it does point the way in which historians can begin to measure at least in relative terms some of the components of a family's resources and needs.

While historians have obtained at least some hard data on the incomes and expenditures of individuals in the past, it is much more difficult to ascertain the decision-making process within families. Of course, some have tried to make inferences about the process by looking only at the behavioral outcomes, but this usually does not reveal very much about how individuals went about reaching those conclusions. Instead, we might use letters or autobiographical accounts for clues as to how families went about making decisions. Oral histories, especially if conducted in a more rigorous and scientific manner, could be used effectively. Though all of these types of sources are highly subjective and must be used carefully, they will provide some useful information about how decisions were made and enforced among family members in the past.

Life-course analysis often studies only individuals and families without paying any attention to their interactions with institutions, such as churches, schools, and factories. An older generation of scholars (Smelser, 1959) did consider how industrialization changes family life, but did not investigate how families adjusted to the new work conditions or modified them. Yet a new generation of scholars, led by the pioneering work of Hareven (1982b), is now exploring how the life course of individuals is affected by changes in the institutional environment.

Hareven's (1982b) analysis of the Amoskeag textile mills in the early twentieth century demonstrates how individuals used their family and kinship ties to adjust to the workplace. She skillfully shows how the operations of the textile mill were in turn modified to accommodate the needs of the kinship networks that played such a large role in recruiting workers to Amoskeag and then socializing them into the industrial regime once they had arrived. Hareven captures the dynamics of the interaction of individuals and institutions by considering how the life course of workers was affected by the changing conditions of work during periods of labor shortages or surpluses. By tracing the differential effects of changes in the economy on the fortunes of the workers, Hareven nicely illustrates the importance of seeing the life course of individuals within their historical and institutional context.

Just as individuals are affected by their families and institutions, they are also influenced by the communities in which they live. Unfortunately, because much of life-course analysis has been done in single community settings, the importance of community influence is often overlooked. Indeed, there is a tendency among many historians (Chudacoff, 1972; Frisch, 1972; Thernstrom, 1964) to generalize from the experiences of their particular case study to the population at large without adequately considering the representativeness of their particular analysis (Vinovskis, 1983b).

The potential importance of the community setting can be seen by looking at the rates of female labor-force participation in different settings in the nineteenth century. An analysis (Mason et al., 1978) of eight Essex County, Mass., communities in 1880 revealed that women were much more likely to work in Lawrence, a textile center employing many females, than in Salem, a commercial city with fewer opportunities for working women. The results of the Essex County analysis were then compared directly with those from Los Angeles (Mason & Laslett, 1983) in 1880 and 1900. While the general age-specific curve for female employment was similar in the Essex communities and Los Angeles, the level of labor-force participation was much lower in Los Angeles in 1880 and 1900. As a result, students of the life course in the past need to pay closer attention to the communities in which individuals lived as this may have affected opportunities such as being able to send their children to school or to enter the labor force.

Similarly, scholars should explore the effects of neighborhood on the life course of individuals. Unfortunately, most urban historians have implicitly treated cities as uniform settings by failing to differentiate the various neighborhoods in which families lived. The analyses (Kaestle & Vinovskis, 1978; Mason et al., 1978) of the eight Essex County communities, for example, do not attempt to distinguish between the experiences of those who grew up in the central business district of Salem and those who lived in the more outlying, residential sections. Yet an investigation (Hareven & Vinovskis, 1975) of Boston in the late nineteenth century found significant differences in marital fertility among individuals living in different wards even after controlling for the effects of their personal characteristics.

Urban historians are now beginning to pay much more attention to the importance of space and location in defining the experiences of residents in nineteenth-century cities. The Philadelphia Social History Project (Burstein, 1981; Greenberg, 1981; Hershberg et al., 1981) uses a grid system measuring approximately 1.25 city blocks on each side to study the effects of neighborhoods on the life course of individuals. Zunz (1982) sampled blocks in Detroit from 1880 to 1920 to investigate changes in the ethnic and occupational composition of neighborhoods and analyzed how this affected individuals growing up in different parts of the community.

Historians have been relatively quick to accept in principle the life-course approach, but are now experiencing considerable difficulty in applying the concept to their research as the result of limitations in data. Life-course analysis assumes the availability of longitudinal data. Analysts of the nineteenth century, however, rely almost exclusively on individual-level, cross-sectional data from the decennial federal manuscript censuses (1850–1880, 1900–1910), often without adequately considering the biases introduced into their studies by the ways in which they interpret their limited data.

Many scholars simply make inferences about the life course of individuals from the cross-sectional census data. But this assumes that the age-specific experiences of individuals at a particular point in time will approximate those of the same age-cohorts over time. Unfortunately, this is often not the case. For example, if one (Vinovskis, 1977) compares the cross-sectional and cohort estimates of tuberculois death rates for Massachusetts males from 1880 to 1930, it is evident that the cross-sectional estimates yield a much higher level of mortality than was actually experienced by those age-cohorts. Therefore, it is hazardous to try to estimate life-course experiences from cross-sectional data—especially when there are reasons to suspect that the age-specific rates of that behavior may have changed over time (Kertzer, 1984; Watkins, 1980).

There is another danger associated with using cross-sectional data to make inferences about life-course development on the basis of a case study of a single community—the biases introduced due to selective migration. Modell et al. (1976) compared the timing of the transitions of leaving school, entering the labor force, leaving the household of origin, marrying, and establishing one's own household in Philadelphia in 1880. They used the age-sepcific rates for these behaviors in Philadelphia to develop a model of the life-course transitions of youth in the late-nineteenth century. One might question, however, the construction of the life course of individuals from their data since many young people undoubtedly migrated to Philadelphia to find a job. The sudden appearance of these individuals in the census would result in incorrect inferences being drawn from the cross-sectional data about the work experiences of those growing up in Philadelphia; the influx of teen-agers seeking work creates the misleading impression that a much larger percentage of those who had lived in that city most of their lives were dropping out of school to go to work. In other words, when the behavior (such as entering the labor force) being investigated is also one of the key factors in the age-specific in- or outmigration to a small geographical area, estimates of the life course of individuals from the age-specific, cross-sectional data will yield an inaccurate picture.

If one does use age-specific, cross-sectional census data to make inferences about the life course, one should at least analyze the age-specific, aggregate, population flows into or out of the community, using the decennial censuses and mortality estimates to obtain a rough idea of the biases that may be introduced by net migration. Using this approach, scholars (Mason et al., 1978) found that young men and women migrated to Lawrence to work in the textile mills but then left as they grew older. As a result, one should not try to make life-course inferences from the age-specific, cross-sectional census data for that community. Similarly, Kaestle and Vinovskis (1980) discovered that the age-specific school attendance pattern of eight Essex County cities and towns in 1860 and 1880 does not reflect the experiences of children actually growing up in those communities since many young people entered or left them specifically to find work.

Some scholars (Glasco, 1977) analyze the life course of individuals by using nineteenth-century New York State censuses which provide data on the length of time an individual has resided in the community. The length of time one has lived in a community is used to make longitudinal inferences about the lives of the residents of those cities and towns. This approach, however, fails to recognize the biases introduced by selective outmigration. Individuals in the higher occupational strata and those who are property owners are less likely to move (Chudacoff, 1972; Thernstrom, 1964). Hence, inferring the life course of individuals on the basis of data from those who stay in an area may provide a very inaccurate guide to the experiences of the population as a whole.

One promising way of constructing a more dynamic picture of the life course is to link the vital records of individuals with their census information. Several historians (Ankarloo, 1978; Chudacoff, 1978b) have linked vital events within one or two years of the census information and shown that many newlyweds lived with their parents for a short time before establishing their own households. So far, most of these studies are limited because they cover such a small portion of the life course. Furthermore. the difficulties of making even such a proximate linkage for a sizable portion of the population reduces the utility of this procedure. Nevertheless, the results of the studies using this linkage technique suggest its usefulness in constructing a more dynamic picture of important life-course transitions than could be developed from cross-sectional data alone.[23]

Another useful way of constructing a longitudinal data set is to link individuals from one decennial census to the next. Despite the considerable difficulties

[23]One particularly promising approach uses census data combined with information from population registers to study European family life (Kertzer, 1984). Although population registers are not available for the study of American family life, perhaps vital records and city directories might be substituted.

involved in such an undertaking, many historians (Griffen & Griffen, 1978; Katz et al., 1982; Thernstrom, 1964) have succeeded in making such linkages and provided important new information on the career patterns of nineteenth-century Americans. Due to the larger turnover in population, however, this method also has serious limitations in terms of representativeness. Some of these shortcomings can at least be minimized by using the cross-sectional data of the entire population to estimate the direction and magnitude of the biases introduced by linking individuals from one census to the next. Furthermore, by also using state censuses which are sometimes available between the federal censuses, one can reduce considerably the attrition rate of the population from one period to the next and thereby greatly increase the representativeness of the investigation. Finally, although tracing the origins or destinations of individuals who migrate seems like an impossible task, Peter Knights (1983) is demonstrating its feasibility when there are ample state and local records available. Indeed. he has traced more than 90% of a sample of outmigrants from Boston between 1860 and 1900.

Overall, the life-course perspective is being adopted by many American family historians, as evidenced by the increasing willingness of scholars to apply that term to their work. Unfortunately, much of the work to date has been rather limited in scope and hampered by the lack of longitudinal data as well as by the lack of conceptual clarity. Indeed, the very looseness of the life-course perspective, both one of its strengths and weaknesses, allows some family historians to utilize this framework without employing the type of rigorous and systematic social-science methods that are essential for answering the questions posed by their research. Nevertheless, the life-course perspective remains one of the most promising avenues for future research in this field as it encourages scholars to use a broader and a more dynamic perspective in analyzing family life in the past.

Acknowledgments

Several scholars who read an earlier version of this chapter made important suggestions for improving it. While I have not always been able to incorporate all of their ideas, I want to thank Glen Elder, Maurine Greenwald, David Kertzer, and John Modell for their assistance.

References

Anderson, M. (1971). *Family structure in nineteenth century Lancashire*. Cambridge, England: Cambridge University Press.

Anderson, M. (1980). *Approaches to the history of the western family*. London: Macmillan.

Ankarloo, B. (1978). Marriage and family formation. In T. K. Hareven (Ed.), *Transitions: The family and the life course in historical perspective* (pp. 113–133). New York: Academic Press.

Berkner, L. (1972). The stem family and the developmental cycle of the peasant household: An eighteenth-century Austrian example. *American Historical Review, 77,* 398–418.

Brumberg, J. J. (1984). "Ruined girls": Changing community responses to illegitimacy in upstate New York, 1890–1920. *Journal of Social History, 18,* 247–272.

Burstein, A. N. (1981). Immigrants and residential mobility: The Irish and Germans in Philadelphia, 1850–1880. In T. Hershberg (Ed.), *Work, space, and family and group experience in the nineteenth century: Essays toward an interdisciplinary history of the city* (pp. 174–203). New York: Oxford University Press.

Censer, J. T. (1984). *North Carolina planters and their children, 1800–1860.* Baton Rouge, LA: Louisiana State University Press.

Chayanov, A. V. (1966). *The theory of peasant economy.* Homewood, IL: R. D. Irwin.

Chudacoff, H. P. (1972). *Mobile Americans: Residential and social mobility in Omaha,* 1880–1920. New York: Oxford University Press.

Chudacoff, H. P. (1978a). New branches of the tree: Household structure in early stages of the family cycle in Worcester, Massachusetts, 1860–1880." In T. K. Hareven (Ed.), *Themes in the history of the family* (pp. 55–72). Lunenberg, VT: Stinehour Press.

Chudacoff, H. P. (1978b). Newlyweds and family extension: The first stage of the family cycle in Providence, Rhode Island, 1864–1865 and 1879–1880. In T. K. Hareven & M. A. Vinovskis (Eds.), *Family and population in nineteenth-century America* (pp. 179–205). Princeton,NJ: Princeton University Press.

Chudacoff, H. P., & Hareven, T. K. (1978). Family transitions into old age. In T. K. Hareven (Ed.), *Transitions: The family and the life course in historical perspective* (pp. 217–243). New York: Academic Press.

Czap, P., Jr. (1983). "A large family": The peasant's greatest wealth: Serf households in Mishino, Russia, 1814–1858. In R. Wall, J. Robin, & P. Laslett (Eds.), *Family forms in historic Europe* (pp. 105–151). Cambridge, England: Cambridge University Press.

Degler, C. N. (1980). Women and the family. In M. Kammen (Ed.), *The past before us: Contemporary historical writing in the United States* (pp. 308–326). New York: Cornell University Press.

deMause, L. (Ed.). (1974). *The history of childhood.* New York: Harper & Row.

Demos, J. (1965). Notes on life in Plymouth Colony. *William and Mary Quarterly (3rd Series), 22,* 264–286.

Demos, J. (1968). Families in colonial Bristol, Rhode Island: An exercise in historical demography. *William and Mary Quarterly (3rd Series), 25,* 40–57.

Demos, J. (1970). *A little commonwealth: Family life in Plymouth Colony.* New York: Oxford University Press.

Demos, J., & Demos, V. (1969). Adolescence in historical perspective. *Journal of Marriage and the Family, 31,* 632–638.

Duvall, E. M. (1967). *Family development.* Philadelphia: J. B. Lippincott.

Duvall, E. M., & Miller, B. C. (1985). *Marriage and family development.* New York: Harper & Row.

Eisenstadt, S. N. (1956). *From generation to generation.* Glencoe, IL: Free Press.

Elder, G. H., Jr. (1978). Family history and the life course. In T. K. Hareven (Ed.), *Transitions: The family and the life course in historical perspective* (pp. 17–64). New York: Academic Press.

Elder, G. H., Jr. (1981a). History and the family: The discovery of complexity. *Journal of Marriage and the Family, 43,* 489–519.

Elder, G. H., Jr. (1981b). History and the life course. In D. Bertaux (Ed.), *Biography and society: The life course approach in the social sciences* (pp. 77–115). Beverly Hills, CA: Sage.

Elder, G. H., Jr. (1983). The life-course perspective. In M. Gordon (Ed.), *The American family in social–historical perspective* (3rd ed., pp. 54–60). New York: St. Martin's Press.

Fischer, D. H. (1978). *Growing old in America* (expanded ed.) New York: Oxford University Press.

Frisch, M. H. (1972). *Town into city: Springfield, Massachusetts and the meaning of community, 1840–1880*. Cambridge, MA: Harvard University Press.

Glasco, L. A. (1977). The life cycles and household structure of American ethnic groups: Irish, German, and native-born whites in Buffalo, New York, 1855. In Tamara K. Hareven (Ed.), *Family and kin in urban communities, 1700–1930* (pp. 122–143). New York: New Viewpoints.

Gordon, M. (1978). *The American family: Past, present, and future*. New York: Random House.

Greenberg, S. W. (1981). Industrial location and ethnic residential patterns in an industrializing city: Philadelphia, 1880. In T. Hershberg (Ed.), *Work, space, family and group experience in the nineteenth century: Essays toward an interdisciplinary history of the city* (pp. 204–232). New York: Oxford University Press.

Greven, P. J., Jr. (1966). Family structure in seventeenth-century Andover, Massachusetts. *William and Mary Quarterly (3rd Series), 23*, 234–256.

Greven, P. J., Jr. (1970). *Four generations: Population, land, and family in colonial Andover. Massachusetts*. Ithaca, NY: Cornell University Press.

Griffen, C., & Griffen, S. (1978). *Natives and newcomers: The ordering of opportunity in mid-nineteenth-century Poughkeepsie*. Cambridge, MA: Harvard University Press.

Haines, M. R. (1981). Poverty, economic stress, and the family in a late nineteenth-century American city: Whites in Philadelphia, 1880. In T. Hershberg (Ed.), *Philadelphia: Work, space, family, and group experience in the nineteenth century: Essays toward an interdisciplinary history of the city* (pp. 245–276). New York: Oxford University Press.

Hareven, T. K. (1974). The family process: The historical study of the family cycle. *Journal of Social History, 7*, 322–329.

Hareven, T. K. (1977). Family time and historical time. *Daedalus, 106*, 57–70.

Hareven, T. K. (1978a). Cycles, courses and cohorts: Reflections on the theoretical and methodological approaches to the historical study of family development. *Journal of Social History, 12*, 97–109.

Hareven, T. K. (1978b). Introduction: The historical study of the life course. In T. K. Hareven (Ed.), *Transitions: The family and the life course in historical perspective* (pp. 1–16). New York: Academic Press.

Hareven, T. K. (1982a). The life course and aging in historical perspective. In T. K. Hareven & K. Adams (Eds.), *Aging and the life course transitions: An interdisciplinary perspective* (pp. 1–26). New York: Guilford Press.

Hareven, T. K. (1982b). *Family time and industrial time: The relationship between the family and work in a New England industrial community*. Cambridge, England: Cambridge University Press.

Hareven, T. K., & Vinovskis, M. A. (1975). Marital fertility, ethnicity, and occupation in urban families: An analysis of South Boston and the South End in 1880. *Journal of Social History, 9*, 69–93.

Hershberg, T., Cox, H. E., Light, D. B., Jr., & Greenfield, R. R. (1981). The "journey-to-work": An empirical investigation of work, residence and transportation, Philadelphia, 1850 and 1880. In T. Hershberg (Ed.), *Philadelphia: Work, space, family and group experience in the nineteenth century: Essays toward an interdisciplinary history of the city* (pp. 128–173). New York: Oxford University Press.

Hill, R. (1964). Methodological issues in family development research. *Family Process, 3*, 186–206.

Hill, R., & Rodgers. R. H. (1964). The developmental approach. In H. T. Christensen (Ed.), *Handbook of marriage and the family* (pp. 171–211). Chicago: Rand McNally.

Hiner. N. R. (1975). Adolescence in eighteenth-century America. *History of Childhood Quarterly, 3,* 253–280.

Hudson, W. W., & Murphy, G. J. (1980). The non-linear relationship between marital satisfaction and stages of the family cycle: An artifact of type I errors? *Journal of Marriage and the Family, 42,* 263–267.

Kaestle, C. F., & Vinovskis, M. A. (1978). From fireside to factory: School entry and school leaving in nineteenth-century Massachusetts. In T. K. Hareven (Ed.), *Transitions: The family and the life course in historical perspective* (pp. 135–186). New York: Academic Press.

Kaestle, C. F., & Vinovskis, M. A. (1980). *Education and social change in nineteenth-century Massachusetts.* Cambridge, England: Cambridge University Press.

Kagan, J. (1984). *The nature of the child.* New York: Basic Books.

Katz, M. B., Doucet, M. J., & Stern, M. J. (1982). *The social organization of early industrial capitalism.* Cambridge, MA: Harvard University Press.

Kertzer, D. I. (1982). Generation and age in cross-cultural perspective. In M. W. Riley, R. P. Abeles, & M. S. Teitelbaum (Eds.), *Aging from birth to death: Sociotemporal perspectives* (Vol. 2, pp. 27–50). Boulder, CO: Westview Press.

Kertzer, D. I. (1984). *Family life in central Italy, 1880–1910: Sharecropping, wage labor, and coresidence.* New Brunswick, NJ: Rutgers University Press.

Kertzer, D. I., & Schiaffino, A. (1983). Industrialization and coresidence: A life course approach. In P. B. Baltes & O. G. Brim, Jr., (Eds.), *Life-span development and behavior* (Vol. 5, pp. 359–391). New York: Academic Press.

Knights, P. R. (1983, October). *Finding out-migrants from Boston: 1860–1900.* Paper presented at the Social Science History Association annual meeting, Washington, D.C.

Laslett, P. (1969). Size and structure of the household in England over three centuries. *Population Studies, 23,* 199–223.

Laslett, P. (1970). The comparative history of household and family. *Journal of Social History, 3,* 75–87.

Laslett, P. (Ed.).(1972). *Household and family in past time.* Cambridge, England: Cambridge University Press.

Laslett, P. (1977). *Family life and illicit love in earlier generations: Essays in historical sociology.* Cambridge, England, Cambridge University Press.

Lebsock, S. (1984). *The free women of Petersburg: Status and culture in a southern town, 1784–1860.* New York: Norton.

Levy, M. J., Jr. (1965). Aspects of the analysis of family structure. In A. J. Coale, L. A. Fallers, & M. J. Levy, Jr. (Eds.), *Aspects of the analysis of family structure* (pp. 1–63). Princeton, NJ: Princeton University Press.

Lewis, J. (1983). *The pursuit of happiness: Family and values in Jefferson's Virginia.* Cambridge, England: Cambridge University Press.

Lockridge, K. A. (1966). The population of Dedham, Massachusetts. 1636–1736. *Economic History Review (2nd Series), 19,* 318–344.

Lockridge, K. A. (1970). *A New England town; the first hundred years: Dedham, Massachusetts, 1636–1736.* New York: Norton.

Lockridge, K. A. (1977). Historical demography. In C. F. Delzell (Ed.), *The future of history* (pp. 53–64). Nashville, TN: Vanderbilt University Press.

Mannheim, K. (1952). *Essays on the sociology of knowledge.* New York: Oxford University Press.

Mason, K. O., & Laslett, B. (1983, April). *Women's work in the American west: Los Angeles, 1880–1900, and its contrast with Essex County, Massachusetts in 1880.* Paper presented at the Population Association annual meeting, Pittsburgh.

Mason, K. O., Vinovskis, M. A., & Hareven, T. K. (1978). Women's work and the life course in

Essex County, Massachusetts, 1880. In T. K. Hareven (Ed.), *Transitions: The family and the life course in historical perspective* (pp. 187–216). New York: Academic Press.

Modell, J., Furstenberg, F. F., Jr., & Hershberg, T. (1976). Social change and transitions to adulthood in historical perspective. *Journal of Family History, 1,* 7–32.

Moran, G. F., & Vinovskis, M. A. (1982). The Puritan family and religion: A critical reappraisal. *William and Mary Quarterly (3rd Series), 39,* 761–786.

Morgan, M., & Golden, H. H. (1979). Immigrant families in an industrial city: A study of households in Holyoke, 1880. *Journal of Family History, 4,* 59–68.

Nock, S. L. (1979). The family life cycle: Empirical or conceptual tool? *Journal of Marriage and the Family, 41,* 15–26.

Nock, S. L. (1981). Family life-cycle transitions: Longitudinal effects on family members. *Journal of Marriage and the Family, 43,* 703–714.

Parsons, T., & Bales, R. F. (1955). *Family, socialization and interaction process.* New York: Free Press.

Rodgers, R. H. (1962). *Improvement in the construction and analysis of family life cycle categories.* Kalamazoo, MI: Western Michigan University.

Rodgers, R. H. (1973). *Family interactions and transaction: The developmental approach.* Englewood Cliffs, NJ: Prentice-Hall.

Ryan, M. P. (1981). *Cradle of the middle class: The family in Oneida County, New York, 1790–1865.* Cambridge, England: Cambridge University Press.

Ryan, M. P. (1982). The explosion of family history. *Reviews in American History, 10,* 181–195.

Segalen, M. (1974). Research and discussion around family life cycle: An account of the 13th seminar on family research. *Journal of Marriage and the Family, 36,* 814–818.

Sieder, R., & Mitteraurer, M. (1983). The reconstruction of the family life course: Theoretical problems and empirical results. In R. Wall, J. Robin, & P. Laslett (Eds.), *Family forms in historic Europe* (pp. 309–345). Cambridge, England: Cambridge University Press.

Smelser, N. J. (1959). *Social change and the industrial revolution.* Chicago: University of Chicago Press.

Smith, D. B. (1980). *Inside the great house: Planter family life in eighteenth-century Chesapeake society.* Ithaca, NY: Cornell University Press.

Spanier, G. B., Sauer, W., & Larzelere, R. (1979). An empirical evaluation of the family life cycle. *Journal of Marriage and the Family, 41,* 27–38.

Stannard, D. E. (1980). *Shrinking history: On Freud and the failure of psychohistory.* NewYork: Oxford University Press.

Stone, L. (1977). *The family, sex and marriage in England, 1500–1800.* New York: Harper & Row.

Thernstrom, S. (1964). *Poverty and progress: Social mobility in a nineteenth-century city.* Cambridge, MA: Harvard University Press.

Thompson, R. (1984). Adolescent culture in colonial Massachusetts. *Journal of Family History, 9,* 127–144.

Tilly, L. A. (1979). Occupational structure, women's work, and demographic change in two French industrial cities, Anzin and Roubaix, 1872–1906. In J. Sundrin & E. Soderlund (Eds.), *Time, space and man* (pp. 107–132). Atlantic Highlands, NJ: Humanities Press.

Velsor, E. V., & O'Rand, A. M. (1984). Family life cycle, work career patterns and women's wages at midlife. *Journal of Marriage and the Family, 46,* 365–373.

Vinovskis, M. A. (1971). American historical demography: A review essay. *Historical Methods Newsletter, 4,* 141–148.

Vinovskis, M. A. (1977). From household size to the life course: Some observations on recent trends in family history. *American Behavioral Scientist, 21,* 263–287.

Vinovskis, M. A. (1978). Recent trends in American historical demography: Some methodological and conceptual considerations. *Annual Review of Sociology, 4,* 603–627.

Vinovskis, M. A. (1982). Aged servants of the lord: Changes in the status and treatment of elderly ministers in colonial America. In M. W. Riley, R. P. Abeles, & M. S. Teitelbaum (Eds.), *Aging from birth to death: Sociotemporal perspectives* (Vol. 2, pp. 105–137). Boulder, CO: Westview Press.

Vinovskis, M. A. (1983a). Home, hearth, and history: American families in the past. In J. B. Gardner & G. R. Adams (Eds.), *Ordinary people and everyday Life: Perspectives on the new social history* (pp. 115–138). Nashville, TN: American Association for State and Local History.

Vinovskis, M. A. (1983b). Community studies in urban educational history: Some methodological and conceptual observations. In R. K. Goodenow & D. Ravitch (Eds.), *Schools in cities: Consensus and conflict in American educational history* (pp. 287–304). New York: Holmes & Krier.

Vinovskis, M. A. (in press). Historical perspectives on the development of the family and parent-child interactions. In J. Altmann, J. Lancaster, & A. Rossi (Eds.), *Parenting across the life span*. New York: Aldine Press.

Wachter. K., Hammel, E., & Laslett. P. (1978). *Statistical studies of historical social structure*. New York: Academic Press.

Wall, R. (1983). Does owning real property influence the form of the household? An example from rural West Flanders. In R. Wall, J. Robin, & P. Laslett (Eds.), *Family forms in historic Europe* (pp. 379–407). Cambridge, England: Cambridge University Press.

Wall, R., Robin, J., & Laslett, P. (Eds.).(1983). *Family forms in historic Europe*. Cambridge, England, Cambridge University Press.

Watkins, S. C. (1980). On measuring transitions and turning points. *Historical Methods, 13,* 181–186.

Wells, R. V. (1985). *Uncle Sam's family: Issues in and perspectives on American demographic history*. Albany, NY: State University of New York Press.

Wrigley, E. A. (1977). Reflections on the history of the family. *Daedalus, 106,* 71–85.

Zunz, O. (1982). *The changing face of inequality: Urbanization, industrial development, and immigrants in Detroit, 1880–1920*. Chicago: University of Chicago Press.

Evaluating Developmental Hypotheses Using Statement Calculus and Nonparametric Statistics

Alexander von Eye
MAX PLANCK INSTITUTE FOR HUMAN DEVELOPMENT AND EDUCATION
Jochen Brandtstädter
UNIVERSITY OF TRIER

Abstract

A system for formulating and evaluating developmental hypotheses is presented. This method combines elements of statement calculus and of nonparametric statistics. The approach involves the following essential steps: (1) casting the hypothesis into a propositional format, (2) determining the corresponding truth table and disjunctive normal form, (3) identifying cells in the pertinent contingency table that are relevant to the evaluation of the proposition under study (so-called hit- and error-cells), and (4) comparing the observed distribution in relevant cells with an expected distribution estimated under a suitably chosen statistical model. Strategies for the estimation of expected values and for the statistical evaluation of propositions are outlined. Furthermore, several descriptive measures for evaluating the predictive efficiency of propositions are presented. The methods introduced are applied to two examples from developmental research. The first example pertains to personal control and emotional evaluation of development in partnership relations. A local hypothesis in which particular states of subjective developmental attainment, personal control over development, and perceived marital support were used as predictors of particular states of depression turned out to be highly effective. The hypothesis allowed for 28.5% more hits in the predictions when applied to the observed frequency distribution as compared with the expected frequency distribution that was estimated under the assumption of independence of predictors and criteria. In the second example tasks operationalizing Piaget's stages of cognitive development were administered to a sample of children at ages 7 and 9. A local hypothesis specifying concepts of developmental constancy and change led to an increase in the hit rates of 32%. The present approach is an extension of the method of prediction analysis (Hildebrand, Laing, & Rosenthal, 1977). Differences to the latter approach reside in the more strict formulation of hypotheses, the use of measures of increase in hits, and the use of the more conservative, nonparametric binomial test.

I. Introduction

Whether development is conceived as an age-related process as in maturational conceptions or as a nonage-related process, as in concepts of duration dependence, developmental research virtually always involves the notion of time (Baltes & Nesselroade, 1979; Featherman, 1985; Lerner, 1984; Wohlwill, 1973). Time is used as a predictor of developmental stages, progress, acceleration, deceleration, or—in more general terms—of constancy and change. In these predictions, the predictors and criteria usually are linked in terms of bi- or multivariate relations or interactions. In bi- or multivariate relations, changes in the time variable are assumed to account for a significant proportion of the variation of the developmental variables under study.

The main characteristic of these relations and interactions is that they are assumed to apply to the entire range of values that can meaningfully be taken by any variable under study. If, for instance, one assumes that wisdom develops ontogenetically as a result of individual experiences and that this kind of process can best be described by, say, a quadratic curve then one usually assumes also that the parameters of this curve hold true for the entire age range. Other examples of parameters of relations that are assumed to display general validity are correlation coefficients, regression coefficients, or coefficients of polynomials used for smoothing developmental curves.

It is one well-known consequence of this assumption of general validity that elements that do not follow the general trend, the so-called outliers, can cause large errors in the estimation of both kind and strength of a relation. Outliers can, for example, increase low correlation coefficients, or even change their sign. Another consequence of the assumption of general validity is that the strength of a relation can be incorrectly estimated if the type of relation changes. For example, sudden leaps or the transition from a linear to a curvilinear type of relation frequently cause underestimations of the strength of the relation when estimated within the framework of the linear model.

In this chapter, a group of methods will be described that can be applied to a broad range of multivariate relations and interactions. In particular, hypotheses that apply to particular subsets of a given data space rather than to the entire data range can be tested. These kinds of hypotheses will be termed local hypotheses. They allow for the consideration of relations that exist only in particular subsets of the data space or outlier cells as well as of relations that meet the general validity assumptions. The methods that will be described here are designed for the analysis of contingency tables.

An example of such local hypotheses can be derived from the development of cyclical psychoses. It is assumed that cyclical psychoses generally do not become manifest before middle adulthood. Although this assumption links the manifestation of cyclical psychoses to age, it might be misleading to assume a (linear) function valid from birth to death relating age to this disorder. Rather, one may exclude childhood, adolescence, and early adulthood from the hypothesis and state that if an individual reaches middle adulthood the probability of his/her displaying cyclical psychoses is increased.

Similar examples can be derived from developmental stages that are clearly linked to clearly circumscribed age ranges. Examples include "the terrible two" or puberty. Furthermore, behavioral changes related to particular discrete events, such as falling in love, moving to another country, or having a car accident may be subject to local hypotheses. The general form of the local hypotheses considered in the present chapter is such that particular discrete events as the onset of a developmental stage are used as predictors of behavioral classes or changes.

Concerning the operations to be executed, three steps are required to evaluate local hypotheses. First, it is necessary to state the hypotheses in a form that allows the determination of those cells of a contingency table that are relevant to the evaluation of the hypotheses. In this chapter, hyoptheses will be stated as logical propositions. The second step involves the determination of a statistical model for the estimation of expected cell frequencies. In the third step the model is compared statistically with the substantive hyoptheses under the null hypothesis of no differences between the observed and the estimated frequencies in relevant cells. The results of this comparison are expressed both in terms of the increase in the number of elements that can be assigned correctly to relevant cells and the statistical significance of the difference between expected and observed frequencies in those cells.

These steps serve as a basis for structuring the following chapter. First, the application of statement calculus in formulating hypotheses with respect to contingency tables will be treated. Second, the statistical tools needed for the evaluation of local hypotheses will be presented. In the last part of this chapter, two data sets from the investigation of action development and cognitive development will be presented, and methodological implications will be discussed.

II. Statement Calculus as a Format for Stating Developmental Propositions

Statement calculus, which can be defined as the algebra of truth values, deals with the logical structure of statements. There are four areas to which statement calculus has been applied that are of interest in the present context of testing developmental hyoptheses. First, statement calculus can be used within a confirmatory approach to formulate developmental hyoptheses. Examples include the prediction of developmental sequences (Froman & Hubert, 1980) or hypotheses on the development of attributions (Brandstädter, Krampen, & Vesely, 1985). In these examples, substantive statements are made and analyzed, using statement calculus before statistical analysis.

Second, statement calculus may be used within an exploratory approach to summarize observed relationships. However, instead of formulating hypotheses before applying statistics, the results of statistical analyses themselves are analyzed here. Examples include the search for types, in which clusters or types can often be translated into logical terms. These terms can, then, be minimized to obtain more parsimonious, logically equivalent expressions (von Eye & Brandtstädter, 1982).

In the third area the status of statement calculus is that of replacing statistics. Wottawa and collaborators (Härtner, Matthes, & Wottawa, 1980; Wottawa, 1984) presented an approach in which *hyp*otheses are systematically *ag*glutinated (HYPAG), that is, single hypotheses are grouped together according to some criteria. The criteria of agglutination include empirical truth of single hypotheses, which means that a certain portion of the sample must be accounted for (the relation of logical truth to empirical hypotheses will be discussed later), and both logical and empirical truth of the synthesized hypotheses, which means that the agglutination must not result in contradictory hypotheses. In HYPAG, there is no null hypothesis with which empirical results can be compared. Therefore, the criteria of empirical evidence and logical truth replace the classical approach of inferential statistics.

In the fourth area the approaches of statement calculus and statistics are combined in such a manner that only those hyoptheses that fulfill certain requirements with respect to their logical and empirical truth are subject to further statistical analysis. In a group of methods called GUHA (*g*eneral *u*nary *h*ypothesis *a*utomation) this way of applying statement calculus and statistics is realized (Hájek, Havránek, & Chytil, 1983). First, statements are generated using a theory of hypothesis formation (Hájek & Havránek, 1978). The application of this theory results in a set of statements that is not redundant, not contradictory, and accounts for a considerable portion of the sample under study. Only these statements are tested for statistical significance.

For the purposes of this chapter, the status of statement calculus in contingency table analysis is that of a tool for formulating and evaluating hypotheses. More specifically, it is used to link theoretical propositions to the data space under study.

A. SOME ELEMENTARY CONCEPTS OF STATEMENT CALCULUS

In the following section, some elementary concepts of statement calculus that are needed in contingency table analysis will be presented (cf. Berztiss, 1975, Klaus, 1973).

Statements and Their Connection. The first concept of importance in the following discussion is that of a *statement*. In classical logic, statements are defined as sentences that are either true or false. Examples of statements include "it is raining" and "2 + 2 = 4." Counterexamples include questions and commands. Since statement calculus does not refer to the content of a statement but only to its truth value, substantive statements usually are replaced by variables.

In order to negate or to combine statements the connectives *negation* ("not"), *disjunction* ("or"), *conjunction* ("and"), *implication* ("if–then"), and *equivalence* ("if and only if", "iff") are generally used. The respective symbols are $-$ (negation), $\vee$ (disjunction), $\wedge$ (conjunction), $\rightarrow$ (implication), and $\leftrightarrow$ (equivalence). Let both p and q be statements, then, these connectives can be explicated as follows:

(1) $\bar{p}$: "*not p*" (or "what has been said in p does not hold true");
(2) $p \vee q$: "p or q" (or "at least one of the two statements holds true"; the logical "or" is not exclusive);
(3) $p \wedge q$: "p and q" (or "p as well as q");
(4) $p \rightarrow q$: "if p then q" (or "p is sufficient for q," "p not without q," "q is necessary for p");
(5) $p \leftrightarrow q$: "q only if p" (or "p is necessary and sufficient for q," "p iff q").

Such statements, generated by linking simpler statements using logical connectives, are termed *composite statements*.

The Truth Table of Propositions. The logical operators just introduced are used also in colloquial speech. However, their colloquial meaning is not necessarily exactly the same as in statement calculus. According to the rules of statement calculus, disjunctions are true if either one of p and q, or both, hold

TABLE I

Definition of Connectives in Statement Calculus

Variables		Connectives				
p	q[a]	$\bar{p}$	$p \vee q$	$p \vee q$	$p \rightarrow q$	$p \leftrightarrow q$
1	1	0	1	1	1	1
1	0	0	1	0	0	0
0	1	1	1	0	1	0
0	0	1	0	0	1	1

[a] 1 = true, 0 = false.

true; and "p and q" is true only if both p and q hold true; "p" is true only if $\bar{p}$ does not hold true, etc. The general rule applied here is that the truth of a composite statement is a function of the truth of the single statements that are connected. The truth functions of the connectives negation, disjunction, conjunction, implication, and equivalence are given in Table I.

The statements in Table I may be interpreted as mathematical functions. Let $\{1,0\}^2 = \{11, 10, 01, 00\}$ be the set of all possible combinations of truth values that can be assumed by two statements, and $\{1,0\}$ the set of the truth values that can be assumed by the statement form, then every connective defines a mapping f of $\{1,0\}^2$ onto $\{1,0\}$. In more general terms, every proposition involving n variables ($n \geqq 2$) defines a mapping f of $\{1,0\}^n$ onto $\{1,0\}$.

Truth tables of composite statements involving more than two variables can be constructed stepwise on the basis of truth tables of two variables. In Table II the example of the trivariate statement $((\bar{p} \vee q) \wedge (q \vee \bar{r})) \rightarrow (p \rightarrow r)$ is developed.

TABLE II

Constructing the Truth Table of a Complex Trivariate Proposition[a]

p	q	r	$((\bar{p} \vee q)$	$\wedge$	$(r \vee \bar{q}))$	$\rightarrow$	$(p \rightarrow r)$
1	1	1	1	1	1	1	1
1	1	0	1	0	0	1	0
1	0	1	0	0	1	1	1
1	0	0	0	0	1	1	0
0	1	1	1	1	1	1	1
0	1	0	1	0	0	1	1
0	0	1	1	1	1	1	1
0	0	0	1	1	1	1	1

[a] see text for further explanation.

The truth value of complex composite statements can be developed stepwise. First, the truth values of the composite statements in the inner parentheses are determined. Applying this rule in Table II, the truth vectors of $\bar{p} \vee q$ (column 1) and $r \vee \bar{q}$ (column 3) are determined first. Then, stepwise the outer parentheses are solved. In Table II the conjunction $(\bar{p} \vee q) \wedge (r \vee \bar{q})$ and the implication $p \rightarrow r$ are the only remaining parentheses after the first step. These are solved next. What remains is the implication connecting the two outer parentheses. The determination of the truth values of this implication completes the development of the entire proposition.

Substantively, it turns out that this particular composite statement is a *tautology*. Irrespective of the truth values assumed by the statements that are connected, tautologies are always true, that is, the truth functions of tautologies show only the value "true" (or 1, as in Table II). In Table II, the tautology of transitivity was developed: If p is sufficient for q and q is sufficient for r, then p is sufficient for r (the law of syllogisms).

The Disjunctive Normal Form. In this section the concept of disjunctive normal form (DNF) will be introduced. This is a key concept in the analysis of contingency tables, because the transformation of a statement into its DNF leads immediately to the identification of cells in a contingency table that are relevant in the evaluation of the truth of that statement. Let V^k be any k-variate statement in statement calculus terms. Then, the DNF is the disjunctive connection of all complete conjunctions for which V^k holds true. Complete conjunctions (or minterms; see Berztiss, 1975) contain all k variables (Klaus, 1973; Klaus & Buhr, 1964).

The DNF of any V^k can be derived immediately from the truth table. The following equivalences can, for instance, be derived from Table I (for the sake of simplicity in the following the "$\wedge$" is omitted from complete conjunctions; it will be written $p\bar{q}$ instead of $p \wedge \bar{q}$, or $p\bar{q}r$ instead of $p \wedge \bar{q} \wedge r$):

(1) $(p \vee q) \leftrightarrow (pq \vee p\bar{q} \vee \bar{p}q)$,
(2) $(p \rightarrow q) \leftrightarrow (pq \vee \bar{p}q \vee \bar{p}\bar{q})$,
(3) $(p \leftrightarrow q) \leftrightarrow (pq \vee \bar{p}\bar{q})$.

The parentheses on the right side of the equivalence signs contain the DNF of the respective statement form on the left side. The reader is invited to extract the DNFs of the following composite statements from Table II: $(\bar{p} \vee q)$; $(r \vee \bar{q})$; $((\bar{p} \vee q) \wedge (r \vee \bar{q}))$.

[1]The DNFs of the composite statements are:

$$(\bar{p} \vee q) \leftrightarrow (pq \vee \bar{p}q \vee \bar{p}\bar{q})$$

$$(r \vee \bar{q}) \leftrightarrow (rq \vee r\bar{q} \vee \bar{r}\bar{q})$$

$$((\bar{p} \vee r) \wedge (r \vee \bar{q})) \leftrightarrow (pqr \vee \bar{p}\bar{q}r \vee \bar{p}\bar{q}\bar{r})$$

A DNF of a k-variate composite statement V^k disjunctively combines those and only those elements of the set $\{1,0\}^k$ of all configurations of truth values of k variables for which V^k assumes the truth value $V^k = 1$, that is, for which V^k holds true. The DNF of $\bar{V}^k$, that is, the negation of V^k, is given by the disjunction of those configurations of $\{1,0\}^k$ for which $\bar{V}^k$ assumes the value 1 or—equivalently—for which V^k assumes the value 0. Let $K_V k \leqq \{1,0\}^k$ be the subset of those complete conjunctions for which V^k-holds true, and $K_{\bar{V}} k \leqq \{1,0\}^k$ the subset of those configurations for which V^k does not hold true. Then, it holds that the intersection $K_V k \cap K_{\bar{V}} k = \emptyset$. This equation shows that none of the configurations meets both V^k and its negation. It also follows from the definition of $K_V k$ and $K_{\bar{V}} k$ that the union $K_V k \cup K_{\bar{V}} k = \{1,0\}^k$, which means that every configuration is necessarily either true or false. It also holds true that $K_V k = \{1,0\}^k$ and $K_{\bar{V}} k = \emptyset$ if V^k is tautological; if V^k is a contradiction the inverse holds true, i.e., $K_V k = 0$ and $K_{\bar{V}} k = \{1,0\}^k$.

In the following section, we will show how the DNF can be used in relating k-variate statement forms to configurations of k variables and—equivalently—to subsets of cells of k-variate contingency tables. It will be shown that the DNF is a useful tool for determining relevant cells of any given proposition.

B. THE CORRESPONDENCE BETWEEN COMPOSITE STATEMENTS AND CELLS OF CONTINGENCY TABLES

In order to test hypotheses that are given as composite statements, two operations are necessary. First, those cells of a given contingency table, which fulfill the composite statement under study, that is, for which the proposition holds true, must be identified. Second, the number of elements in these cells must be tested against some null hypothesis. In the following sections the correspondence between composite statements and contingency table cells will be treated.

Before beginning with this topic, however, a notation will be introduced. The variables under study will be denoted with capital letters (A, B, C . . .). The number of states that can be assumed by a given variable will be denoted by the respective lowercase letters. The states themselves will be denoted by combinations of lowercase letters with subscript. The cross-tabulation of $d > 1$ variables will be denoted by these variables. Thus, if A, B, and C are cross-tabulated the respective table will be called the A×B×C table or the A×B×C matrix. If only dichotomous variables are analyzed, the resulting matrix will also be called a 2^d matrix or 2^d table.

The Identification of Hit- and Error-cells in Cross-classifications. The relation between hypotheses that are formulated in statement calculus terms and those cells of contingency tables that fulfill these hypotheses is established using the DNF. Let, for instance, a composite statement V be given through which d

dichotomous (or dichotomized) variables $A, B, \ldots, L$ are connected. These variables can assume the values $A = \{a_1, a_2\}$, $B = \{b_1, b_2\}$, . . . , and $L = \{l_1, l_2\}$. From the truth table of $V(A, B, \ldots, L)$ the DNF of $V(A, B, \ldots, L)$ can be derived. Let the contingency table under study be denoted by $A \times B \times \ldots \times L$. Then those elements (minterms) of the DNF for which $V = 1$ correspond to those cells of $A \times B \times \ldots \times L$ that fulfill the hypotheses. Accordingly, those cells not fulfilling the hypotheses are immediately identified. These are the cells for which V is false and—equivalently—$\bar{V}$ holds true.

In the following expressions, T_V will denote the set of cells for which $V = 1$; these cells will be termed *hit-cells* of V_i. Accordingly, F_V denotes the complementary set of cells for which $V = 0$. These cells will be termed *error-cells*. For the complementary sets T_V and F_V it holds that $T_V \subseteq A \times B \times \ldots \times L$; $F_V \subset A \times B \times \ldots \times L$; $T_V \cup F_V = A \times B \times \ldots \times L$; $T_V \cap F_V = \emptyset$. If V represents a tautology, then $T_V = A \times B \times \ldots \times L$ and $F_V = \emptyset$; if V represents contradiction, thus $T_V = \emptyset$, and $F_V = A \times B \times \ldots \times L$. Obviously, every composite statement defines a unique set of hit- and error-cells in a given contingency table. Conversely, every set of hit- and error-cells corresponds to a class of logically equivalent statements.

In the following example let us consider the trivariate composite statement, $V(A,B,C){:}(a_1 \rightarrow c_1) \wedge (a_2b_1 \rightarrow c_2) \wedge (a_2b_2 \rightarrow (c_1 \vee c_2))$.In Table III the truth table of this composite statement is given. In this table the truth function of V is developed according to the same rules as in Table II. It turns out that the set of configurations for which $V(A,B,C) = 1$ contains the following elements: $K_{V(A,B,C)} = \{111,121,212,221,222\}$. This set leads immediately to the disjunctive normal form of $V(A,B,C)$: $a_1b_1c_1 \vee a_1b_2c_1 \vee a_2b_1c_2 \vee a_2b_2c_1 \vee a_2b_2c_2$.

TABLE III

Truth Table of the Composite Statement
$V(A,B,C){:}(a_1 \rightarrow c_1) \wedge (a_2b_1 \rightarrow c_2) \wedge (a_2b_2 \rightarrow (c_1 \vee c_2))$

Variables[a]			(1)	(2)	(3)	(4)
A	*B*	*C*	$a_1 \rightarrow c_1$	$a_2b_1 \rightarrow c_2$	$a_2b_2 \rightarrow (c_1 \vee c_2)$	(1)∧(2)∧(3)
1	1	1	1	1	1	1
1	1	2	0	1	1	0
1	2	1	1	1	1	1
1	2	2	0	1	1	0
2	1	1	1	0	1	0
2	1	2	1	1	1	1
2	2	1	1	1	1	1
2	2	2	1	1	1	1

[a]for categories, only subscripts are given; in the truth table, 1 denotes true, 0 denotes false.

Cross-classifications of Polytomous Variables. In the examples given so far, cross-classifications of dichotomous (binary) variables were treated. However, without leaving the framework of classical two-value logic, the present approach can also be applied to polytomous variables. Let the variables $A = \{a_1,a_2,a_3\}$ and $B = \{b_1,b_2,b_3\}$ be given. Then, the categories of A and B can be looked at as variables of statement calculus that can assume the truth values 0 and 1. A value of 1 (= true) is assigned if an observation realizes a given category of a given variable; also, the value 0 (= false) is assigned. It follows that a truth table can be constructed that contains $2^6 = 64$ configurations of truth values.

We require these configurations to be mutually exclusive and exhaustive. This requirement can be expressed by the following format condition, F:

$$(\bar{a}_1 \leftrightarrow (a_2 \vee a_3)) \wedge (\bar{a}_2 \leftrightarrow (a_1 \vee a_3)) \wedge (\bar{a}_3 \leftrightarrow (a_1 \vee a_2)) \wedge$$
$$(\bar{b}_1 \leftrightarrow (b_2 \vee b_3)) \wedge (\bar{b}_2 \leftrightarrow (b_1 \vee b_3)) \wedge (\bar{b}_3 \leftrightarrow (b_1 \vee b_2)) \wedge$$
$$(\bar{c}_1 \leftrightarrow (c_2 \vee c_3)) \wedge (\bar{c}_2 \leftrightarrow (c_1 \vee c_3)) \wedge (\bar{c}_3 \leftrightarrow (c_1 \vee c_2)).$$

Using the truth table of F the subset of configurations can be determined that fulfill F and, therefore, are structurally admissible. The result is, not surprisingly, that this subset contains only those configurations that are also in the cross-classification $A \times B$. In the present example the resulting nine configurations are:

(1) $a_1\bar{a}_2\bar{a}_3b_1\bar{b}_2\bar{b}_3$; (2) $a_1\bar{a}_2\bar{a}_3\bar{b}_1b_2\bar{b}_3$; (3) $a_1\bar{a}_2\bar{a}_3\bar{b}_1\bar{b}_2b_3$; (4) $\bar{a}_1a_2\bar{a}_3b_1\bar{b}_2\bar{b}_3$; (5) $\bar{a}_1a_2\bar{a}_3\bar{b}_1b_2\bar{b}_3$; (6) $\bar{a}_1a_2\bar{a}_3\bar{b}_1\bar{b}_2b_3$; (7) $\bar{a}_1\bar{a}_2a_3b_1\bar{b}_2\bar{b}_3$; (8) $\bar{a}_1\bar{a}_2a_3\bar{b}_1b_2\bar{b}_3$; (9) $\bar{a}_1\bar{a}_2a_3b_1b_2b_3$, or, shorter,
(1) a_1b_1; (2) a_1b_2; (3) a_1b_3; (4) a_2b_1; (5) a_2b_2; (6) a_2b_3; (7) a_3b_1; (8) a_3b_2; (9) a_3b_3.

Within the subset of structurally admissible configurations all logical operations that were treated so far can be used. Let, for instance, the variables $A = \{a_1,a_2,a_3\}$, and $B = \{b_1,b_2,b_2\}$ and the composite statement $V_{(A,B)}$:$(a_1 \rightarrow b_2) \wedge (a_2 \rightarrow b_1) \wedge a_3 \rightarrow (b_1 \vee b_3)$ be given. Hence, the truth table, which is reduced to nine admissible configurations, yields DNF: $a_1b_2 \vee a_2b_1 \vee a_3b_1 \vee a_3b_3$. This last expression also defines the hit-cells of $V_{(A,B)}$. The negation of $V_{(A,B)}$ can be expressed by $a_1b_1 \vee a_1b_3 \vee a_2b_2 \vee a_2b_3 \vee a_3b_2$. Accordingly, this expression defines the error-cells of $D_{(A,B)}$. In Table IV the structure of hit- and error-cells of $V_{(A,B)}$ is given. The present example shows that truth tables are not always necessary for the identification of the structure of hit- and error-cells, because the composite statement assigns a subset of categories of B to every category of A: If a_1, then b_2 (hit-cell: a_1b_2, error-cells a_1b_1 and a_1b_3); and: If a_2, then b_1 (hit-cell: a_2b_1, error-cells a_2b_2 and a_2b_3); and: If a_3, then b_1 or b_3 (hit-cells: a_3b_1 and a_3b_3, error-cell: a_1b_2).

A set of composite statements that connect categories of predictor variables with categories of criteria in an implicative manner, may be termed *prediction system*. If a hypothesis is formulated as a prediction system hit- and error-cells

TABLE IV

Hit- and Error-Cells[a] of the Composite Statement $V(A,B){:}(a_1 \rightarrow b_2) \wedge (a_2 \rightarrow b_1) \wedge (a_3 \rightarrow (b_1 \vee b_2))$

	b_1	b_2	b_3
a_1	X		X
a_2		X	X
a_3		X	

[a]Error-cells are crossed out.

can be immediately recognized in the way shown. Accordingly, any composite statement can be transformed into a prediction system using a truth table: If the table identifies the corresponding hit- and error-cells as cells of a contingency table, for every predictor category the implied criterion category can be immediately identified.

III. Empirical Evaluation of Prediction Hypotheses

Two issues will be covered in the following sections. First, several types of prediction will be distinguished. Second, some statistical criteria for the evaluation of prediction hypotheses will be discussed.

A. TYPES OF PREDICTION

The first task of this section is to distinguish between conditional and unconditional predictions. Second, labels for multivariate predictions will be introduced. Third, the consequences of different ranges of conditional predictions will be discussed.

Conditional and Unconditional Predictions. In order to develop criteria for the evaluation of composite statements conditional predictions must be distinguished from unconditional predictions. If conditional predictions are made, hypotheses or—equivalently—prediction rules are used in which states of variables are connected with states of other variables in an implicative manner. These hypotheses are of the "if–then" type. The general form of these hypotheses is $H(E_P \rightarrow E_C)$, where E_P denotes a predictive event, that is, the state of either a single predictor or a configuration of states of several predictors, and E_C denotes a predicted event, that is, the state of either a single criterion or a configuration of states of several criteria. The form $H(E_P \rightarrow E_C)$ can be interpreted as the proposition: "If E_P was observed then E_C was also observed." Statistically, it will be tested whether these predictions are fulfilled in a sufficient number of cases, where "sufficient" denotes statistical significance.

In unconditional predictions there are no implicative connections of variables. Because there is no grouping of variables into predictors or criteria, every variable has the same status. An event E is predicted without any specification of preceding causes or conditions. It should be noted that the distinction between conditional and unconditional statements is not a formal, logical one, but rather a pragmatic one. In statement calculus every implication can be transformed into a statement in which only the elementary connectives of negation, conjunction, and disjunction are used and vice versa. An example is the implication $a \rightarrow b$ which is equivalent to $\bar{a} \vee b$; both statements hold true for $a \wedge b$, $\bar{a} \wedge b$, and $\bar{a} \wedge \bar{b}$, that is, the logical implication is true even if a was not realized (see Table I).

In the present context, for pragmatic reasons, conditional predictions will be evaluated with respect to only those instances for which E was observed. Whereas the statement $a \rightarrow b$ holds true also for both $\bar{a} \wedge b$ and $\bar{a} \wedge \bar{b}$, the corresponding prediction rule $a \rightarrow b$ should be evaluated only with respect to those instances where the predictive event was realized. Furthermore, it follows that the concept of hit-cells and error-cells must be differentiated to deal appropriately with conditional predictions. If conditional prediction rules are evaluated the set of hit-cells can be decomposed into two subsets. One subset contains hit-cells in a strict sense, that is, cells for which the predictive event was observed. The second subset contains hit-cells in a weaker sense. These are cells that define events that do not formally contradict the prediction but without the predictive event being observed. Those cells will be called irrelevant cells and will be explained in more detail.

In developmental psychology, conditional predictions are frequent in investigations in which time is involved as a variable. If, for instance, cross-sectional studies are done, age or membership in a birth-cohort can be treated as predictive conditions for reaching developmental states. An analysis of this kind is not necessarily equivalent to correlating age with behavior measures because the predicted states do not necessarily vary monotonously with age. Other examples occur in longitudinal designs in which the sequence of intraindividual observation points can be used to predict states at later points in time, or from time-lag designs in which the membership in certain birth-cohorts can be used as an indicator (predictor) of social change across time. In both cases there is no need for the assumption that a relation remains the same across the entire time interval under study. One can, for example, assume that social change was generated by a particular event. This assumption would, then, lead to the prediction that there is a relation between time and behavioral measures that is observable only from a given point in time on. This kind of relation has been termed a local association

(Havránek & Lienert, 1984; von Eye & Brandtstädter, 1982). In later sections of this chapter, examples of such local associations will be given in detail.

Because of their general importance in developmental psychology, conditional predictions will be emphasized in the remainder of this chapter. In the next section, criteria for the evaluation of conditional predictions will be introduced.

Types of Uni- and Multivariate Predictions. Conditional predictions involving either more than one predictor, more than one criterion, or both more than one predictor and more than one criterion can also be made. However, the most simple case involves only one variable on either side. This case will be called *uni-univariate* (or *U–U*) prediction. Increasing the number of variables on the predictor side leads to *multi-univariate* (or M–U) predictions.

An increase in the number of criteria leads to *uni-multivariate* (or U–M) predictions, which are comparable to multivariate regression and multivariate analysis of variance. If both the number of predictors and the number of criteria are greater than one, *multi-multivariate* (or M–M) predictions result.

Unconditional predictions can also be made in multivariate data spaces. However, since there is no need for a classification of variables when unconditional predictions are made, there is also no classification of prediction types. It is sufficient to talk about uni-, bi-, or multivariate unconditional predictions, depending on the number of variables under study.

B. STATISTICAL CRITERIA FOR THE EMPIRICAL EVALUATION OF CONDITIONAL PREDICTIONS

In the evaluation of a prediction of the general form $H(E_P \rightarrow E_C)$ the following criteria may be considered:

1. The conditional probability of E_C, given E_P, must be greater than the conditional probability of $\bar{E}_C$, given E_P:

$$C_1: p(E_C|E_P) \overset{!}{>} p(\bar{E}_C|E_P) \tag{1}$$

Because of $p(E_C|E_P) = 1 - p(\bar{E}_C|E_P)$, criterion C_1 can be expressed equivalently by

$$C_1: p(E_C|E_P) \overset{!}{>} .50. \tag{2}$$

For pragmatic reasons, this criterion can be replaced by a weaker form. In its present form, this criterion requires that the probability of a predicted developmental state, E_C, be greater than the probability of some alternative developmental state, $\bar{E}_C$. When the number of developmental states that can follow E_P is greater than two, C_1 implies that the probability of E_C is greater than the joint probability of all alternative developmental states. However, conditional predictions can also be meaningful if the probability of E_C is greater than that of any single alternative event. Obviously, this is possible even if $p(E_C|E_P) \leqq .50$. In particular developmental contexts—for example, in the prevention of disorders or diseases—it might be appropriate to deal with events E_C, even if $p(E_C|E_P)$ is very small, as long as the inequality $p(E_C|E_P) > p(E_C|\bar{E}_P)$ holds (see Brandtstädter & von Eye, 1982).

2. From a pragmatic perspective, the prediction $H(E_P \rightarrow E_C)$ is only meaningful if there is a statistical relation between E_P and E_C. This relation is defined by the following criterion:

$$C_2\text{: } p(E_C|E_P) \overset{!}{>} p(E_C). \tag{3}$$

C_2 requires that E_P have a particular predictive value such that the probability of E_C given E_P is greater than the a priori probability of E_C. Because of $p(E_C) = p(E_C|E_P)\ p(E_P) + p(E_C|\bar{E}_P)\ p(\bar{E}_P)$ criterion C_2 implies the requirement

$$p(E_C|E_P) \overset{!}{>} p(E_C|\bar{E}_P). \tag{4}$$

Let A and B be any events. Then, because of $p(A|B) = p(A \wedge B)/p(B)$, criterion C_2, which is given in Formula (3), can be rewritten equivalently as

$$p(E_C \wedge E_P) \overset{!}{>} p(E_C)\ p(E_P), \tag{5}$$

as

$$\frac{p(E_C \wedge E_P)}{p(E_C)\ p(E_P)} \overset{!}{>} 1, \tag{6}$$

or as

$$\frac{p(E_C \wedge E_P)}{p(E_C)\ p(E_P)} - 1 \overset{!}{>} 0 \tag{7}$$

These inequalities are fulfilled if and only if E_C and E_P are statistically related to each other. Examples of relations that lead to this inequality include positive correlations and association coefficients. Formula (6) shows that C_2 is also fulfilled if the observed relative frequency of the joint event $E_P \wedge E_C$ is greater than the probability of this event when estimated under the assumption of statistical independence of E_P and E_C.

It is important to note in the present context that if a is statistically related to b, then b is also statistically related to a. The following relation holds true:

$$C_3\text{: } p(E_C|E_P) = \frac{p(E_P|E_C)}{p(E_P)}\ p(E_C). \tag{8}$$

It follows from this equation that $p(E_C|E_p) > p(E_C)$ is fulfilled if $p(E_p|E_C) > p(E_P)$ also holds true.

Equation (8) shows $p(E_C|E_P)$ is fulfilled only if $p(E_P|E_C) > P(E_P)$ also holds true. It follows, then, that if for a given data set the prediction $H(E_P \rightarrow E_C)$

satisfies C the prediction $H(E_C \rightarrow E_P)$ does also satisfy C_2. (Note that the joint event $E_P \wedge E_C$ is a "hit" with respect to both prediction directions.) However, this ambiguity can be avoided by introducing the additional criterion:

$$C_3: p(\bar{E}_C|E_P) \overset{!}{<} p(\bar{E}_C). \tag{9}$$

C_3 stipulates that a prediction rule $H(E_P \rightarrow E_C)$ should also satisfy the requirement that the conditional probability of $\bar{E}_C$ given E_P be smaller than the a priori probability of E_C. (Note that the joint event $E_P \wedge \bar{E}_C$ is an error with respect to $E_P \rightarrow E_C$, but only an irrelevant event with respect to the inverse prediction.) Again, Formula (8) can be rewritten equivalently as

$$\frac{p(\bar{E}_C \wedge E_P)}{p(\bar{E}_C)p(E_P)} \overset{!}{>} 1, \tag{10}$$

and

$$1 - \frac{p(\bar{E}_C \wedge E_P)}{p(\bar{E}_C)p(E_P)} \overset{!}{>} 0. \tag{11}$$

It is easy to show that C_2 is fulfilled if and only if C_3 is fulfilled: Because of $p(E_C|E_P) = 1\text{-}p(\bar{E}_C|E_P)$ Formula (3) can be rewritten as

$$1\text{-}p(\bar{E}_C|E_P) \overset{!}{>} 1\text{-}p(\bar{E}_C). \tag{12}$$

Obviously, this inequality is fulfilled if C_3 is also fulfilled. Nevertheless, criteria C_2 and C_3 must be interpreted in different ways and should, therefore, both be considered when evaluating a given prediction. The left-hand side of inequality (11) will be interpreted as a measure of the proportionate reduction in errors (PRE), whereas the left-hand side of inequality (7) will be interpreted as a measure of the proportionate increase in hits (PIH).

Both criteria C_2 and C_3 imply statistical dependency between the variables involved in the prediction. Therefore, they constitute a necessary condition of the prediction rule being either accepted or rejected (cf. Stegmüller's, 1973, criteria for the statistical justification of prognoses). C_1 is not sufficient to accept a given prediction rule. Nevertheless, C_1 can be used supplementarily if both C_2 and C_3 are fulfilled. If, for any given prediction rule H, only criteria (3) and (9) are fulfilled it may be called *confirmed in a weak sense*. If, however. C_1 is also fulfilled, H may be called *confirmed in a strong sense*.

IV. Statistical Evaluation

In the following sections statistical methods will be presented to evaluate developmental hypotheses. It is assumed that these hypotheses are formulated in statement calculus terms and that a contingency table of two or more variables is given. The statistical methods that will be introduced include descriptive measures that take the relative frequency of cases in those cells into account that are relevant for evaluating a given proposition. These measures can also be interpreted as measures of practical significance (see Bredenkamp, 1970).

In addition to these measures, tests of statistical inference will be presented that can be used for evaluating the relative frequency of cases in favor of the hypotheses with respect to populations. All tests in this chapter are of the null-hypothesis rejecting type. The reason for the selection of "classical" significance tests is that a decision whether a prediction H leads to greater hit-rates (or lower error-rates) than alternative assumptions is attempted. The basic idea behind the descriptive measures and the tests is that the number of elements in relevant cells is compared with the expected number of elements. This number is estimated using a suitably chosen model in which the relations in the set of variables under study are specified with respect to H. It is important to note that this strategy of evaluation implies a particular interpretation of H. If H were treated as a deterministic theoretical statement, only one case contradicting H would be sufficient to invalidate it. Accordingly, all error-cells would have to be empty if H is to be accepted. However, in the present context of research on human development this would be an unrealistic requirement. Instead, measures will be presented to account for the predictive efficiency of a given H. This present approach implies that H be interpreted as a prediction rule that is not necessarily rejected if there is a certain number of observations that are inconsistent with H.

A. STATISTICAL EVALUATION OF DEVELOPMENTAL HYPOTHESES: DEFINITION OF THE PROBLEM

In this section it will be assumed that a predictive statement is given with which a subset of cells of the contingency table under study is assigned to T_V, the hit-cells, and the complementary set of cells is assigned to F_V, the error-cells. Let a cell of the contingency table under study assume the value

$$\omega = \begin{cases} 1 & \text{if it defines an event for which } V \text{ holds true,} \\ 0 & \text{otherwise} \end{cases} \tag{13}$$

Then, the number of elements for which V holds true is given by $H = \sum_i \omega_i f_i$, where i counts the cells of the contingency table. Accordingly, $E = n - H$ is the number of elements in the error-cells, where n denotes the sample size.

After determining the number of elements for which V holds true one needs a reference number to which this number can be compared. This reference number can be defined on the basis of the following considerations. The composite statement is used to postulate that elements are assigned only to the hit-cells. This postulate constitutes the deterministic facet of the methods discussed in this chapter. However, errors are not assumed to lead necessarily to a rejection of a given composite statement. As long as the number of errors does not exceed a limit that is determined by a statistical model, the composite statement will still be considered as valid. This interpretation of hit- and error-cells implies that composite statements have the status of an assignment rule according to which elements are placed into contingency tables. To determine the effectiveness of this assignment rule it will be applied to two frequency distributions. The first of these is the observed frequency distribution that reflects the empirical relations between predictors and criteria. The second distribution is given by expected values that are estimated under the assumption of independence between predictors and criteria.

Let a composite statement be defined. Then, application of equation (13) yields the numbers of elements for which V holds true in the respective frequency distributions. Let Σ_1 denote the number of elements in those cells for which V holds true in the observed frequency distribution, and Σ_2 the number of the respective elements in the expected frequency distribution. Then, the null hypothesis under which Σ_1 is compared with Σ_2 is

$$\Sigma_1 = \Sigma_2. \tag{14}$$

Equation (14) describes a null hypothesis in the classical sense. It implies that differences between the frequency distributions in the hit-cells are random in nature. The alternative hypothesis is

$$\Sigma_1 > \Sigma_2. \tag{15}$$

The relation expressed in inequality (15) implies that the composite statement is retained if it allows one to assign correctly more elements to the hit-cells in the observed than in the expected frequency distribution. Accordingly, statistical tests have to be applied in their one-tailed form. They become meaningless if $\Sigma_1 \leqq \Sigma_2$. If both Σ_1 and Σ_2 denote frequencies in error-cells the relation in (15) must be inverted.

B. MODELS FOR ESTIMATING EXPECTED FREQUENCY DISTRIBUTIONS

As was pointed out in the last section the prediction form that is used to test a developmental hypothesis can be interpreted as an assignment rule or a prediction rule. In order to derive a basis for statistical comparisons, assumptions about relations among the variables under study will be made and applied to estimate the expected cell frequencies in hit- and error-cells. Assumptions of this kind are made in the applications of many methods of contingency table analysis. Examples include configural frequency analysis (CFA; Krauth & Lienert, 1973) and the method of loglinear models (Bishop, Fienberg, & Holland, 1975; Clogg &

Shockey, 1984). In the application of these methods, virtually all assumptions about relations in groups of variables can be taken as a basis to estimate expected cell frequencies. The set of assumptions against which the observed frequencies are tested, is called a *model.*

Before giving examples of such models, rules will be introduced to denote models in a concise form: (1) Variables that are allowed to be statistically related are jointly put in brackets and (2) Higher-order relations of variables (relations in triplets, quadruplets of variables and so forth) imply that the same variables are assumed to be related also at lower levels; it follows from this hierarchical concept that the denotation of lower-order relations is redundant and, therefore, can be omitted, if higher-order relations are assumed.

In a first example of the application of these rules, let us assume that the four variables *A, B, C,* and *D* display main effects, and that there are no variable relations whatsoever, that is, that these variables are totally independent. Thus, the model is [A],[B],[C],[D]. In a second example, let the same four variables be given and the model imply that *A, B,* and *C* are related as a triplet, and that *C* and *D* are associated as a pair. Accordingly, the model can then be denoted by [*A*,*B*,*C*],[*C*,*D*]. In a third example, let us observe a sample of subjects with respect to three variables—*A, B,* and *C*—three times. Consequently, one possible model may imply the assumption that the variables are totally independent, and that the variables are autocorrelated from only one point in time to the next. This model can be illustrated as $[A_1,A_2],[A_2,A_3],[B_1,B_2],[B_2,B_3],[C_1,C_2], [C_2,C_3]$, in which subscripts denote observation points.

However. one particular case cannot be covered by the foregoing rules. This instance concerns the case in which the model represents the assumption that there are no effects at all. This assumption implies the existence of equally distributed cell frequencies. This model will be denoted by [-].

Model Specification. The importance of these models to the methodology presented in this chapter results, first, from their status as a basis of statistical decisions about the significance of the gain in the number of hits obtained by the composite statement. Models do not represent the predictive hypothesis *V* under study; rather, existing substantive knowledge and theoretical assumptions must be incorporated so as not to overestimate the value of the composite statement and to "give the null hypothesis a chance." Substantively, these models can be interpreted in terms of associations or correlations. If relation (15) holds true, it can be concluded that the assumptions in the model are not complex enough to account for the entire frequency distribution in the contingency table, or—equivalently—that there are at least locally (i.e., in particular sectors of the data space) significant deviations from the assumed distribution.

The second reason why these models are important to the testing of developmental hypotheses is that they represent concepts of association that are basically different from those realized by the application of composite statements. The concept of association realized in the alternative assignment rules (i.e., in the models) involves the entire range of values that can be assumed by any variable. This concept represents the usual idea of what an association or a correlation is. The concept of association realized by application of composite statements is different in two ways. First, not necessarily all predictor levels are linked to levels of the criteria. Second, it is possible to link both more than one criterion level to one predictor level and more than one predictor level to one criterion level. Therefore, predictions that differ in precision can be dealt with, using the same methodology. The most precise prediction is the one in which one predictor level is linked to only one criterion level. The least precise and, therefore, trivial prediction allows the criterion to assume any state after a particular state of the predictor is realized. In both correlation and association analysis relations that do not represent maximal precision lead to lower coefficients rather than being identified as particular types of relations.

To summarize, the model specification plays two roles. First, it provides the basis for null hypothesis testing by taking into account knowledge about variable relations. Second, it realizes a particular concept of local association. Furthermore, the model specification implies the estimation of expected values. This issue will be treated in the next section.

Estimation of Expected Values. In this section, the estimation of expected values will be treated from a pragmatic perspective. Rather than discussing the statistical properties of estimation techniques, formulas will be presented that cover those models that are most frequent in developmental research. Most of these formulas represent maximum likelihood estimations which are well known as being consistent, asymptotically normally distributed, and asymptotically efficient (cf. Fienberg, 1981; Haberman, 1973; Hildebrand, Laing, & Rosenthal, 1977).

The algorithms presented in this section are used to estimate the expected values from the marginals of the contingency table under study. However, when more complex models are assumed, closed forms for the estimation algorithms can no longer be given, and iterative procedures must be used. Procedures for virtually any model are available as computer programs. Even some of the better-known program packages provide estimation procedures. Examples include the BMDP (Dixon et al., 1981), which provides a program for the fitting of log-linear models in which expected values are estimated. This program provides estimations of expected values even if structural zeroes. that is cells that can for logical reasons not be frequented, prevail. Examples of iterative techniques are given in Fienberg (1981). These techniques fulfill the restrictions imposed by the models sequentially.

The simplest model to be presented herein is based on the assumption that there are no effects at all. This assumption corresponds to the zero-order model [-] introduced in the last section. The model implies equally distributed expected frequencies. Thus, expected frequencies can be estimated by

$$e_{ijk\ldots} = n/(a \cdot b \cdot c \ldots), \tag{16}$$

where n signifies the sample size, $a, b, c, \ldots$, the number of categories of the variables $A, B, C, \ldots$, and $i = 1, \ldots, a$, $j = 1, \ldots, b$, $k = 1, \ldots, c$.

The model of total independence of variables is the second simplest in terms of complexity of assumptions. In the application of this first-order model, expected values are estimated by

$$e_{ijk\ldots} = (1/n)^{d-1} f_{i\ldots\ldots} \cdot f_{.j\ldots\ldots} \cdot f_{..k\ldots} \cdot \ldots, \tag{17}$$

where d signifies the number of variables and the $f_{\ldots\ldots}$ the marginal frequencies of the categories of the variables under study.

Both models presented so far are global, that is, the assumptions regarding variable relations apply to all variables in the same manner. A first regional model in which particular assumptions apply to particular subsets of variables can be formulated under the assumption that one variable, say A, shows a main effect, whereas all remaining variables have no effects at all. The short notation of this model is $[A]$. The cell frequencies expected under this model can be estimated by

$$e_{ijk\ldots} = (b \cdot c \cdot \ldots)^{-1} f_{i}, \tag{18}$$

where $i = 1, \ldots, a$, $j = 1, \ldots, b$, $k = 1, \ldots, c$, etc. A more complex regional model is constituted by the assumption that two variables, say A and B, are independent of each other, and that only these two variables have main effects, whereas the remaining variables have no effects. The short notation of this model is $[A],[B]$; it leads to the following formula for the estimation of expected cell frequencies:

$$e_{ijk\ldots} = (n \cdot c \cdot \ldots)^{-1} f_{i\ldots\ldots} \cdot f_{.j\ldots} \tag{19}$$

where $i = 1, \ldots, a$, $j = 1, \ldots, b$, $k = 1, \ldots, c$, and so on.

In developmental research the last two models are frequently used. They imply the assumption that either one variable, as in model $[A]$, or two, as in model $[A][B]$, determine the variation of all other variables. The generalization of these models to a greater number of variables that have main effects is straightforward. Basically, these models reflect the usual dichotomy of independent and dependent variables or predictors and criteria. When the methodology presented in this chapter is applied and hypotheses are tested against these models, the basic question is whether predictions of particular states of dependent variables or criteria lead to higher hit-rates than the assumption of a general dependency of one group of variables upon the other.

In an even more complex model three instead of two groups of variables are defined. Examples in which three groups of variables are used include the application of variable groups from different hierarchical levels (cf. the concept of embeddedness; Lerner, 1984). Let *A, B*, . . . belong to a first group of variables, *Q, R*, . . . to a second group of variables, and *X, Y*, . . . to a third group of variables. Then, one model that takes the status of the variable groups into account can be illustrated as [*A*,*B*, . . .],[*Q*,*R*, . . .],[*X*,*Y*, . . .]. This model implies that, at a first level, relations of any order may exist in each of the variable groups, and that, at the second level, the groups are totally independent of each other.

To simplify the notation, variables within brackets may be treated as one single dummy variable (or metavariable), so that the matrix formed by these variables can be interpreted as three-dimensional. The first metavariable has $a \times b \times$ . . . states. Accordingly, the second metavariable has $q \times r \times$ . . . states, and the third metavariable has $x \times y \times$ . . . states. Let MV_i denote the resulting metavariables ($i = 1, \ldots, 3$). Then, the expected cell frequencies can be estimated by

$$e_{ijk} = mv_{1i} \cdot mv_{2j} \cdot mv_{3j} / n^2 \tag{20}$$

where $i = 1, \ldots, mv_1$, $j = 1, \ldots, mv_2$, and $k = 1, \ldots, mv_3$. Obviously, Formula (20) is the trivariate case of Formula (17).

In all examples of models presented in this chapter, the expected cell frequencies can be estimated explicitly from the marginals. Models with this characteristic are called elementary models (Goodman, 1970). More examples of such models are given by Fienberg (1981) or Upton (1978). If more complex models are formulated, expected values can be estimated by only using iterative procedures. These procedures will not be discussed in detail in the present chapter; instead, reference is made again to the widely available program packages.

In Table V, numerical examples are given in which an imaginary three-dimensional data set is used. Expected frequencies under five different models are estimated from the marginals of the variables *A*, *B*, and *C*. All variables are dichotomous, that is $a = b = c = 2$. The models in Table V, from left to right, represent increasingly complex assumptions. The model [-] leads to equally distributed expected frequencies. No information from the marginals is used. In model [*A*] the different probability of lying in A_1 compared with A_2 is taken into account. This information determines the distribution of expected frequencies in that every single cell under A_1 is estimated to contain more elements than every single cell under A_2 by a factor of $\frac{47}{38}$. This model can be interpreted as the assumption that variable *A* accounts for the variation of both *B* and *C*. Let, for instance, *A* denote the length of time spent by a person in a given job, and *B* and *C* the duration dependent variables income and probability of moving. Then, model [*A*] implies that both income and probability of moving are determined uniquely by how long somebody has had a given job.

TABLE V

Estimated Cell Frequencies in a Three-Dimensional Data Cube under 5 Different Models

Variables				Models				
A	*B*	*C*	o	[−]	[*A*]	[*A*],[*B*]	[*A*],[*B*],[*C*]	[*AB*],[*AC*],[*BC*]
1	1	1	20	10.63	11.75	12.16	14.88	16.63
1	1	2	6	10.63	11.75	12.16	9.45	9.37
1	2	1	9	10.63	11.75	11.34	13.87	12.37
1	2	2	12	10.63	11.75	11.34	8.80	8.63
2	1	1	8	10.63	9.50	9.84	12.03	11.37
2	1	2	10	10.63	9.50	9.84	7.64	6.63
2	2	1	15	10.63	9.50	9.16	11.21	11.63
2	2	2	5	10.63	9.50	9.16	7.12	8.37

$A_1 = 47$, $A_2 = 38$, $B_1 = 44$, $B_2 = 41$, $C_1 = 52$, $C_2 = 33$

In model [*A*],[*B*] two variables are used as predictors of the states that can be assumed by a criterion. Here, the information on the marginals of variable *C* is not taken into account, and this leads to $a \cdot b = 2 \cdot 2 = 4$ different expected values. In model [*A*],[*B*],[*C*] the marginals (main effects) of all three variables are taken into account. Therefore, $a \times b \times c$ different expected values can result. Model [*A*],[*B*] can be interpreted again as taking the status of variables as predictors and criteria into account. In Model [*A*],[*B*],[*C*] all variables have the same status. They are assumed to be totally independent.

In model [*AB*],[*BC*],[*AC*] variable relations are taken into account for the first time.[2] It is assumed that all three variables have main effects and that the variables are pairwise associated. This particular model may be used to exemplify two aspects of the estimation of expected values that may be of interest in development research. The first aspect has to do with taking into account pairwise associations. If the researcher is interested in whether in repeated measurement designs there are relations among variables that go beyond what can be measured by autocorrelation coefficients, he or she can estimate the cell frequencies by taking the autocorrelations into account, that is, pairwise correlations of the variables observed at consecutive points in time. If there are substantial deviations of the observed from the resulting estimated cell frequencies there must be relations that go beyond the usually high correlations across time. The second aspect concerns the degree to which model assumptions meet the relations in data sets. Table II shows that different models can indeed yield estimated

[2]The algorithm of the estimation of expected cell frequencies under this model is not described in this chapter. However, it is possible to estimate the cell frequencies under this model from the marginals (von Eye & Lienert, 1985).

cell frequencies that differ clearly. Furthermore, Table II shows that the more complex the models are, the closer the observed frequencies lie to the expected ones on the average. This result reflects the fact mentioned above that the number of possibilities to deviate from a given model decreases when the model's complexity increases. Whereas, for example, in model [-] in principle any kind of effects can cause the differences between observed and expected cell frequencies, in model [*AB*],[*AC*],[*BC*] only the (saturated) model [*ABC*] is left.

Selection of Models. If unconditional predictions are analyzed there is no general strict rule that can be followed when a model (i.e., an alternative assignment rule) is to be selected. However, there are two rules of thumb that can be applied in order to give the null hypothesis a chance so as not to be rejected or—put in other terms—so as not to overestimate the predictive efficiency of the developmental hypotheses under study. The first rule is that the status of variables as members of groups of variables be taken into account. This rule implies first, that at least higher-order relations within particular groups of variables can be taken into account when the expected cell frequencies are estimated. Second, this rule implies that regional models are used more often than global ones when groups of variables can be distinguished, and—equivalently—that the often unrealistic assumption of total independence is replaced by more complex and more realistic assumptions. The second rule is that well-known empirical relations between variables be taken into consideration. It is unrealistic, and leads to a clear overestimation of effects, if well-established empirical relations are assumed not to exist when expected frequencies are estimated.

In the analysis of conditional predictions there is always the distinction between predictors and criteria. Therefore, the basic model that takes the status of variables as either predictors or criteria into account has the form "[predictor variables],[criterion variables]." In this form, relations of any order among the predictors may exist as well as relations of any order among the criteria. However, one assumes that there exists independence between these two variable groups. (Remember that a conditional prediction presupposes that the observed frequencies in relevant cells deviate from the expected frequencies that are generated under this assumption.)

The main characteristic of this model is that there is only one way of deviating from it. Since within both groups of variables, predictors and criteria, any order of relation may be present, deviations from this model necessarily are due to relations between these groups of variables. In general, any kind of relation between predictors and criteria may prevail. However, using the basic model, it cannot be decided what kind of relation led to the deviation.

It should be noted that the basic model discussed in this chapter is an approach that is based on the Hildebrand et al. (1977) prediction analysis. Other approaches can be derived from the basic model by taking into account all first-order relations between predictors and criteria. Deviations from this model imply that at least second-order relations among predictors and criteria are present. Models in which higher-order relations among predictors and criteria are considered can be interpreted accordingly. Another class of models can be developed under the quasi-independence assumption (see Goodman, 1968). Under this assumption error cells are not used in the estimation of appropriate expected values. Goodman and Kruskal (1974) discussed this approach and presented descriptive measures of the prediction success that are constructed parallel to the ones discussed in the next section.

Contributions of single variables or groups of variables to the overall prediction success can be estimated through specific decompositions. The estimation of these contributions can be accomplished through a number of systematic steps in which the effect of every single predictor, of every pair of predictors, in general of every n-tuplet of predictors ($n = 1, \ldots, d$-1) is analyzed with respect to the prediction success. Let P be the set of the predictors under study, C the set of all criteria, P_A and P_B two nonempty and nonoverlapping subsets of P. Then, the contribution of P_A to the success of the prediction hypothesis H ($E_P \rightarrow E_C$) can be evaluated using the model "[P_A, P_B], [P_B, C]" for the estimation of expected values. The background of this approach will be described elsewhere (Brandstädter & von Eye, in press).

C. DESCRIPTIVE MEASURES FOR EVALUATION OF HYPOTHESES

In this section, two groups of parameters will be presented to evaluate hypotheses that are formulated in statement calculus terms. In the first group there are measures that describe the extent to which the application of a predictive statement leads to better results for the observed than for the expected cell frequencies. In these measures, Σ_1, the observed number of elements in hit- and error-cells is compared with Σ_2, the expected number of elements in these cells. In particular, a measure of the *p*roportionate *r*eduction in *e*rror (PRE; Goodman & Kruskal, 1954; Hildebrand et al., 1977) is compared with two measures of the *p*roportionate *i*ncrease in *h*its (PIH). In the second group there are measures that focus on more general qualities of hypotheses. In particular, the measures of scope and precision will be discussed (cf. also Hildebrand et al., 1977).

PRE- and PIH-measures. The measure of the *p*roportionate *r*eduction in *e*rror, PRE, describes the extent to which errors in assigning elements to the observed frequency distribution are avoided if compared with the expected frequency distribution. To calculate PRE for a given prediction hypothesis V, a parameter ω must be defined such that

$$\omega = \begin{cases} 1 & \text{in cells for which } V \text{ does not hold true (error cells)} \\ 0 & \text{else.} \end{cases}$$

The sums Σ_1 and Σ_2 introduced above can, then, be computed by

$$\Sigma_1 = \sum_{ijk\ldots} o_{ijk\ldots} \ \omega_{ijk\ldots} \tag{21}$$

and

$$\Sigma_2 = \sum_{ijk\ldots} e_{ijk\ldots} \ \omega_{ijk\ldots} \tag{22}$$

respectively, where o signifies observed cell frequencies and e expected cell frequencies. Using these sums, PRE is defined as

$$\text{PRE} = \frac{\Sigma_2 - \Sigma_1}{\Sigma_2} = 1 - \frac{\Sigma_1}{\Sigma_2}\ . \tag{23}$$

Multiplied by 100, PRE can be interpreted as the percentage of errors that are committed *less* when V is applied to the observed rather than to the expected frequency distribution. An analogous interpretation is also possible, when PRE < 0; however, in this case assignment to the expected frequency distribution leads to fewer mistakes.

PRE was first introduced as a measure of asymmetric similarity (Goodman & Kruskal, 1954). It has the following properties:

1. PRE is undefined if only one configuration of the criteria is realized in the population;
2. $-\infty <$ PRE $\leqq +1$;
3. PRE $= 0$ only if the application of the predictive statement does not lead to any advantage in the observed frequency distribution when compared with the frequency distribution used to estimate Σ_2; and
4. PRE $= 1$ only if the observed frequency distribution is entirely determined by the statement form, i.e., if $\Sigma_1 = 0$.

The measure of the proportionate increase in hits, PIH, describes the extent to which elements are more often correctly assigned to the observed as compared with the expected frequency distribution. Before measuring PIH, a parameter α must be defined such that

$$\alpha = \begin{cases} 1 & \text{in cells for which } V \text{ holds true (hit cells)} \\ 0 & \text{else.} \end{cases}$$

This definition does not change the form of Formulas (21) and (22); however, these sums denote here the numbers of elements correctly assigned rather than the numbers of errors committed by applying the assignment rules. Using Σ_1 and Σ_2, a first measure, PIH_1, can be defined in a manner analogous to PRE:

$$\mathrm{PIH}_1 = \frac{\Sigma_1 - \Sigma_2}{\Sigma_2} = \frac{\Sigma_1}{\Sigma_2} - 1 \tag{24}$$

Multiplied by 100, PIH_1 can be interpreted as the percentage of increase in the number of hits that can be obtained in the observed as compared with the expected frequency distribution. The properties of PIH_1 are

1. PIH_1 is undefined if only one configuration of the criteria in the population is realized;
2. $-1 \leqq \mathrm{PIH}_1 < +\infty$;
3. $\mathrm{PIH}_1 = 0$ only if the application of the statement form to the observed frequency distribution does not lead to any advantage; and
4. $\mathrm{PIH}_1 = n/\Sigma_2 - 1$ only if the distribution in the observed frequency distribution is entirely determined by the statement form.

As is the case with PRE, PIH can be interpreted for both positive and negative values.

A second measure, focusing on the relative increase in hits, PIH_2, can be constructed such that its maximum cannot exceed $\mathrm{PIH}_2 = 1$. If one takes the maximal increase in hits as reference value, PIH_2 can be expressed as

$$\mathrm{PIH}_2 = \mathrm{PIH}_1/\mathrm{PIH}_{1,\max} = (\Sigma_1 - \Sigma_2)/(n - \Sigma_2), \tag{25}$$

where $\mathrm{PIH}_{1,\max} = n/\Sigma_2 - 1$.

PIH_2 expresses the increase in hits relative to the maximal increase in hits. The properties of this measure are identical to the properties of PIH_1, except for the range of possible values which is $-\Sigma_2/(n-\Sigma_2) \leqq \mathrm{PIH}_2 \leqq +1$. For any given contingency table, both PIH_1 and PIH_2 can be transformed into each other. Nevertheless. it may be helpful to consider both measures, because increases in hits that are a multiple of the expected number of hits can still be small when compared with the maximal number of hits and vice versa. PIH_2 yields the same results as PRE, as long as the sets T_V and F_V are exhaustive, that is, as long as there are no irrelevant cells. If there are irrelevant cells the information provided by PIH_2 focuses only on the hit-cells in a strict sense.

Scope and Precision of Predictions. Hypotheses that are equally efficient in terms of PRE or PIH may nevertheless differ qualitatively in important respects. Intuitively, it is clear that a hypothesis that predicts exactly one out of several alternative events—a sharp hypothesis—has a priori a lower chance to be consistent with the data than a less-concise hypothesis predicting a greater number of alternative events. Furthermore, a hypothesis with a given PRE or PIH efficiency seems to have a higher informative value if it excludes many observations that statistically have a high a priori probability to occur. To account for this qualification, the measures of scope and precision (as proposed by Hildebrand et al.,

1977) may be considered for the evaluation of predictions in addition to the PRE and PIH measures just discussed.

The scope (Sc) of a prediction is formally defined by

$$Sc = \frac{1}{n} \sum_{i=1}^{p} f_i \text{ for all } i \text{ for which at least one } \omega = 0, \tag{26}$$

where i counts the predictor configurations and $\omega = 0$ denotes error-cells. The measure Sc can be interpreted as that portion of a population to which a composite statement can be applied. If all predictor configurations are used at least once, and if these are not tautological statements, then $Sc = 1.0$ (or 100%). This property can also be described by the fact that, in principle, all members of a population must be potential members of hit-cells in order to obtain $Sc = 1.0$. Sc is minimal if only one person is covered by the composite statement. If no one is covered, the composite statement is not admissible. The range of admissible values of Sc is, then, $1/n \leqq Sc \leqq 1$. The definition of Sc given here is compatible with the definition by Hildebrand et al. (1977). However, in the present context, Sc can also be applied to multivariate designs in which more than two groups of variables are simultaneously analyzed.

The same difference is obtained when the precision of a composite statement—as defined in the present context—is compared with the definition by Hildebrand et al. (1977). The precision of a composite statement is determined by the number of states of the criterion variable that contradict it. If, for instance, one state of a variable is linked to only one state of a second variable, a statement results that is more precise than if two states of the second variable were linked to one state of the first one. The implication "if a then b" for instance, is very precise because only one state of the criterion is linked to the predictor. The implication "if a then b or $\bar{b}$" is, obviously, not precise at all. In the formal description, the precision P_r is given by

$$Pr = \frac{1}{n} \sum_{ijk\ldots} e_{ijk\ldots} \cdot \omega_{ijk\ldots} = \frac{1}{n} \Sigma_2. \tag{27}$$

where $\omega = 0$ denotes error-cells. The range of admissible values is

$$0 \leqq Pr \leqq (n - f_e)/n,$$

where f_e denotes the expected frequency of a single cell.

D. INFERENTIAL TESTING OF PREDICTIONS

The null hypothesis presented in Formula (14) and the alternative hypothesis presented in Formula (15) imply comparisons between observed and expected frequencies. In this section, the nonparametric binomial test will be introduced as a method which allows the evaluation of these hypotheses. This test can be applied to every design under any model. For particular designs and particular models more powerful tests have been presented which are based on the estimation of variances of the test statistics (see Hildebrand et al., 1977; Rudinger, Henning, & Schmitz–Scherzer, 1984). However, because of its general applicability, the binomial test will be used in the present context.

Let Σ_1 denote the observed frequency of elements for which V holds true, and Σ_2 the expected frequency. Let, furthermore, $p = \Sigma_2/n$ denote the expected relative frequency of hits. Consequently, P', the point probability of Σ_1 hits is

$$P'(\Sigma_1) = \binom{n}{\Sigma_1} p^{\Sigma_1} q^{(n-\Sigma_1)} \tag{28}$$

where $q = 1 - p$. When the alternative hypothesis in Formula (15) is to be tested, the one-sided tail probability of Σ_1 can be computed by

$$P(\Sigma_1) = \sum_{i=\Sigma_1}^{n} \binom{n}{i} p^{i}\, q^{(n-i)}. \tag{29}$$

Obviously, the application of Formula (29) is meaningful only if $\Sigma_1 > \Sigma_2$.

If, according to a commonly accepted rule of thumb, $np \geqq 10$ the binominal, distribution can be approximated sufficiently exact by the normal distribution. The resulting test statistic is

$$z = \frac{\Sigma_1 - np}{(npq)^{1/2}} = \frac{\Sigma_1 - \Sigma_2}{(npq)^{1/2}}, \tag{30}$$

where the numerator must be positive in order to fulfill the relation expressed in (15). If $5 \leqq np \leqq 10$ correction for continuity is recommended, that is, a subtraction of 0.5 from the numerator. Tables of z are given in standard statistics textbooks.

V. Empirical Applications

In this section, examples from two areas of developmental research will be given. In the first example, data collected from a research project on "Personal control and emotional evaluation of development in partnership relations" (Brandtstädter, Krampen, & Heil, 1986) will be analyzed. In the second example data from a longitudinal project on cognitive development of children[3] will be analyzed (Edelstein, 1983; Schröder, 1984). Before we present these examples, however, the sequence of steps to take when applying statement calculus to the testing of developmental hypotheses will be summarized.

[3]The authors are indebted to Wolfgang Edelstein for the as yet unpublished data set.

The first step in the confirmatory testing of developmental hypotheses is the formulation of these hypotheses both in substantive and in statement calculus terms. In order to simplify the identification of hit-, error-, and irrelevant cells, the particular hypotheses must be formulated as complete conjunctions. Together, the partial hypotheses form the aggregate hypothesis to be tested using either Formula (29) or (30). The second step determines the model against which the hypotheses are tested. In the model, relations of variables are postulated. These relations determine the estimation of expected values.

The third step is the estimation of descriptive PRE and PIH measures. These measures describe the extent to which it is advantageous to assign elements to cells of a contingency table according to the assignment rule given by the model. In addition, the scope and the precision of the hypothesis can be determined. The fourth step tests the hypothesis inferentially. This step is necessary only if the observed number of elements in the hit-cells is greater than the expected number. Attention is to be given to the results obtained when applying PRE in the evaluation of the hypothesis, which can differ from the results for PIH. This difference comes about from the fact that only hit-cells in PIH—in a strict sense—are used to support the hypothesis.

A. STUDY I: PERSONAL CONTROL AND EMOTIONAL EVALUATION OF DEVELOPMENT IN PARTNERSHIP RELATIONS

The data to be discussed in this section were collected in a research project on subjective control on development and perceptions of development in partnerships (Brandtstädter et al., 1986). Subjects ($N = 950$) comprising 475 couples—ranging from 30 to 60 years of age—answered a questionnaire dealing with the relation between development-related action orientations and emotional attitudes toward personal development and aging.

From the questionnaire data, several aggregate variables were derived. The following analyses involve aggregate variables related to: (1) Subjective developmental attainment (SDA), (2) personal control over development (PCD), (3) perceived marital support (PMS), and (4) depressive outlook toward future development (DEP) (for details of the questionnaire format and the construction of aggregate variables, see Brandtstädter et al., 1986). The first three of these aggregate variables were dichotomized at the median. Subjects with median ties were randomly assigned either to the upper or the lower median category. Subscript 1 denotes higher scores and subscript 2 lower scores. The depression variable was trichotomized. The first category of the depression variable, DEP_1, denotes absence of depression, DEP_2 little depression, and DEP_3 high depression.

The following analyses are based on the assumption that the four variables under study form two groups. The first group includes the variables *SDA, PCD,* and *PMS*. This group is assumed to predict *DEP,* the only variable in the second group. In the present context, the first step in data analysis consists of the formulation of particular local hypotheses in statement calculus terms. In short, these hypotheses are given here immediately in formal notation (the substantive background is given by Brandtstädter et al., 1986):

$$
\begin{array}{lllr}
\text{H:} & (\text{SDA}_1 \wedge \text{PCD}_1 \wedge \text{PMS}_1) \rightarrow & \text{DEP}_1 & \& \\
& (\text{SDA}_1 \wedge \text{PCD}_1 \wedge \text{PMS}_2) \rightarrow & (\text{DEP}_1 \vee \text{DEP}_2) & \& \\
& (\text{SDA}_1 \wedge \text{PCD}_2 \wedge \text{PMS}_1) \rightarrow & (\text{DEP}_1 \vee \text{DEP}_2) & \& \\
& (\text{SDA}_1 \wedge \text{PCD}_2 \wedge \text{PMS}_2) \rightarrow & \text{DEP}_2 & \& \\
& (\text{SDA}_2 \wedge \text{PCD}_1 \wedge \text{PMS}_1) \rightarrow & (\text{DEP}_1 \vee \text{DEP}_2) & \& \\
& (\text{SDA}_2 \wedge \text{PCD}_1 \wedge \text{PMS}_2) \rightarrow & \text{DEP}_2 & \& \\
& (\text{SDA}_2 \wedge \text{PCD}_2 \wedge \text{PMS}_1) \rightarrow & \text{DEP}_2 & \& \\
& (\text{SDA}_2 \wedge \text{PCD}_2 \wedge \text{PMS}_2) \rightarrow & \text{DEP}_3. &
\end{array}
$$

The second step of the confirmatory analysis of developmental hypotheses involves the definition of a model that has the status of an alternative assignment rule.

In the notion introduced above, a model for the estimation of expected values that takes the structure of the given prediction system into account has the format [*SDA, PCD, PMS*], [DEP]. This model assumes under the null hypothesis two kinds of relations among variables. First, the predictor variables *SDA, PCD,* and *PMS* are assumed to be associated. This assumption includes associations of any possible order—associations in pairs of variables and in the triplet of variables. The second kind of relation that is implied by this model concerns the two groups of variables. It is assumed that there is no relation between the group of predictors and the criterion (null hypothesis).

In this model, the three predictor variables may be treated as one metavariable with 2×2×2 states; the expected cell frequencies may be estimated using Formula (19). In Table VI the observed and the expected cell frequencies are given. Hit-cells are underlined.

In the third step descriptive measures are determined. The results suggest that 28.5% fewer *S*s are misclassified (*PRE*) if *H* is applied to the observed rather than to the expected frequency distribution. In addition, the number of correctly assigned subjects increases by 34.3% (PIH_1), an amount that covers 28.5% of the maximal increase in hits (PIH_2). The values of *PRE* and PIH_2 do not differ numerically because there are no irrelevant cells.

Substantively, the present results suggest that the assumption of independence between predictors and criteria is violated in the set of hit-cells. Therefore, it can be concluded that there exists a predictor–criteria relationship that allows for an effective prediction of a depressive outlook toward future development on the basis of perceptions of the development of partnership relations. However, the

TABLE VI

Analysis of the Aggregate Hypothesis H in the Matrix of the Variables SDA, PCD, PMS, and DEP[a]

Configurations[b]				Model: [SDA, PCD, PMS], [DEP][a]	
SDA	PCD	PMS	DEP	o	e
1	1	1	1	95	53.5
1	1	1	2	49	62.6
1	1	1	3	22	50.0
1	1	2	1	61	36.4
1	1	2	2	43	42.6
1	1	2	3	9	34.0
1	2	1	1	31	26.7
1	2	1	2	42	31.3
1	2	1	3	10	25.0
1	2	2	1	17	35.1
1	2	2	2	48	41.1
1	2	2	3	44	32.8
2	1	1	1	37	31.6
2	1	1	2	37	36.9
2	1	1	3	24	29.5
2	1	2	1	23	33.8
2	1	2	2	48	39.6
2	1	2	3	34	31.6
2	2	1	1	23	35.8
2	2	1	2	41	41.8
2	2	1	3	47	33.4
2	2	2	1	19	53.1
2	2	2	2	50	62.2
2	2	2	3	96	49.7

[a]See text for further explanation.
[b]Hit-cells are underlined.

present results do not imply that H is better than any other hypothesis. If we ask which hypothesis describes appropriately the relations in the present data set, search methods within the framework of log-linear modeling can be used (e.g., Wermuth, 1976). In the present context, however, the focus is not on the explanatory search of best-fitting models; rather, it is on the confirmatory evaluation of a given hypothesis.

The results for the descriptive measures scope and precision are $Sc = 1.00$ and $Pr = 0.55$. The former value indicates that the hypothesis involves no tautological or empty predictions and covers, in principle, the entire population under study. The value of $Pr = 0.55$ is relatively low. This result is due to the fact that in three predictions two out of three states of the criterion are linked to only one state of the metapredictor.

In the inferential evaluation of the *PIH* and *PRE* measures, Formula (30) can be applied. The result is $z = 9.64$ and $P(z) < 1 \cdot 10^{-7}$, a value that is smaller than α, which was a priori set to $\alpha = 0.05$.

B. STUDY II: DEVELOPMENT OF CONCRETE OPERATIONS

The data to be discussed in this section were collected in a project on child development and social structure (Edelstein, 1983). One facet of this longitudinal project is the investigation of cognitive development in the Piagetian tradition (Schröder, 1984). Children ($n = 113$) were presented with tasks at the concrete operation level at both age 7 and age 9. At age 7 the tasks covered the concepts of invariance, inclusion, and logical multiplication; at age 9 the children were administered again the same tests on inclusion and logical multiplication. The basic assumption behind the following analysis is that there is a specified acquisition sequence of these tasks. More specifically, it is assumed that there are two types of sequential patterns: (1) patterns that imply developmental constancy, that is, nothing changes with respect to the repeatedly administered inclusion and multiplication tasks; (2) patterns where one or both of the repeatedly administered tasks are mastered (Schröder, 1984). Each of the tasks was scored dichotomously (task solved vs. task not solved). Thus, $2^5 = 32$ different developmental patterns are possible. However, only a subset of patterns meets constraints 1 and 2. Incompatible with these constraints are all patterns where the tasks of inclusion and logical multiplication are mastered at age 7 but not at age 9.

Let IV_i denote the invariance task, $I7_i$ the inclusion task at age 7, $I9_i$ the inclusion task at age 9, $M7_i$ the logical multiplication task at age 7, and $M9_i$ the logical multiplication task at age 9 (where $i = 0$ denotes task unsolved and $i = 1$ task solved). Then, the nine admissible sequential patterns yield the following prediction system:

$$
\begin{aligned}
\text{H:}\quad & (IV_0 \wedge I7_0 \wedge M7_0) \rightarrow (I9_0 \wedge M9_0) \vee (I9_1 \wedge M9_0) \vee (I9_1 \wedge M9_1)\ \& \\
& (IV_1 \wedge I7_0 \wedge M7_0) \rightarrow (I9_0 \wedge M9_0) \vee (I9_1 \wedge M9_0) \vee (I9_1 \wedge M9_1)\ \& \\
& (IV_1 \wedge I7_1 \wedge M7_0) \rightarrow (I9_1 \wedge M9_0) \vee (I9_1 \wedge M9_1)\ \& \\
& (IV_1 \wedge I7_1 \wedge M7_1) \rightarrow (I9_1 \wedge M9_1).
\end{aligned}
$$

Since the goal of the investigation is the specific prediction of performance at age 9 from the performance at age 7, the model [*IV*,*I7*,*M7*],[*I9*,M9] can be taken as a basis of the estimation of expected values.

In Table VII the observed and the expected cell frequencies are given in which the latter were estimated by using Formula (17) in its bivariate version, omitting the third and the succeeding factors. Because of the large number of irrelevant cells in Table VII the discrepancy between *PRE* and the *PIH* measures is large. *PRE* = 0.318 suggests that almost 32% of the misclassifications can be avoided

TABLE VII

Analysis of the Aggregate Hypothesis in the Variables IV, I7, M7, I9, and M9

Configurations[b]					model [IV,I7,M7],[I9,M9][a]	
IV	I7	M7	I9	M9	o	e
1	1	1	1	1	4	1.4
1	1	1	1	2	1	0.5
1	1	1	2	1	6	5.0
1	1	1	2	2	2	5.8
(1	1	2	1	1	0	0.4)
(1	1	2	1	2	0	0.1)
(1	1	2	2	1	2	1.5)
(1	1	2	2	2	2	1.8)
(1	2	1	1	1	0	)
(1	2	1	1	2	0	)
(1	2	1	2	1	0	)
(1	2	1	2	2	0	)
(1	2	2	1	1	0	)
(1	2	2	1	2	0	)
(1	2	2	2	1	0	)
(1	2	2	2	2	0	)
2	1	1	1	1	9	5.1
2	1	1	1	2	1	1.9
2	1	1	2	1	16	17.5
2	1	1	2	2	19	20.3
(2	1	2	1	1	0	2.1)
(2	1	2	1	2	0	0.8)
(2	1	2	2	1	10	7.3)
(2	1	2	2	2	9	8.5)
2	2	1	1	1	0	1.6
2	2	1	1	2	1	0.6
2	2	1	2	1	5	5.4
2	2	1	2	2	8	6.3
2	2	2	1	1	0	2.0
2	2	2	1	2	2	0.7
2	2	2	2	1	5	7.0
2	2	2	2	2	11	8.1

[a]See text for further explanation.
[b]Hit-cells are underlined; irrelevant cells are in parentheses.

if *H* is applied to the observed frequency distribution. This value reflects a significant proportionate reduction in errors. (Note that here the significance test described by Hildebrand et al., 1977, was used.) The *PIH* measures describe the advantage of *H* less favorably. Altogether, there is only a 6.2% increase of correctly classified *S*s, an amount that covers 12.40% of the maximally possible increase. In terms of signficance test statistics, this increase in the hit rate corresponds with $z = 0.932$, of which the probability is $P(z) = 0.18 > \alpha$.

The precision of *H* assumes the low value of 0.129, which is due to both the large number of irrelevant cells and the relatively large number of states of the metacriterion that is linked to some of the metapredictor configurations. The scope if 0.796, which as a value, is also relatively small. However, it is not as small as one might expect with respect to the large number of irrelevant cells. Since half of these cells are empty, the scope value is less affected than might be expected.

The present example was chosen to illustrate two problems in developmental research, the first of which emerges when longitudinal data are analyzed. The present chapter presents various ways of treating longitudinal data, one being the treatment of repeated measurements as separate variables the relations of which are under study and which was chosen in the last example because there were only two observation points. This number of observations usually leads to the null hyopthesis of independence of the first from the second observations. If, however, the same variables are measured more than twice, the assumption of total independence cannot be justified. At the least, first-order autocorrelations should be taken into account in the model formulation; that is, the adjacent observations should be allowed to be associated.

The second problem is more pertinent to the methodology presented in this chapter. In the present example, the interpretation of *PRE* suggests the conclusion that the application of *H*—in contrast to the model—allows a considerably more effective assignment of *S*s to the observed frequency distribution. On the other hand, the interpretation of the *PIH* measures suggests the conclusion that *H* does not lead to significantly better classifications. A decision favoring one of these results can be made on the basis of the cells that are included in the estimation of these measures. In the computation of *PRE,* only events that logically contradict *H* are treated as error-cells; in the computation of *PIH* measures, only events that—in a strict sense—correspond with *H* are treated as hit-cells. The present example makes obviously more sense in referring the interpretation to *PIH* measures, because the cells that are technically labeled as irrelevant must substantively be interpreted as inadmissible developmental sequences.

VI. Summary and Discussion

In this chapter an approach which allows the consideration of a broad range of relations is introduced. On the one hand, relations can be analyzed that are assumed to hold true for the entire range of admissible values of all variables under study; these kinds of relations correspond with the relations that are usually analyzed when correlations or covariances are estimated. On the other hand, particular relations, which are assumed to apply to only a subset of admissible values, as well as particular relations which apply to groups of variables rather than to pairs, can be examined.

In order to describe and evaluate statistically these assumed relations, statement calculus was applied in the process of hypothesis formulation. The application of statement calculus requires that the investigator formulate in the most explicit way the kind of relations he or she assumes to exist. By constructing the truth table of a hypothesis in terms of statement calculus the investigator can immediately identify those cells of contingency tables that contain elements which are consistent with the hypotheses under study.

The methods introduced herein were applied to the confirmatory analysis of conditional predictions. In conditional predictions, predictor states are connected by an "if–then" statement to particular states of criterion variables. The present approach, however, can also be applied to unconditional predictions in which the realization of variable states is postulated without any contingency upon other variables.

Furthermore, application of these methods in exploratory contexts, that is, in the derivation of predictions from a given data set, is possible. In these applications, different amounts of knowledge can be taken into account. First. if in conditional predictions the status of each variable as predictor or criterion is known, the search can be restricted to models in which this status is considered. Second, if only unconditional hypotheses seem admissible, the search can be restricted to a particular subset of models. Generally, knowledge about the status of variables leads to a reduction in the number of models that are to be considered.

The methodology presented in this chapter can be further developed when considering relations to the method of log-linear models. The methods for estimating expected values used herein can be interpreted as simple log-linear models. It still needs to be discussed whether other log-linear models that treat all variables as responses, logit-models that are particularly suited for analyzing dependence–independence relationships, or estimation procedures under quasi-independence assumptions might enable one to evaluate particular hypotheses appropriately.

Furthermore, the framework of log-linear models allows for the analysis of ordinal or continuous data. In the approaches applying statement calculus and *PRE*-measures to developmental data sets (e.g., Froman & Hubert, 1980) as well as in this chapter expected frequencies have been estimated using procedures from log-linear modeling that presuppose qualitative data. However, if time is introduced in the analysis as a variable per se, or if ordinal variables, such as grades in school, are analyzed, the information contained in the data might be better exhausted when log-linear models that take the level of measurement into account are considered (Clogg & Shockey, 1984).

Acknowledgments

The authors are indebted to Paul B. Baltes, Heather Chipuer, Clifford C. Clogg, Roger A. Dixon, Dan P. Keating, Jack J. McArdle, John R. Nesselroade, and Christopher Winship for helpful comments on earlier versions of this chapter. This was completed while Alexander von Eye was visiting professor of human development at The Pennsylvania State University. The support of the college is gratefully acknowledged.

References

Baltes, P. B., & Nesselroade, J. R. (1979). History and rationale of longitudinal research. In J. R. Nesselroade & P. B. Baltes (Eds.), *Longitudinal research in the study of behavior and development* (pp. 1–39). New York: Academic Press.

Berztiss, A. T. (1975). *Data structures. Theory and practice.* New York: Academic Press.

Bishop, Y. M. M., Fienberg, S. E., & Holland, P. W. (1975). *Discrete multivariate analysis: Theory and practice.* Cambridge, MA: MIT Press.

Brandtstädter, J., Krampen, G., & Heil, F. E. (1986). Personal control and emotional evaluation of development in partnership relations during adulthood. In M. M. Baltes & P. B. Baltes (Eds.), *The psychology of control and aging* (pp. pp 265–296). Hillsdale, NJ: Lawrence Erlbaum Associates.

Brandtstädter, J., Krampen, G., & Veselý. H. (1985). Attribution und sprachliche Kompetenz: Zur Bewährung attributionstheoretischer Annahmen bei Grundschülern mit unterschiedlichem sprachlichen Entwicklungsstand. *Sprache und Kognition, 3,* 130–138.

Brandtstädter, J., & von Eye, A. (1982). Aussagenlogische Analyse von Kontingenztafeln: I. Methodologische Vorüberlegungen. *Trierer Psychologische Berichte, 9,* 1–18.

Brandtstädter, J., & von Eye, A. (in press). *Hypothesenvaluation in der multivariaten Prädiktionsanalyse.* Psychologische Beiträge.

Bredenkamp, J. (1970). Über Maße der praktischen Signifikanz. *Zeitschrift für Psychologie, 177,* 310–318.

Clogg, C. C., & Shockey, J. W. (1984). Multivariate analysis of discrete data. In J. R. Nesselroade & R. B. Cattell (Eds.), *Handbook of multivariate experimental psychology* (2d ed.). New York: Plenum Press.

Dixon, W. J., Brown, M. B., Engelman, L., Franke, J. W., Hill, M. A., Jennrich, R. I., & Toporek, J. D. (1981). *BMDP statistical software 1981.* Berkeley: University of California Press.

Edelstein, W. (1983). Das Projekt kindliche Entwicklung und soziale Struktur. In K. E. Grossmann & P. Lütkenhaus (Eds.), *Bericht über die 6. Tagung Entwicklungspsychologie in Regensburg* (Vol. 2, pp. 275–277). Regensburg, Germany: University of Regensburg.

Featherman, D. (1985). Individual development and aging as a population process. In J. R. Nesselroade & A. von Eye (Eds.), *Individual development and social change: Explanatory analysis.* New York: Academic Press.

Fienberg, S. E. (1981). *The analysis of cross-classified categorical data.* Cambridge, MA: MIT Press.

Froman, T., & Hubert, L. J. (1980). Application of prediction analysis to developmental priority. *Psychological Bulletin, 87,* 136–146.

Goodman, L. A. (1968). The analysis of cross-classified data: Independence, quasi-independence and interactions in contingency tables with or without missing entries. *Journal of the American Statistical Association, 63,* 1091–1131.

Goodman, L. A. (1970). The multivariate analysis of qualitative data: Interactions among multiple classifications. *Journal of the American Statistical Association, 65,* 226–256.

Goodman, L. A., & Kruskal, W. H. (1954). Measures of association for cross classifications. *Journal of the American Statistical Association, 49,* 732–764.

Goodman, L. A., & Kruskal, W. (1974). Empirical evaluation of formal theroy. *Journal of Mathematical Sociology, 3,* 187–196.

Haberman, S. J. (1973). The analysis of residuals in cross-classified tables. *Biometrics, 29,* 205–220.

Hájek, P., & Havránek, T. (1978). *Mechanizing hypothesis formation. Mathematical foundations for a general theory.* Berlin: Springer.

Hájek, P., Havránek, T., & Chytil, M. K. (1983). *Metoda GUHA. Automatiká tvorba hypotéz.* Prague, Czechoslovakia: Academia.

Härtner, M., Matthes, K., & Wottawa, H. (1980). Computerunterstützte Hypothesenagglutination zur Erfassung komplexer Zusammenhänge. *EDV in Medizin und Biologie. 11,* 53–59.

Havránek, T., & Lienert, G. A. (1984). Local and regional vs. global contingency testing. *Biometrical Journal, 26,* 483–494.

Hildebrand, D. K., Laing, J. D., & Rosenthal, H. (1977). *Prediction analysis of cross classifications.* New York: John Wiley.

Klaus, G. (1973). *Moderne Logik. Abriß der formalen Logik.* Berlin, GDR: VEB Deutscher Verlag der Wissenschaften.

Klaus, G., & Buhr, M. (1964). *Philosophisches Wörterbuch.* (Band 2). Leipzig, GDR: VEB Verlag Enzyklopädie.

Krauth, J., & Lienert, G. A. (1973). *KFA. Die Konfigurationsfrequenzanalyse und ihre Anwendung in Psychologie und Medizin.* Freiburg, Germany: Alber.

Lerner, R. M. (1984). *On the nature of human plasticity.* Cambridge, England: Cambridge University Press.

Rudinger, G., Henning, H. J., & Schmitz–Scherzer, R. (1984). Das Projekt Anakonda. *Bonner Methoden Berichte, 1,* 1–25.

Schröder, E. (1984). *Zur Erklärung intraindividueller Veränderung konkreter Operationen: Eine empirische Evaluation der Entwicklungslogik konkreter Operationen anhand multinomialer qualitativer Verfahren.* Unpublished master's thesis, Technical University of Berlin.

Stegmüller, W. (1973). *Personelle und statistische Wahrscheinlichkeit.* Berlin: Springer.

Upton, J. G. (1978). *The analysis of cross-tabulated data.* New York: John Wiley.

von Eye, A., & Brandtstädter, J. (1982). Systematization of results of configural frequency analysis by minimizing Boolean functions. In H. Caussinus, P. Ettinger, & J. R. Mathieu (Eds.), *Compstat 1982, Pt. 2: Short communications, summaries of posters* (pp. 91–92). Vienna: Physica.

von Eye, A., & Lienert, G. A. (1985). Die Konfigurationsanalyse XX. Typen und Syndrome zweiter Ordnung (Komplextypen). *Zeitschrift für Klinische Psychlogie und Psychotherapie, 32,* 345–354.

Wermuth, N. (1976). Model search among multiplicative models. *Biometrics, 32,* 253–264.

Wohlwill, J. F. (1973). *The study of behavioral development.* New York: Academic Press.

Wottawa, H. (1984). *Strategien und Modelle in der Psychologie.* Munich: Urban & Schwarzenberg.

Expression through Affect and Words in the Transition from Infancy to Language

Lois Bloom, Richard Beckwith, Joanne Bitetti Capatides, and Jeremie Hafitz

TEACHERS COLLEGE, COLUMBIA UNIVERSITY

Abstract

The emergence of language at the end of infancy has a profound effect on the individual's development throughout the life span. In this chapter, we suggest a model to explain why and how infants acquire language, and present data from a research study demonstrating the usefulness of the methodology derived from that model. In our theory, we propose that children acquire the forms of speech for expressing the contents of states of mind. In our methodology, we use attributions of the contents of states of mind underlying children's expressions for understanding how the one system of expression already available to infants, affect, is related to the acquisition of words as a new system for expressing meaning. Both affect and words expressed desires more often than beliefs, and desires for events that involved the child as actor more often than other persons. Whereas affect was the predominant form of expression to begin with, by the time of a vocabulary spurt toward the end of the single-word period, words expressed the majority of propositions in every category except one; the category of beliefs that involved other persons and their actions toward the child continued to be expressed more often with affect than with words.

This chapter introduces a theory of language development which departs from the commonly held view that language is acquired by children as a tool for achieving purposes and goals. We suggest that tool use should not be central to a theory of language development. We propose, instead, that children acquire the forms of speech for expressing the contents of states of mind and for interpreting the speech of others so as to attribute states of mind to them (see Bloom & Beckwith, 1986, for the full account of this theoretical perspective). In what follows here, we begin by summarizing the theory and its relation to other views of child language, and describe how the theory has been translated into the methodology of our research. We then describe that research project and report results from one study that demonstrate the usefulness of the methodology and validate aspects of the theory.

Our investigation into the transition in language development from prelexical vocalizing to the use of conventional words has been concerned with two questions that have dominated efforts to explain the emergence of language in the last decade. One question concerns how developments in cognition contribute to developments in language. We know that certain properties of mentally represented objects and events develop in roughly the same period in which children begin to say words, in the second year of life, but the connections between developments in cognition and developments in language remain obscure (e.g., Bloom, Lifter, & Broughton, 1985).

The second question we have asked is how developments in affect relate to developments in language in this same period. Infants develop in their capacities for affective experience and expression (Campos, Barrett, Lamb, Goldsmith, & Stenberg, 1983; Lewis & Michaelson, 1983; Sroufe, 1979). Emotional expression and language are two communication systems available to the child for the transmission of meaning in the second year of life. Since some affective expressions are in place virtually from birth, and affective communication is developmentally prior to language, a reasonable question to ask is how the emergence of words might be related to communication with affect (e.g., Adamson & Bakeman, 1982; Bullowa, 1979; Stern, 1977). Our research project, then, has been concerned with how the two systems of expression, affect and language, relate to one another, and how both relate to cognition more generally.

I. Intentionality and Language Development

The research has been grounded in a theoretical model of Intentionality and language development (Bloom & Beckwith, 1986), which proposes that children acquire language in order to express what they are thinking about in their consciously active, mental states. We are calling these states of mind *Intentional states* in the philosophical tradition of Brentano, as followed by Dennett (1978), and Searle (1983), among others. While we have borrowed the term from philosophy, the construct that it represents is common to both philosophy and psychology. For example, because we argue that the child is operating on presently active states of mind to acquire language, we are talking about awareness (e.g., Klatzky, 1984; Yates, 1985) and children's working memory (e.g., Case, 1974; Pascual–Leone, 1970); and because the contents of Intentional states are derived from the data of perception and memory, the developments which allow the child to have such mental states depend on developments in infant memory and recall (e.g., Mandler, 1983; Moscovitch, 1984).

We propose that any successful effort toward an understanding of language development must be grounded in a theory which takes an Intentional stance (Dennett, 1978), that is, a theory that explains behaviors as expressions of beliefs and desires, and a methodology that makes explicit the attributions of such states of mind to the actions of speaking and interpreting. This stance is already implicit in child language research, even though the emphasis is on observable behaviors most often. For instance, in speech act theory, the speech act that is observed is a linguistic expression (having a behavioral/physical aspect) of an underlying mental state. Hence, researchers concerned with speech acts can easily believe they are dealing with "objective," that is, non-mental phenomena. However, Intentional states are the "sincerity conditions" for their corresponding speech acts; for instance, making a statement about *X* expresses the belief in *X;* issuing a directive to do *Y* expresses the desire that *Y* be done. The direction of influence is from Intentionality to language (Searle, 1983).

The states of mind underlying expression include psychological *attitudes* and *contents* that those attitudes are about. Beliefs are basic to the psychological attitudes of mental states and encompass a range of epistemic attitudes (e.g., know, think, expect, wonder, guess), depending on ontological certainty/ uncertainty. These enable a range of desires (e.g., want, need, hope, intend) (see Danto, 1973; Davidson, 1984). In infancy, the contents of awareness are constrained to the data of perception, but with developments in the knowledge store and in procedures for recalling aspects of knowledge from memory, the child can represent in awareness objects and events that are not available in perception. Thus, mentally present contents can include events and objects recalled from the past, perceived in the present, and/or anticipated in the future.

The word "intentionality" has been used in several contexts in language acquisition research. In the proposal that language development depends on mothers attributing intentions to their infants during interaction, intentions are desires for a goal or a change of state. By expressing these attributions for her child, the mother provides experiences with the kinds of language that can achieve the goal (Bruner, 1975, 1981; Ryan, 1974), and influence the behaviors of other persons (McShane, 1980). When speech act theory was applied to prespeech vocalizations and single-word speech, intention was invoked as the "primitive force" or purpose for uttering the word (Bates, Benigni, Bretherton, Camaioni, & Volterra, 1979; Dore, 1975; as in the "illocutionary force" of Austin, 1962). In both of these views, children acquire language as a tool to use in their interactions with others and the model of language development that is suggested is an *instrumental* one.

Others have described the intentionality of the infant in terms of directedness, with directedness defined as repeated or sustained actions that incorporate other persons toward a goal in a communication event. Studies of directedness have identified the development of communication with behaviors that are "intended" by the infant in the sense of being voluntary and purposive (Bates, 1976; Bruner, 1981; Dore, 1975; Greenfield, 1980; Harding & Golinkoff, 1979). They have, for the most part, proposed that children acquire language as a tool for achieving purposes and goals in communication, again suggesting an instrumental model of language development.

Desires to achieve a goal or to communicate are *one* sort of Intentional state; desires do not comprise all mental states nor do the actions resulting from desire comprise all actions. Many of the Intentional states that we can hold in mind are beliefs, and the actions of their expression reflect the way we *believe* the world to be rather than the way we *desire* it to be. Thus, language expresses, and the child acquires language in order to express, many sorts of mental states with a range of beliefs, including but not limited to the beliefs entailed in desires. When language is viewed as a tool for achieving goals, the focus is on end states and the effect the child's behaviors have on the context. Tool use, however, is subordinate to the general symbolic capacity of humans (Burke, 1935; Piaget, 1972/1973), and it is the symbolic capacity which allows us to recall and represent aspects of events from memory and anticipate new events. A focus on mental contents, then, allows us to inquire into the capacities that are required for expression. The theory of language development that results, in this view, is a *mental* theory rather than an *instrumental* one.

Introducing Intentionality into a model of language development is compatible with and, indeed, *it functions to integrate* the many theories that we have in child language. We have already noted studies that describe the attributions mothers make of their infants' desires for goals and intentions to communicate. The present theory is consistent with these and with other accounts that explain the development of communication in social contexts (e.g., Bates, 1976; Dore, 1975; Ervin–Tripp, 1973; Halliday, 1975), but with a shift in emphasis from end states to mental states. Because the contents of mental states derive from aspects of knowledge stored in memory, the theory is relevant as well to theories that argue for the importance of children's early conceptual development in the development of language (e.g., Bates et al., 1979; Bloom, 1970, 1973; Bloom et al., 1985; Clark, 1983; Gopnik & Meltzoff. 1985; Nelson, 1974; Nelson & Lucariello, 1985; Sinclair, 1970). And because expression is basic to the theory we are proposing, and children acquire language as the mode of expression par excellence, the theory embraces explanations of how children analyze formal properties of speech (e.g., Braine, 1976; Maratsos & Chalkley, 1980; Peters, 1983; Slobin, 1982).

But each of these theories deals with only one or another fragment of the acquisition process, and, by themselves, they are insufficient. The several aspects of learning addressed by separate theories come together in the child's construction and expression of Intentional states, and only together can they explain the development of language. Intentionality, as the "leading edge" of the mind, intervenes between events in the context and knowledge about the world in memory. It is that aspect of cognition through which percepts and knowledge recalled from memory are related to one another, and both are related to words and sentences. In taking this stance, we offer a theory of language development which integrates the social interaction, cognitive, and linguistic theories that we have for understanding language development.

II. Translation between Theory and Method

Our use of Intentionality in a theory of language development was motivated by three basic assumptions. First, what individuals think about in their conscious states of mind underlies their actions (including actions of speaking and interpreting), which, in turn, determines their development (e.g., Brandtstädter, 1984; Piaget, 1954). Second, children endeavor to express what they are thinking about, and to interpret the speech of others so as to discover what others are thinking about. And third, children actively engage in acquiring words and constructing the grammar of a language in that endeavor.

Expression, is basic to the theory we are proposing. We already know that language is expression, but other modes of expression are also available to the child, and are available to us as observers before language begins. We know from the work of others that infants' actions can be interpreted as meaningful before words appear (Bates et al., 1979), so that actions are one sort of expression. Affect displays are in place before any words are acquired, and they allow us to say something more than simply that the display is apparent. At the least, we can say that the child is experiencing some emotional state or is feigning that state. The affect display is the public aspect of the constellation of things associated with the emotion, as a manifestation of that emotion. Given that the child has at least these three modes of expression—action, language, and affect—the question that concerns us has to do with what we are licensed to attribute to the child engaging in them. (We will not have anything to say here about action as expression, but see Lifter & Bloom, 1985, for another sort of analysis of children's actions with objects.)

The issue of what we are licensed to attribute to displays of emotions is likely to be as problematic as the dissension surrounding rich interpretation of child language (e.g., Bloom, Capatides, & Tackeff, 1981; Golinkoff, 1981; Howe, 1976), which is, indeed, an argument concerning the license to attribute. Rich interpretation involves assigning semantic-conceptual categories to the words in an expression based on the conditions under which the expression was uttered. If certain categories are attributed some criterial number of times, then the category is considered to have psychological reality for the child. The categories assigned in rich interpretation are based on our understanding of language qua language, child language, and cognitive development. What understanding can we bring to attributions based on affect expressions?

Affect expressions are often seen as expressions of such discrete emotions as disgust, joy, and happiness (as in Darwin). As such, we should be capable of attributing at least these discrete emotions to the displays in question. Whether individual expressions of these discrete emotions would relate in any interesting ways to language development, we do not know, and we are not familiar with any theoretical or empirical work that makes such claims. And so this attribution, while possible, may not be interesting.

Another possibility, and the one which we pursue here, is to attribute what these emotions are about in the same way that we attribute what the child's words are about. The object of an emotion must have been the occasion for that emotion, and hence its expression. In observing contextualized affect displays it is often possible to know what caused the emotion; for example, negative emotions are often caused by discomfort and pain. But discomfort and pain do not exhaust our resources; as any actively involved care-giver knows, all possible sources of discomfort can be removed and yet the child will express a negative affect. We know from the theoretical work of Campos et al. (1983) and Stein and Jewett (in press), among others, that there are many other causes of emotion. For example, negative emotions are often associated with negative outcomes of plans or perceived obstacles to plans. Conversely, positive emotions are often associated with positive outcomes of plans. A child's emotion may be disgust about a pie, or fear about a snake, or joy about achieving some goal. The point is that the things the child's emotions are about are frequently part of the context so that thought about those things can be attributed to the child.

Affect can serve as an index according to which planfulness may be attributed, and in a given context, the elements that comprise the plan may also themselves be evident and thus attributable. In other contexts, our understanding of emotions and observations of the objects that cause emotions will guide the attributions that we make.

These assumptions led us to devise a coding scheme for ascribing mental contents underlying infants' expressions through affect and words. No doubt other schemes are equal to the task, but the one that we present here has allowed us to inquire into developmental relations between these different forms of expression. The format we devised for coding attributions of mental states underlying both word and affect expression is schematized in Fig. 1.

The first level, Level I, is an attribution of the child's psychological *attitude*, and Level II is an attribution of the contents of mind toward which the psychological attitude, either belief or desire, was directed. These contents were coded as *propositions*. Thus, using the child's expression and the context of the expression, we endeavored to attribute (I) the child's psychological attitude, either a desire or belief; and (II) the contents of these desires and beliefs.

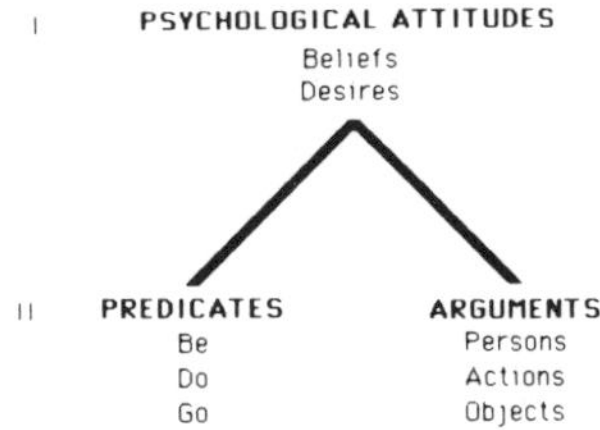

Fig. 1. Components of intentional state coding.

The fact that we coded the contents of mental states in propositional form, that is, as predicate argument structures, should not be construed as our holding a propositional theory of mind. We chose to maintain certain relationships within a propositional format for coding onto a computer, and this was not limiting since an effable system can be implemented in propositions. That is, anything that one can be conscious of can be represented in propositions and this holds whether the conscious material, itself, is in propositional form. We do not suppose that our attributions are replicas of any sort; that is, they need not look like what underlies the expressions on which we base our attributions.

The two psychological attitudes we attributed to the children were *beliefs* and *desires*—whether the child desired the event to be the case or believed the event to be the case. We coded belief and desire because they are the most fundamental of the psychological attitudes, and expressions based on belief or desire are relatively easy to distinguish and therefore to code. A belief marks reality as it is from the child's point of view; that is, a belief matches the world as the child sees or imagines it to be. A desire marks an intention to make some change in the world; that is, a desire matches the way the world ought to be according to the child (see Searle, 1983). For example, we attributed a desire to the child if the child appeared to be thinking about doing an action, obtaining an object, or fulfilling some other kind of goal (and also coded whether the child was considering the desire in terms of achieving or failing to achieve the goal). We attributed a belief to the child if the child was considering an object or action without trying to influence or change the events in the context.

The contents of what the child was thinking about were coded as propositions, with the three predicates *be* (static state), *do* (dynamic state), and *go* (locative change of state), in relation to persons (self and other), objects, and actions as arguments. *Be* was attributed if the child appeared to be thinking about a static event, for example, as when the child noticed the mother smiling, or looked up at the clock on the wall. *Do* was attributed to the contents of the child's mental state if the child appeared to be thinking about a dynamic event, for example, giving the doll a kiss, or sliding on the slide. *Go* was attributed if the child seemed to be thinking of a dynamic event that resulted in a change of location (or possession), for example, walking across the room to the snack table, or giving the doll to the mother. Thus, *be, do,* and *go* named static, dynamic, and change of place events.

The arguments of these predicates were specified from a finite list of the persons, objects, and common actions that occurred in the playroom. Persons included the child, mother, and research assistants. The objects included the toys, the furniture, and the snack items which were always introduced into the playroom. Since the same groups of toys were introduced during each playroom visit and since the children interacted only with these known objects, we were usually able to specify accurately both the objects and the actions in our attributions.

So, in research with children on the threshold of language, we suggest keeping in mind that several modes of expression are available to the young child and we are licensed to make attributions on the basis of each of them. To make these attributions, our research practices do not need to change significantly. We need only acknowledge and make explicit the practice of making attributions based on language as expression and then to expand the conditions under which we engage in this practice. Our coding scheme is just one way in which to implement such a strategy but it is only through this strategy that we are capable of looking at some of the relations between diverging forms of expression.

Our inclusion of Intentionality in a model of language development, and our proposal that changes in the contents of mental states of awareness drive the construction of language, lead to the following assumptions. The first is that children will acquire words and language structures as the contents of their mental states become increasingly *discrepant* from the data of perception. In infancy, the contents of awareness are constrained to the data of perception; with developments in knowledge and procedures for retrieval and recall, the infant can access objects and events from memory for the contents of mental states that do not match the data from perception, so that expression becomes necessary for interpretation by others. For example, the child holding out a bottle to a caregiver can depend on the shared perception between them for understanding. But in a situation when the child's mental contents include a bottle that is not also available to perception, saying the word becomes necessary for communication.

The second assumption is that as the contents of Intentional states become increasingly *complex,* the child will require correspondingly more complex language for their expression. That is, the more complex the contents of mental states become, the more the child will need to know of the language for both expressing and interpreting the expressions of others. One of the clearest examples of this is in the acquisition of complex sentences which generally begins between 2 and 3 years of age. With development of the ability to hold the content underlying two sentences in mind, the child searches for the forms of the language for expressing these contents and the connections between them (Bloom, Lahey, Hood, Lifter, & Fiess, 1980).

The third assumption, and the one that is relevant to the purpose of the study reported here, is that *different contents* of Intentional states will require different modalities of expression. That is, qualitative differences in the contents of mental states—as opposed to changes in discrepancy and complexity—will underly the difference between expression through words and expression through an affect display.

III. Affective and Linguistic Expression

Two of the modes of expression available to the young child—words and affect displays—were the subject of the study presented here. We have asked how attributions of the contents of mind expressed through affect, were related to those that were expressed with words, in the period when words first emerged and as the children's vocabularies increased.

A. THE RESEARCH PROJECT

Subjects. Our subjects are 14 infants—7 girls and 7 boys—from a range of ethnic and economic backgrounds. Our selection criteria were that the children were first-born, from English-speaking families, with mothers who were not employed outside of the home when they began their participation in the study.

The most striking thing about our subject population is the diversity among the infants and their mothers. We are confident that we have tapped a wide range of the general population in metropolitan New York. Ten of the children are white; three are black; and one is of mixed ethnicity (Dominican Hispanic and Native American). Four families earned less than $10,000; three earned between $10,000 and 30,000; and seven earned more than $30,000. (The threshold of poverty in the United States in 1981 was an income of $9287 a year for a family of four, and the median income for 1981 was $22,390; Herbers, 1982).

Data Collection. The data were collected through monthly playroom observations, from 8 to 26 months; home visits monthly from 8 to 15 months and at 3-month intervals thereafter; and parents' diaries. Both the playroom sessions and home visits were video-recorded and the primary data for this analysis were the child/mother interactions in the playroom.

The playroom was furnished with a child-size table and two chairs. and a plastic slide. The video camera was mounted on a movable tripod 3 feet high, and one of the investigators followed the activities, moving the camera as needed. Each mother was asked to play with her child as she would if she had a free hour at home. A group of toys was in place in the middle of the floor when the mother and child entered the room. A different group of toys was brought into the room every 10 minutes thereafter. The same toys were presented with the same schedule to all of the children; the toys were chosen so as to counterbalance: (1) possible boy/girl interest (e.g., truck, doll); and (2) potential for manipulative/enactment play (e.g., stacking blocks, miniature cutlery). After the first half-hour, if the child had not already requested it, a snack of juice and cookies, with coffee or tea for the mother, was brought in. The fact that only one month's observation with one subject was missed (due to a family vacation) in the entire course of data collection attests to the fact that both the mothers and the children looked forward to and enjoyed these sessions.

Data Processing. We identified two developmental reference points in these children's transition from infancy to language for the study reported here. Both were defined for the children individually on the basis of their language development: *First words,* which was operationalized as the first use of one conventional word at least two times; and a *vocabulary spurt,* which was a sharp increase in the number of different words from one month to the next, and operationalized as the first increase of at least 12 new words in a 4-week period, after the child had already acquired at least 20 words. Imitations of mothers' words and self-repetitions were not used in identifying the language achievements. Each of the developmental reference points consisted of three sessions: the target session during which the criterion for either first words or vocabulary spurt was met, the preceding session, and the following session. Thus, the two developmental reference points: first words and vocabulary spurt each extended over 3 months. The children's ages at each of the target sessions were 13.7 months (mean; range = 10–18 months) for first words, and 19.2 months (mean; range = 13–25 months) for vocabulary spurt.

Computerized Coding. The equipment we use is schematized in Fig. 2. The hardware itself is, for the most part, commercially available. Only their combination is unique. We use Apple II Plus computers, Sony Betamax SLO–383 stereo-editing decks, FOR.A TCR–3100 SMPTE time-code readers, and a simple multiplexing circuit made to interface the 32-bit time-code readers and the 8-bit Apples. We also use a FOR.A SMPTE time-code generator to record a discrete audio signal 30 times every second, 1 for each frame, on track one of the videotape.

The coded input is stored in a file from which data can be retrieved sequentially according to the time code. These files are then transferred from the Apple to an IBM–XT for analysis. For this analysis, each of three observations (the first word, first word + 1 month, and vocabulary spurt target) was coded according to three independent coding schemes, each in a separate pass. The computer–

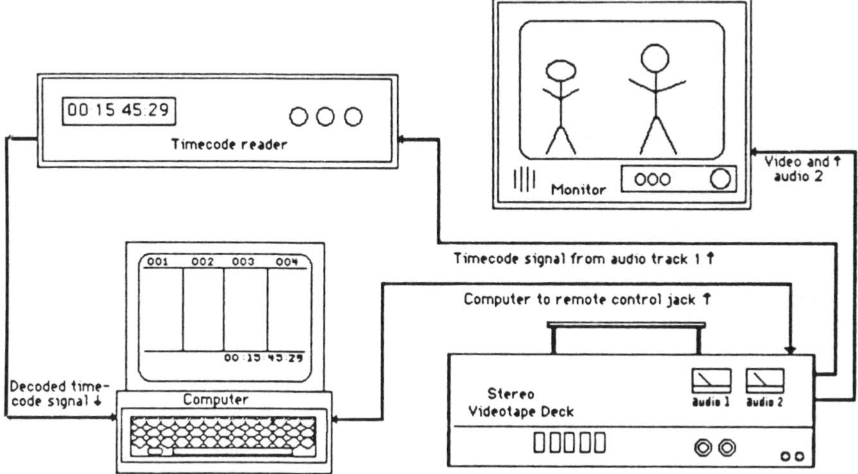

Fig. 2. Hardware used in coding data.

video interface enabled these successive passes to be merged according to time code, preserving the temporal relations in the data. First, all of the child's words and non-word vocalizations were transcribed; second, all instances of shifts in affect expression were identified and coded for their valence and intensity; and third, all words and all nonneutral affective expressions (i.e., positive and negative affect shifts) were coded for attributions of underlying intentional state.

Coding Expression of Affect. Because affect is always present, every change in expressed affect was recorded in the stream of the child's behavior. The coding scheme that we devised for this study yielded a continuous record of changes in expressed affect or what we are calling *affect shifts,* and the duration of affect states from one shift to another. An affect shift was defined as any observable change in the child's affect expression, which included changes in facial expression, body tension and posture, and affective vocalization (whining, laughing, and the like). These affect expressions were coded for their *valence,* whether neutral, negative, positive, mixed positive/negative, or equivocal hedonic tone. A neutral expression was defined by the face being in a resting or baseline position without any facial movement, as described by Ekman and Friesen (1975, 1978). A mixed affect display included elements of both positive and negative valence; equivocal affect was neither positive, negative, nor neutral, as happened with expressions of surprise or excitement. Nonneutral affect expressions were also coded for *intensity,* with three levels of nonneutral affect: one, two, and three degrees of intensity, indicating the fullness of display of an expression. Thus, the coding scheme for describing the quality of expressed affect included the three levels of intensity (1, 2, 3) and five categories of valence (neutral, negative, and positive valence, mixed and equivocal).

The emotional signal carries two kinds of information, categorical and gradient (Stern, Barnett, & Spieker, 1983). Categorical information is the particular emotion being expressed, such as joy, sadness, or anger; gradient information includes such properties of the expression as hedonic tone and intensity. The coding scheme used in this study captured the gradient properties of emotional expression and did not identify or label discrete emotional categories. This does not preclude coding for categorical information at a subsequent time.

An emotion is a multidimensional construct that includes, at least, a representation of an eliciting situation, and an internal physiological state, feeling, and experience (e.g., Lewis & Michaelson. 1983). When we describe the affect expressions of the children in this study, we are actually describing that aspect of their emotions that is public. The public expression of emotion provided information that is well suited to our purposes. Our concern is with affect and its expressive properties. Care givers respond to their children on the basis of the affect expressions that they observe and the attributions that they make. The valence and intensity of facial and vocal expressions are readily apparent to an observer; they are not so microscopic that they require extensive training in order to be identified. In effect, they are the kind of attributions that naïve observers (e.g., care givers) make in the interactions of daily life. Thus, we believe that the scheme we devised was psychologically real for the observers, as well as for the children whom they observed.

The photographs reproduced in Figs. 3, 4, 5, 6, 7 were coded according to this scheme for coding affect. They are reproduced here for purposes of illustration only, they were not part of the actual data of this study. The photos were taken informally for another purpose and they are included here to provide examples that are as good as static photos can be of each of the affect shifts that were coded from the video display. In actuality, the dynamic video display, with repeated viewings, provided many more cues for the coding decisions than could be captured with still photos. Examples of negative affect (−1, −2, and −3) are presented in Fig. 3; examples of positive affect (+1, +2, and +3) are presented in Fig. 4; and four examples of neutral affect, two from each of two children at different ages, are presented in Fig. 5.

Examples of mixed affect, in which the child's expression included elements of both positive and negative valence are presented in Fig. 6; and examples of equivocal affect, in which the affect was neither positive, negative, nor neutral, are presented in Fig. 7.

3A

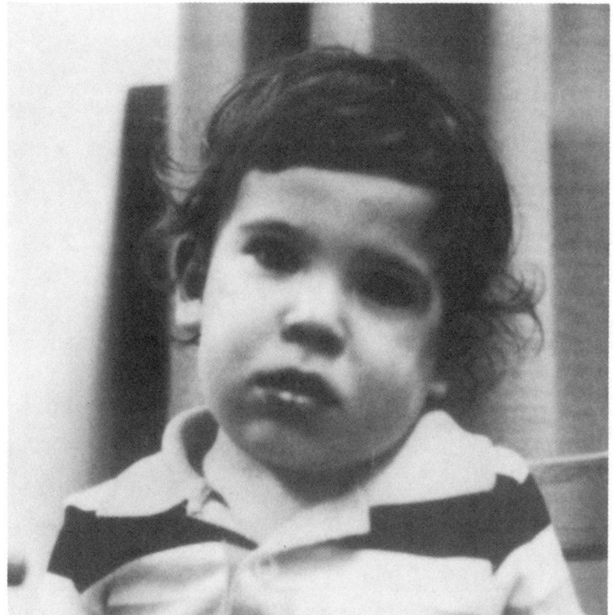

MINUS ONE (- 1)

3B

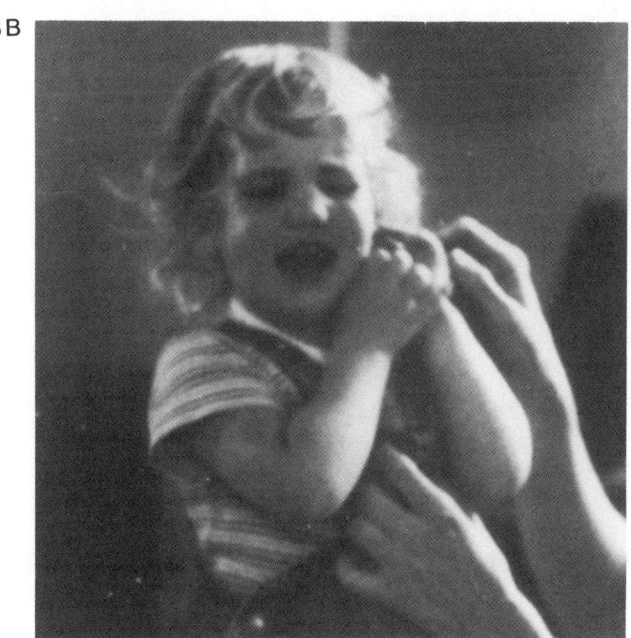

MINUS TWO (- 2)

Fig. 3. Examples of negative affect expression.

3C

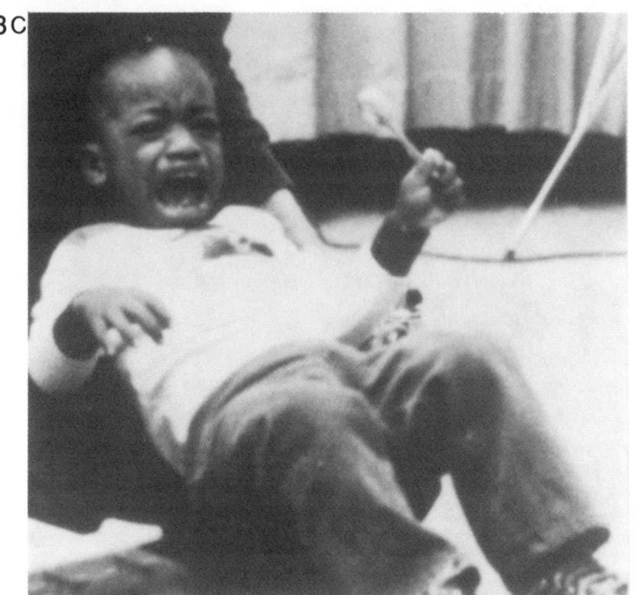

MINUS THREE (- 3)

Fig. 3. (*continued*)

4A

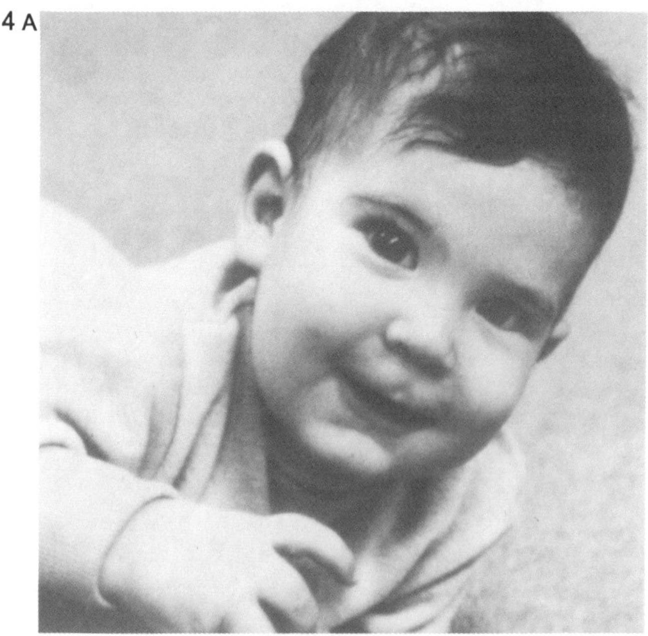

PLUS ONE (+ 1)

Fig. 4. Examples of positive affect expression.

4B

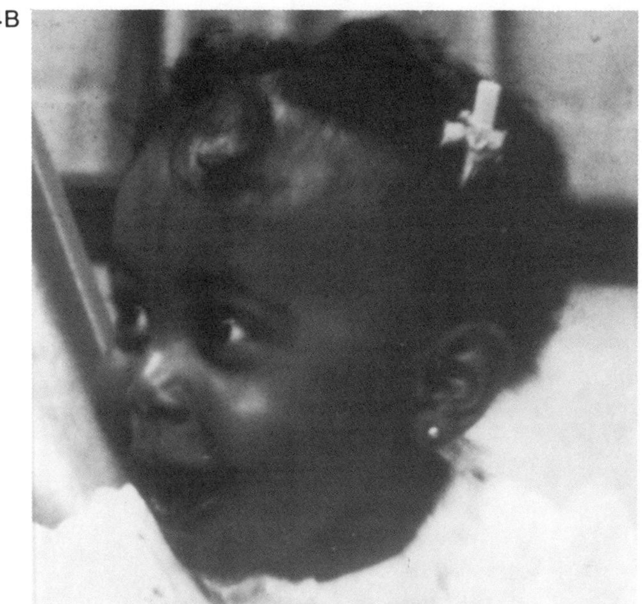

PLUS TWO (+ 2)

4C

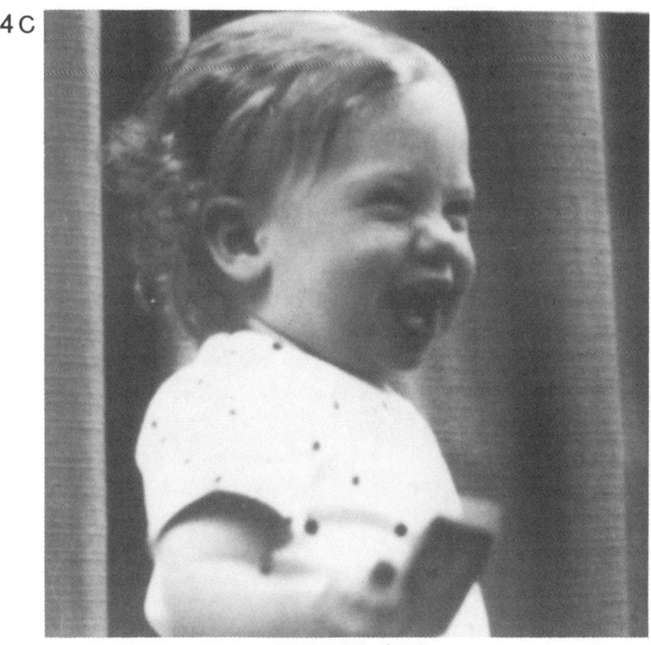

PLUS THREE (+ 3)

Fig. 4. *(continued)*

5A

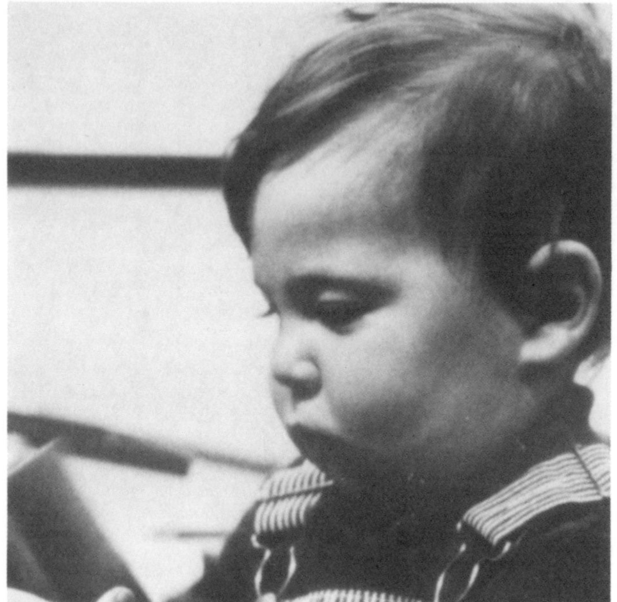

13 months

5B

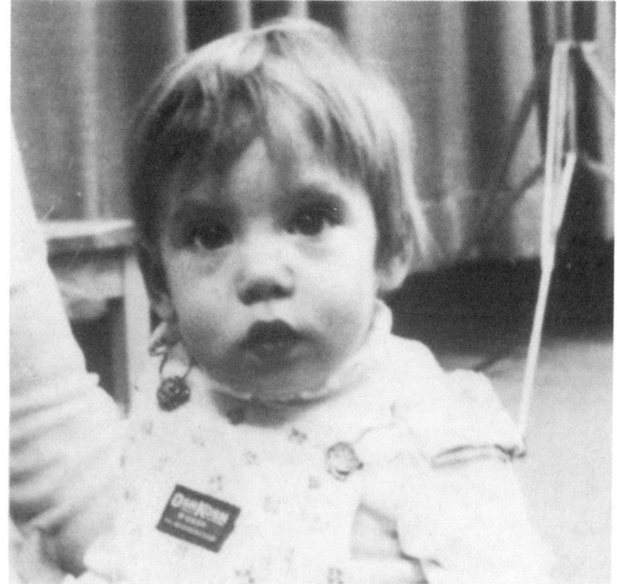

11 months

Fig. 5. Examples of neutral affect expression.

5C

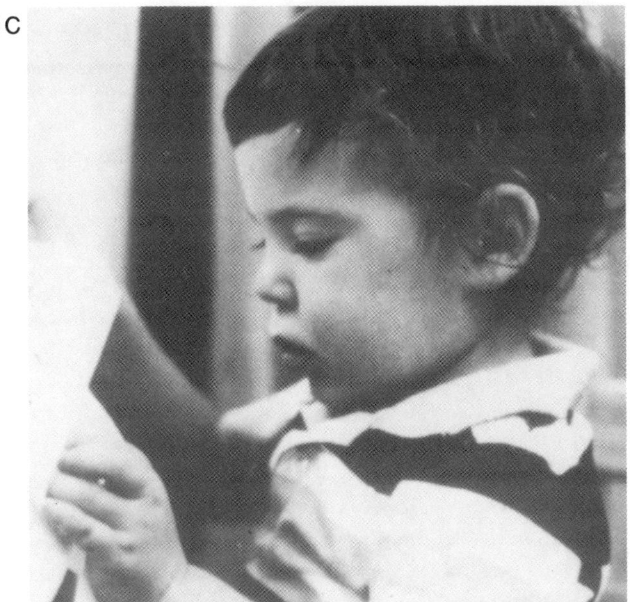

17 months

5D

22 months

Fig. 5. (*continued*)

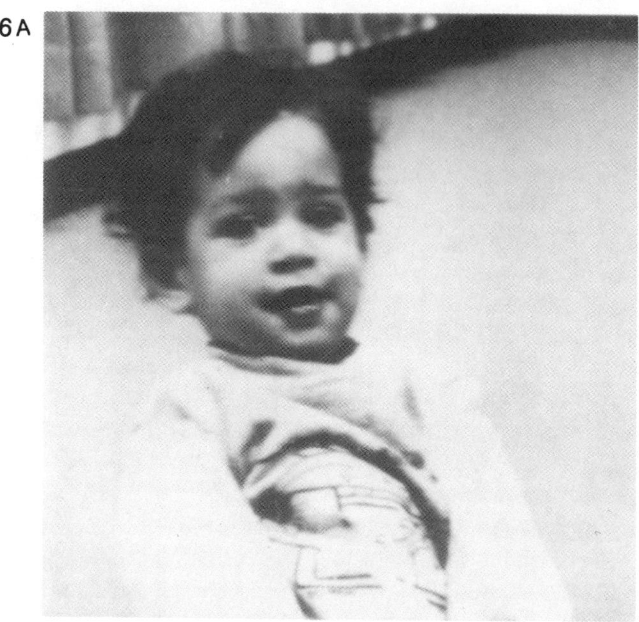

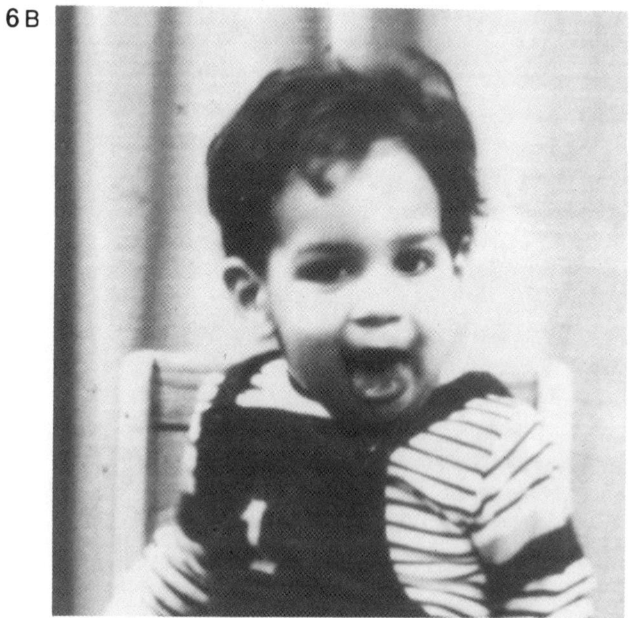

Fig. 6. Examples of mixed affect expression: both positive and negative elements.

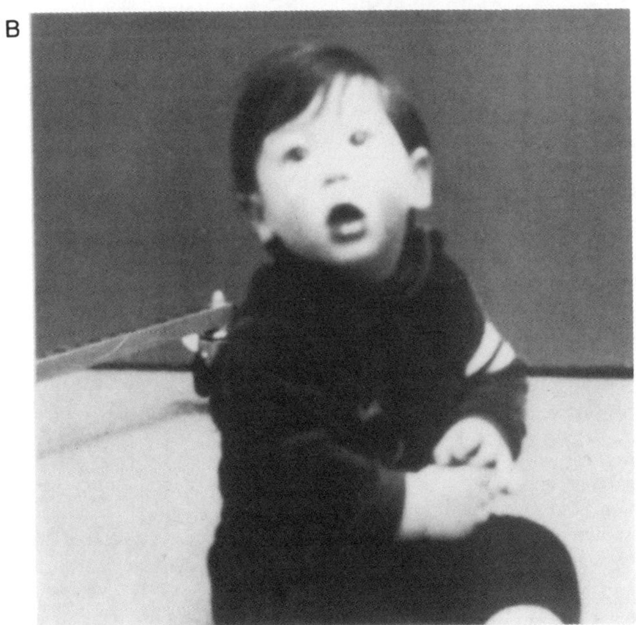

Fig. 7. Examples of equivocal affect expression: neither positive, negative, nor neutral.

Reliability for coding was high. Coders were trained in pairs and after training their accuracy was assessed by calculating the agreement of each pair with a segment of data that had been coded by the two senior research assistants who were responsible for implementing the code (J. Capatides and J. Hafitz). The reliability (Pearson product–moment correlation) ranged from .98 to 1.0 for the three pairs. After working in pairs for several weeks, reliability was assessed for the individual coders working independently, and agreement ranged from .98 to .99 between the members of the pairs. Thereafter, coders worked independently.

Coding Attributions of Intentional States. A separate pass was made through the data for coding attributions of the contents of the children's intentional states, according to the scheme presented earlier (see Fig. 1). Attributions were made and coded for every word and every nonneutral affect shift. Coding the contents of mental states would be an unreasonable task—that is, we would never be able to verify what the child was thinking of at any one point in time. But it was possible to do what care givers do routinely when they interact with children. For instance, when a baby whimpers, the care giver might attribute desire for a bottle or an inability to obtain a toy. We have made the same sorts of attributions to the children, attributions of what the child is thinking about when the child displays a shift in affect or says a word. In coding these attributions we use the kinds of cues that care givers use: what the child says, what the child does, what has been said or what is subsequently said, what is observable in the context, and what we know of the child from past experience. Moreover, we can do what the care-giver cannot do. We can use our videotapes to watch and listen to the moments that surround an expression, over and over, and we can look ahead as well as backwards for relevant cues (Hafitz & Bloom, 1985).[1]

Coders were initially trained in pairs and worked together until reliability between them was obtained. This was done by having each member of the pair code a portion of the data separately, then comparing the codings, and then resolving differences. For the reliability measures for the final analyses, the percentage of agreement between independent coders ranged from .79 to .93 for each of the coding decisions in the attributions (i.e., attitude, progress toward achieving a goal of a desire, the predicate, the objects specified in the argument,

[1]We did not have the mothers of the children view the video records and attribute meaning to their own children's words and affect expressions for several reasons. For one, we wanted our mothers to be naïve with respect to the purposes of the study and so avoided including them in any interpretive procedures which might have influenced their interactions with their children in the recording sessions (or at home, between visits to our laboratory). For another, the time required (away from their children) would have placed unreasonable demands on the mothers; they were already contributing two days each month to the project (one laboratory session and one home visit). In addition, the mothers would have differed in their accuracy and objectivity and reliability among them could not have been assessed.

the number of propositions attributed, time, and directedness). Several analyses of how the children's words expressed these attributions are under way. The study presented here concerns the qualitative comparisons between the contents of these attributions as expressed through words and affect.

Each expression of affect in the first 30 minutes of the *first word* and *vocabulary spurt* target observations; all of the words in the 2 hours that made up the first word target and subsequent first word + 1-month observations; and all of the words in the first half-hour of the vocabulary spurt target observation, were coded for attributions of intentional states. Because words were sampled for 2 hours in the two first word observations (because words were infrequent in the first words and first words + 1 observations) and for only 1 half-hour in the vocabulary spurt observation, the following measures were taken to control for the differences in sampling time. The frequencies of words and attributions for words from the two first word observations were divided by four, so that results are presented here for 30 minutes of interaction for words and for affect, at each time (first words and vocabulary spurt). In addition, when word and affect occurred in the same expression, the attribution was counted twice, that is, added to the frequencies of both word and affect.[2]

The attributions that were made of the children's intentional states provided us with a heuristic for comparing the profiles of meaning that were conveyed with affective exprcssions and with words, at two times in the children's single-word period—when words first emerged, and at the time of a precipitous increase in the number of different words.

IV. Results

The numbers of words and affect shifts that occurred at the two different times are presented in Table I. The numbers of propositions in the attributions that were made of the mental states underlying these words and affect shifts are also presented in Table I. Each expression could have had one or more propositions (along with a psychological attitude) attributed to it. For example, when a child tried to put the cow into a block and turned to the mother for help saying "cow," two propositions were coded: the desire that the child put the cow in (failing to achieve the goal), and the desire that mother do it (with the expectation that she would achieve the goal). Thus, in the analyses that follow, the numbers of propositions are compared for expression by words and affect, at two times, first words and vocabulary spurt. Each of the coding passes was performed independently of the others; persons doing the coding for attributions of Intentional states

[2]The incidence of words occurring at the same time as a positive/negative affect display was low; words occurred with neutral affect primarily (.76 at first words and .64 at vocabulary spurt; Bloom, Capatides, & Beckwith, in preparation).

TABLE I

Frequency of Expressions and Attributed Propositions[a]

	Expressions	Propositions
First Words		
Age: $\bar{X}$ = 13.7 months		
Range: 10–18 months		
Affect	1029 (.88)	1448 (.85)
Words	135 (.12)	265 (.15)
Vocabulary Spurt		
Age: $\bar{X}$ = 19.2 months		
Range: 13–25 months		
Affect	1023 (.48)	1688 (.43)
Words	1092 (.52)	2251 (.57)

N = 14

[a]30 minutes of interaction at first words and vocabulary spurt.

were unaware at the time that the number of propositions in these attributions would be the unit of analysis for this study.

At the most global level, one can compare the frequencies of words and affect shifts, and the propositions that were attributed to them, at the two times. At the time of first words, a total of 1713 propositions were attributed and 85% of these were attributed to expressions of affect. By the time of the vocabulary spurt, the relative contributions from affect and words to the expression of propositions had shifted, and only 43% of the propositions were attributed to expressions of affect. This shift reflected the approximately eightfold increase in both the numbers of words and the numbers of propositions attributed to words. At the same time, however, the numbers of affect shifts and propositions attributed to affect shifts increased only slightly. Thus, expression per se increased in the period, but only with the children's emerging use of words.

The frequency in these attributions of the two psychological attitudes, beliefs and desires, are compared in Table II. The relative frequency of beliefs and desires was the same for both kinds of expression at the time of the vocabulary spurt: Approximately two-thirds were desires, while one-third were beliefs. This finding was the same at first words for affect, when affect expressions predominated, but words, which were just beginning to emerge, tended to express beliefs somewhat more.

The relative frequency with which different categories of propositional content were attributed to words as compared with affect shifts is presented in Table III. The categories of propositions included persons, either child or mother (or, on occasion, an investigator) in their arguments. Because of the exploratory nature of this analysis and the lack of independence between word and affect expression

TABLE II

Frequency of Beliefs and Desires Attributed to Children's Expressions[a]

	First Words			Vocabulary Spurt		
	Belief	Desire	*n*	Belief	Desire	*n*
Affect	.33	.67	1448	.32	.68	1688
Words	.43	.57	265	.36	.64	2251

N = 14
[a]*n* = Number of propositions attributed.

(given that propositions attributed to concurrences were counted twice), these data are treated here only descriptively.

At the time of first words, affect expressed the greater proportion (.84 overall) of each category of proposition, which reflected the preponderance of affective expressions over words. Two categories diverged from this overall relative frequency. One was the child's expression of BELIEF with the contents [be,do,go/child]—the belief category in which the proposition included an event that did

TABLE III

Distribution of Contents of Beliefs and Desires Attributed to Children's Expressions[a]

	Belief			Desire		
	be, do, go/ mother	do/ mother say	be, do, go/ child	be, do, go/ mother	be, do, go/ child	Total
First Words						
	n = 386	*n* = 155	*n* = 50	*n* = 174	*n* = 948	1713
Affect	.90	.65	.57	.83	.87	.84
Words	.10	.35	.43	.17	.13	.16
Vocabulary Spurt						
	n = 459	*n* = 733	*n* = 152	*n* = 478	*n* = 2117	3939
Affect	.56	.32	.30	.39	.45	.43
Words	.44	.68	.70	.61	.55	.57

N = 14
[a]*n* = number of propositions attributed.
Note. The categories of content are abbreviated here; they should be read: predicate (either *be, do, go*) ''in relation to'' content (that includes mother or child). The category *mother say* represents the child acknowledging or otherwise taking into account what someone has just said; *n* = 0 under *desire*.

not involve another person. Examples included the following: A child accidentally dropped a block, and said ''uhoh;'' a child fell down, and whimpered; and a child looked up at the clock on the wall and said ''ticktock.'' Thus, contents in this category, which was the least frequent category, included fortuitous events with the child as actor, and objects that the child noticed and attended to (underlying commenting and naming utterances). The second was the category [BELIEF[do/mother say]], the proposition attributed when the child acknowledged or otherwise took into account the mother saying something (as happened with an imitation or contingent responding).

At the vocabulary spurt, however, words expressed the greater proportion of each category of propositions except one, reflecting the increase in the number of words compared with number of affect shifts. The exception was the category]BELIEF[be,do,go/mother]], in which the proposition was a belief that included an event that did include another person (the mother most often). For example, a mother smiled at her child and the child smiled back or the child watched the mother rolling the truck down the slide and said ''down.'' Desires, in contrast, were expressed relatively more often with words than with affect, whether the desired event in the proposition included the child or the mother as actor.

V. Discussion

The data presented here are surely insufficient to validate the theory we propose, and represent only one of several analyses currently in progress. However, this study does elucidate the methodology we have devised and can validate certain aspects of the theory. The two questions that motivated our research concerned how (1) developments in cognition contribute to developments in language, and (2) the two systems of expression, affect, and language, relate to one another, and both relate to cognition more generally.

Affect displays and language both permit an observer to make an attribution of the state of mind of the expressor. In the present study, we used the contents of the attributions of these states of mind as a heuristic for comparing the meanings that the children expressed with affect and with words.

The same propositional contents could be attributed to both affect displays and words; both had to do with similar kinds of events. We suggest that this result was due to certain developments in the children's cognition which determined contents of states of mind in general. In the model that we have constructed, the cognitive developments that are required for the child to have such states of mind occur in the contents of memory, and in the ability to recall elements of knowledge in memory in relation to the data of perception (Bloom & Beckwith, 1986). These developments in cognition make possible the mental contents underlying both affect and words.

However, the model also predicts that the two forms of expression develop to express qualitatively different contents. While the same categories of contents were attributable to both affect and words, we interpret differences between them in their relative frequencies as qualitative differences. While words came to assume most of the responsibility for expressing the contents of intentional states at the vocabulary spurt, the children continued to express their beliefs about other persons and their actions toward the child primarily through expressions of affect.

Two other findings in Table III deserve mention. One is that more than half the propositions attributed to the child were in the category [DESIRE[be,do,go/child]], at both times. The children's expressions—affect shifts primarily at Time 1 and words primarily at Time 2—most often concerned desires for themselves to be, to do, or to go. Thus, the children in this study did not acquire words as tools for manipulating actions by other persons; overwhelmingly they expressed their own desires to act in achieving purposes and goals.

In addition, the second least frequent category at Time 1 became the second most frequent category at Time 2: [BELIEF[do/mother say]], attributed when the child acknowledged or otherwise took into account the adult saying something. For example, a mother said "You're a funny bunny" and the child smiled; or the mother said "Let's put the baby on the slide" and the child said "slide;" or the mother said "We have to go home now" and the child said "no." The shift in the relative frequency of this category indicated that the children acquired words in this period for interpreting and responding to the speech of others as well as for expressing their own contents of mind.

A major result of this study was that the frequency of affect displays, and propositions attributed to them, did not increase appreciably over time, while the frequency of words and propositions attributed to words increased substantially. We interpret this stability in affect expression as an indication that the children were already able to express how they felt about the contents of mental states—through their facial expression, body posture, and affective vocalizations—before words appeared. Words, in contrast, were acquired in order to express what those contents were. Thus, words did not replace affect, but emerged as a new system for expressing aspects of the contents of mental states—with names of persons. objects, and actions primarily—while affect continued to express the children's feelings about those contents.

We conclude that affect and language coexist as complementary systems of expression. The forms of the two systems are fundamentally different (e.g., Sapir, 1921). and their developmental histories differ as well. Some forms of affect are available from birth, and in early infancy an affect display is virtually a symptom of the emotion it is an expression of. The units of language, in contrast, have to be learned and they are arbitrary. Affective expression was already in place and was the far more frequent form of expression at the time that first words appeared. The number of affect shifts and number of propositions attributed to these affect shifts increased only slightly, while words and the propositions attributed to them increased eightfold. Thus, while affective expression was developmentally prior to language, it was surpassed by the expressive power of words by the time of the vocabulary spurt.

We conclude that cognition, affect, and language are related to one another by virtue of the relevance of developments in each to the contents of awareness in the developing mind of the child. The child's cognition encompasses all the elements of memory. The ability to access elements of memory in relation to the data of perception determines the contents of mental states. These contents, in turn, underlie the child's expressions through affective displays and language. The instrumental function of language, like many of its functions, happens in the interaction between persons. Words are the tools of such interaction only in light of the influence they have on the actions of other persons. But the origins of these end states are in the minds of the participants.

Introducing Intentionality in a theory of language development emphasizes the mind of the child and its development. In this view, the control of language development is in the mind and action of the child, rather than in the events of the external context, or the support that the child receives in familiar interactions with adults. The theory that we are proposing places the emphasis on how the development of the child's cognitive capacities influences the contents of mental states, which, in turn, determine what the child expresses and interprets of what others express. Events in the context and interactions with others are vital to this development, but it is the *child's* understanding of these external events that is the critical explanatory factor.

Acknowledgments

The research reported here was made possible by a grant from the Spencer Foundation, for which we are grateful. We thank Margaret Honey, Tresmaine Roubaine, and Joy Vaughn, who helped to collect the data; Virginia Brennan, Pia Wikstrom, Suzanne Gottlieb, Geraldine MacDonald, Mariette Newton–Danilo, Lisa Spiegel, and Joy Vaughn for their help with transcription and coding; and Karin Lifter and Matthew Rispoli for their considerable assistance in all phases of data collection and processing. Our warmest appreciation goes to the children and their mothers for their devoted participation and enthusiasm for the project; they were a delight.

References

Adamson, L., & Bakeman, R. (1982). Affectivity and reference: Concepts, methods, and techniques in the study of communication development of 6- to 18-month old infants. In T. Field & A. Fogel (Eds.), *Emotion and early interaction* (pp. 213–236). Hillsdale, NJ: Lawrence Erlbaum Associates.

Austin, J. (1962). *How to do things with words.* New York: Oxford University Press.

Bates, E. (1976). *Language in context.* New York: Academic Press.

Bates, E., Benigni, L., Bretherton, I., Camaioni, L., & Volterra, V. (1979). *The emergence of symbols: Communication and cognition in infancy.* New York: Academic Press.

Bloom, L. (1970). *Language development and language disorders.* Cambridge, MA: MIT Press.

Bloom, L. (1973). *One word at a time: The use of single word utterances before syntax.* The Hague: Mouton.

Bloom, L., & Beckwith, R. (1986). *Intentionality and language development.* Unpublished manuscript.

Bloom, L., Capatides, J., & Beckwith, R. (in preparation). *Developments in expression: Saying words and conveying affect.*

Bloom, L., Capatides, J., & Tackeff, J. (1981). Further remarks on interpretive analysis: In response to Christine Howe. *Journal of Child Language, 8,* 403–411.

Bloom, L., Lahey, M., Hood, L., Lifter, K., & Fiess, K. (1980). Complex sentences: Acquisition of syntactic connectives and the meaning relations they encode. *Journal of Child Language, 7,* 235–261.

Bloom, L., Lifter, K., & Broughton, J. (1985). The convergence of early cognition and language in the second year of life: Problems in conceptualization and measurement. In M. Barrett (Ed.), *Single word speech* (pp. 149–180). London: John Wiley.

Braine, M. (1976). Children's first word combinations. *Monographs of the Society for Research in Child Development, 41,* (Serial No. 164).

Brandtstädter, J. (1984). Action development and development through action. *Human Development, 27.* 115–118.

Brentano, F. (1966). *The true and the evident.* O. Kraus (Ed.), London: Routledge & Kegan Paul.

Bruner, J. (1975). The ontogenesis of speech acts. *Journal of Child Language, 2,* 1–19.

Bruner, J. (1981). Intention in the structure of action and interaction. In L. Lipsett (Ed.), *Advances in infancy research* (Vol. 1, pp. 41–56). Norwood, NJ: Ablex.

Bullowa, M. (1979). *Before speech: The beginning of interpersonal communication.* Cambridge, England: Cambridge University Press.

Burke, K. (1935). *Permanence and change: An anatomy of purpose.* Berkeley, CA: University of California Press.

Campos, J., Barrett, K., Lamb, M., Goldsmith, H., & Stenberg. C. (1983). Socioemotional development. In P. Mussen (Ed.), *Handbook of child psychology* (Vol. 2, pp. 783–915). New York: John Wiley.

Case, R. (1974). Structures and strictures: Some functional limitations on the course of cognitive growth. *Cognitive Psychology, 6,* 544–574.

Clark, E. (1983). Meanings and concepts. In J. Flavell & E. Markman (Eds.), *Cognitive development.* In P. Mussen (Ed.), *Handbook of child psychology* (Vol. 3, pp. 787–840). New York: John Wiley.

Danto, A. (1973). *Analytical philosophy of action.* Cambridge. England: Cambridge University Press.

Davidson, D. (1984). *Inquiries into truth and interpretation.* Oxford, England: Clarendon Press.

Dennett, D. (1978). *Brainstorms.* Montgomery, VT: Bradford Books.

Dore, J. (1975). Holophrases, speech acts, and language universals. *Journal of Child Language, 2,* 21–40.

Ekman, P., & Friesen, W. (1975). *Unmasking the face: A guide to recognizing emotions from facial cues.* Palo Alto, CA: Consulting Psychologists Press.

Ekman, P., & Friesen, W. (1978). *Facial action coding scheme.* Palo Alto, CA: Consulting Psychologists Press.

Ervin–Tripp, S. (1973). *Language acquisition and communicative choice: Essays by Susan M. Ervin–Tripp.* Stanford, CA: Stanford University Press.

Golinkoff, R. (1981). The case for semantic relations: Evidence from the nonverbal and verbal domains. *Journal of Child Language, 8,* 413–437.

Gopnik, A., & Meltzoff, A. (1985). Words, plans, things and locations: Interactions between semantic and cognitive development in the one-word stage. In S. Kuczaj & M. Barrett (Eds.), *The development of word meaning* (pp. 199–223). New York: Springer–Verlag.

Greenfield, P. (1980). Toward an operational and logical analysis of intentionality: The use of discourse in early child language. In D. Olson (Ed.), *The social foundations of language and thought* (pp. 254–279). New York: W. W. Norton.

Hafitz, J., & Bloom, L. (1985). *After the first word: Intentionality and language.* Paper presented to the biennial meeting of the Society for Research in Child Development, Toronto, Canada.

Halliday, M. (1975). *Learning how to mean—Explorations in the development of language.* London, England: Edward Arnold.

Harding, C., & Golinkoff, R. (1979). The origins of intentional vocalizations in prelinguistic infants. *Child Development, 50,* 33–40.

Herbers, J. (1982). Poverty rate 14%, termed highest since '67. *The New York Times* (Vol. 131, July 20, pp. A1 and A18). New York: The New York Times Company.

Howe, C. (1976). The meanings of two-word utterances in the speech of young children. *Journal of Child Language, 3,* 29–47.

Klatzky, R. (1984). *Memory and awareness: An information-processing perspective.* New York: W. H. Freeman.

Lewis, M., & Michaelson, L. (1983). *Children's emotions and moods: Developmental theory and measurement.* New York: Plenum Press.

Lifter, K., & Bloom, L. (1985). *Mental representation in object play.* Paper presented to the biennial meeting, Society for Research in Child Development, Toronto, Canada.

Mandler, J. (1983). Representation. In P. Mussen (Ed.), *Handbook of child psychology* (Vol. 3, pp. 420–494). New York: John Wiley.

Maratsos, M., & Chalkley, M. (1980). The internal language of children's syntax: The ontogenesis and representation of syntactic categories. In K. Nelson (Ed.), *Children's language* (Vol. 2, pp. 127–214). New York: Gardner Press.

McShane, J. (1980). *Learning to talk.* Cambridge, England: Cambridge University Press.

Moscovitch, M. (Ed.). (1984). *Infant memory: Its relation to normal and pathological memory in humans and other animals.* New York: Plenum Press.

Nelson, K. (1974). Concept, word and sentence: Interrelations in acquisition and development. *Psychological Review, 81,* 267–285.

Nelson, K., & Lucariello, J. (1985). The development of meaning in first words. In M. Barrett (Ed.), *Single word speech* (pp. 59–86). London, England: John Wiley.

Pascual–Leone, J. (1970). A mathematical model for the transition rule in Piaget's developmental stages. *Acta Psychologica, 32,* 301–345.

Peters, A. (1983). *The units of language acquisition.* Cambridge, England: Cambridge University Press.

Piaget, J. (1954). *The construction of reality in the child.* New York: Basic Books.

Piaget, J. (1972/1973). *The child in reality: Problems of genetic psychology.* New York: Penguin.

Ryan, J. (1974). Early language development: Towards a communicational analysis. In M. Richards (Ed.), *The integration of the child into the social world* (pp. 185–213). London, England: Cambridge University Press.

Sapir, E. (1921). *Language.* New York: Harcourt, Brace.

Searle, J. (1983). *Intentionality: An essay in the philosophy of mind.* Cambridge, England: Cambridge University Press.

Sinclair, H. (1970). The transition from sensory-motor to symbolic activity. *Interchange, 3,* 119–126.

Slobin, D. (1982). Universal and particular in the acquisition of language. In E. Wanner & L. Gleitman (Eds.), *Language acquisition: The state of the art* (pp. 128–172). Cambridge, England: Cambridge University Press.

Sroufe, A. (1979). Socioemotional development. In J. Osofsky (Ed.), *The handbook of infant development* (pp. 462–516). New York: John Wiley.

Stein, N., & Jewett, J. (in press). A conceptual analysis of the meaning of basic negative emotions: Implications for a theory of development. In C. Izard & P. Read (Eds.), *Measurement of emotion in infants and children* (Vol. 2). New York: Cambridge University Press.

Stern, D. (1977). *The first relationship.* Cambridge, MA: Harvard University Press.

Stern, D., Barnett, R., & Spieker, S. (1983). Early transmission of affect: Some research issues. In J. Call, F. Galenson, & R. Tyson (Eds.), *Frontiers of infant psychiatry* (pp. 74–84). New York: Basic Books.

Yates, J. (1985). The content of awareness is a model of the world. *Psychological Review, 92,* 249–284.

Stability of Type A Behavior from Early Childhood to Young Adulthood

Laurence Steinberg
UNIVERSITY OF WISCONSIN–MADISON

Abstract

This chapter presents data on the homotypical and heterotypical stability, from early childhood to young adulthood, of overt Type A behaviors in a sample of individuals who had been interviewed during the course of the New York Longitudinal Study. The Type A behavior pattern, characterized by competitiveness, easily aroused hostility, and achievement-striving, has been established as a major risk factor for coronary heart disease. Data were derived from four sources of information: (1) measures of temperament derived from interviews conducted with the children's mothers when the youngsters were ages 3 and 4; (2) measures of Type A behaviors derived from interviews conducted with the youngsters' elementary schoolteachers during the first or second grades (7 years), (3) measures of Type A behaviors derived from interviews conducted with the participants during adolescence (16 years), and (4) measures of Type A behaviors derived from interviews with the participants during young adulthood (21 years).

Among the major findings discussed are that: (1) the Type A behavior pattern is actually composed of two distinct, but related, dimensions of personality—a prosocial dimension, best characterized as achievement-striving, and an antisocial dimension, best characterized as impatience–aggression; (2) the correlation between the prosocial and antisocial components of the Type A pattern shifts, as individuals age, from significantly positive (during elementary school), to unrelated (during adolescence), to significantly negative (during young adulthood); (3) Type A behaviors show an impressive degree of stability, among both males and females, over the period between adolescence and adulthood, but an equally impressive degree of instability between childhood and adolescence; (4) the Type A behavior pattern is likely to have dispositional underpinnings that are present even during individuals' earliest years, with certain aspects of temperament emerging repeatedly as related to the Type A behavior pattern; and (5) that although the underlying dispositional substrate may be present from early childhood onward, individual differences in the manifestation of this substrate *as*

Type A behavior become increasingly stable during the period from elementary school through young adulthood. Overall, the findings are consistent with the notion that the Type A pattern is the product of an *interaction* between an underlying behavioral style and a particular set of socialization experiences.

I. Introduction

Over the past two decades, the Type A behavior pattern has been convincingly established as a major risk factor for coronary heart disease. The Type A pattern, now richly described in the psychological, medical, and epidemiological literature, is characterized by extremes of aggressiveness, easily aroused hostility, a sense of time urgency, and competitive achievement-striving (Matthews, 1982). Now that the association between adult Type A behavior and coronary heart disease has been confirmed, researchers have begun more recently to turn their attention to the study of the development and etiology of the behavior pattern, with an eye toward understanding the underpinnings of the Type A construct and the treatment and prevention of coronary-proneness.

One line of research in this spirit has been the examination of Type A behaviors in children. Matthews and her colleagues for example, have demonstrated in a series of studies that it is possible to measure during childhood behavior that is analogous to adult Type A behavior—that is, competitive achievement-striving, impatience, and easily aroused anger—and that scores on a questionnaire measure of Type A behavior developed for use with children are meaningfully related to children's behavior in situations designed to elicit the Type A pattern. For example, children categorized as Type A are more likely than their Type B peers to behave impatiently and aggressively, work harder in the absence of a deadline, exert greater efforts to excel in achievement situations, choose to evaluate their performance in achievement situations against the performances of superior competitors, and exert stronger efforts to maintain control when threatened with the possibility of failure (Matthews, 1979; Matthews & Angulo, 1980; Matthews & Siegel, 1983; Matthews & Volkin, 1981).

Demonstrating that Type A children exist is one thing; demonstrating that these children grow up to be Type A adults is quite another. For, despite the burgeoning literature on the identification of children who exhibit overt Type A behaviors, these studies do not explicitly link Type A behavior prior to adolescence (when its consequences for coronary disease have not been established) with Type A behavior during adulthood (which has been shown to be predictive of coronary disease). Thus, we do not know whether the constellation of behaviors that has come to be labeled "Type A" when observed among adults necessarily has, as its early developmental precursor, an analogous behavior pattern.

While it is reasonable to propose that the behavioral manifestations of an underlying disposition (for instance, having a Type A "personality") are similar during different developmental periods, such is not always the case. Many characteristics in which the underlying psychological core is thought to be relatively stable over time show behavioral manifestations that vary greatly from one developmental era to another. For example, although we assume that a healthy sense of autonomy during the preschool years has at least some of its origins in infancy, the behavioral manifestations of this underlying characteristic could not be more dissimilar during the two developmental eras. To draw upon a distinction made by Kagan (1980), while some characteristics (e.g., aggression) are *homotypically* stable over time (that is, the observable manifestations of the characteristic are similar across different periods), other characteristics (e.g., dependency)—with underlying psychological cores that may be just as stable—are *heterotypically* stable (that is, the observable manifestations are dissimilar across different periods). Although most recent research on the development of the Type A behavior pattern has proceeded from the assumption that the pattern is homotypically stable, this assumption may not prove to be correct. For example, one recent report (Bergman & Magnusson, 1983) links young adult Type A behavior with aggression and overambition among adolescent boys (consistent with the notion that the pattern is homotypically stable), but not with these traits and, instead, with hyperactivity among adolescent girls (consistent with the view that the pattern may be heterotypically stable). It may be the case that, owing to achievement-related conflicts experienced by many adolescent girls, studies of Type A behaviors during adolescence may yield findings for females that are somewhat more difficult to interpret (cf. Steinberg, 1986).

Previous studies of Type A behaviors have suggested that the Type A pattern is actually composed of several more or less distinct components, although the specific components have varied somewhat from one study to another. Matthews and Angulo (1980) report, for example, that among elementary schoolchildren, Type A behavior ratings derived from the Matthews Youth Test of Health (MYTH) cluster into two orthogonal factors: competitive achievement-striving and impatience–aggression. The Jenkins Activity Scale (JAS), perhaps the most widely used paper-and-pencil measure of Type A behavior among adults, yields three factor-analytically derived subscales: speed-and-impatience, hard-driving competitiveness, and job involvement (Jenkins, Zyzanski, & Rosenman, 1971). Steinberg (1985, 1986), using data collected as a part of the New York Longitudinal Study, also found that Type A behaviors clustered into two distinct components similar to those observed by Matthews. Indeed, the accumulating evidence that Type A behavior is multidimensional prompted Matthews (1982), in a recent review, to propose that "future research should take care to assess *individual Type A behaviors*" (p.316, emphasis added).

Viewing Type A behavior as a multidimensional construct has several important implications for developmental research examining the developmental course of the behavior pattern. First, it is possible that the components of the Type A behavior pattern cluster differently at one point in the life span than at another; thus, in order to examine the continuity of the behavior pattern across developmental eras, it is necessary to examine the structure of the Type A behavior pattern at different ages and construct Type A profiles accordingly. Second, different dimensions of the behavior pattern themselves may show different degrees (and different patterns) of stability during various developmental eras. Thus, it is important to ask whether some dimensions of the Type A pattern are more stable than others. Third, it is possible that the different components of the Type A behavior pattern may be differentially predictable from early measures and, as well, that the different components of the Type A pattern may have quite different precursors.

Existing longitudinal studies of relevant personality dimensions (e.g., achievement-striving, competitiveness, anger arousal) provide indirect evidence that at least some aspects of the Type A behavior pattern should be expected to enjoy differential degrees of continuity between adolescence and adulthood, and that most aspects of the behavior pattern may be more stable among males than females (Block, 1971; Kagan & Moss, 1962). For example, the greater stability of Type A behaviors among males may be attributable to the more consistent and continuous socialization of both achievement and aggression that males are likely to receive across different developmental eras (cf. Kagan & Moss, 1962). Among girls, the aspect of Type A behavior shown to be most stable is reactivity (Bronson, 1967). Taken together, these studies suggest that it may be important to examine the developmental course of the Type A pattern separately for males and females.

Few studies exist that have examined the stability of Type A behavior directly. Matthews and Avis (1983) report that Type A behavior assessed via the MYTH is relatively stable over 1-year intervals during the elementary school years. While suggestive of continuity in the behavior pattern, their findings, unfortunately, do not establish the stability of Type A behaviors over a period of time during which changes in the form or expression of such behaviors might more reasonably be expected to occur. More important, it remains to be demonstrated that the behavior pattern is stable between two developmental eras in which individuals change environments (and, presumably, their exposure to stimuli likely to elicit the behavior pattern).

The present report has two foci: the stability, from childhood to adulthood, of overt Type A behaviors, and the role of early childhood temperament in the development of adult Type A behaviors. Analyses pertaining to the first of these two concerns provide evidence relevant to the question of homotypical stability. Specifically, this report examines the stability, over time, of the Type A behavior pattern measured and conceptualized similarly across different developmental eras. Analyses pertaining to the second concern—the role of early childhood temperament in the development of Type A behavior—provide evidence relevant to the question of heterotypical stability. That is, these analyses examine a variety of predictors which, while not identical to adult Type A behavior, reasonably may be presumed to be important precursors or contributors to the adult pattern.

II. Method

A. SUBJECTS

The subjects of this study were drawn from a sample of 133 individuals, now young adults, who comprise the core sample of the ongoing New York Longitudinal Study (NYLS). The NYLS was initiated in 1956 by Alexander Thomas and Stella Chess. Originally, the sample consisted of 138 individuals, but in the early years of the study, 5 subjects were dropped, or withdrew, from the study. Remarkably, there has been no further sample attrition since that time, some 25 years ago.

Detailed information on the sample and its recruitment has been reported elsewhere by the principal investigators of NYLS (Thomas & Chess, 1977; Thomas, Chess, & Birch, 1968; Thomas et al., 1963). The core NYLS sample is composed of 66 males and 67 females from 84 middle- or upper-middle-class, predominantly Jewish families residing in the New York metropolitan area. Although the sample is in no way representative of the general population, it represents an interesting group within which to examine the development of Type A behaviors, because of the likely emphasis that these highly educated, highly successful, urban families placed on achievement-striving during the course of their children's socialization.

The data presented in this report were derived from four sources of information: (1) measures of temperament derived from interviews conducted with the children's mothers when the youngsters were ages 3 and 4; (2) measures of Type A behaviors derived from interviews conducted with the youngsters' elementary schoolteachers during the first or second grades (mean age, 7 years, 2 months); (3) measures of Type A behaviors derived from interviews conducted with the participants during adolescence (mean age, 16 years, 9 months); and (4) measures of Type A behaviors derived from interviews with the participants during young adulthood (mean age, 21 years, 0 months). Virtually all subjects were enrolled in school (high school or college) at the time of the adolescent and young adult interviews.

Measures of temperament were available for 126 individuals (95%) (63 males, 63 females). Complete interview transcripts were available for 101 individuals during childhood (76%) (52 males, 49 females), for 96 individuals (72%) at adolescence (46 males, 50 females), and for 108 (81%) individuals at young adulthood (53 males, 55 females). For purposes of examining interrelations among measures, information on *both* temperament and childhood Type A behavior was available for 91 individuals (44 males, 47 females); on both temperament and adolescent Type A behavior, for 85 individuals (42 males, 43 females); and on both temperament and young adult Type A behavior, for 89 individuals (43 males, 46 females). Complete, codable transcripts for *both* childhood and adolescence were available for 84 individuals (44 males, 40 females); for both childhood and young adulthood, 77 individuals (40 males, 37 females); and for both the adolescence and young adult interview dates, 73 individuals (35 males, 38 females). Reductions in sample size from the original NYLS sample of 133 to the present samples of bewteen 91 and 73 are due chiefly to the loss of individuals who had completed only one of the two measures of interest, rather than to large-scale attrition over the course of the NYLS investigation.

B. MEASURES

Early Childhood Temperament. The original investigators of the NYLS assigned scores on nine dimensions of temperament to each youngster on the basis of annual interviews conducted with each child's mother during each of the child's first 5 years. In the present analysis, temperament scores for years 3 and 4 were averaged to yield early childhood scores. Temperament scores from years 1 and 2 were not used because previous studies (e.g., Kagan & Moss, 1962), and preliminary analyses of the present data, suggested that measures of temperament taken prior to 3 years of age are typically not strongly related to measures of personality during adulthood. It was decided not to use fifth-year temperament scores in order to ensure that the measure of temperament predated the youngsters' entry into elementary school. The nine dimensions of temperament included in the original assessment battery were: *activity level, rhythmicity, approach/withdrawal, adaptability, intensity of reaction, sensory threshold, quality of mood, persistence, and distractability.* Further information on the assessment and scoring of temperament may be found in Thomas and Chess (1977), and information concerning intercorrelations among the nine temperament dimensions can be found in Steinberg (1985).

Type A Behavior. The original directors of the NYLS were not interested in the development of Type A behaviors per se. But their interest in temperament and adjustment over the life cycle led them to include in their impressive battery of measures a series of interview schedules designed to elicit information on a range of topics relevant to the study at hand (e.g., achievement-striving, aggression, susceptibility to frustration). It was therefore possible to return to the original interview transcripts, review a sample of them with an eye toward determining which, if any, relevant information might be extracted, and then develop a coding scheme to fit the aims of the present study. Thus the reader should note that the Type A data discussed in this report were coded specifically for this study from interviews designed by other investigators and conducted for other research purposes. Childhood, adolescent, and young adult interview transcripts were all approximately 20 pages long.

Existing measures of Type A behavior available for use with children, adolescents and young adults (e.g., the Jenkins Activity Scale [Jenkins, Rosenman, & Friedman, 1967]; the Matthews Youth Test for Health [Matthews & Angulo, 1980]; the Hunter–Wolf A–B Rating Scale [Hunter et al., 1982]) were reviewed in order to guide the selection of variables. Although there continues to be debate over the relative importance of various traits as components of the Type A pattern (and, in particular, over whether achievement-striving is, or is not, a key component) it was decided to cast a wide net over the array of potentially relevant attributes.

All interviews were coded by a single rater, a member of a team of researchers who had been working with the NYLS archive for some time. Thus, the rater was a highly experienced judge who was quite familiar with the style and nature of the interviews and with the design and intent of the NYLS. Childhood, adolescent, and young adult interviews were coded independently; codings of each wave of transcripts were separated by at least a 3-month interval, and all identifying information was removed from interview transcripts in order to minimize contamination.

Childhood Measures. Because the childhood interviews were conducted with the participants' elementary schoolteachers, the data set presented an opportunity to operationalize childhood Type A behavior in a way as similar as possible to that used by Matthews and her colleagues in the development of the MYTH, the most widely used measure of Type A behavior during childhood. The MYTH includes 17 items for which teachers are asked to characterize their students' behavior on a five-point scale (from extremely uncharacteristic to extremely characteristic). The items may be found in Table I. After a preliminary review of the elementary schoolteacher interview transcripts, it was decided that it was indeed possible to code the transcripts for the 17 items contained in the MYTH, rating the teacher's description of each child's behavior on a five-point scale, from extremely characteristic to extremely uncharacteristic.

The reader should note that although the information coded from the teacher interviews is quite similar to that obtained via the MYTH, the data were gathered and presented in a different manner from that used by Matthews and her colleagues. In both instances, teachers, rather than parents or the individuals under investigation, provide the assessment of Type A behavior, on the assumption that many of the behaviors assumed to comprise the Type A pattern are displayed relatively frequently in school settings. But in the standard use of the MYTH, teachers provide their assessments by completing a structured questionnaire used to rate students on the 17 predetermined items. In the present study, in contrast, interviews covering a variety of topics and originally conducted for multiple purposes (of which the assessment of Type A behavior was *not* one of them) were recoded, using Matthews's 17-item scheme. In a subsequent section of this report, the comparability of information derived from the MYTH and from the present approach is discussed; at this juncture, suffice it to say that the clustering of items obtained through a factor analysis of the interview-derived data in the present study was virtually identical to that reported by Matthews in her studies using MYTH.

Adolescent and Young Adult Measures. Identical interview protocols and coding schemes were employed for the adolescent and young adult data. On the basis of existing measures of Type A behavior, as well as previous studies of Type A behavior, and after reviewing the adolescent and young adult interview transcripts, 14 variables were selected for inclusion in the coding scheme used to assess Type A behavior during these developmental eras: *Perseveres, Concentrates Intently, Self-Motivated, Strives to Achieve, Assumes Leadership Positions, Competitive, Serious About Schoolwork, Impatient, Hurries/Rushes, High Activity Level, Impulsive, Easily Annoyed, Easily Angered, and Easily Frustrated.* These variables resemble in spirit, but not necessarily language, those components of Type A behavior generally measured via standard assessment instruments.

For each variable, a global score was assigned on the basis of the information contained in the entire interview, using a five-point scale ranging from very characteristic (5) ("This trait is mentioned frequently and prominently . . . a characterization of this individual would not be complete without reference to this trait.") to very uncharacteristic (1) ("This trait is not at all a part of this person's character; if anything, its opposite is true."). Coders were instructed to use the scale midpoint (3) in cases in which a trait, or behaviors relevant to a trait, were discussed but where the trait seemed "neither characteristic nor uncharacteristic of this person." The "characteristic/uncharacteristic" continuum was chosen in order to maximize comparability between the coding scheme employed in the present study and the format of several existing measures of Type A behavior (cf. the MYTH, the JAS). In each of these measures, individuals are rated (either by themselves or by others) as to their usual or characteristic behavior. Recall that the MYTH asks teachers to judge how "characteristic" each of 17 items is of the student being evaluated; similarly, the JAS asks respondents to report how they "usually," "ordinarily," or "frequently" behave.

C. RELIABILITY

A second rater was employed in order to establish reliability; reliability was calculated on the basis of the two coders' ratings for 20 childhood interviews, randomly selected from the males' and females' interviews (10 male and 10 female), and on the basis of 10 (5 male and 5 female) randomly selected young adult interviews (the young adult and adolescent interview protocols and coding schemes were identical).

With regard to the childhood interviews, agreement among raters on whether codable information for a specific variable was present in the transcript averaged 87% across the 14 variables. Exact agreement on codings for codable variables (i.e., variables for which information was determined to be present) averaged 44%. Reliabilities determined by essential percentage of agreement (instances in which the two raters agreed within one point of each other [cf. Kagan & Moss, 1962]) averaged 92%. On only two of the 17 items was essential agreement below 75%: "This child likes to argue or debate" (essential agreement = 70%); and "It is important for this child to win, rather than to have fun in games or schoolwork" (essential agreement = 71%). Average rater reliability as determined by product–moment correlation was .74, with only two of the correlations falling below .62: "This child gets irritated easily" ($r = .43$); and "This child tends to get into fights" ($r = .56$).

With regard to the adolescent and young adult interviews, rater agreement on whether codable information for a specific variable was present in the transcript averaged 75% across the 14 variables. Exact rater agreement on codings for codable variables (i.e., variables for which information was determined to be present) averaged 66%. Reliabilities determined by essential percentage of agreement averaged 94%; raters agreed within one point of each other in 100% of the cases for 12 of the 14 variables, the two exceptions being "easily angered" (essential agreement = 71%) and "impulsive" (essential agreement = 50%). Average rater reliability as determined by product–moment correlation was .87. Only the reliability coefficient for the variable "impulsive" fell below .70. However, because this variable was used infrequently in subsequent analyses, its low level of rater agreement does not present a major problem.

III. Results and Discussion

A. STRUCTURE OF THE TYPE A BEHAVIOR PATTERN

The first step in the analysis was to examine the childhood, adolescent and young adult Type A data via factor analyses, separately for each developmental period. Because these results have been reported elsewhere (Steinberg, 1985;

1986), their presentation here will be brief. However, the reader should note that somewhat different procedures were followed for the treatment of the childhood data, on the one hand, and the adolescent and young adult data, on the other. In both cases, intercorrelation matrices of the relevant set of variables were subjected to factor analytical procedures using principal components analyses with orthogonal rotation of factors. In the case of the childhood data, the number of factors was limited to two and the data for males and females were treated together (in order to examine comparability between the present data and those reported by Matthews & Angulo, 1980). In the case of the adolescent and young adult data, no previous factor analyses could serve as bases of comparison and hence no limit was imposed on the number of rotated factors to be extracted (all factors with eigenvalues above 1.0 were rotated). The analyses were conducted separately for males and females within each period.

Childhood Data. Table I presents the loadings for the two factors obtained in the present analysis and for those reported by Matthews and Angulo (1980). The factor analyses of the data for elementary schoolchildren resulted in two factors

TABLE I

Factor Loadings of MYTH (Form O) Items and Interview-derived Elementary School Type A Items

	MYTH[a]		Interview	
Item	Factor I	Factor II	Factor I	Factor II
1. Competitive in games	.725	.304	.786	.308
2. Works quickly and energetically	.449	.095	.338	.043
3. Impatient when waiting	.250	.617	.147	.648
4. Does things in a hurry	.239	.354	.360	.052
5. Takes a lot to anger	−.073	−.546	−.174	−.760
6. Interrupts others	.116	.688	.312	.454
7. Leads in activities	.764	−.045	.412	.122
8. Easily irritated	.155	.790	.184	.831
9. Performs better when competing with others	.686	.094	.632	.206
10. Likes to argue/debate	.270	.763	.292	.624
11. Patient with slower children	−.005	−.594	−.023	−.632
12. Tries to better others	.794	.162	.819	.158
13. Can sit still long	.178	−.500	−.069	−.402
14. Important to win, rather than have fun	.544	.448	.672	.257
15. Others look to as leader	.813	−.187	.320	−.112
16. Competitive	.775	.336	.814	.310
17. Gets into fights	.169	.735	.037	.822

[a]Factor loadings for MYTH–Form O, reported in Matthews and Angulo (1980).

which closely resemble those reported by Matthews and her colleagues. One factor is best characterized as competitive achievement-striving and the other as impatience–aggression. Indeed, the similarity of factor loadings between those obtained in the present analysis and those reported in studies using the MYTH in its standard format is remarkable, given the differences in sample and procedures used to generate the two sets of data. The similarity lends credibility both to the coding scheme employed in the present analysis and to the two-factor (achievement-striving and impatience–aggression) conceptualization of Type A behavior in the literature on children.

For each child, scores on two subscales were calculated using unweighted item scores: Following Matthews, scores on items 1, 2, 7, 9, 12, 14, 15, and 16 were summed to yield a competitive achievement-striving subscale; scores on the remaining items were summed to yield an impatience–aggression subscale. Both subscales were combined to yield an overall Type A score. In cases in which data were missing for a specific item, the item mean for that gender was substituted in the calculation of the individual's subscale scores. (This substitution procedure was followed for the adolescent and young adult analyses as well.)

For purposes of comparison with findings reported by Matthews and Angulo (1980), the reliability coefficients (alpha) of the competitive achievement-striving, impatience–anger, and Type A scales used in the present study are .66, .74, and .76, respectively. Not unexpectedly, the alphas reported by Matthews are somewhat higher (.82, .79, and .82, respectively). Finally, in the present study, the correlation between the competitive achievement-striving and impatience–anger subscales is r (101) = .45 ($p < .001$). Matthews and Angulo report a comparable between-scale correlation of .41.

Adolescent Data. The factor analysis of the data for adolescent males resulted in two factors closely resembling those derived from the elementary school data. The first factor is best characterized as competitive achievement-striving; the second, as impatience–aggression. For each adolescent boy, scores on two subscales were calculated using unweighted item scores: *Competitive Achievement Striving* and *Impatience–Anger*. Overall *Type A* scores were computed by summing the subscale scores. The factor analysis of the data for adolescent females resulted in three factors with eigenvalues greater than 1.0 after rotation. The analysis revealed a competitive achievement-striving cluster among girls that is similar to that extracted from the boys' data. However, the makeup of the second and third factors suggests that impatience and anger are less interrelated among adolescent girls than among boys. For girls, therefore, three subscale scores were computed: *Competitive Achievement-Striving, Impatience,* and *Anger*. (In some subsequent analyses, the impatience and anger subscales were combined to yield an impatience–anger score for adolescent girls in order to examine sex differences on comparable dimensions.) Overall *Type A* scores were computed by summing the subscale scores.

Among adolescent boys, the competitive achievement-striving and impatience–anger dimensions are unrelated [$r(46) = .08, p > .05$]; among girls, competitive achievement-striving and anger are, similarly, not significantly correlated [$r(50) = -.18, p > .05$], but competitive achievement-striving and impatience are *negatively* correlated [$r(50) = -.24, p < .05$].

Young Adult Data. Among the young adult males, achievement-striving and competitive drivenness cluster on two different factors; the third factor, impatience–aggression, is similar to that extracted from the adolescent boys' data. These three clusters parallel those derived from studies of Type A behavior among adults employing the Jenkins Activity Scale (job involvement, hard-driving competitiveness, and speed-and-impatience; Jenkins et al., 1971). It is not entirely clear why the pattern of variables should change between adolescence and young adulthood; it may be the case that as individuals move into adulthood (and leave high school environments that often explicitly link achievement with competition), achievement per se begins to be more tied to internally produced performance standards and less to direct competition with others. The analysis yields two factors for young adult females: The first factor appears to be best characterized as achievement-striving while the second factor appears to be best labeled impatience–aggression. The reader should note that, as was the case for young adult males, competitiveness, which loaded on the achievement-striving factor in the analysis of the adolescent data, did not load highly on the achievement factor extracted in the analysis of the young adult female data.

Among males and females both, the achievement-striving and impatience–anger dimensions are significantly *negatively* correlated [for males, $r(53) = -.25, p < .05$; for females, $r(55) = -.31, p < .01$]. In order to ensure that differences in the correlation between the Type A components across developmental periods are not due to differences among the three samples (owing to differential rates of subject participation at different assessment points), these correlations were recalculated using only those subjects for whom all three Type A assessments were available (33 males and 28 females). The results remain essentially unchanged.

Taken together, the three sets of factor analyses lend strong support to the notion that the Type A behavior pattern is composed of two distinct dimensions of personality: a prosocial dimension, best characterized as achievement-striving, and an antisocial dimension, best characterized as impatience–aggression. This bidimensional structure is evident in studies of males as well as females, and is apparent during the early years of elementary school, during the middle years of adolescence, during early adulthood, and during middle adulthood. Furthermore, the two-factor structure is found in studies using different methods of data collection, in studies using standardized measures of the Type A construct as well as studies based on secondary analyses of data not initially collected for purposes of examining Type A behavior, and in studies that rely on the subjective self-reports of participants as well as studies that rely on the characterizations of individuals by others. Researchers would do well to heed Matthews's (1982) recommendation that we focus on *aspects* of the Type A pattern rather than consider the pattern as a unidimensional phenomenon. It also should be said that the fact that meaningful clusters of Type A behaviors comparable to patterns found in studies employing measures designed specifically for the assessment of this construct can be extracted from an existing data archive should encourage investigators to pursue the study of Type A behavior over the life span using other appropriate longitudinal data bases.

The preceding analyses indicate that individuals who are "strivers" are also likely to be competitive, self-motivated, persevering leaders; and individuals who are easily annoyed are also likely to be impatient, easily frustrated, and quick to anger. But—and this is a very important "but"—the two dimensions are not necessarily linked; that is to say, individuals who are strivers are not necessarily impatient and angry. This is especially the case during young adulthood, and represents a finding that has important etiological and developmental implications. With regard to the former, it indicates that some individuals are able to maintain high levels of achievement-striving (which may benefit themselves and society) without having to suffer the consequences of impatience, anger, and irritability (which probably benefit neither). Moreover, in light of some speculation that it is specifically the antisocial component of Type A behavior, and not the prosocial component, that is most strongly related to coronary disease, the finding that the two dimensions function somewhat independently suggests that individuals may be able to maintain hard-working, achievement-striving profiles without endangering their health.

It is also interesting to consider developmental changes in the relation between the two dimensions. In the present report, the correlation between the prosocial and antisocial components of the Type A pattern shifted, as subjects aged, from significantly positive (during elementary school), to unrelated (during adolescence), to significantly negative (during young adulthood). The pattern suggests that the behaviors which have come to be viewed as comprising the Type A pattern become increasingly more differentiated over the life span. Whereas for children, striving is often accompanied by an irritable sort of impatience, the two dimensions are separated over the course of late childhood and adolescence. Perhaps as individuals become socialized into "appropriate" achievement roles they learn, for example, that one can work energetically and strive to succeed without being impatient with others or frustrated by occasional impediments to one's progress. Indeed, it may well be the case that individuals learn, with age and experience, that the antisocial aspects of the Type A pattern (e.g., being easily annoyed) actually interfere with the prosocial aspects of the pattern (e.g., striving to succeed). Persons for whom achievement becomes or remains exceedingly important throughout adolescence may shed their impatient and angry ways as they move into an educational and occupational structure that rewards success but presents strong sanctions against the expression of negative affect.

That certain sets of traits appear to cluster together consistently over time—that is, that factor analyses performed on similar sets of data collected during different developmental eras yield similar patterns of loadings—has several important implications for studying the development of Type A behavior over the life span. The clear support for the bidimensional nature of the Type A pattern suggests that studies of the antecedents, consequences, and stability of Type A behavior over the life span begin with the assumption that the prosocial and antisocial components of the behavior pattern may well have different antecedents, different consequences, and different degrees of stability. It is to the last of these issues that I now turn.

B. STABILITY (AND INSTABILITY) OF TYPE A BEHAVIOR CLUSTERS

The stability across childhood, adolescence, and young adulthood, of the factor-analytically derived prosocial and antisocial Type A behavior clusters was examined separately for males and females by correlating subscale scores derived from the elementary school data with comparable scores derived from the adolescent and young adult data, and by correlating scores derived from the adolescent data with comparable subscale scores derived from the young adult data. These correlations are presented in Table II.

Overall, Type A behaviors show an impressive degree of stability over the period between adolescence and adulthood, but equally impressive *instability* between childhood and adolescence, among both males and females. Indeed, virtually all of the correlations between conceptually similar clusters (e.g., achievement-striving with achievement-striving) measured during adolescence and young adulthood reach statistical significance (the only exception is the correlation between adolescent impatience and young adult impatience–anger among females), whereas virtually none of the correlations between conceptually different clusters (e.g., achievement-striving with impatience–anger) attains significance.

On the other hand, *none* of the correlations between childhood and adolescent Type A behaviors reaches statistical significance, and, among males, some of the correlations between childhood and young adult Type A behaviors are actually negative. For example, the correlation between achievement-striving assessed in childhood and again in young adulthood is $r(40) = -.26$, $p<.05$, and the correlation between overall Type A scores in childhood and young adult achievement-striving is $r(40) = -.26$, $p<.05$. Interestingly, both overall Type A scores as well as competitive achievement-striving assessed during childhood are signif-

TABLE II

Pearson Correlations Among Childhood, Adolescent, and Young Adult Type A Behavior Clusters

		Males Childhood		
		Competitive Achievement Striving	Impatience Anger	Type A Total
Adolescence	Achievement Striving	.08	−.07	.00
	Impatience—Anger	−.01	−.17	−.12
	Type A Total	.06	−.15	−.07
		Childhood		
		Competitive Achievement Striving	Impatience Anger	Type A Total
Young Adulthood	Achievement Striving	−.26[a]	−.18	−.26[a]
	Competitive—Drivenness	−.10	−.01	−.06
	Impatience—Anger	.31[a]	.14	.26[a]
	Type A Total	−.06	−.04	−.06
		Adolescence		
		Competitive Achievement Striving	Impatience Anger	Type A Total
Young Adulthood	Achievement Striving	.75[d]	−.09	.60[d]
	Competitive—Drivenness	.31[a]	−.20	.16
	Impatience—Anger	−.17	.34[a]	.04
	Type A Total	.55[d]	.01	.48[c]
		Females Childhood		
		Competitive Achievement Striving	Impatience Anger	Type A Total
Adolescence	Achievement Striving	.08	−.01	.03
	Impatience	.11	.15	.14
	Anger—Irritation	.02	.04	.04
	Type A Total	.12	.08	.10

(*continued*)

TABLE II (*Cont.*)

		Childhood			
		Competitive Achievement Striving	Impatience—Anger	Type A Total	
Young Adulthood	Competitive Achievement Striving	.17	.22	.22	
	Impatience—Anger	−.05	−.09	−.08	
	Type A Total	.08	.09	.10	
		Adolescence			
		Competitive Achievement Striving	Impatience	Anger Irritation	Type A Total
Young Adulthood	Competitive Achievement Striving	.41[b]	.16	.25	.26
	Impatience—Anger	.08	−.07	.35[a]	.25
	Type A Total	.32[a]	.04	.12	.37[a]

[a] $p<.05$, one-tailed
[b] $p<.01$, one-tailed
[c] $p<.005$, one-tailed
[d] $p<.001$, one-tailed

icantly positively correlated with young adult impatience–anger among males [$r(40) = .26$, $p<.05$. and $r(40) = .31$, $p<.05$, respectively]. Among females, in contrast, childhood indicators of Type A behavior and impatience–anger are predictive (albeit marginally so) of young adult achievement-striving [$r(37) = .22$, $p<.10$, and $r(37) = .22$, $p<.10$, respectively].

When we examine the correlations between the adolescent and young adult assessments, we find that, generally speaking, the striving clusters appear to be more stable than the impatience–anger clusters, especially among males. Stability coefficients for the impatience–anger clusters are of about the same magnitude for males and females, although it is worth pointing out that among females, the adolescent anger cluster is a significant predictor of young adult impatience–anger, while the adolescent impatience cluster is not. Overall Type A scores also show moderate stability, although somewhat higher among males [$r(35) = .48$, $p<.005$] than females [$r(38) = .37$, $p<.05$]. For purposes of comparison, the reader should bear in mind that Matthews and Avis (1983) report *one-year* stability coefficients of approximately .57 and .53 for the MYTH scores of elementary schoolboys and -girls, respectively. Limiting these analyses to only those subjects for whom all three Type A assessments are available does not alter the results.

C. STABILITY (AND INSTABILITY) OF TYPE A CLASSIFICATIONS

Many previous studies of Type A behavior have categorized individuals as Type A or Type B according to their relative standing on the measure of Type A behavior employed. Although it may make more intuitive sense to conceive of Type A behavior as a continuous, rather than dichotomous variable (at least it does to this author), the historical precedent for distinguishing between "Type A" and "Type B" individuals is sufficiently strong to warrant examining the stability issue from this vantage point as well. To this end, individuals were classified into Type A and Type B groups at adolescence and at young adulthood on the basis of median-splits within the male and female subsamples for each age. Contingency analyses indicated that among males, Type A classifications remained highly stable over the period from adolescence to young adulthood [$\chi^z(1)$ 8.06, $p < .005$]; nearly three-quarters of males scoring above the median at adolescence scored above the median as young adults. This is true not only for overall Type A scores, but for achievement-striving as well (the median-split analysis yields $\chi^z(1) = 7.90$, $p < .005$; this was not the case for impatience–anger, however (i.e., males scoring above the median on this dimension as adolescents did not necessarily score above the median as young adults).

Among females, Type A classifications were *not* stable between adolescence and adulthood [$\chi^z(1) = .422$, n.s.], although, interestingly, median-split classifications with regard to achievement-striving and impatience–anger were [$\chi^z(1) = 6.73$, $p < .01$; and $\chi^z(1) = 5.09$, $p < .05$, respectively]. This finding further supports the view that the antisocial and prosocial dimensions of the Type A pattern function quite independently of each other. Combining the two dimensions and examining only overall Type A scores would not reveal what happens to be an interesting developmental pattern: Even though women who are highly achievement-striving or highly impatient and angry as adolescents are likely to be so as young adults; remaining high on one dimension is not associated with remaining high on the other.

In view of the correlational findings reported earlier, it is not surprising to find that Type A classifications made on the basis of the elementary school data are not at all predictive of classifications made during adolescence or young adulthood. Neither of the median-split analyses of overall Type A scores (i.e., childhood to adolescence or childhood to young adulthood) suggested stability of classifications. This is also the case for analyses examining individuals scoring above or below the median on achievement-striving and impatience–anger.

These analyses were repeated after trichotomizing the samples and including only the highest and lowest tertiles; again, however, no significant trends emerged.

As indicated earlier, assessments of Type A behavior made during adolescence, in contrast to those made during childhood, are predictive of Type A behavior during young adulthood. However, the findings indicate that the achievement-striving component of the pattern may be more stable than the impatience–anger component. Whether this differential stability is peculiar to the specific developmental eras studied, or whether it is also characteristic of other life-span periods, awaits further investigation. It may prove to be the case that the greater stability of the achievement component is attributable to its more consistent socialization over the course of development. Alternatively, it may be the case that stability in achievement-striving may be attributable to stability in individuals' roles over this period of time (i.e., remaining students) and the resultant similarity in the demands that they probably faced.

The observed sex differences are consistent with previous longitudinal studies of personality (Block, 1971; Bronson, 1967; Kagan & Moss, 1962) and with the general proposition that differential stability between the genders is likely to be found in traits and behaviors for which there are sex differences in the clarity and consistency with which socialization standards are enforced. Because women are likely to feel more conflict than men over the expression of competition, anger, and striving, women's display of Type A behavior may be less consistent over time. This may prove especially true in studies involving adolescence, a time during which many young women may receive mixed messages concerning their display of achievement-related behaviors (cf. Bardwick & Douvan, 1971; Rosen & Aneshensel, 1976). It may be the case that, after adolescence, women's Type A behaviors remain just as stable as do men's.

In the present study, Type A classifications made during the early elementary school years were of no value in predicting Type A classifications in adolescence or young adulthood—a finding that may have important implications for researchers who believe that assessing youngsters' Type A behavior during elementary school has predictive significance. It suggests that although the apparent structure of Type A behavior observed among elementary schoolchildren resembles the structure of Type A behavior observed among adults—a conclusion derived from previous research and clearly supported by the present study—this does not guarantee that individual differences in the behavior pattern remain stable over the same developmental period. Yes, there are Type A children—that is, children who, like Type A adults, are competitive, achievement-striving, impatient, and angry—and yes, these children can be reliably identified. But, no, these children do not necessarily grow up to be Type A adults.

The absence of stability found in the present study does not mean that investigators should abandon the goal of identifying, before adulthood, individuals likely to develop the adult Type A pattern. The present findings suggest only that this goal may not be best realized through research that assumes *homotypical* stability in the Type A pattern, that is, through research that attempts to identify potential Type A adults by searching for children who exhibit Type A behaviors. An alternative approach to examining the developmental antecedents of adult Type A behavior is to study the developmental histories of individuals who exhibit Type A behaviors as adults. Rather than limiting such analyses to the relation between adult Type A behaviors and their homotypical antecedents, one may instead examine developmental precursors assumed to be conceptually linked (if not identical to) the adult behaviors of interest.

Early childhood temperament was selected as the heterotypical antecedent of interest in the present study of Type A behavior, for two reasons. First, early childhood temperament has been shown to be a predictor and moderator of psychological functioning in both home (Thomas, Chess, & Birch, 1968) and school (Gordon & Thomas, 1977), the latter being an important setting for the display of Type A behaviors during childhood and adolescence. These and other previous longitudinal studies have shown that measures of personality and behavioral style taken during the early childhood years are often related to psychological functioning during young adulthood (e.g., Kagan & Moss, 1962). Although the studies did not examine the role of temperament in the display of Type A behavior, they nevertheless indicate than an individual's behavioral style early in life may have an enduring effect on his or her personality and social behavior over the life span.

Second, and more important, several theorists have hypothesized that an underlying factor best characterized as *nonspecific hyperreactivity* may contribute to the development and expression of Type A behavior (cf. Matthews, 1982). Some have argued that this hyperreactivity is psychological in nature—that, for example, Type A individuals, owing to their socialization histories, have a propensity toward behavioral reactivity which may be especially sensitive to certain social and environmental stimuli, such as threats to personal control (e.g., Glass, 1977) or ambiguous standards for performance evaluation (e.g., Matthews & Siegel, 1983). Others have suggested that the hyperreactivity may reflect an underlying constitutional dimension related to excessive autonomic arousal (cf. Krantz & Manuck, 1984). In either case (and the two views are not incompatible with one another), hyperreactivity may be construed as an aspect of an individual's behavioral style, or temperament. That is, both temperament and hyperreactivity can be seen as reflections of *how* one does what one does, rather than *what* one does (cf. Thomas & Chess, 1977). To the extent that the adult Type A pattern may be a particular manifestation of a certain behavioral style (having more to do with how an adult does what he or she does than with what he or she does), it is interesting to ask whether there are meaningful stylistic precursors of the adult pattern. It is this question to which I now turn.

D. EARLY CHILDHOOD TEMPERAMENT AND ADULT TYPE A BEHAVIOR

Before turning to the results of analyses examining the relation between temperament and Type A behavior, a few words are in order regarding what one might reasonably expect to find in such an investigation. Given current thinking about the behavioral style underlying the Type A pattern, it is logical to hypothesize that *some* of the variance in adult Type A behavior might be attributable to early childhood temperament. However, it seems unlikely that there exists a one-to-one correspondence between behavioral hyperreactivity and Type A behavior, for several reasons.

First, Type A behavior is likely to be just one of many possible manifestations of the underlying behavioral style; that is, while most Type A individuals might be expected to be behaviorally hyperreactive, not all hyperreactive individuals would be expected to manifest their hyperreactivity in Type A behavior. The translation of an underlying behavioral style into an overt manifestation is subject to the influence of many mediating factors, which, when unmeasured, will muddy the waters of data analysis.

Second, it seems clear from previous research and theory on Type A behavior that some of the factors contributing to the development of the pattern are *not* in the domain of behavioral style, but may be related to such factors as achievement-training, self-esteem, and self-evaluation. Matthews and Siegel (1983), for example, report that Type A children have higher standards for the evaluation of their own performance than do Type B youngsters and hypothesize that "the development of Type A is most likely to be generated by parental and school pressures in young elementary-school-aged children" (p. 139). Bracke (1985) reports that parents of Type A young adolescents, in comparison with parents of Type B youngsters, expect more early achievement behaviors, are more punitive in response to their children's unsatisfactory performances, are more likely to compare their children's performances with those of other individuals, and exert greater control over their children's behavior in task situations.As the author notes, "Collectively, these parental behaviors could promote an achievement orientation characterized by high need for success, striving for performance superior to others accompanied by a pervasive and underlying anxiety and insecurity" (p. 7).

One hypothesis that I am currently investigating is that Type A behavior is neither the direct result of a certain set of socialization experiences nor the direct result of a certain behavioral style, but rather, the result of an interaction between the two. Specifically, the working hypothesis is that sorts of socialization pressures described by Matthews and Siegel and Bracke may produce Type A behavior only in those individuals who have the necessary behavioral style; and, conversely, that possessing the hyperreactive behavioral style may result in adult

Type A behavior only among individuals who are socialized in the particular fashion thought to produce the behavior pattern. In the present study, temperament, but not childhood socialization, is examined. For this reason, although it is hypothesized that there exists a *significant* relation between temperament and Type A behavior, it is not expected that the relation will be *substantial.*

The relation between early childhood temperament and young adult Type A behavior was examined through two sets of analyses, each conducted separately for males and females. First, each dimension of temperament was correlated with each of the Type A behavior clusters. Because several temperament dimensions were significantly intercorrelated, it was decided to examine these correlations both with and without controlling for each of the other temperament dimensions. Second, regression analyses were performed in order to examine the relations between the temperament dimensions, considered together, and each of the Type A clusters.

The zero-order correlations between each of the temperament dimensions and the Type A clusters are presented in Table III. The results of the partial correlational analyses are presented in Table IV.

As can be seen in Tables III and IV, the correlations between early childhood temperament and young adult Type A behavior are generally quite modest, although the reader should bear in mind that correlations of this magnitude are not atypical in longitudinal investigations of personality spanning considerable lengths of time. It is also worth noting that the zero-order and partial correlational analyses are consistent with one another. Although some specific correlations attain significance in one analysis and not the other, this is the exception, rather than the rule, and, more important, the overall pictures painted by each analysis are generally very similar. It does not appear that significant relationships between temperament dimensions and Type A behavior clusters have been suppressed through the computation of partial correlations. Although the number of significant correlations in Tables III and IV exceeds that expected to be found simply by chance, in the absence of clear hypotheses concerning specific dimensions of temperament and Type A behavior, the reader should view the results presented here as exploratory and preliminary. Most important, perhaps, is the consistency with which activity level, adaptability, approach/withdrawal, sensory threshold, and for females, quality of mood, emerge as important dimensions of temperament in the prediction of Type A behavior.

The results of the regression analyses are presented in Table V. In these analyses, scores on the young adult Type A behavior clusters were regressed on the complete set of temperament variables. Stepwise regression was employed, with variables entered one at a time until the F value for the overall regression equation fell below statistical significance. Because several of the temperament variables are significantly intercorrelated (and thus raise a problem of multicolinearity), the regression analyses were not performed in order to derive esti-

TABLE III

Correlations of Young Adult Type A Behaviors with Early Childhood Temperament Dimensions

Temperament Dimension	Achievement Striving	Competitive Drivenness	Impatience Anger	Total Type A
		Males		
Activity Level	−.39[c]	−.07	−.01	−.28[b]
Rhythmicity	−.02	.05	.00	.02
Adaptability	.28[b]	−.08	−.24[a]	−.00
Approach/Withdrawal	.07	.21[a]	−.01	.16
Sensory Threshold	.22[a]	.05	−.27[b]	−.01
Intensity	−.25[b]	.07	.20	.00
Quality of Mood	.00	.13	−.10	−.02
Distractibility	.09	−.01	−.17	−.04
Persistence	−.18	.06	−.05	−.10
		Females		
Activity Level	.27[b]	——	−.15	.09
Rhythmicity	−.08	——	−.04	−.10
Adaptability	.10	——	−.26[b]	−.15
Approach/Withdrawal	.26[b]	——	−.11	.11
Sensory Threshold	−.18	——	−.20	−.34[c]
Intensity	−.08	——	−.03	−.09
Quality of Mood	−.01	——	−.17	−.16
Distractibility	.02	——	.07	.08
Persistence	−.13	——	−.00	−.11

Note: Positive correlations indicate stronger relationship in the direction of the name of the temperament dimension (e.g., males scoring high in achievement-striving were more likely to have a lower activity level as youngsters).

[a]$p<.10$
[b]$p<.05$
[c]$p<.01$

mates of the unique contributions of each of the temperament dimensions to the prediction of the Type A behavior clusters. Rather, the purpose of the regression analysis was to determine the maximum predictive power of various dimensions of temperament taken together.

Among males, the combination of low activity level, high adaptability, low rhythmicity, negative mood, and high approach in early childhood yields a multiple correlation of .50 with achievement-striving in young adulthood [$F(5,38) = 2.50$, $p<.05$]. The regression of competitive-drivenness on the temperament variables does not reach statistical significance. Young adult impatience–anger is best predicted by a single early childhood temperament dimension: low sensory threshold [$F(1,42) = 3.40$, $p<.10$; $R = .27$]. (Although not statistically significant, the combination of low sensory threshold, high intensity, low persistence, low distractability, and low adaptability yields a multiple correlation of .38 with impatience–anger.) Finally, the regression of males' total Type A score on low activity level, high approach, and high intensity yields a multiple correlation of .39 [$F(3,40) = 2.37$, $p<.10$]. Thus, for males, about 15% of the variance in young adult Type A behavior can be explained by early childhood temperament.

TABLE IV

Partial Correlations of Young Adult Type A Behaviors with Early Childhood Temperament Dimensions

Temperament Dimension	Achievement Striving	Competitive Drivenness	Impatience Anger	Total Type A
		Males		
Activity Level	−.36[c]	−.18	−.12	−.35[c]
Rhythmicity	−.15	.08	.06	−.01
Adaptability	.24[a]	−.16	−.16	−.04
Approach/Withdrawal	.13	.22[a]	.11	.26[b]
Sensory Threshold	.07	.06	−.21[a]	−.03
Intensity	−.05	.14	.17	.14
Quality of Mood	−.19	.07	.03	−.05
Distractibility	−.03	−.01	−.14	.08
Persistence	.01	.06	−.18	−.06
		Females		
Activity Level	.25[b]	——	−.15	.06
Rhythmicity	−.13	——	.02	−.09
Adaptability	.26[b]	——	−.20	.01
Approach/Withdrawal	.36[c]	——	−.03	.28[b]
Sensory Threshold	−.27[b]	——	−.15	−.36[c]
Intensity	−.13	——	−.02	−.13
Quality of Mood	−.29[b]	——	−.08	−.31[b]
Distractibility	.13	——	.08	.18
Persistence	−.05	——	−.14	−.18

Note: Correlation of temperament dimension with Type A behavior controlling for all other temperament dimensions. Positive correlations indicate stronger relationship in the direction of the name of the temperament dimension (e.g., males scoring high in achievement-striving were more likely to have a lower activity level as youngsters).

[a]$p<.10$

[b]$p<.05$

[c]$p<.01$

TABLE V

Multiple Correlations Between Young Adult Type A Scores and Early Childhood Temperament Measures

Adult Variable	Temperament Composite	Multiple R
	Males	
Achievement-striving	Low Activity Level	.50[b]
	High Adaptability	
	Negative Quality of Mood	
	High Approach	
	Low Rhythmicity	
Competitive-drivenness	High Approach	.32
	Low Adaptability	
	Low Activity Level	
	High Intensity	
Impatience–anger	Low Sensory Threshold	.27[a]
	Low Sensory Threshold	.38
	High Intensity	
	Low Persistence	
	Low Distractibility	
	Low Adaptability	
Total Type A Score	Low Activity Level	.39[a]
	High Approach	
	High Intensity	
	Females	
Achievement-striving	High Activity Level	.51[a]
	High Approach	
	Low Sensory Threshold	
	High Adaptability	
	Negative Quality of Mood	
	Low Intensity	
	Low Rhythmicity	
Impatience–anger	Low Adaptability	.27[a]
	Low Adaptability	.37
	Low Activity Level	
	Low Sensory Threshold	
	Low Persistence	
Total Type A Scores	Low Sensory Threshold	.51[b]
	High Approach	
	Negative Quality of Mood	
	Low Persistence	
	Low Intensity	
	High Distractibility	

[a] $p < .10$
[b] $p < .05$

For females, a somewhat stronger relationship emerges between young adult Type A behavior and early childhood temperament. The regression of achievement-striving on the combination of high activity level, high approach, low sensory threshold, high adaptability, negative mood, low intensity, and low rhythmicity yields a multiple correlation of .51 [$F(7,39) = 1.98, p < .10$]. Impatience–anger among females is best predicted by one temperament dimension: low adaptability; the multiple correlation is .27 [$F(1,45) = 3.16, p < .10$]. (It is worth noting, however, for purposes of comparison with the findings for males, that the combination of low adaptability, low activity level, low sensory threshold, and low persistence yields a multiple correlation of .37.) The multiple correlation between total Type A scores and the combination of low sensory threshold, high approach, negative mood, low persistence, low intensity, and high distractibility is .51 [$F(6,40) = 2.34, p < .05$]. For females, then, nearly 25% of the variance in young adult Type A behavior is explained by measures of temperament taken during early childhood.

Comparable regression analyses were conducted with childhood and adolescent Type A scores as the dependent variables of interest. Among boys, childhood achievement-striving is unrelated to early childhood temperament. However, the combination of negative mood. high approach, and low sensory threshold yields a multiple correlation of .44 in the prediction of childhood impatience–anger [$F(3,44) = 3.52, p < .05$]. This same combination, along with *high* activity level, is also predictive of overall Type A behavior among elementary schoolboys [$R = .43, F(4,43) = 2.44, p < .10$]. Among elementary schoolgirls, childhood achievement-striving is predicted by a combination of high activity level and high adaptability [$R = .32; F(2,42) = 2.43, p < .10$]. Neither childhood impatience–anger nor overall Type A score is predicted by early childhood temperament. As is the case during young adulthood, therefore, negative mood, high approach, and low sensory threshold emerge as possible contributors to the impatience–anger component of the Type A pattern, particularly among males, while it appears that high activity level and high adaptability may contribute to the development of the achievement-striving component of Type A behavior, particularly among females.

Among adolescent boys, the combination of *low* activity level, *high* sensory threshold, *low* approach, negative mood, and high adaptability yields a multiple correlation of .46 [$F(5,37) = 2.01, p < .10$]. (Recall that low activity level, negative mood, and high adaptability were significant predictors of males' young adult achievement-striving as well.) Adolescent boys' impatience–anger is not significantly predicted by early childhood temperament. The combination of low activity level, high sensory threshold, and low approach is predictive of adolescent boys' overall Type A scores [$R = .42, F(3,39) = 2.75, p < .10$].

Adolescent girls' achievement-striving is significantly predicted by the combination of high rhythmicity, high adaptability, low distractability, high activity level, low approach, and negative mood [$R = .56$, $F(6,37) = 2.85$, $p<.05$]. (Recall that negative mood and high adaptability were also predictive of females' achievement-striving during young adulthood.) Adolescent girls' impatience–anger is best predicted by the combination of low rhythmicity, low approach, high activity level, and, as was the case among young adult women, low adaptability [$R = .45$, $F(4,39) = 2.42$, $p<.10$]. Early childhood temperament is not predictive of adolescent girls' overall Type A scores.

All in all, the strength of the relationship between Type A behaviors displayed in childhood, adolescence, and young adulthood and measures of temperament taken many years earlier indicates that the Type A behavior pattern is likely to have dispositional underpinnings that are present even during individuals' earliest years. It is not clear, of course, to what extent measures of temperament assessed in early childhood reflect constitutionally endowed predispositions, socialized aspects of personality, or, more likely, the combination of both. Indeed, studies have not indicated that Type A behavior has a substantial genetic component (Matthews, 1982). Thus, while the findings presented here certainly do not indicate that Type A behavior is simply an adult manifestation of an immutable behavioral style that is either inborn or fixed early in life, the results nevertheless suggest that certain temperamental attributes, identifiable early in childhood, may predispose individuals toward the development of the Type A pattern. This lends support to the notion that at least part of the Type A pattern may have its roots in the domain of behavioral style.

It appears for the most part that early childhood temperament becomes increasingly predictive of Type A behavior as individuals get older—an interesting finding, since one would typically expect to find that the relation between two variables would weaken as their measurement was separated by increasing amounts of time. One interpretation of this pattern of findings, consistent with the data presented earlier on the stability of the behavior pattern, is that the Type A behavior pattern becomes increasingly stable over time. That is, although the underlying dispositional substrate may be present from early childhood onward, individual differences in the manifestation of this substrate *as Type A behavior* become increasingly stable during the period from elementary school through young adulthood.

This suggestion is consistent with the notion that the Type A pattern is the product of an *interaction* between an underlying behavioral style and a set of socialization experiences. The contribution of the underlying behavioral style to the Type A pattern remains present over the life span. But with time, individuals who may share the same behavioral style select different environments, encounter different sets of experiences, and are subjected to different sorts of socialization pressures—all of which may have implications for the development and expression of Type A behavior. The pattern may become more stable because individuals who perceive themselves and are perceived by others as Type A may select, and be directed toward, experiences which reinforce and strengthen the behavior pattern. Metaphorically speaking, the inner core of the Type A snowball may consist of the underlying behavioral style; whether the snowball moves along a path likely to add to its girth depends on certain key (but not yet fully understood) socialization experiences in the family and in school; and the wider the snowball becomes, and the greater its velocity, the more likely it is to continue along the same path.

Early childhood temperament accounts for approximately 25% of the variance in young adults' achievement-striving, approximately 13% of the variance in young adults' impatience–anger, and between 15% and 25% of the variance in young adults' overall Type A behavior scores. For purposes of comparison, it is worth noting that the multiple correlations reported here between temperament at ages 3 and 4 and Type A behavior during the early 20s equal or exceed the correlations, presented earlier, between Type A behavior assessed in childhood or adolescence and again in adulthood, or between other behaviors similar to Type A behaviors (e.g., aggression, overambition) assessed in early adolescence and Type A behaviors assessed in adulthood (Bergman & Magnusson, 1983). Indeed, the magnitude of the multiple correlations reported here between temperament and Type A behavior over a 20-year span (.39 for boys and .51 for girls) actually are not remarkably lower than the *one-year* stability coefficients for Type A scores reported by Matthews and Avis in their study of elementary schoolchildren (1983). These findings further support the notion, advanced earlier, that researchers interested in the development of Type A behavior may profit from examining antecedents of the behavior pattern that are not necessarily analogous to adult Type A behavior.

Several specific dimensions of temperament stand out as being especially predictive of Type A behaviors. For young adult males and females, achievement-striving is associated with high adaptability, negative mood, high approach, and low rhythmicity during early childhood; perhaps these attributes underly the successful, yet somewhat antisocial, striving and drivenness characteristic of the achievement behavior associated with the Type A pattern. Impatience–anger, in both genders, has as its antecedents low sensory threshold, low persistence, and low adaptability—a combination that, intuitively, seems a reasonable foundation out of which the easily "triggered" aspect of Type A behavior may develop; indeed, it is easy to imagine youngsters who have a low threshold for stimulation, have difficulty being persistent, and adapt poorly to new situations as impatient, irritable, and easily angered adults.

Although the early childhood predictors of later Type A behaviors do vary somewhat across the three developmental eras, certain aspects of temperament emerge repeatedly as related to the Type A behavior pattern; these dimensions may comprise the critical underlying behavioral style. Among males, these dimensions of temperament are low activity level, negative mood, high adaptability, low sensory threshold, and high approach. Among females. the dimensions of temperament are high activity level, high adaptability for achievement-striving but, low adaptability for impatience–anger, and negative mood. These particular combinations can be seen as representing logical heterotypical antecedents to the Type A pattern.

Bearing in mind the findings concerning temperament and Type A behavior, it is worth returning to the stability issue for a moment. The argument advanced earlier is that the Type A pattern begins to stabilize during early adolescence and is *not* stable between childhood and adulthood. It is important to ask whether the lack of stability between childhood and adolescence, and between childhood and adulthood, found in the present investigation is a spurious finding, owing, perhaps, to the use of a nonstandard procedure for the assessment of Type A behavior, or, to differences in the sources of data used in generating childhood and adolescent or young adult assessments. The reader will recall that, unlike the procedures followed by Matthews and other researchers employing the MYTH, Type A assessments in the present study were derived from a secondary analysis of teacher interviews conducted by other researchers for other purposes, while the adolescent and young adult assessments were derived from interviews with the subjects themselves.

Several lines of evidence in the present report suggest that the instability should not be summarily dismissed as a methodological artifact, however. With regard to the fact that childhood assessments were derived using a nonstandard procedure, the reader should recall three points. First, the comparability of factor loadings obtained in this study and those reported for the MYTH provides support for the construct validity of the coding scheme used in the present investigation. Along similar lines, the correlation between factors reported in this study is also very similar to that obtained with the MYTH. Finally, the alpha coefficients and measures of reliability among raters reported in the present study, while not overwhelming, are at least comparable to those reported by investigators using the MYTH (Jackson & Levine, 1983; Matthews & Volkin, 1981).

The issue of "source variance" is more difficult to address. One might argue that the higher stability coefficients between the adolescent and adult assessments of Type A behavior than between the childhood and adolescent, or childhood and adult, assessments are due to the fact that the adolescent and adult assessments both derive from interviews with subjects while the childhood data derive from interviews with the subjects' teachers. Measures derived from similar sources would be expected to be more highly correlated than measures derived from different sources. In order to examine this possibility, an additional set of analyses was performed using *temperament* ratings derived by the original NYLS investigators from the elementary school interviews in an effort to predict young adult and adolescent Type A scores. If the low correlation between childhood and later Type A scores is indeed due to "source variance," we would expect to find the same problem of source variance operating here and hypothesize that temperament scores derived from the teacher interviews are *not* predictive of later Type A behavior.

This is not the case, however. Regression analyses indicate that measures of temperament taken during the early elementary school years generally are significantly predictive of young adult Type A behaviors. Among males, for example, elementary school temperament accounts for approximately 30% of the variance in young adult Type A scores, 11% of the variance in young adult achievement-striving, and close to 20% of the variance in young adult impatience–anger (the first and third regression equations are significant at $p<.05$). Among females, elementary school temperament accounts for about 20% of the variance in young adult Type A scores, 23% of the variance in young adult achievement-striving, and 15% of the variance in young adult impatience–anger (all three equations are significant at or beyond $p<.10$). As is the case in analyses employing early childhood temperament scores, the analyses using elementary school data once again point to low sensory threshold, low adaptability, negative mood, and high approach as important temperamental underpinnings of the Type A behavior pattern. More to the point, however, despite the fact that the temperament assessments were derived from interviews with persons other than the subjects themselves, they nevertheless are significantly related to assessments of Type A behavior derived from self-report measures several years later.

The lack of stability between childhood and later assessments of Type A behavior does not mean, of course, that Type A classifications made during childhood are without etiological value. It may be the case that the *health* outcomes of childhood Type A behavior are important independent of whether the behavior pattern itself persists over time. For instance, it has been shown that early adolescents classified as Type A individuals show greater systolic blood pressure variability and greater heart-rate variability than their Type B peers. Such variability may damage the inner layer of coronary arteries and increase the likelihood of the development of arteriosclerosis and coronary heart disease (Matthews & Siegel, 1982). It is not known, however, whether such hemodynamic variability is maintained over time in the absence of a maintained Type A style, or, more importantly, whether hemodynamic variability during childhood is, in and of itself, a cause of coronary heart disease during adulthood. Both issues await prospective longitudinal investigation. Until such questions are resolved, researchers should not abandon the assessment of Type A behavior during childhood but should proceed with the proper amount of caution.

IV. Summary and Concluding Comments

The main findings to emerge from the present set of analyses may be summarized as follows:

1. The Type A behavior pattern is composed of two distinct, but related, dimensions of personality: a prosocial dimension, best characterized as achievement-striving, and an antisocial dimension, best characterized as impatience–aggression. This bidimensional nature of the Type A pattern is evident among males as well as females, and is apparent during a wide range of developmental eras.

2. The correlation between the prosocial and antisocial components of the Type A pattern shifts, as individuals age, from significantly positive (during elementary school), to unrelated (during adolescence), to significantly negative (during young adulthood). What this pattern suggests is that the behaviors that have come to be viewed as comprising the Type A pattern become increasingly more differentiated over the life span. Whereas for children, achievement-striving is often accompanied by an irritable sort of impatience, the two dimensions are separated over the course of late childhood and adolescence.

3. Overall, Type A behaviors show an impressive degree of stability over the period between adolescence and adulthood, among both males and females. Indeed, virtually all of the correlations between conceptually similar clusters (e.g., achievement-striving with achievement-striving) measured during adolescence and young adulthood reach statistical significance, whereas virtually none of the correlations between conceptually different clusters (e.g., achievement-striving with impatience–anger) attains significance.

4. On the other hand, Type A behaviors show an equally impressive degree of *instability* between childhood and adolescence. None of the correlations between childhood and adolescent Type A behaviors reaches statistical significance, and, among males, some of the correlations between childhood and young adult Type A behaviors are actually negative.

5. The strength of the relationship between Type A behaviors displayed in childhood, adolescence, and young adulthood and measures of temperament taken many years earlier indicates that the Type A behavior pattern is likely to have dispositional underpinnings that are present even during individuals' earliest years. Certain aspects of temperament emerge repeatedly as related to the Type A behavior pattern. Among males, these dimensions of temperament are low activity level, negative mood, high adaptability, low sensory threshold, and high approach. Among females, the dimensions of temperament are high activity level, high adaptability for achievement-striving but low adaptability for impatience–anger, and negative mood.

6. Although the underlying dispositional substrate may be present from early childhood onward, individual differences in the manifestation of this substrate *as Type A behavior* become increasingly stable during the period from elementary school through young adulthood. This pattern is consistent with the notion that the Type A pattern is the product of an *interaction* between an underlying behavioral style and a set of socialization experiences.

Several words of caution regarding the generalizations one might draw from this investigation are in order. First, because the sample of individuals studied in this research comprise a very homogeneous and special group, it would be unwise to generalize the findings presented here to populations of individuals whose socioeconomic and regional backgrounds differ from those of the sample studied in this research.

Second, it is important to note that the data on temperament were provided by the youngsters' parents and therefore may indicate more about the parents' perceptions of their children's behavior than about the actual behaviors themselves. Thus, it may be the case that children whose parents *perceive* them to be "approachers," or to have a low sensory threshold, are socialized in ways that help foster Type A behavior.

Finally, it is not clear whether the results obtained in the present analysis would be replicated if comparable analyses were conducted using standardized measures of Type A behavior. Although this is an important concern that will need to be addressed in future studies of the behavior pattern, it is worth pointing out that even among researchers using so-called "standard" measures of Type A behavior there exist considerable differences of opinion as to which of the different measures should be considered "standard." Indeed, one recent report (Jackson & Levine, 1983) indicates that intercorrelations among existing measures are not at all high. More research directly examining sources of method variance in the assessment of Type A behavior is sorely needed.

It would be imprudent to suggest on the basis of the data presented in this report that all children with certain sets of temperamental attributes inevitably will grow up to be Type A adults. Rather, it is more likely the case that environmental forces encountered in the family and in school interact with certain temperamental dispositions to encourage the development of Type A behavior. Further research is needed in order to understand how early temperamental dispositions grow into adult behavioral manifestations. For the time being, however, it does appear safe to say at a minimum that some of the roots of the adult Type A behavior pattern are visible early in childhood, and that some of the pattern's antecedents appear to lie in domain of temperament.

It also would be erroneous on the basis of the data presented, of course, to draw the conclusion that the Type A pattern is best conceived as a more or less immutable trait or predisposition after adolescence. Stability over time in any characteristic may be reflective of both intraindividual stability on the dimension in question as well as environmental stability—and, in all likelihood, of the combined effects of both (cf. Scarr, 1981). It may well be the case that the continuity in Type A behaviors found among the achievement-oriented, middle-class New Yorkers who comprise the core sample of the New York Longitudinal Study is due in large measure to continuity in the contexts in which the behavior pattern may be elicited. Adolescents with predispositions toward hard-driving, competitive, achievement-striving may, as young adults, seek and find achievement "niches" compatible with, and encouraging of, their behavioral style; certainly there is no shortage of such niches in the New York metropolitan area. But whatever the mechanism through which Type A behavior may be maintained over time—through the persistence of a behavioral style, through continuity in socialization, or through a tendency for individuals to maintain patterns of niche-picking that reinforce already existing styles of behavior—the findings suggest that it may be possible to identify individuals early in their development who may end up driving themselves toward serious coronary disease as adults.

Acknowledgments

This research was carried out during the author's tenure as a William T. Grant Foundation faculty scholar under the foundation's program in the Mental Health of Children. I am exceedingly grateful to Athena Droogas for her painstaking coding of the interview transcripts, to Jacqueline Lerner and Richard Lerner for their assistance in obtaining access to the New York Longitudinal Study archive, and to four anonymous reviewers for their comments on an earlier draft of this chapter. Data from the New York Longitudinal Study were made available through a grant from the MacArthur Foundation to Jacqueline V. Lerner and Richard M. Lerner. Author's address: Child and Family Studies, 1430 Linden Drive, University of Wisconsin, Madison, WI 53706.

References

Bardwick, J., & Douvan, E. (1971). Ambivalence: The socialization of women. In V. Gernick & B. Moran (Eds.), *Women in sexist society: Studies in power and powerlessness* (pp. 225–241). New York: Basic Books.

Bergman, L., & Magnusson, D. (1983). Type A-related behavior in childhood and adult Type A behavior: A longitudinal study. Unpublished report (No. 612). Department of Psychology, University of Stockholm, Sweden.

Block, J. (1971). *Lives through time*. Berkeley, CA: Bancroft.

Bracke, P. (1985). Parental child-rearing practices and the development of Type A behavior in children. Unpublished Ph.D. dissertation, Department of Psychology, Stanford University, Stanford, CA.

Bronson, W. (1967). Adult derivatives of emotional expressiveness and reactivity-control: Developmental continuities from childhood to adulthood. *Child Development, 38,* 801–817.

Glass, D. (1977). Stress, behavior patterns, and coronary disease. *American Scientist, 65*(2), 177–187.

Gordon, E., & Thomas, A. (1977). Children's behavioral style and the teacher's appraisal of their intelligence. *Journal of School Psychology, 5,* 242–300.

Hunter, S., Wolf, T., Sklov, M., Webber, L., Watson, R., & Berenson, G. (1982). Type A behavior pattern and cardiovascular risk factor variables in children and adolescents: The Bogalusa heart study. *Journal of Chronic Disease, 35,* 613–621.

Jackson, C., & Levine, D. (1983). *Comparison of two measures of Type A behavior in children.* Paper presented at the annual meeting of the American Psychological Association, Anaheim, CA.

Jenkins, C., Rosenman, R., & Friedman, M. (1967). Development of an objective psychological test for determination of the coronary-prone behavior pattern in employed men. *Journal of Chronic Disease, 20,* 371–379.

Jenkins, C., Zyzanski, S., & Rosenman. R. (1971). Progress toward validation of a computer-scored test for the Type A coronary-prone behavior pattern. *Psychosomatic Medicine, 33,* 193–202.

Kagan, J. (1980). Perspectives on continuity. In O. G. Brim, Jr., & J. Kagan (Eds.), *Constancy and change in human development* (pp. 26–74). Cambridge, MA: Harvard University Press.

Kagan, J., & Moss, H. (1962). *Birth to maturity.* New York: John Wiley.

Krantz, D., & Manuck, S. (1984). Acute psychophysiologic reactivity and risk of cardiovascular disease; A review and methodologic critique. *Psychological Bulletin, 96,* 435–464.

Matthews, K. (1979). Efforts to control by children and adults with the Type A coronary-prone behavior pattern. *Child Development, 50,* 842–847.

Matthews, K. (1982). Psychological perspectives on the Type A behavior pattern. *Psychological Bulletin, 91,* 293–323.

Matthews, K., & Angulo, J. (1980). Measurement of the Type A behavior pattern in children: Assessment of children's competitiveness, impatience–anger, and aggression. *Child Development, 51,* 466–475.

Matthews, K., & Avis, N. (1983). Stability of overt Type A behaviors in children: Results from a one-year longitudinal study. *Child Development, 54,* 1507–1512.

Matthews, K., & Siegel, J. (1982). The Type A behavior pattern in children and adolescents: Assessment, development, and associated coronary-risk. In A. R. Baum & J. E. Singer (Eds.), *Handbook of psychology and health* (Vol. 2, pp. 99–116). Hillsdale, NJ: Lawrence Erlbaum Associates.

Matthews, K., & Siegel, J. (1983). Type A behaviors by children, social comparison, and standards for self-evaluation. *Developmental Psychology, 19,* 135–140.

Matthews, K., & Volkin, J. (1981). Efforts to excel and the Type A behavior pattern in children. *Child Development, 52,* 1283–1289.

Rosen, B., & Aneshensel, C. (1976). The chameleon syndrome. *Journal of Marriage and the Family, 38,* 605–617.

Scarr, S. (1981). Testing for children: Assessment and the many determinants of intellectual competence. *American Psychologist, 36,* 1159–1166.

Steinberg, L. (1985). Early temperamental antecedents of adult Type A behaviors. *Developmental Psychology, 22,* 1171–1180.

Steinberg, L. (1986). Stability (and instability) of overt Type A behaviors from childhood to young adulthood. *Developmental Psychology, 23,* 393–402.

Thomas, A., & Chess, S. (1977). *Temperament and development.* New York: Brunner/Mazel.

Thomas, A., Chess, S., & Birch, H. (1968). *Temperament and behavior disorders in children.* New York: New York University Press.

Thomas, A., Chess, S., Birch, H., Hertzig, M., & Korn, S. (1963). *Behavioral individuality in early childhood.* New York: New York University Press.

Some Implications of the Trait–State Distinction for the Study of Development over the Life Span: The Case of Personality

John R. Nesselroade
PENNSYLVANIA STATE UNIVERSITY

Abstract

The distinction between trait-like and state-like dimensions of individual differences has long been recognized by students of behavior. Within the last 30 years or so, much conceptual and empirical work has arisen from the trait–state distinction; work that has helped to clarify a number of substantive and methodological issues. The development of measures of particular state concepts (e.g., state anxiety) has made it possible to study relationships among constructs in a more refined and sensitive manner than can be done with trait measures only.

Recognition of the information that state assessments bring to the study of behavior leads to some major implications for research on development from a life-span perspective. That state mediates behavior in important ways seems well established. The likelihood that state *changes* are involved in mediating other *changes* (e.g., in memory functioning) warrants significant investments in improving state concepts and measurement systems for use in the study of development over the life span.

In truth, should we not hear a tale as strange
that so much tells of sameness, naught of change?
—anonymous

I. Introduction

The most general aim of this chapter is to present a perspective on selected issues of constancy and change and to examine some of its implications for the study of development over the life span. The perspective draws from one set of roots anchored in the issues, themes, and empirical research of life-span development (Baltes, 1986; Baltes & Schaie, 1973; Brim & Kagan, 1980; Featherman, 1983; Goulet & Baltes, 1970; Lerner, 1984; Nesselroade & Reese, 1973).

A second, but equally integral set of this chapter's roots taps into a substantial deposit of theoretical and empirical work on intraindividual change and interindividual differences by researchers in personality. Cattell, for example, to supplement his program of research on stable personality and ability traits, began working on the definition and measurement of dimensions of relatively short-term change (states) some 40 years ago (Cattell, Cattell, & Rhymer, 1947). In the intervening years a large number of researchers have focused their attention on various aspects of state definition and measurement (e.g., Allen and Potkay, 1981; Cattell, 1966b, 1973; Curran & Cattell, 1976; Gottschalk & Gleser, 1969; Hertzog & Nesselroade, in press; Horn, 1972; Lebo & Nesselroade, 1978; Nesselroade & Bartsch, 1977; Nesselroade & Ford, 1985; Spielberger, Gorsuch, & Lushene, 1969; Spielberger, Lushene, & McAdoo, 1977; Thorne, 1966; Zevon & Tellegen, 1982; Zuckerman & Lubin, 1965).

Clearly, the task for developmental researchers is to understand both constancy and change across the life span. Attending solely to one *or* the other is not sufficient. The line of argument to be advanced is that the trait–state distinction found in the personality research literature bears directly on constancy and change issues that developmentalists need to recognize in conducting research activities.

An exhaustive discussion of the trait–state distinction is not possible here and the writer has elected to examine selected aspects from a particular conceptual and methodological vantage point. In contrast to the temporal and cross-situational stability connoted by the label traits (Epstein & O'Brien, 1985), states can be defined as dimensions of endogenously produced (e.g., hormonal) or exogenously produced (e.g., social) intraindividual variability or change. Some writers (e.g., Gottschalk & Gleser, 1969) further distinguished states from other change dimensions (moods, emotions, affects, etc.) on the basis of such features as rates of change, pervasiveness, intensity, and duration. For our discussion the explicit recognition of subspecies is not required and the term *states* will be used to identify relatively short-term change dimensions in general. The writer would like to acknowledge, however, a vast literature on mood and emotion, for example, that cannot be adequately represented herein.

State concepts have made an important contribution to substantive research in personality by offering an enriched characterization of interindividual differences, to advances in measurement by helping to clarify reliability estimation, construct validity, and other psychometric issues, and to research methodology by providing some alternate ways to conceptualize stability and change. There is not a large body of literature to sift, organize, and discuss with respect to the current role of state concepts in the study of life-span development and behavior.

However, these concepts have seen some involvement in discussions of measurement issues (Lachman, Baltes, Nesselroade, & Willis, 1982; Nesselroade, 1984), structural analysis (Baltes & Nesselroade, 1973; Baltes, Nessleroade, & Cornelius, 1978), and the ontogenesis of change patterns (Baltes & Nesselroade, 1973). In this chapter the attempt will be made to demonstrate further how the trait–state distinction can inform the study of life-span development.

In general, the posture that many researchers (e.g., Costa & McCrae, 1980; Sealy & Cattell, 1966) have taken in studying personality from a developmental perspective falls within a long tradition of scholarship that emphasizes trait-like concepts and the relative stability of interindividual differences. Research on the *stability* of personality dimensions has helped to fuel the current round of controversies that have been a major concern of personality researchers for decades (e.g., Block, 1977; Cattell, 1979; Epstein, 1979; Epstein & O'Brien, 1985; Magnusson & Endler, 1977; Mischel, 1968, 1979). Now, in addition to ''mere'' structures, we talk about process orientations, person–situation interactions, and prototypes. The distinction between trait and state, however, points out that focusing these discussions solely on traits and changes in traits misses much of the richness of behavior and behavior change manifested by developing organisms.

II. The Trait–State Distinction

A. CONCEPTUAL ASPECTS OF THE DISTINCTION

Historical Notes. Eysenck (1983) pointed out that in 45 BC Cicero drew a distinction between an anxious temperament and state anxiety and between irascibility (the trait) and anger (the state). Leaping ahead a couple of millenia to 1946, Karen Cattell braved the rigors of serving as a subject day after day for several weeks in the first published P-technique study as R. B. Cattell and his colleagues began their collection and analysis of state data (Cattell et al., 1947). For the next 30 or so years, a fair amount of multivariate research and measurement instrument development by a number of investigators occurred but the work on personality states did not receive wide attention and acceptance.

A number of state research and instrument development programs got under way in the 1960s (e.g., Gottschalk & Gleser, 1969; Spielberger et al., 1969; Thorne, 1966; Zuckerman & Lubin, 1965) and the following 20 or so years of state research has spawned literally dozens of measurement scales and devices. The distinction received its ''official'' blessing in the early seventies when, in the *Annual Review of Psychology,* Singer and Singer (1972) hailed, as a major new trend, the shift toward constructing instruments to differentiate anxiety as a persisting disposition from anxiety as a short-term reaction to stress. The distinction was further reified by a three-paper exchange concerning the arbitrariness of the trait–state distinction (Allen & Potkay, 1981, 1983; Zuckerman, 1983).

Role of States in Personality Theory and Research. State, in the sense we are using the term, connotes a "dynamic" quality in that people are, at any particular time, located at some level or value on the state dimension but are poised for movement or change to another level. They are variably distributed across a range of possible values on each of a number of state dimensions. Therefore, because some individuals are high, some are low, and some are at moderate levels, state variability does not exist only as a difference in level between two times of measurement but, rather, it is present in the variation among persons at any given moment. From a measurement point of view, a person is many values at the same time, some of which can be quite temporary. This notion is consistent with one of the hopes for state measurement expressed by Singer and Singer (1972), namely, that state measures would aid future research by providing a more complex description of persons in both the laboratory and naturalistic settings. Similarly to the concept of potential energy, state conceptions are meaningfully applied at any one point in time and, in their variety, provide a richness to the characterization of individuals at a particular instance of observation that trait concepts alone cannot give.

What of the formal aspects of the role of states in individual differences? There is a variety of possibilities but here we will consider two as illustrated in Fig. 1, using anxiety as a substantive focus. The two possibilities are: (1) states as aspects of variability superimposed on the same dimensions as traits (Panel a); and (2) states as parallel or coordinate constructs to stable, trait-like ones, the two kinds of which "interact" to influence phenomena such as "anxious" behaviors (Panel b). With respect to (1), the state aspect of variability is the more fundamental of the two. Trait, in turn, is defined in terms of stable individual differences characteristics of state such as proneness to manifest state behaviors (e.g., Spielberger et al., 1977), or simply as average state level across situations or occasions (e.g., Patterson & Bechtel, 1977). With respect to (2) (states as coordinate with traits) neither state nor trait assumes preeminence over the other. In fact there is no requirement of a trait counterpart for each state, or vice versa. Rather, the central ideas are: (a) that both trait and state level contribute to the manifest behavior of the individual, (b) some manifest behaviors may be essentially state indicators, others essentially trait indicators, and still others may be indicators of both trait and state, and (c) state level and, thus, manifest state behaviors can fluctuate markedly over time and situations.

Thus, state variation can be involved in the measured differences among persons in at least two ways: (a) through "established" dimensions such as moods, emotions, etc., and (b) through confounding state variation with variation that is usually construed to reflect stable individual differences. In the

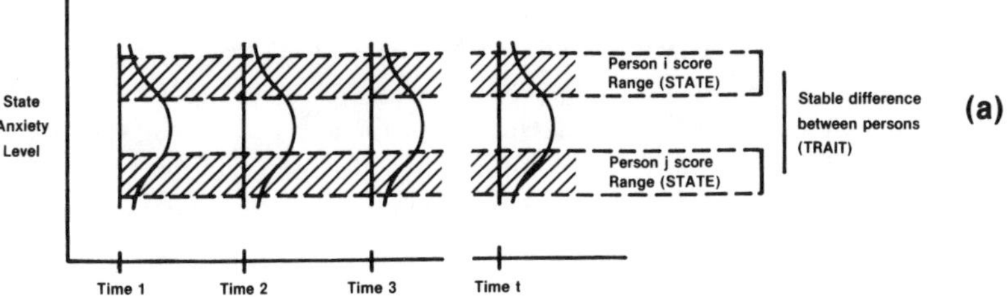

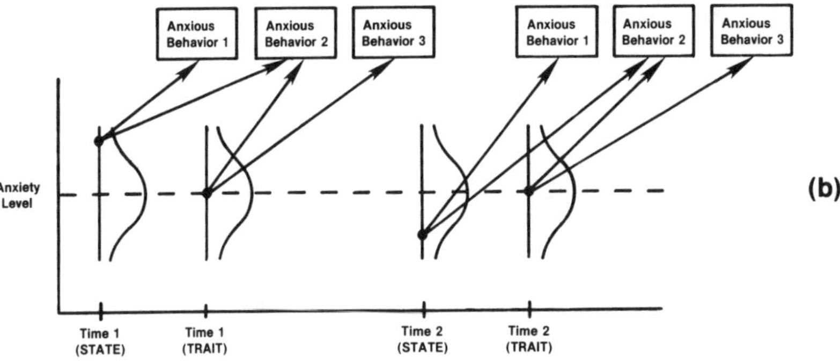

Fig. 1. Two roles of states in accounting for differences among individuals: (a) aspects of variability on the same dimensions as trait variation; (b) dimensions of intraindividual variability that are coordinate with stable, trait-like dimensions and which combine with them to account for behavior.

former case, states enhance the variety, quality, and comprehensiveness of personality descriptions. In the latter case, such confounding can seriously threaten the validity of psychological measures. For example, Roberts and Nesselroade (1986) examined locus of control—putatively a stable personality trait—in a study designed to permit the assessment of short-term intraindividual variability. Their subjects reported coherent, day-to-day fluctuations on the locus of control scales with *internality,* especially, manifesting consistent changes. Patrick and Zuckerman (1977) demonstrated that by explicitly measuring need achievement as if it were a state, they could predict from it to other behavior with a level of precision not possible with need achievement measures representing a trait orientation. In cases where both state and trait variability are manifested in measurements and the assumption is that one is measuring a trait dimension only, the state variability may impede personality research—both the search for stability and for systematic change—until the situation is recognized and corrected.

There is an additional aspect of the confounding of trait and state variability that deserves to be emphasized. State variability can either inflate *or* attenuate test–retest stability estimates of observable variables depending, for example, on the similarity of state-evoking circumstances at the two occasions (situations) of measurement. This possibility bears directly on the interpretation of data-based stability estimates involved in discussions of person–situation interaction phenomena.

Lawfulness with State Measurements. Although an individual's trait score may be assumed to be stable over considerable intervals of time, changes in situations, etc., no such expectations necessarily hold for the person's location on a state dimension. Thus, an individual's pattern of state scores needs, additionally, to be characterized by a certain time, or situation, or occasion of measurement. Because of the potential lability of the scores, state measures tend to be seen as not so useful in traditional psychometric-based prediction schemes. Exception is taken by writers such as Cattell (1973, 1979) and Zuckerman (1976), for example, who argue strongly for the inclusion of state variation in the prediction of behavior.

There are at least two ways to deal constructively with the lability aspects of states. One is the psychometric and largely descriptive pursuit of using change measures in prediction systems. The other, which is more in the causal–explanatory vein, involves searching for the conditions that regulate lability. Lability is not something indeterminate but, rather, something that can be represented in terms of lawful relationships.

First, to the prediction strategy. Are there ways in which state measures, even with their lability, can contribute to the prediction of future behavior? Or, in other terms, can one capitalize on individual differences in intraindividual changes? We will briefly identify some possibilities that look promising. For instance, Cattell (1979) proposed the inclusion in prediction schemes of terms representing one's proneness or liability to manifest a given state score (e.g., high anxiety) in a given situation as modulators of trait-based predictions. Zuckerman (1976) argued that state level averaged over several occasions of measurement is a more valid predictor of future behavior than are more traditional trait measures (see Fig. 1a). Patrick and Zuckerman (1977) reported higher predictive validity for state scores averaged over four separate occasions than for conventional trait scores. Zuckerman's argument is that averaging measured state levels provides a more valid assessment than the usual "cortical integration" of prior states over some indefinite period of time that subjects are expected to do in completing the customary self-report trait measure.

Proneness to manifest a given state score and average state score, of course, begin to sound more and more like "trait" and, as noted above, that is how several researchers have elected to define trait (Patterson & Bechtel, 1977; see also Epstein, 1979; Epstein & O'Brien, 1985; Zuckerman, 1976). If such a maneuver significantly improves longer-term prediction it is difficult to object to it on pragmatic grounds. The practice needs to be assessed, however, from a theoretical stance and on the surface, at least, it bears on the question of arbitrariness of the trait-state distinction already mentioned. For example, it is possible that for some state dimensions individuals would tend to average out to the same level, provided a fully representative sampling of state scores is used. Then, as concerns those averages (trait values) there would be decreased individual differences to use in prediction equations.

From a different tradition, Bower (1981) and Bower, Gilligan, and Monteiro (1981) recently reported a series of experiments on state-dependent learning and memory. In these studies the learner's state at the time of encoding was found to influence the nature of subsequent free recall. Thus, state level as measured at one time (encoding) can be a predictor of behavior at a later time (recall). In the "real world," for example, high levels of affect (e.g., as manifested in an emotional outburst at a traffic light) may be followed quite predictably by a display of highly selective recall when the story is subsequently related—just ask your spouse!

A second general strategy for apprehending the lawfulness of state fluctuations is to try to account for intraindividual change and interindividual differences and similarities in those change patterns. What are the major dimensions of state change? What are their antecedents, their consequents, their correlates? How do they change in nature and number across the life span? Here is where developmentalists have the opportunity to advance the understanding of behavior and behavior change with a combination of simulation, correlational, and manipulative, experimental work aimed at further explication of trait-versus-state issues and the joint consideration of matters of constancy and change. In simulation studies, for example, Baltes and Nesselroade (1973) and Baltes et al. (1978) demonstrated how easily state change patterns with high lability could be produced in developmental data by means of quite simple manipulations of environmental influences.

For the developmentalist, one of the principal objectives is to understand both the ontogeny of change dimensions and their role in personality and behavioral processes. Is there a developmental pattern? Do we, for example, begin life with a few, prewired emotional patterns that then differentiate with experience into the multidimensional adult personality? At very late portions of the human life span is there a reintegration of these patterns analogous to that postulated in the integration–differentiation–reintegration conception of human ability development and change? In the extreme, for example, do affective states coalesce into one general "feeling good" versus "feeling bad" dimension? Do developmental changes in state dimensions impinge on developmental changes in other attributes? Careful study of such questions requires both some guiding theory and the appropriately sensitive measuring instruments; instruments, for example, that have been constructed with a view to the differences between trait and state characteristics discussed earlier.

We are in the process of completing some empirical checks on the validity of the 8-State Battery (Curran & Cattell, 1976) for measuring state change in older adult subjects. The specific purposes have been to check on the factorial structure of the scales and to obtain some indication of the amount of score lability in both scales and latent variables over the interval between measurements. These studies have involved fitting the coordinate trait–state model identified in Fig. 1(b) to empirical data. Two studies have involved repeated administrations of five of the eight scales: *anxiety, fatigue, depression, effort stress,* and *regression* to older adults. One study involved a 2-week interval and the other a 1-month interval. The major line of analysis has involved fitting occasion-invariant factor-loading patterns to the subscales and estimating the test–retest stability coefficients for the latent variables under the condition of invariance (Nesselroade, 1977; Nesselroade & Bartsch, 1977).

In both studies the anxiety and fatigue state scales were found to retain their factorial structures across time but the effort stress, depression, and regression scales tended to collapse into one more global affect dimension which, however, retained the factorial invariance property. Outcomes regarding anxiety and fatigue are summarized in Figs. 2 and 3.

As noted, these inquiries assume a state model of the type depicted earlier in Fig. 1b. The estimated stability coefficients for the 2-week and 1-month intervals vary by attribute but, in general, are comparable with those found to give a clean separation of state and trait by Nesselroade and Cable (1974). The stabilities are

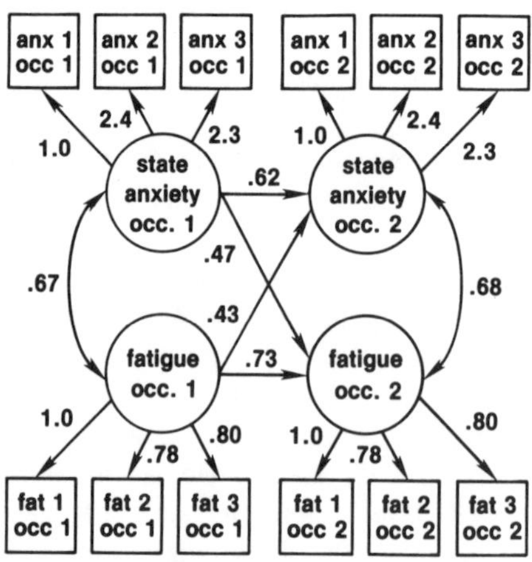

Fig. 2. Fit of factor model with cross-occasion invariant loadings to older adults' state data ($X^2 = 48.01$; $df = 46$, $p < .39$). Time between occasions is two weeks. Numerical values among state anxiety and fatigue constructs (circles) are correlation coefficients. (anx 1 = Spielberger A-state scale; anx 2 = Cattell–Nesselroade State Anxiety scale—Form A; anx 3 = Cattell–Nesselroade State Anxiety Scale—Form B; fat 1, fat 2, and fat 3 are four-item fatigue subscales based on the 12-item fatigue scale of the Curran–Cattell 8-State Questionnaire). (After Nesselroade, Mitteness, & Thompson, 1984.)

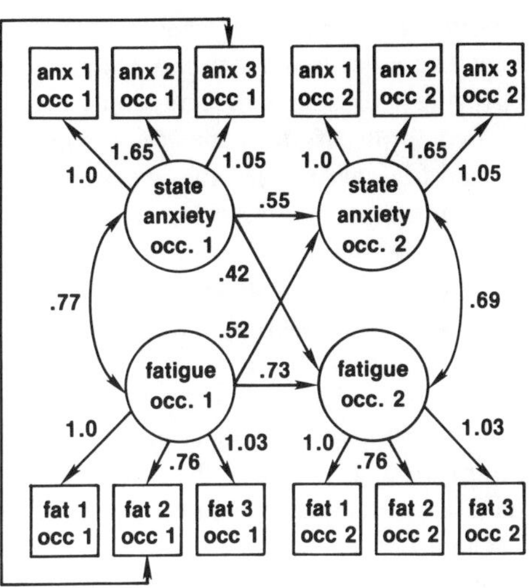

Fig. 3. Fit of factor model with cross-occasion invariant loadings to older adults' state data ($X^2 = 76.98$; $df = 45$; $p < .0021$). Time between occasions is one month. Numerical values among state anxiety and fatigue constructs (circles) are correlation coefficients. All scales are from Curran-Cattell 8-State Battery. Each of the Curran-Cattell scales consists of 12 items. These were parceled up into subscales of four items to obtain the three markers for each construct. Note that model fitted includes correlated error between one anxiety and one fatigue subscale at occasion one.

also considerably lower than one would predict from a trait model, given the reliabilities of measurement.

Although the factorial validity of the Curran and Cattell (1976) scales was testable, we cannot draw definitive conclusions about the stabilities nor the sensitivity of the scales for registering changes from these data. The anxiety and fatigue subscales do seem to be factorially valid and warrant further examination of their other characteristics. The apparent coalescing of effort stress, depression, and regression could represent a property of the measures, of the participants, or both. These alternatives need to be investigated more systematically if we are to differentiate among them.

B. METHODOLOGICAL ASPECTS OF THE DISTINCTION

The trait–state distinction can be made somewhat more precise if we consider it in relation to selected methodological topics. Here we will briefly examine some relevant measurement and data analytical aspects of the distinction.

Issues at the Measurement Instrument Level. Somewhat different psychometric and validation criteria need to be applied to the development and evaluation of state measurement instruments than are generally considered to be appropriate for trait-like measures (Baltes, Reese, & Nesselroade, 1977; Cattell, 1973; Nesselroade, Pruchno, & Jacobs, 1985). Most notably, concepts of reliability and stability must be distinguished carefully because of the potential lability of scores in state measurements. Reliability characterizes the measurement process whereas stability, in the sense in which we are using the term, describes the nature of a psychological phenomenon or process.

Figure 4 illustrates the situation with data from four repeated administrations of two forms of state anxiety measure (Nesselroade et al., 1985). The four administrations spanned two weeks. The estimated reliabilities (based on alternate form intercorrelations) of the measures are in excess of +.90 at all measurement occasions, but the test–retest stabilities estimated for both the scales and the latent variable, state anxiety, vary around zero. Thus, these data show that it is possible to measure a highly labile attribute in a highly reliable manner.

A major implication of Fig. 4 is that stability coefficients (e.g., test–retest correlations) of tests should not be used either: (1) to estimate reliability in the state domain; or (2) to discriminate state from trait measures without additional information. If one uses the ordinary test–retest correlation coefficient to estimate the reliability of state measures, one confounds process lability of the phenomenon to be studied with measurement error associated with the instrument and low stability may be erroneously interpreted as low reliability. It is also possible for state level either to remain firm over time or, due to contextual similarity, to be manifested at similar levels at the two occasions of measurement. In either case the stability coefficient would be high even though what is being measured reflects a state rather than a trait dimension.

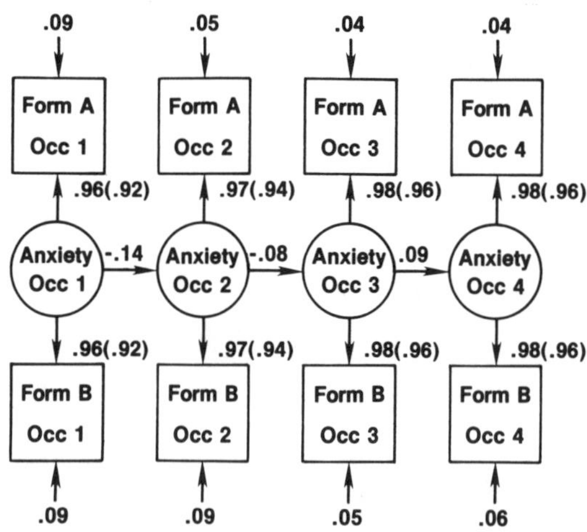

Fig. 4. Conceptual model and coefficients fitted to four-occasion repeated measures application involving parallel forms of state anxiety scale ($X^2 = 17.926$; $df = 18$; $p < .46$). From top to bottom, within each occasion, numbers are: (1) unique variance—Form A; (2) loading (and estimated scale reliability)—Form A; (3) loading and estimated scale reliability)--Form B; (4) unique variance—Form B. The three numbers between pairs of occasions are stability coefficients. (After Nesselroade, Pruchno, & Jacobs, 1985.)

Thus, the development and use of highly reliable measures remains of paramount importance, perhaps it is even more important in the case of state measurement, because process lability is a plausible alternative to "measurement error" in accounting for lack of temporal stability. Just as theory dictates that stability will be high with valid trait measures, it should be low (or lower) with valid state measures *when* circumstances change differentially for members of a group whose stability is being studied. Otherwise, test–retest correlations might actually be quite high and are therefore not a useful way to discriminate trait from state unless one accounts for situational circumstances (Bartsch & Nesselroade, 1973).

In addition to concerns regarding the distinction between reliability and stability, matters of validity are also important in particular ways with regard to the trait–state distinction. Obviously, the traditional psychometric concerns with content and construct validity are no less salient in the case of state measurement devices than they are for trait measures. Because of the potential lability of state measurements, predictive validity issues require more elaboration and care than is the case for measurement with instruments that reflect stable, trait-like attributes (e.g., see Cattell, 1973). One line of research that has tried to bridge the gap between *expectations* of stability across time and situations and *findings* of lability is the development of situation-specific measures of personality attributes (e.g., Endler, Hunt, & Rosenstein, 1962). Lachman et al. (1982), for example, reported on the development of a situation-specific measure of personality for the domain of intellectual aging. Such approaches to more fine-grained measurement have shown considerable promise for increasing the predictive validity of personality measures. Some balance must be sought, however, for if it is carried to the extreme a program of measurement instrument construction based on situation specificity runs counter to the scientific objective of parsimony. In any case, the importance of dealing with critical validity issues for the trait–state distinction to be delineated further cannot be underestimated.

Issues at the Latent Variable Level. Alternative ways to discriminate trait and state range from the application of empirical methods of scale construction with emphasis on content and stability–lability criteria (Zuckerman & Lubin, 1965) to multivariate methods, such as discriminant function analysis (Horn, 1972; Horn & Little, 1966) and a variety of factor-analytical procedures (Nesselroade & Bartsch, 1977; Nesselroade & Cable, 1974). Major tools for distinguishing between trait and state constructs in multivariate-correlational approches to the study of personality have included R-, P-, and dR-technique analyses (Cattell, 1963). The three covariation techniques are defined in the context of the covariation chart or data box (Cattell, 1966a) represented in Fig. 5.

As is well known, R-technique involves sampling both persons and variables relatively extensively but drawing at only one measurement occasion. Using

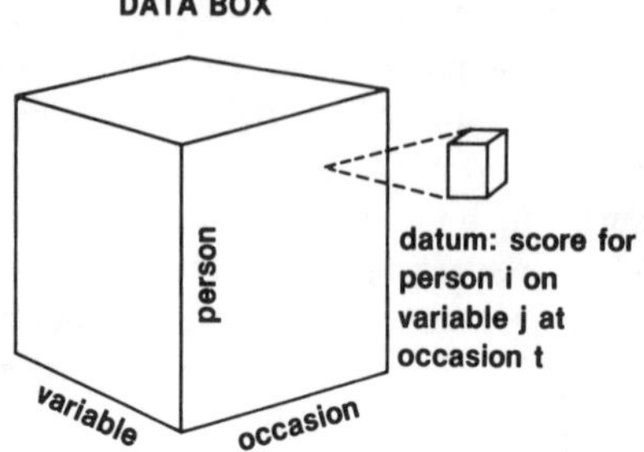

Fig. 5. The basic "data box" of Cattell stressing the nature of a datum. Different covariation techniques (e.g., R, P, dR) involve selecting data differentially in regard to the person, variable, and occasion dimensions.

these cross-sectional data, variables are intercorrelated and factor-analyzed to determine dimensions of individual differences. The most plausible directions for generalization from these cross-sectional observations, assuming reasonable sampling, are to other measures and other persons. Generalizations to other measurement occasions from the single instance involved is patently risky, but the relatively common interpretation of R-technique factors as *stable* traits implicitly amounts to just such a generalization regarding time.

Somewhat less well known, perhaps, P-technique (Cattell & Scheier, 1961; Nesselroade & Ford, 1985; Zevon & Tellegen, 1982) involves the relatively extensive sampling of variables and occasions (say, 100 occasions or more), but the measurements are made repeatedly on only one person. Variables are intercorrelated over occasions and factored to determine dimensions of intraindividual change. The approach, which is longitudinal in nature, was identified by Bereiter (1963) as "the logical way to study change." Stability, as represented in the person's mean scores computed over occasions, is discarded in the calculation of the covariances among variables. These covariances reflect the degree to which the variables change together and the factors provide a dimensional representation of the patterns of change. The most plausible directions for generalization are to other measures and other occasions of measurement. Generalization to other persons from the one person measured is obviously risky. Yet, from a nomothetic standpoint, it is necessary to ascertain the generality of P-technique factors (Nesselroade & Ford, 1985; Zevon & Tellegen, 1982). Recently conducted P-technique studies have deliberately incorporated several concurrent replications of persons for this purpose (e.g., Hooker et al., 1985; Lebo & Nesselroade, 1978; Roberts & Nesselroade, 1986; Zevon & Tellegen, 1982).

In its main sampling dimensions dR-technique (differential-R technique) is like R-technique (Cattell, 1963). Individuals and variables are sampled but instead of one measurement occasion, the participants are measured, then remeasured, and difference scores are computed, intercorrelated, and analyzed. Thus, the data represent one change rather than one occasion of measurement.

The resulting factors are interpreted as dimensions of change (e.g., states) but, as noted below, this interpretation is not without risk in some applications.

What are the relationships among these three approaches? Historically, the tendency has been to infer that R-technique resulted in trait dimensions and P- and dR-techniques resulted in state dimensions. It is not that simple. P-technique does rather straightforwardly produce state dimensions. The dR-technique can result in state dimensions, too, but it can also yield a kind of trait-like factor on which individuals' scores remain stable over time but the pattern of relationships between variables and factors changes (see e.g., Harris, 1963; Nesselroade & Bartsch, 1977). Of the three approaches, R-technique is the most ambiguous in outcome in that it produces whatever patterns (trait, state, or both) contribute to interindividual differences at that particular occasion of measurement (Nesselroade & Bartsch, 1977). However, because only a single occasion of measurement is involved, one cannot determine from the patterns themselves whether a given dimension is a state or a trait unless the variables themselves provide clear validity cues, that is, unless one has truly valid, distinct trait and state markers.

A device that has proven to be helpful both in representing trait-versus-state notions and in understanding the relationships between covariation schemes such as R- and dR-technique and the trait and state concepts is the representation shown in Fig. 6. The fourfold table is bounded by two types of factor pattern (invariant and noninvariant) and two kinds of factor scores (stable and fluctuant). The former characterizes whether or not the relationships between observable and latent variables remain constant over time. The latter identifies the nature of factor score stability or the extent to which individuals retain their rank order on the latent variables over time (see Baltes & Nesselroade, 1973; Nesselroade & Bartsch, 1977).

Within the cells of the fourfold table, traits and states are thus identified in idealized form. Traits (cell a) are defined by invariant patterns of loadings and stable factor scores. States (cell b), somewhat in contrast, are invariant patterns of loadings and fluctuant factor scores. The emphasis on metrically invariant loadings is perhaps unduly restrictive (see e.g., Horn, McArdle, & Mason, 1983), but for our purposes here it provides for a conceptually clean discrimination between the two kinds of dimensions in relation to the nature of the implied scores. Cell c is construable as a condition of genetypical continuity with phenotypical change and cell d as the condition of discontinuity. Figure 6 indicates one possible course of developmental change leading from less to more organization in terms of state and trait. For additional discussion of these concepts in relation to developmental stability and change see Baltes and Nesselroade (1973) and Nesselroade and Bartsch (1977).

For the present discussion, in the case of both traits and states observable variables relate to latent variables in temporally invariant ways (invariant loading patterns) but trait scores show stability; state scores fluctuate. Although temporal

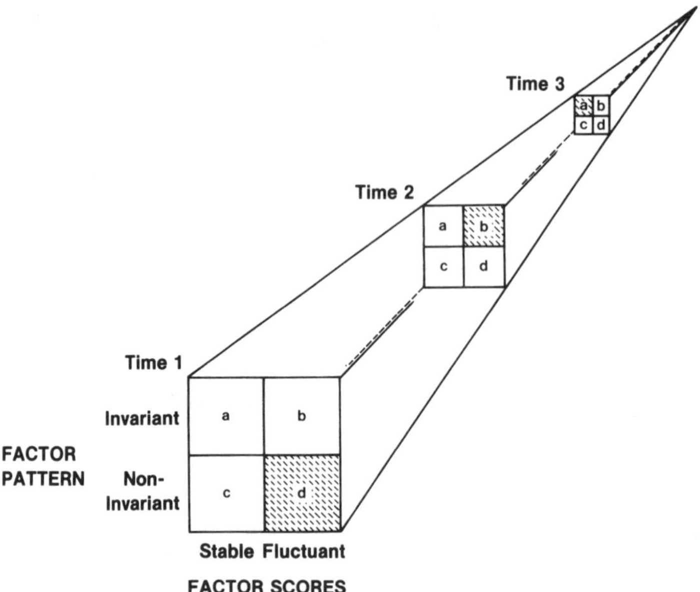

Fig. 6. Combinations of temporally defined kinds of factor patterns and factor scores that identify trait and state dimensions. (After Baltes & Nesselroade, 1973.)

stability, per se, is not accepted as sufficient to define traits, as the current debate between such protagonists as Epstein (1979; see also Epstein & O'Brien, 1985) and Mischel (1979) attests, in generalized form it includes transsituational constancy.

The fourfold table of Fig. 6, which is presented primarily as a heuristic device for identifying descriptive, correlational information, can serve as a vehicle to illustrate some of the aspects of the trait–state distinction that Allen and Potkay (1981) consider to be arbitrary. It makes an interpretational difference whether one has succeeded in manipulating stability (Bartsch & Nesselroade, 1973; Nesselroade & Cable, 1974) or has only a set of test–retest data, the influences on which are unknown. In the latter case, if purported state measures show high stability one has to infer a similarity in the evoking conditions at the occasions or else a state of the appropriate duration. If a purported state measure shows low stability, it may be because of individual differences in the changes from one occasion to the next or it may be due to low reliability of measurement. Thus, in either the high- or the low-stability situation, one has an explanation and thus need not reject the state measurement notion. The difficulties in falsifying the state–trait distinction are at the heart of Allen and Potkay's (1981) criticism that it is arbitrary.

Relationships between R- and dR-technique Factors. Based on the fourfold table (Fig. 6), Nesselroade and Bartsch (1977) presented a set of mathematical expectations concerning the relationship between R- and dR-technique factors. The findings of principal concern are: (a) Both state and trait factors as defined in the fourfold table can emerge in R-technique analysis; (b) trait dimensions, as defined in the fourfold table, do indeed disappear when one factor-analyzes difference scores (dR-technique); and (c) factor-loading patterns of states, as defined in the fourfold table, will be found if one uses dR-technique. Moreover, with proper scaling of factor variances, the loading patterns of state factors in difference scores will be the same as if they had been isolated in separate (occasion 1 and occasion 2) R-technique analyses. The model of state and trait that was assumed in developing these expectations is that of Fig. 6.1(b), namely, coordinate state and trait dimensions.

The expectations concerning states and traits in R- and dR-technique analyses that have been described were clearly borne out in an empirical investigation (Nesselroade & Cable, 1974) summarized in Table I and Fig. 7. In that study subjects were administered four state and four trait-marker tests at each of two occasions of measurement. The separate occasion factor-loading patterns (R-technique) clearly identify both a trait and a state factor. In the dR-technique analysis, however, only one factor emerged and, according to expectation, it loaded only the state marker variables. Further supporting evidence came from

TABLE I

Factor Loading Patterns of State and Trait Anxiety Marker Variables on Two Occasions of Measurement (R-Technique) and for Difference Scores (dR-Technique)

	Occasion 1 Factors		Occasion 2 Factors		Difference Score Factor
Variable	I (state)	II (trait)	I (state)	II (trait)	I (state only)
1. State Anxiety	.75	−.07	.63	.05	.78
2. State Anxiety	.76	−.11	.69	−.05	.78
3. State Anxiety	.53	.21	.72	−.01	.57
4. State Anxiety	.60	.09	.62	.01	.55
5. Trait Anxiety	.12	.65	.06	.66	.15
6. Trait Anxiety	−.01	.80	.07	.71	.15
7. Trait Anxiety	.20	.71	.13	.79	.10
8. Trait Anxiety	.18	.70	.19	.75	.16

[a]After Nesselroade and Cable, 1974.

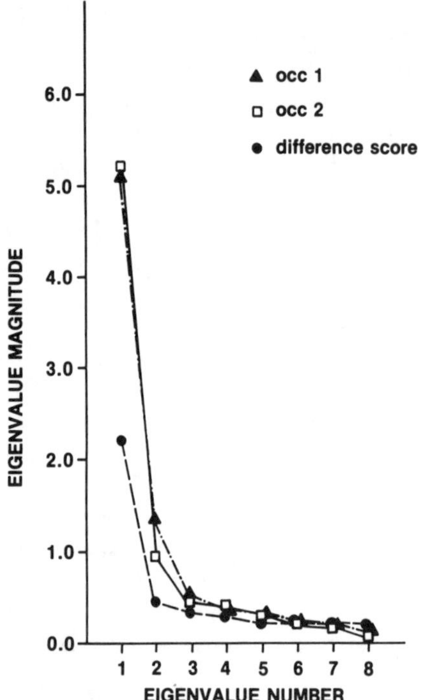

Fig. 7. Roots of covariance matrices showing differences in number of factors in R- versus dR-technique analyses involving trait and state measures. (After Nesselroade & Cable, 1974.)

the number of factors to be extracted in each analysis as indicated by the latent roots of the respective covariance matrices. These are presented in Fig. 7.

The differences between test–retest stabilities for the actual measures were of the following magnitude: State measures exhibited test–restest correlations in the range of +.57 to +.68; those for trait measures fell between +.83 and +.87. Thus, although the stabilities of state and trait measures did not overlap, the state stabilities were not dramatically low. Yet, the separation of state and trait factors by R- and dR-techniques was sharply produced both in the numbers of factors as reflected in the eigenvalues of the respective covariance matrices and in the factor-loading patterns. Such a clear separation of state and trait concepts within one analysis helps to vitiate the claim of arbitrariness leveled against the trait–state distinction by Allen and Potkay (1981).

Relationships between R- and P-technique Factors. Similar issues need to be explicated in the cases of other facets of the covariation chart. For example, the relationship between R- and P-technique factors is also a matter of some interest both to students of stability and change and to methodologists. Although at a conceptual level one can speculate on such relationships it is somewhat more difficult to work out a formal expectation for them because they are derived from orthogonal slices of the data box. As far as state dimensions are concerned, however, there are models of selection and selection effects (Nesselroade, 1983, in press) that indicate circumstances under which factor-loading patterns should be the same regardless of whether they are derived from measuring many people one time or one person many times. At the extreme, for instance, imagine a dimension on which each person, over many occasions, varied over the entire range of possible scores. Then, assuming representative sampling of persons, measurement of many persons on one occasion (R-technique) should give the picture of complete variability just as one might witness it in observing one person over many occasions (P-technique)—assuming a representative sampling of occasions!

III. P-Technique Approach to the Study of Changes

To emphasize further the promise of state concepts in personality research, the author would like to examine P-technique (Cattell, 1963; Nesselroade & Ford, 1985; Zevon & Tellegen, 1982) in more detail. As was noted before, in P-technique one approaches the study of intraindividual change and variability by focusing on the measurement of one person on many occasions, each time administering the complete battery of measures. One can then examine the underlying structure of such data by covarying the measures over occasions to ascertain the extent to which they change together. Interest can center on "steady state" variability, temporary or permanent changes in "steady state" variability, or all of these possibilities (Nesselroade & Ford, 1985).

Factor analysis or other multivariate techniques can be used to develop a dimensional representation of the change patterns defined across the set of measures involved. If the person shows either no change on the variables or no covariation in the changes then the analysis results in no factors. If there are changes and they are correlated among variables across occasions then a factor solution summarizing the covariation is obtained. The loading pattern for one individual's data can be compared with that of other individuals to determine the degree of generality represented in the change patterns (Lebo & Nesselroade, 1978; Zevon & Tellegen, 1982). Recent developments in P-technique methodology have made it possible to study the time-lagged nature of the interrelationships of variables and factors (McArdle, 1982; Molenaar, 1985).

With regard to the study of personality from a developmental perspective, P-technique represents a source of considerable promise (Hertzog & Nesselroade,

1986; Nesselroade & Ford, 1985). Developmentalists need to look for similarities and differences among individuals not only in configurations of more or less stable attributes, but in patterns of change also (Baltes et al., 1977). This contention holds for shorter-term as well as for longer-term changes. Marx (1956; see also Skinner, 1953), for example, argued for carefully formulating the nature of the single case before looking across cases for similarities and differences, and the argument has been elaborated in relation to P-technique by Zevon and Tellegen (1982) and Nesselroade and Ford (1985). Although they do not use the label *P-technique,* Lazarus and DeLongis (1983) recently made a strong pitch for such intensive, intraindividual designs in the study of stress and coping in aging. Similarly, Hoyer (1974) has stressed the importance of this general approach in the study of adult development and aging.

IV. Discussion and Conclusion

The study of development from a life-span orientation focuses on intraindividual changes and interindividual differences and similarities in those intraindividual changes (Baltes et al., 1977). Intraindividual changes cannot be usefully studied without some attention being given to stable features of the organism as well. Concepts and methods that enable developmentalists to study systematically both change and stability are, therefore, to be desired. The trait–state distinction, as we have identified and discussed it in this chapter, has provided researchers with some valuable conceptual and methodological tools with which to approach the task of making sense out of change and stability.

A. SOME SUMMARY ASSERTIONS

Before recognizing some implications for life-span developmental research that can be drawn from work with the trait–state distinction, there are several worthwhile generalizations to be made from the information just reviewed. First, at a given point in time, we are what we are—then. What we will be 10 minutes, 10 days, or 10 years from now is only partly accounted for by, and predictable from, what we are now and were before. Obviously, the attempt to predict future status with trait-like concepts represents an effort to capitalize on stability characteristics. There are other dimensions of differences among people, however; these are dimensions of relatively short-term change and changeability (e.g., Anxiety, Fatigue, Effort Stress, Depression, Hostility, etc.) that, nevertheless, characterize the individual at a particular time and are involved in determining behavior. These are many and varied, but a precise and comprehensive description and understanding of the behaving, developing organism depends on utilizing these dimensions as well as traditional trait-like ones. At the very least, we need to know under what conditions and for what purposes any subset of attributes (trait, state, or otherwise) can safely be ignored.

Second, the utilities of state and trait dimensions differ in respect to several criteria. As developmentalists, we are interested in understanding the processes by which both states and traits come about, change, and are maintained. Zuckerman (1976), however, emphasized that whereas state measures are of interest in their own right, the utility of stable, trait measures derives from the extent to which they predict, or account for other aspects of behavior. This viewpoint is illustrated to some extent by Costa and McCrae (1980) in arguing for the use of neuroticism, extraversion, and openness to experience as a stable framework of traits within which to account for age-related changes in coping and adaptation. The levels of stability they find suggest to them that it is not in the traits themselves that important adult development is occurring but rather, that the stable differences on these traits may predict the nature of changes on other variables.

It is reasonable to ask: How is such a high level of stability maintained? Explaining stability when there is any reason for expecting change is as important as accounting for change. Clearly, bereft of such stability, state dimensions do require explication of their antecedents, their consequents, and their correlates if they are to become integrated into comprehensive theories of personality functioning, individual differences, etc.

Third, there is no serious contender to sampling occasions and circumstances thoroughly if we are to ''plumb'' the dimensions of intraindividual variability and change accurately and comprehensively. That is an argument for appropriately designed and executed longitudinal research (Baltes et al., 1977; Lazarus & DeLongis, 1983; McCall, 1977; Nesselroade & Baltes, 1974).

B. IMPLICATIONS OF THE TRAIT-STATE DISTINCTION FOR LIFE-SPAN RESEARCH

What are some implications of these assertions? First, there is a host of obvious and general, but certainly nontrivial implications such as the need to refine concepts, to improve operational definitions of state dimensions, and to integrate the concepts more thoroughly into personality theory in general. There is a richness and complexity to the state dimensions that characterizes the personality differences evident among people at a given point in time that is not captured if one focuses solely on measures of traits. These differences in anxiety, hostility, depression, or fatigue, are involved in social interactions between children and adults, middle-aged people and their old parents, patients and staff in care facilities, and so on. Developing a clearer understanding of, for example, their number, nature, age-correlated change patterns is both scientifically and humanly desirable.

There are implications of a more specific nature arising from work with the trait–state distinction that deserve emphasis. Four areas in particular seem well worth singling out. They are: measurement, research design, modeling, and substantive research and theory.

Measurement. Regardless of how attractive one makes the names of variables, concepts, and their hypothesized linkages, empirical research demands that key concepts and variables be representable in measures. Developmental phenomena such as change (and stability) can be hypothesized, but they cannot be tested against data unless the concepts of interest can be measured. Research stemming from the trait–state distinction has helped to clarify several key measurement issues that are pertinent to the systematic study of change and stability. We will identify three.

First, the distinction between reliability and stability enables researchers to separate the psychometric properties of the measurement instrument or process from the properties of the attribute being measured. This paves the way to developing more valid measures of psychological constructs for use in developmental research. For example, reliability can be established without confounding it with stability of the construct being measured. Stability can then be investigated as a phenomenon rather than imposed to some extent by the measurement instrument.

Second, the demonstration of highly reliable measurement of changeable attributes supports the development and use of measurement procedures that are more sensitive to change than are instruments that are developed and evaluated in terms of how stable individuals' scores tend to remain over x units of time. For the developmentalist, increased sensitivity of measures is important both in correlational investigations of stability and change and in manipulative, experimental settings.

Third, the use of state measures in concert with trait measures can give a much richer picture of the nature and extent of individual differences at one point in time and across multiple points in time. The apparent multidimensionality of developmental change requires that batteries of measures be available to approach the study of development as patterns defined across many variables simultaneously.

Research Design. Findings deriving from research on the trait–state distinction have some clear implications for the design and conduct of developmental research. The implications drawn above with regard to measurement apply directly to many aspects of designing correlational research, whether cross-sectional or longitudinal in nature. For example, longitudinal research to examine stability of personality attributes will produce different conclusions depending on the sensitivity to changes of the measures used, said differently, depending on the bias of the measures toward stability.

With respect to manipulative, experimental research design, valid state measures can serve as useful probes to validate the effectiveness of treatments designed to elicit a particular response pattern. They can also serve as covariates, especially in those cases where transitory state variability may intrude upon the planned design. Many state measures are brief while being highly reliable and a judiciously chosen set can provide a much richer characterization of the differences among experimental subjects at or very close the administration of a treatment condition.

Modeling. Developmentalists are relying more and more on the use of structural modeling procedures to analyze longitudinal data. Many of these modeling applications have rather uncritically assumed the autoregressive nature of the data and proceeded to fit models accordingly. Hertzog and Nesselroade (in press) examined this practice from the perspective of the trait–state distinction and concluded that there is a tacit but very strong association between trait concepts and autoregressive models. They demonstrate that autoregressive models do not necessarily fit longitudinal data involving state measures. They conclude that because extant individual differences, even at one occasion of measurement, reflect state as well as trait variability, researchers should be alert to the possibility that alternatives to autoregressive models may be needed if longitudinal data are to be understood.

Substantive Research and Theory. The trait–state distinction helps to emphasize that the study of personality from a life-span perspective involves explaining and accounting for more than personality traits. It also emphasizes that there are other concepts besides traits to be used in accounting for and predicting manifest behavior and behavior change (Cattell, 1979, 1980). The enhanced ability to structure individual differences that state measurement concepts and instruments provide enables researchers to approach the study of personality from more of a systems perspective than has been the case with strictly trait orientations. For example, distinctions between steady state "hum," temporary changes in steady state, and permanent changes in steady state, are important for developmentalists to make in describing the status of the organism across significant periods of time. Not all observed intraindividual variability should be construed as change, let alone as development (Nesselroade & Ford, 1985).

Psychologists will continue to use single-occasion trait measures to try to predict behaviors of various kinds (e.g., achievement, smoking, life satisfaction, etc.). To the extent that adulthood and older age is a time of increased frequency and intensity of illness, for example, the stage is set for increased state variation.

Given that circumstance, the objective of prediction using stable, trait-like systems is further jeopardized. The evidence reviewed here indicates that such predictions can be improved by taking into account state measures and their interactive relationships to traits. For example, as was mentioned there are indications that the use of average state level is an avenue to the improvement of predictions from individual differences measures (Epstein, 1979; Epstein & O'Brien, 1985; Patrick & Zuckerman, 1977). Another approach is to administer state measures along with trait measures and to use the state levels to "correct" the trait scores for state confounding (Cattell, 1979).

To illustrate the utilization of state and trait information consider blood pressure, for instance, which is often used as a trait-like indicator of systemic conditions. A plausible example of state–trait confounding is that one's blood pressure reading is high because of anxiety that the blood pressure reading will be high. One solution to such confounding is to take several readings and average them to obtain a "trait" value, a practice of many physicians. Alternatively, a valid measure of state anxiety might be used to adjust the reading to a "trait" value. In the first case, state variability that confounds trait is treated somewhat like measurement error in classical test theory and averaged out to reveal "true" trait scores. In the second case, trait and state are conceptualized as coordinate dimensions and state may be regressed out of trait (or vice versa) to raise the validity of scores.

Acceptance of multidimensionality and development of appropriate measures and more sophisticated models of trait and state relationships should lead to improvements in trait-performance predictions. For example, in accounting for older person's adaptations to being relocated, the utilization of state measures offers one possibility for capturing more of the apparent differences between persons that may be involved. The implications of an increase in state anxiety may be quite a different matter from an increase in trait anxiety, but without proper measurement and utilization of scores, potential gains in understanding the processes involved will not be realized.

A second illustration of these ideas is found in the arena of learning and memory. State dependent learning has been a topic of investigation for decades. The research designs, at least in studies involving pharmacological agents, have tended not to be internally valid (Overton, 1974) and the effects somewhat illusory. In the area of human learning and memory, for example, anxiety has long been implicated as a salient antecedent but until recently the trait–state distinction has not proven to be particularly important in that connection (Mueller, 1976). Recent work by Bower and colleagues (Bower, 1981; Bower et al., 1981), however, has revealed some impressive consistency in links between affective state ("happy vs. sad," essentially) and learning and free recall effects. These studies are of considerable significance to researchers in personality and in various aspects of aging for several reasons.

First, the data clearly signify the importance of knowing the status of the organism at a particular moment (e.g., at encoding or free recall) as opposed to relying solely on trait scores that may have been obtained quite some time ago and are simply presumed to be stable. For instance. in the case of what Bower (1981) calls congruity (i.e., a match between emotional tone of material to be learned and subject's emotional state), state at time of encoding is a predictor of subsequent free recall performance.

Evidence of the involvement of states in learning and memory has potentially far-reaching implications for students of development, provided that there are age-related changes in state variability, in state change patterns, etc. Age-related changes in state mechanisms could be involved in age-related changes in learning and memory functioning. For example, depression may be implicated in memory changes in older adulthood. To the extent that performance factors (such as mood) are involved in age differences and changes in memory, for example, it becomes important to be able to control for state variation in doing research on these cognitive functions. That, in turn, requires that valid, reliable measures of change dimensions be readily available. In any case, to some extent it seems that a fuller understanding either of personality or of learning depends on advances in the other area (Cattell, 1979). Thus, we cannot resist asking what subleties in our understanding of cognitive performance await the more precise and complete development of the psychological states domain?

Current interest in older adults as learners and information on how to facilitate their learning (Willis, 1985) is a timely adjunct for the exploration of intervention at the state-mediation level (Nesselroade, 1986). There may be some important leverage to be gained from the state–cognition linkages for intervention work on adult learning and memory functioning, for example. Perhaps material to be learned can be packaged advantageously in alternative ways designed to be congruent with modal affective states of potential learners.

The success of any scholarly research or professional intervention plan or strategy involving individual differences depends in part on how well we are able to structure the domain of mood and state variability and what we find out about the correlates, antecedents, and consequents of state characteristics. Clearly, with its focus on interindividual differences in intraindividual variability the study of development across the life span stands to benefit from more differentiated conceptualization and careful empirical research springing from the trait–state distinction.

Acknowledgment

This chapter is based on a presidential address to the Division of Adult Development and Aging, American Psychological Association. The author gratefully acknowledges the generous support provided by the Max Planck Institute for Human Development and Education, Berlin, during preparation of the manuscript. He is also very thankful to Roger Dixon, Alexander von Eye, Reinhold Kliegl, Margie Lachman, and three anonymous reviewers for their many insightful comments and suggestions for improving it. Joy Barger deserves special mention for her patient help in producing the final manuscript.

References

Allen, B. P., & Potkay, C. R. (1981). On the arbitrary distinction between states and traits. *Journal of Personality and Social Psychology, 41,* 916–928.

Allen, B. P., & Potkay, C. R. (1983). Just as arbitrary as ever: Comments on Zuckerman's rejoinder. *Journal of Personality and Social Psychology, 44,* 1087–1089.

Baltes, P. B. (1986). Theoretical propositions of life-span developmental psychology: On the dynamics between growth and decline. Unpublished manuscript, Max Planck Institute for Human Development and Education, Berlin.

Baltes, P. B., & Nesselroade, J. R. (1973). The developmental analysis of individual differences on multiple measures. In J. R. Nesselroade & H. W. Reese (Eds.), *Life-span developmental psychology: Methodological issues* (pp. 219–251). New York: Academic Press.

Baltes, P. B., Nesselroade, J. R., & Cornelius, S. W. (1978). Multivariate antecedents of structural change in development: A simulation of cumulative environmental patterns. *Multivariate Behavioral Research, 13,* 127–152.

Baltes, P. B., Reese, H. W., & Nesselroade, J. R. (1977). *Life-span developmental psychology: Introduction to research methods.* Monterey, CA: Brooks/Cole.

Baltes, P. B., & Schaie, K. W. (Eds.). (1973). *Life-span developmental psychology: Personality and socialization.* New York: Academic Press.

Bartsch, T. W., & Nesselroade, J. R. (1973). Test of the trait–state distinction using a manipulative factor analytic design. *Journal of Personality and Social Psychology, 27,* 58–64.

Bereiter, C. (1963). Some persisting dilemmas in the measurement of change. In C. W. Harris (Ed.), *Problems in measuring change* (pp. 3–20). Madison, WI: University of Wisconsin Press.

Block, J. (1977). Advancing the psychology of personality: Paradigmatic shift or improving the quality of research. In D. Magnusson & N. S. Endler (Eds.), *Personality at the crossroads: Current issues in interactional psychology* (pp. 37–63). Hillsdale, NJ: Lawrence Erlbaum Associates.

Bower, G. H. (1981). Mood and memory. *American Psychologist, 36,* 129–148.

Bower, G. H., Gilligan, S. G., & Monteiro, K. P. (1981). Selectivity of learning caused by affective states. *Journal of Experimental Psychology: General, 110,* 451–473.

Brim, O. G., Jr., & Kagan, J. (Eds.). (1980). *Constancy and change in human development.* Cambridge, MA: Harvard University Press.

Cattell, R. B. (1963). The structuring of change by P- and incremental-R techniques. In C. W. Harris (Ed.), *Problems in measuring change* (pp. 167–198). Madison, WI: University of Wisconsin Press.

Cattell, R. B. (1966a). The data box: Its ordering of total resources in terms of possible relational systems. In R. B. Cattell (Ed.), *Handbook of multivariate experimental psychology* (pp. 67–128). Chicago: Rand McNally.

Cattell, R. B. (1966b). Patterns of change: Measurement in relation to state–dimension, trait change, lability, and process concepts. In R. B. Cattell (Eds.), *Handbook of multivariate experimental psychology* (pp. 355–402). Chicago: Rand-McNally.

Cattell, R. B. (1973). *Mood and personality by questionnaire.* San Francisco: Jossey–Bass.

Cattell, R. B. (1979). *Personality and learning theory. Vol. 1.* New York: Springer.

Cattell, R. B. (1980). *Personality and learning theory. Vol. 2.* New York: Springer.

Cattell, R. B., Cattell, A. K. S., & Rhymer, R. M. (1947). P-technique demonstrated in determining psycho-physiological source traits in a normal individual. *Psychometrika, 12,* 267–288.

Cattell, R. B., & Scheier, I. H. (1961). *The meaning and measurement of neuroticism and anxiety.* New York: Ronald Press.

Costa, P. T., Jr., & McCrae, R. R. (1980). Still stable after all these years: Personality as a key to some issues in adulthood and old age. In P. B. Baltes & O. G. Brim, Jr. (Eds.), *Life-span development and behavior* (Vol. 3, pp. 66–102). New York: Academic Press.

Curran, J. P., & Cattell, R. B. (1976). *Handbook for the 8-state questionnaire.* Champaign, IL: Institute for Personality and Ability Testing.

Endler, N. S., Hunt, J. McV., & Rosenstein, A. J. (1962). An S–R inventory of anxiousness. *Psychological Monographs, 76*(Whole No. 536).

Epstein, S. (1979). The stability of behavior: I. On predicting most of the people much of the time. *Journal of Personality and Social Psychology, 37,* 1097–1126.

Epstein, S., & O'Brien, E. J. (1985). The person–situation debate in historical and current perspectives. *Psychological Bulletin, 98,* 513–537.

Eysenck, H. J. (1983). Cicero and the state–trait theory of anxiety: Another case of delayed recognition. *American Psychologist, 38,* 114.

Featherman, D. L. (1983). The life-span perspective in social science research. In P. B. Baltes & O. G. Brim, Jr. (Eds.), *Life-span development and behavior* (Vol. 5, pp. 1–57). New York: Academic Press.

Gottschalk, L. A., & Gleser, G. C. (1969). *The measurement of psychological states through the content analysis of verbal behavior.* Berkeley, CA: University of California Press.

Goulet, L. R., & Baltes, P. B. (Eds.). (1970). *Life-span developmental psychology: Research and theory.* New York: Academic Press.

Harris, C. W. (1963). Canonical factor models for the description of change. In C. W. Harris (Ed.), *Problems in measuring change* (pp. 138–155). Madison, WI: University of Wisconsin Press.

Hertzog, C., & Nesselroade, J. R. (in press). Beyond autoregressive models: Some implications of the trait–state distinction for the structural modeling of developmental change. *Child Development.*

Hooker, K., Nesselroade, D. W., Nesselroade, J. R., & Lerner, R. M. (1985). *The structure of intraindividual temperament in the context of mother-child dyads: P-technique factor analysis of short term change.* Unpublished manuscript. Department of Individual and Family Studies, Pennsylvania State University.

Horn, J. L. (1972). State, trait, and change dimensions of intelligence. *British Journal of Educational Psychology, 42,* 159–185.

Horn, J. L., & Little, K. B. (1966). Isolating change and invariance in patterns of behavior. *Multivariate Behavioral Research, 2,* 219–228.

Horn, J. L., McArdle, J. J., & Mason, R. (1983). When is invariance not invariant: A practical scientist's look at the ethereal concept of factor invariance. *Southern Psychologst, 1*(4), 179–188.

Hoyer, W. J. (1974). Aging as intraindividual change. *Developmental Psychology, 10,* 821–826.

Lachman, M. E., Baltes, P. B., Nesselroade, J. R., & Willis, S. L. (1982). Examination of personality–ability relationships in the elderly: The role of the contextual (interface) assessment mode. *Journal of Research in Personality, 16,* 485–501.

Lazarus, R. S., & DeLongis, A. (1983). Psychological stress and coping in aging. *American Psychologist, 38,* 245–254.

Lebo, M. A., & Nesselroade, J. R. (1978). Intraindividual differences dimensions of mood change during pregnancy identified in five P-technique factor analyses. *Journal of Research in Personality, 12,* 205–224.

Lerner, R. M. (1984). *On the nature of human plasticity.* Cambridge, MA: Harvard University Press.

Magnusson, D., & Endler, N. S. (1977). Interactional psychology: Present status and future prospects. In D. Magnusson & N. S. Endler (Eds.), *Personality at the crossroads: Current issues in interactional psychology* (pp. 3–35). Hillsdale, NJ: Lawrence Erlbaum Associates.

Marx, M. (1956). Sources of confusion in attitudes toward clinical theory. *Journal of General Psychology, 55,* 19–30.

McArdle, J. J. (1982). *Structural equation modeling of an individual system: Preliminary results from "A case study of episodic alcoholism."* Unpublished manuscript, Psychology Department, University of Denver.

McCall, R. B. (1977). Challenges to a science of developmental psychology. *Child Development, 48,* 333–344.

Mischel, W. (1968). *Personality and assessment.* New York: John Wiley.

Mischel, W. (1979). On the interface of cognition and personality: Beyond the person–situation debate. *American Psychologist, 34,* 740–754.

Molenaar, P. C. M. (1985). A dynamic factor model for the analysis of multivariate time series. *Psychometrika, 50,* 181–202.

Mueller, J. H. (1976). Anxiety and cue utilization in human learning and memory. In M. Zuckerman & C. D. Spielberger (Eds.), *Emotions and anxiety: New concepts, methods, and applications* (pp. 197–229). Hillsdale, NJ: Lawrence Erlbaum Associates.

Nesselroade, J. R. (1977). Issues in studying developmental change in adults from a multivariate perspective. In J. E. Birren & K. W. Schaie (Eds.), *Handbook of the psychology of aging* (pp. 59–69). New York: Van Nostrand Reinhold.

Nesselroade, J. R. (1983). Temporal selection and factorial invariance in the study of change and development. In P. B. Baltes & O. G. Brim, Jr. (Eds.), *Life-span development and behavior* (Vol. 5, pp. 59–87). New York: Academic Press.

Nesselroade, J. R. (1984). Concepts of intraindividual variability and change: Impressions of Cattell's influence on life-span developmental psychology. *Multivariate Behavioral Research, 19,* 269–286.

Nesselroade, J. R. (1986). Selection and generalization in investigations of interrelationships among variables: Some commentary on aging research. *Educational Gerontology.*

Nesselroade, J. R. (in press). Sampling and generalizability: Adult development and aging research issues examined within the general methodological framework of selection. In K. W. Schaie, R. T. Campbell, W. M. Meredith, & S. C. Rawlings (Eds.), *Methodological issues in aging research.* New York: Springer.

Nesselroade, J. R., & Baltes, P. B. (1974). Adolescent personality development and historical change: 1970–1972. *Monographs of the Society for Research in Child Development, 39*(1, Whole No. 154).

Nesselroade, J. R., & Bartsch, T. W. (1977). Multivariate perspectives on the construct validity of the trait–state distinction. In R. B. Cattell & R. M. Dreger (Eds.), *Handbook of modern personality theory* (pp. 221–238). Washington, DC: Hemisphere.

Nesselroade, J. R., & Cable, D. G. (1974). "Sometimes, it's okay to factor difference scores"—the separation of trait and state anxiety. *Multivariate Behavioral Research, 9,* 273–282.

Nesselroade, J. R., & Ford, D. H. (1985). P-technique comes of age: Multivariate, replicated, single-subject designs for research on older adults. *Research on Aging, 7,* 46–80.

Nesselroade, J. R., Mitteness, L. S., & Thompson, L. K. (1984). Short-term changes in anxiety, fatigue, and other psychological states in older adulthood. *Research on Aging, 6,* 3–23.

Nesselroade, J. R., Pruchno, R., & Jacobs, A. (1986). Reliability versus stability in the measurement of psychological states: An illustration with anxiety measures. *Psychologische Beitraege, 28,* 255–264.

Nesselroade, J. R., & Reese, H. W. (Eds.). (1973). *Life-span developmental psychology: Methodological issues.* New York: Academic Press.

Overton, D. A. (1974). Experimental methods for the study of state-dependent learning. *Federation Proceedings, 33,* 1800–1813.

Patrick, A. W., & Zuckerman, M. (1977). An application of the state–trait concept to the need for achievement. *Journal of Research in Personality, 11,* 459–465.

Patterson, G. R., & Bechtel, G. C. (1977). Formulating situational environment in relation to states and traits. In R. B. Cattell & R. M. Dreger (Eds.), *Handbook of modern personality theory* (pp. 254–268). Washington, DC: Hemisphere.

Roberts, M. L., & Nesselroade, J. R. (1986). State variability in locus of control measures: P-technique factor analyses of short-term change. *Journal of Research in Personality, 20,* 529–545.

Sealy, A. P., & Cattell, R. B. (1966). Adolescent personality trends in primary factors measured on the 16 P.F. and the HSPQ questionnaires through ages 11 to 23. *British Journal of Social and Clinical Psychology, 5,* 172–184.

Singer, J. L., & Singer, D. G. (1972). Personality. *Annual Review of Psychology, 23,* 375–412.

Skinner, B. F. (1953). *Science and human behavior.* New York: Macmillan.

Spielberger, C. D., Gorsuch, R. L., & Lushene, R. (1969). *The state–trait anxiety inventory (STAI) test manual, form X.* Palo Alto, CA: Consulting Psychologists Press.

Speilberger, C. D., Lushene, R. E., & McAdoo, W. G. (1977). Theory and measurement of anxiety states. In R. B. Cattell & R. M. Dreger (Eds.), *Handbook of modern personality theory* (pp. 239–253). Washington, DC: Hemisphere.

Thorne, F. C. (1966). Theory of the psychological state. *Journal of Clinical Psychology, 22,* 127–135.

Willis, S. L. (1985). Toward an educational psychology of the older adult learner: Intellectual and cognitive bases. In J. E. Birren & K. W. Schaie (Eds.), *Handbook of the psychology of aging* (pp. 818–847). New York: Van Nostrand.

Zevon, M. A., & Tellegen, A. (1982). The structure of mood change: An idiographic/nomothetic analysis. *Journal of Personality and Social Psychology, 43,* 111–122.

Zuckerman, M. (1976). General and situation-specific traits and states: New approaches to assessment and other constructs. In M. Zuckerman & C. D. Spielberger (Eds.), *Emotions and anxiety: New concepts, methods, and applications* (pp. 133–174). Hillsdale, NJ: Lawrence Erlbaum Associates.

Zuckerman, M. (1983). The distinctions between trait and state scales is not arbitrary: Comment on Allen and Potkay's "On the arbitrary distinction between traits and states." *Journal of Personality and Social Psychology, 44,* 1083–1086.

Zuckerman, M., & Lubin, B. (1965). *Manual for the multiple affect adjective check list.* San Diego, CA: Educational and Industrial Testing Service.

Stability and Change in Self over the Life Course

L. Edward Wells and Sheldon Stryker
DEPARTMENT OF SOCIOLOGY
INDIANA UNIVERSITY

Abstract

From a symbolic interactionist perspective, the *self* is a central feature for understanding human experience. The explanation of behavior is premised on its essential reflexivity and intentionality. At the same time, the self is necessarily a *social* process, situated within social, physical, and temporal orders which provide essential parts of its substance and meaning. In these terms, symbolic interactionist and life-course perspectives provide complementary frameworks for the analysis of human experience and behavior. The former provides a systematic means to deal with both the socially common and the individually unique features of human biographies, without resorting to either deterministic or aleatory accounts. The life-course perspective provides a natural and coherent framework for dealing with the inherent temporality of the self and for interpreting the patterns of change and constancy that characterize people's selves over time. An explicit synthesis of these perspectives remains undeveloped and incomplete, however, making a systematic explication of the relationship between self and life-course processes especially important. *Identity theory,* as a specific theoretical development from structural symbolic interactionism, provides an apt framework for examining the connections of the self to the life course. The life course is viewed sociologically as the systematic movement in and out of social roles with age—a process which reflects a variable mixture of biological, cultural, historical, and interactional conditions. In aggregate, it reflects the successive choices made by persons as they make transitions between age-linked categories. Correspondingly, identity theory views the operation of the self in terms of the interactional choices which persons make as a consequence of their social roles and relationships. In these terms, individual selves and biographies will reflect general sequences of identity *transitions* (movement into and out of roles) and identity *transformations* (changes in the meaning and salience of ongoing role-identities) over the life course. Thus, this chapter explicates a synthesis of identity theory and life course ideas to examine how the process and content of self may be linked to the social structures and categories of aging. Finally, the chapter focuses specifically on the ways in which life-course passage may affect the identity content of people's selves, the structural organization of selves (e.g., scope, permeability, salience hierarchies), and the important processes of self-evaluation and self-esteem.

I. Introduction

How are the social and psychological processes that constitute the phenomenon of the self affected—initiated, conditioned, stabilized, altered, or ended—by events that make up the life course of individuals? How may the content of self be shaped by the timing and sequencing of these events, as they are organized on either an individual or collective level by the interplay of social structural, interactional, and age-related (including biological) variables? These questions indicate our concern: to suggest the potential utility for sociology and for social psychology—as measured by both theoretical and research fertility—of examining the self as a consequence of life-course dynamics.

Our concern is also to suggest some of the reciprocal side of the life-course/self relationship. The thesis is straightforward: Just as self theorists benefit from viewing the self in the context of the life course,[1] so life-course theorists benefit from being more explicitly sensitive to the self and to role of the self in organizing the life course. Life-course theorists are increasingly aware that no few patterns of timing or ordering of life course events will obtain for all or even most persons in any given society (e.g., Atchley, 1975; Neugarten & Hagestad, 1976; Runyan, 1984); in fact, very considerable individual-level variability is the rule. Incorporating self into thinking about the life course is the means for a principled theoretical account of such ''idiosyncratic'' variation. That account recognizes that the human being is something other than an automaton passively responding to social and/or biological imperatives, yet without resorting to randomness (or aleatory models) as a way to reconcile theory with observed reality.

[1]Life-course considerations have not been absent from works on the self; examples of the incorporating of such considerations include Gordon (1971, 1976), Rosenberg (1979), Bush and Simmons (1981), Mortimer and Simmons (1978). However, interest generally has been limited to self at particular junctures of the life course: to childhood, adolescence, or old age, or to particular points of transition, such as leaving school or retirement.

II. A Structural Symbolic Interactionist Framework

Our approach to the reciprocal relationship of self and life course is defined by a framework and a theory. The framework is that of a structural symbolic interactionism (Stryker. 1980, in press-a) while the theory represents a specific substantive development from that framework—i.e., identity theory (Stryker & Serpe, 1982).[2] The specific implications of this theory and framework will be developed later; however, we note at the outset some essential considerations.

The symbolic interactionist framework develops from the premise that human behavior is fundamentally *minded* and *situated* activity, and from the argument that an adequate description or explanation of human behavior must take these features into account. To say that behavior is "minded" is to recognize that it can be conscious[3] (involving active awareness of the elements in situations of interaction—persons, things, and events—as objects), interpretive (involving responses to those elements in terms of their meanings rather than simply as physical cues), and intentional (involving anticipations, purposes, and choices). The critical implication of the minded character of behavior is that human conduct can be and frequently is reflexive in substantial and important degree; it involves a self, or alternatively phrased, it involves a process in which persons become objects of their own consciousness and activity. People can and often do take themselves into account—are both subject and object—in the social production of behavior. This is what we mean by "the self"—in simple generic terms, the capacity for and the process of reflexive experience.[4]

[2]We cannot provide a complete discussion of either the structural symbolic interactionist framework or identity theory here; we must be content with a selective discussion of the elements of each that are particularly relevant to the task at hand. Also, we must explicitly recognize that there are various symbolic interactionist frameworks, not a single well-defined position. The various frameworks, however, have much in common; these commonalities are emphasized here. For reviews of symbolic interactionism in its various guises as well as for statements of a structural symbolic interactionist position and of identity theory, see Stryker (1980) and Stryker and Statham (1985).

[3]There is no claim that human behavior is invariably minded—conscious, interpretive and intentional—only that it is frequently so and that minded behavior is a distinctive and important human characteristic. Inferentially, then, there is no claim that human behavior invariably involves self (is always reflexive), only that it often and vitally does.

[4]This description of "self" is both more restricted and more general than in many discussions of the self. It is more specific and limited than using self to refer to the "entire person from a psychological perspective" (McCrae & Costa, 1982). Such a conceptualization expands the idea of self beyond reflexivity to include the whole of personality, stretching it so thinly that it defies rigorous analysis. On the other hand, the self for us is broader and more inclusive than the "self-concept" (referring to the particular perceptions, identities, and attitudes which persons hold about themselves). As we are using it, the self is a generic concept, encompassing both the *processes* of reflexive activity and the specific *contents* (or products) of this experience. When using the language of self without modification we mean both the process and the (temporary or enduring) content that

To say that behavior is "situated" is to underscore a basic contention that human behavior is invariably embedded in some larger contexts or fields that provide essential parts of the meaning and substance of that behavior. Human activity cannot be isolated from the contexts in which it is embedded without distorting its meaning and therefore its comprehension. This activity is not simply framed by its contexts but is substantively constituted by them. Consequently, the understanding and explanation of human behavior requires taking into account the contexts within which it occurs.

A. THE CONTEXTUALITY OF ACTION

Traditionally, symbolic interactionism emphasized the *social* (interactional) context of behavior, focusing on the immediate situations and momentary encounters within which behavior is produced. A structural symbolic interactionism broadens the vision of the social context to incorporate the larger cultural and structural conditions that shape the immediate situations and momentary encounters (Stryker, 1980, 1983). Clearly, such social contexts are necessary concerns in any analysis of human behavior as the activity of purposive, symbol-creating and -using, culture-bearing creatures. Just as clearly, there are other sorts of contexts within which behavior is simultaneously embedded, and these must also be taken into account in any reasonably complete analysis of that behavior. While less attention has been directed by symbolic interactionists to these other contextual issues, recent and emerging literatures indicate that this is changing.[5]

One such context is the physical-spatial: Actions and experiences are embedded in space, in a literal sense "taking place" within a physical environment only partly reducible to social and cultural definition. Recent analyses of places and physical objects as elements of self-identities (e.g., Hormuth, 1984; Proshansky, Fabian, & Kaminoff, 1983; Rochberg–Halton, 1984), as well as developments within "human geography" (e.g., Tuan, 1982; LaGory, 1982) or microecology (e.g., Ball, 1973; Rowles & Ohta, 1983) provide examples of a developing concern with the impact of physical context on social action.

---

results from the process. When necessary to draw the distinction, we will use the terms self-processes and self-concepts.

[5]The term "context" generally is used by sociologists to refer holistically to the operation of all variables in single situations or environments of behavior. Our discussion of social, temporal, physical/spatial, and biological contexts separates out facets of such environments and views them as constituting distinctive analytical frames for the relation of self to life course. In this chapter, we emphasize the social and temporal contexts as most immediately constitutive of what we consider the life course. We do not deny the clear importance of physical and biological issues for a life-course view but must accept some practical limits on what can be addressed in a single essay.

Another context is biological, recognizing that behavior is always "embodied." It is the product of living organisms whose anatomical and physiological features affect significantly the possibility or the probabilities for particular actions. In contrast with the either–or quality of traditional debate about "nature versus nurture" and early interactionist dogma that radically deemphasized biological considerations, recent analyses suggest a fluid and transactional relation between biological and social variables. viewing neither as preeminent or determinant and recognizing that each impinges on the other, jointly constraining human experience. The biological context figures importantly in recent interactionist analyses of emotion (e.g., Hochschild, 1983; Kemper, 1978), or of gender and sexuality (e.g., Laws & Schwartz, 1977; Rossi, 1985; Victor, 1978).

A third contextual dimension is time, because actions and events are finite occurrences taking place within temporal orders. They occur within ongoing chronological, biographical, and historical streams, the location and timing of events within these streams affecting what happens, why and how it happens, and its consequences. Human activity is distinguished by being not only "in time" (i.e., subject to time in some objective sense) but also "aware of time" (i.e., responsive to the social and psychological meaning of time in phenomenal terms). This feature directly implicates interest in a life-span or life-course perspective, because such a perspective reflects an insistence upon explicitly considering the temporal framework of human experience. While relatively unappreciated and undeveloped,[6] time and temporality have long been fundamental elements of interactionism, for example, in the emphasis on social process (rather than state) permeating the writings of early interactionists from the Scottish moral philosophers (Bryson, 1945) to the pragmatic philosophers (Dewey, 1940; James, 1890). We note especially Mead's (1932, 1938) analyses of the past and the present as phenomenal aspects of behavior and his emphases upon evolutionary emergence (Mead, 1934). The interactionist framework does not simply provide a license for linking the self to the life course; it requires that linking.

The symbolic interactionist framework directs us to see behavior as the product of ongoing interplay between society and self, understanding society as a congeries of symbolic interactions based in a consensually named and categorized world of events and involving the co-orientation of active, self-conscious persons. A structural symbolic interactionism employs the interaction–self–be-

[6]Traditional symbolic interactionism, given its focus on the immediate situation of interaction, tended to view temporality as bounded by the initiation and ending of an episode of interaction (Strauss, 1978; Goffman, 1959, 1967). Structural symbolic interactionism, with its emphasis on the larger social structural contexts within which episodes of interaction occur, opens the way for a consideration of broader expanses of historical as well as biographical time.

havior paradigm, but embeds that social process in wider contexts, that include social structural, physical–spatial, biological, and temporal contexts. It brings this seemingly disparate set of variables to bear theoretically in a more-or-less unified account of human behavior: It visualizes their impact as occurring through interaction, patterned and recurrent as well as momentary and emergent, by altering the probabilities of particular kinds of people interacting in particular ways with particular interactional resources for particular purposes. From the standpoint of a structural symbolic interactionism, a key to understanding and explaining behavior as meaningful activity is to be found in the self; a key to understanding and explaining variation in self is to be found in the forms and content of social interaction; and a key to understanding and explaining interaction is to be found in the contextual constraints within which interaction occurs. The language of constraints does not imply a determinism: Biology is not destiny, nor is sociology, but the probability of becoming a surgeon is still altered by the fact of maleness or femaleness for both biologically related and social reasons.

B. IDENTITY THEORY: BASIC CONCEPTS

Identity theory (Stryker, 1981, in press-a) emphasizes linkages among particular factors of society, self, and behavior. The behavior it seeks to explain is *choice* among courses or lines of behavior where the latter represent differential expectations attached to or symbolic of various social roles. Identity theory is concerned with understanding rather stable and enduring lines of activity as well as more occasional actions. Its prototypical question is: Why is it that on weekend afternoons on which it is possible to choose among these alternatives, one man opts for taking his daughter to the zoo, a second spends his time at the office catching up on work, and a third plays golf with his buddies?

According to identity theory, the answer to this kind of question is to be found substantially in the relative salience of various identities among the self-concepts of interactants. That is, the content of the self is conceptualized in identity theory as partly comprised by a set of identities or internalized role designations,[7] as many identities as the positions occupied and the roles enacted by a person in organized sets of social relationships. Further, these identities are conceptualized as being organized into a hierarchy of salience, where the latter is defined by the

[7]Identity theory does not assert that cognitive representations of roles are all there is to self-concepts, only that such cognitive representations are a behaviorally relevant modality of self whose importance can be exploited in a systematic way. Further, the theory not only recognizes that there are other modalities—e.g., in the form of affect and in the form of cognitions not strictly tied to roles—of self, but aspires to incorporate these other dimensions into the theory itself. For an early and very limited instance of this, see Stryker (1968); for a latter and better developed instance, see Stryker (in press-a).

different probabilities of identities being invoked (or "coming into play") in a given situation or across a number of situations. Identity theory proposes that the probability of a particular choice (as opposed to possible alternative choices) reflects the locations in a salience hierarchy of the identities that the choices symbolize or represent.

Identity theory takes matters a step further by proposing that the location of an identity within a salience hierarchy will reflect the social commitments of persons to the role that underlies that identity, where commitment represents the degree to which important social relationships are premised on particular identities. Commitment is defined by the social and personal costs entailed in no longer fulfilling a role that is the basis for a given identity. The theory recognizes two potentially independent forms of such commitments: (a) interactional commitment, referring to the number or extensiveness of relationships involving that identity; and (b) affective commitment, referring to the affect or intensiveness attached to the potentially lost relationships and activities (Stryker, in press-a).[8]

As a final element, identity theory recognizes that interpersonal commitments are constrained by the larger social structure that brings together or keeps people apart and that affords or forecloses the possibilities for various kinds of activities. The larger social structure does not determine but does importantly shape the probabilities that different choices will be made. It represents the framework of opportunities, resources, meanings, and values within which commitments are established, maintained, and foregone.

C. IDENTITY THEORY: THE SELF AND THE LIFE COURSE

The theoretical utility of invoking identity theory for viewing the self in the life course becomes evident at this juncture. It provides a way to delimit meaningfully the intersection between two exceedingly broad concepts. The "life course," as a broad, heuristic gloss for all the events and experiences that regularly happen to people between birth and death, is too complex to be adequately comprehended by any one view. Innumerable perspectives are possible; each highlights certain features and ignores others (Runyan, 1984). None is inclusive or preeminent; the analytical value of each is relative to the specific questions it addresses (along with the kinds of answers it provides). The pre-

[8]The connections between the concept of commitment as elaborated in identity theory and the concepts of "role set" and "role involvement" as elaborated by Merton (1957) are apparent. However, we forgo an explication of the connections at this point, given our particular focus in this chapter. Our emphasis here is on the "complete role set" corresponding to occupancy of a particular position (or status, in Merton's terms) rather than on internal divisions or structures within a role set. Identity theory has dealt with the latter issues using the concept of "structural overlap" (see Stryker, 1980).

dominant sociological view (e.g., Bush & Simmons, 1981; George, 1980; Neugarten & Datan, 1973; Riley, Johnson, & Foner, 1972) represents the life course as a matter of the successive enterings and leavings of social roles through the life span.[9] This provides a "structural" view of the life course which we share. Clearly, the life course viewed in this way involves patterns of extension, contraction, and alteration of the personnel implicated in networks of social interaction. From the standpoint of identity theory, such structurally induced changes in social relationships must impact self—particularly in the form of the structure of identity salience—and this in turn must help us to understand and to explain lines of action taken by persons as they move through the life course.

The invocation of structural symbolic interactionism and identity theory limits our analysis of the self. The self is an important construct from a variety of theoretical perspectives and in a variety of more specific and focused theories, among them, for example, cognitive schematic theories (Kihlstrom & Cantor, 1984; Markus & Sentis, 1982), social behavioristic frameworks (Bandura, 1977; Bem, 1972), social comparison theories (Suls & Mullen, 1982), cybernetic theory (Carver & Scheier, 1981), field theory (Wicklund & Gollwitzer, 1982), self-esteem theories (Brockner, 1983; Kaplan, 1980), and developmental theories (Edelstein & Noam, 1982; Leahy, 1983). Variables flowing out of these alternative perspectives provide an exceedingly large and rich set of conceptual tools with which to examine the self in the life course. Indeed, they provide an embarrassment of riches, too extensive and diverse to be encompassed meaningfully in any simple review. Our presumption of a particular theoretical perspective limits the variables and ideas that we consider, but usefully grounds our analysis. At this point, a more catholic statement of the reciprocal links between life course and self seems unwarranted.

Even within the restrictions implied by our decision, we must disclaim comprehensiveness of attention: There is a very large number of aspects, elements, and dimensions of self or self-related attributes relevant from a symbolic interactionist frame, attention to which we forgo. We do not discuss these aspects, not

[9]The life-course/life-span distinction is difficult to maintain as a clear, inviolable dichotomy, as Bush and Simmons (1981) note. The differences are matters of degree rather than of kind, of relative emphasis on individual versus social frames in characterizing the shapes of people's lives. From this perspective, a life span represents more of an individual project (reflecting developmental sequences and psychological operations), more of an endogenous personal structure which an individual has or experiences. In contrast, a life course represents more of a social agenda or timetable for life events (reflecting age grades, age norms, and age roles), an exogenous social sequence which individuals "move through" during their lives. This distinction reflects the differing disciplinary origins for these ideas—life-span study evolving out of developmental psychology while life-course analysis evolved out of sociological concern with the social structure of aging and age stratification. Despite their overlap and affinity, the life-span/life-course differences seem important enough to us that we will try to maintain the distinction here.

because they are uninteresting, but because we cannot say much about them at this point. We also take for granted in this chapter the relevance of self for behavior, and do not seek to demonstrate that relevance. There exists a reasonably large, reasonably sophisticated body of empirical literature, inspired by a variety of theoretical frames including symbolic interactionism, that makes the necessary case; and we refer the reader to that literature: Gecas (1982), Lynch, Norem–Hebeisen, and Gergen (1981), Rosenberg (1979, 1981), Suls (1982) Suls and Greenwald (1983), Wegner and Vallacher (1980), Wylie (1979).

D. A RELATED APPROACH: ACTION THEORY

As already suggested, the approach taken in this chapter, defined by identity theory and its parent, the structural symbolic interactionist framework, has a distinctively American intellectual heritage. While its sources can be traced to European social thought, specifically to Adam Smith, David Hume, Adam Ferguson and others who collectively have been labeled the Scottish moral philosophers (Bryson, 1945), its essential development has been through American pragmatic philosophy and American social psychology as practiced by sociologically trained successors to George Herbert Mead.

This approach, more or less uniquely American in its evolution, is hardly unique in many of its fundamentals. It shares an outlook with intellectual traditions, both American and European, that have evolved more or less independently of it, each with its own relatively distinctive sources and contributors along the way. It is useful to recognize this fact, for recognizing it suggests the important inference that it is not some quirk of a given intellectual tradition that has led to its assumptions, conceptualizations, methodological posture, and theoretical propositions. Rather, it suggests that there is something in the common object of thinking and study that accounts for the commonalities of the diverse traditions. Recognizing this fact is important as well because it can serve to facilitate communication across intellectual boundaries that might otherwise remain inviolate.

By the same token, it is useful to recognize that the differing intellectual traditions incorporate at least somewhat disparate elements. Recognition of convergence should not be permitted to obscure important differences, for then communication can involve mutual learning as well as mutual self-congratulation.

We cannot undertake a comparison between the approach that underlies this chapter and the variety of related yet different alternative approaches it is possible to take to the relation of life course and self. To do that would involve a discussion of a more traditional symbolic interactionism, phenomenology, ethnomethodology, ethogeny, "*verstehende soziologie,*" "sociorationalism," interpretive sociology, hermeneutics, among other approaches to social life and individual behavior. Obviously, and if nothing else, space limits preclude that discussion.

However, many of the strands suggested by the labels for diverse intellectual traditions just given appear to be coming together under the rubric of *action theory,* or an action perspective. While there are American sources and contributors, contemporary action theory is largely an European emergent, with at least some roots in a self-conscious European departure from a social psychology as practiced by American psychologists (Israel & Tajfel, 1972), with other roots in Marx, in Weber, in British language philosophy, as well as in more orthodox developmental and social psychology and sociology. Representations of this emerging action perspective are to be found in the sociological work of Giddens (1984) and the social psychological work of Harre (1982) and Secord (1982). Most immediately pertinent as an instance of the action perspective, because of its application to a life-span developmental psychology, is the work of Brandtstädter (1984). Using Brandtstädter's (1984) presentation of the action perspective, we proceed with a comparison of that perspective with the approach described in this chapter, which incorporates structural symbolic interactionism and identity theory. The premises and arguments presented are essentially interdependent and are not listed in order of importance or generality.

Both the approach of this chapter and the action perspective contain strong presumptions of human agency. A view of human behavior as agentic argues an important degree of voluntarism, of the possibility of choice, in that behavior. Such a view does not necessarily reject all conventional conceptions of causality, and can coexist with the recognition of serious constraint on the exercise of choice. Nevertheless, it implies the need for models that incorporate the proactive human, and depart from strict mechanistic, deterministic formulations. In the context of discussions of life course and life span, the common emphasis on agency implies that lives are not something that people have but rather that which they do; consciousness, personality, human experience and social order all are states of doing rather than being, constituted by processes and activities.

A second common theme involves viewing action as purposive or goal-directed, often oriented to distant or long-term ends. Such a view, clearly, implies an emphasis on persons as rational beings. That emphasis, however, does not extend to ignoring the potential of affect in accounts of human behavior or social interaction.

Agency and intentionality imply reflexivity. That is, both approaches suggest that human action folds back on itself, that actors monitor their own actions as well as the actions of others, taking both into account in the course of their social behavior. Self-consciousness, self-control, and self-direction thus become characteristic of human behavior.

Intelligibility is yet another common theme. Action is seen as being meaningful, as having significance in Mead's terms. A subjective, interpretive dimension is thus an intrinsic, defining quality of human action. Intelligibility also implies an emphasis on the accountability of action: Action has a normative character and is to be understood with reference to rules, norms, and roles.

Still another commonality is a virtual equation of action and interaction, in the specific sense that all individual action—by virtue of the social bases of meaning, of intelligibility—is understood to be embedded in and constituted by a social context which is interpersonally, social structurally, culturally, and historically specified. There is, then, a view of action as simultaneously individual and social, as well as a view of social systems as simultaneously the media and the product of individual and social action. The individual and the social are taken both to constitute and reproduce one another. There is also the recognition that action is constrained and mediated by social structural and cultural—especially linguistic—systems; language is taken to be the instrument making human action possible and producing (as well as exemplifying) that action. To reemphasize the interdependency of these characteristic themes of both the framework of this chapter and the action perspective, language is taken to provide or make possible the reflexivity of action as well as its normative character.

An emphasis on temporality, on shorter- or longer-term process, represents another common theme. All action is understood to occur in a space–time nexus; all action and knowledge is understood to be historically conditioned.

This last implies one final similarity to be remarked: Both the action perspective and the framework of this chapter recognize a dimension of historical specificity in human activity. Nevertheless, and despite such recognition, both adopt a "quasi-nomological" stance, assuming that it is reasonable to aspire to fairly general knowledge about the generating conditions of human action and interaction that in important degree transcend the specifics of historically and culturally generated events.

Obviously, then, the framework underlying this chapter and the action framework have a good deal in common. There are also differences of some significance, albeit differences more in degree than in kind, apart from the separate intellectual heritages already noted. These differences are largely conceptual and have to do mainly with specifications introduced by identity theory into highly abstract conceptualizations present in the action perspective. They reflect also the level of explicitness with which these more specific conceptualizations are recognized and utilized in theoretical, "causal" arguments.

More specifically, the approach of this chapter contains an explicit recognition of the significance of social structure, both large-scale and small, in constraining and channeling the actions that persons actually undertake (as differentiated from those they conceivably could take or even those that they may consider taking). It also contains a more concrete and nuanced view of social structure than is found in Brandtstädter's formulation of the action perspective, incorporating societal-level social differentiations and organizational structures, social networks, and structures of dyadic interaction into its theoretical statements. In general, the view of social structure appearing in action-theoretical statements tends to the somewhat more ephemeral, frequently remaining on the level of general assertions about the import of the "social," or of "society," in human activities. One consequence of a more explicit and nuanced treatment of social structure is to permit more precise propositions regarding its causal significance in such activities as well as more precise research examination of the validity of these propositions. In addition, social structure in the approach taken in this chapter tends to be seen as exercising more constraint, as having somewhat more external, causal force over human affairs than is true in the action perspective.

Also recognized more explicitly, as well as accorded more theoretical and research consideration, in the frame of this chapter as compared with the action perspective are the correlative concepts of role and self. These concepts are often only implicitly contained in statements of the action perspective. Their explicit presence as well as their postulated interdependence provide a major link between a structural symbolic interactionism and identity theory. In other words, they enable movement from the level of general framework to specific theory with rather immediate consequences in the form of empirical expectations open to research evidence. The same point can be made in reverse in respect to the shortcomings of the action perspective as it is thus far formulated: The concepts that permit a specification of the society–person link remain somewhat mysterious in action perspective formulations.

That these differences exist are not surprising, since they reflect the differing purposes underlying the development of a structural symbolic interactionism and identity theory as compared with the action perspective. It should be clear, in any event, that these differences announce no fundamental incompatibility; rather, they suggest only what it may be that those taking an action perspective can find useful in the approach of this chapter.

III. The Relevance of Self for Life-Course Theorizing

While our attention is primarily on the impact of life-course events on the self, we wish to consider also the reciprocal import of self for the life course. In particular, what does or can the concept of self, as explicated within an interactionist framework, contribute to life-course analysis as a substantive body of theory and research? Much of our answer to this question is couched at a very general, almost metatheoretical, level for two reasons. First, it is at that level that thinking about self can have a functional yet immediate impact. Second, while a good deal of extant theory, conceptualization, and research permits us to explicate how the life course operates through the self to organize individual biographies, there is far less research indicating how biographical conditions operate through the self to organize the broader life course.[10] In principle, we could ''simply reverse'' the explanatory course that leads from larger social process to personal experience; in practice, that proves extraordinarily difficult.

Theorizing about how the life course—the social structures of aging and age grading that organize movement into and out of social roles—links to the psychological structures and behavioral events in individual biographies has in general operated with a ''black box.'' In common with other efforts in the arena of ''social structure and personality,'' attention has focused on the structure of the life course and on the ultimate, individual-level personality or behavioral correlates of that structure, without specifying the mechanisms by which the former works its impact on the latter. Opening up the ''black box'' (without doing so we can have no causal explanation of that impact) involves what House (1981) has termed the ''proximity principle.'' Social structures do not directly impinge on individuals, whether these social structures are in the form of social class, the organization of power in a society, or structures developed out of age-graded processes; rather, social structures affect individuals by conditioning the kinds of interactions and relationships within which individuals exist as social actors. Thus, accounting for the impact of the social structure of life courses means explicating ''proximate'' interactional events through which individual lives are actually lived. The concept of self provides an important component of the interactional interface between society and person.

It is important, because the self is necessary to account fully for the process of ''internalization'' as the means by which social norms are transformed into individual goals, dispositions, and meanings. Much human activity is not simply and directly under external social control but is autonomously or ''self''-produced. Where human conduct cannot be accounted for as simply a collection of momentary, automatic, habituated movements prompted by external cues and schedules, reflexivity and intentionality must be incorporated into theoretical explanations of that conduct. This requirement magnifies as the conduct being explained extends over long temporal spans and across varying sets of activities: Whereas momentary actions might be explained by impulse or reflex, accounting for the appearance of intentional, long-range plans and purposive sequences of discontinuous behaviors clearly demand some form of reflexive agency. Humans as biological organisms become ''persons'' (in the sense of competent. acting participants in the ongoing social order) by developing selves, and thus are able to engage in minded, reflective behavior, to take into account the perspectives of others, to coordinate their behaviors with others, and to participate in complex

[10]Extant work is mostly restricted to the impact of individuals' experience on their selves (e.g., Bem, 1972), rather than on how self-processes may aggregate to affect larger social structures. For nascent attempts at the latter, see Collins, 1981; Giddens, 1984; Stokes and Hewitt, 1976; Stryker and Statham, 1985.

institutionalized social processes. While individual, these selves are thoroughly social products. As Mead (1934) depicted them, they represent the incorporation of the social process within the conduct of the individual, the process by which social order is reproduced in individual identity, consciousness, and behavior. The relation of the life course (as with other social structures) to individual persons necessarily implicates the self.

In addition, the self represents a mechanism for a principled indeterminacy in the process through which the social order shapes the content of individual lives and personality, providing a way to avoid the problems of a deterministic or oversocialized conception of persons as mere replicas of social order, a conception which frequently plagues sociological accounts. Without intentionality and personal agency, individual variation and uniqueness represent only slippage, error, or noise in the socialization process; they are not theoretically intelligible. The self, in the form of an active, ongoing I–me dialogue, provides a theoretically meaningful source for novelty, emergence, and individuality. While the self includes a "me" as an acquired and socialized object, it also includes an "I" as an impulsive, creative subject. The self cannot be reduced to either; it represents the ongoing interaction between the two. This conceptualization is readily reflected in the idea that behavior includes some (variable) element of *choice*—that behavior is not merely conditioned reaction but also reflects selectivity and agency. With the development of mind and self, this activity becomes self-conscious, self-controlled, and "willful"; it is socially orderly yet it retains a creative, unpredictable element. The corollary of social indeterminacy in this sense is individual autonomy. The paradoxical and dialectical character of the self provides an essential means to comprehend both the social determination of personality and its indeterminacy and uniqueness.

Beyond providing the analytical bases for an explanation of the indeterminacy in individual lives, the self helps to account for the reciprocality between the life course (as a social order) and the person (as an individual being). Life changes are not all exogenously caused, but may be substantially self-produced. They result from a person's goals, feelings, perceptions, interpretations, aspirations, and evaluations. For instance, decisions to shift jobs or occupations in mid-career, go back to school, have another child, or even take up jogging will in part reflect the self-perceived fit between where one is and where one aspires to be. Adolescents may make occupational or educational choices that are at odds with the sensible paths chosen for them by parents and counselors but which seem more self-relevant. Such choices (reflecting self-values, self-definitions, self-expectations) clearly can have biographical consequences for the person making them. They can close off and open up a range of subsequent choices, activities, and possibilities available to the person.

Individuals not only help shape their own biographies, but they also affect the life course as a larger process constructed out of many individual life choices. In interactional terms, choices made by an individual alter the biographies of other persons, conditioning their options and opportunities through the material and social interdependencies that link people's lives together. One person's choices can change the pattern of resources and experiences available to spouse, parents, children, relatives, friends, even strangers. In more macrosocial terms, the choices made by individuals combine to form jointly the larger structures of society, since the social order must be produced and reproduced in the (inter)actions of individuals, even as it constrains these (inter)actions. As individuals make new or altered choices, the aggregate result of these choices is a new social ordering—a systematic change in the life course as a broader social phenomenon. As individuals decide to postpone having children (as a result of self-defining goals, expectations, and perceptions), the molar effect of such choices may be an increase in the age at which persons customarily have children and a shift in the age norms for parenthood. Where the self constitutes the agency of selection, intention, and choice, it becomes a mechanism through which both social order and social change are produced in individual lives.

The presence of the self in human activity is variable, not constant. There is variation in the degree to which persons respond to themselves reflexively (i.e., act self-consciously and mindfully) in the course of their behaviors. The self as reflexive consciousness is absent from some and perhaps much human behavior.[11] Why can this variability in the "existence" of self as well as its manifestation in the range of behaviors of the person be clarified by locating self in the life course? Often overlooked by interactionists promoting an action conception of human behavior, much human behavior is habitual and not minded. As the pragmatic philosophers noted (providing the foundations for symbolic interactionism), thinking arises in response to blocked activity and to the emergence of a problem in the course of conduct. When problems occur, habit will not suffice to complete activity or to continue a course of conduct: thinking, searching out alternatives via symbolic manipulations, is required to do so. The reflexive thinking that brings self into being is premised on the disruption of habit. Where habit suffices, self does not enter behavior and in a sense does not even exist. Self, then, is a variable process; that is, the ability to engage in such reflexive

[11]People do not always behave in an autonomous, conscious, creative way; much behavior might be viewed as automatic, conditioned, or overlearned habits. Correspondingly, we are not suggesting that all (or even most) behavior is freely "chosen" but simply that we are most concerned with what happens when choices do come up. Clearly, across situations and activities, autonomy and mindfulness of behavior will be variably present. Part of the theoretical problem of a social psychology is to explicate the occasions and sources of such variability. The issue of when and in what ways behavior can be regarded as "minded" or conscious is itself a controversial matter on which numerous views are possible; a substantial debate exists on this issue per se (see for example, Bem, 1972; Carver & Scheier, 1981; Harre, 1982; Langer, 1978; Secord, 1982).

behavior as well as the propensity to do so is tied to processes that extend and evolve across the life course.

In principle, choice, while indeterminate, is not in itself unpredictable—at least in a probabilistic sense. Indeed, identity theory takes personal and behavioral choice as its object of explanation. The existence of realistic choice in the experience of human beings, however, does suggest why fixed linear sequences of events will not adequately serve as a framework for life-course analyses. Many of the transitions that define the life course are perhaps best represented as choice or branching points: The high school graduate must decide whether to go on to college, enter the job market, or join the military; married couples increasingly can choose to become parents, adopt a child, or remain childless. To the degree that individual lives offer situations that permit and even require choice, the generalized life course resembles a branching tree; every choice made at one point in a time-ordered sequence opens up a different set of choices (and choice probabilities) at later points (Atchley, 1975). It seems possible to model the process being described as stochastic (e.g., Runyan, 1978, 1984); for some purposes, such a model may be perfectly adequate and useful. However, this does not grant randomness full sway. Indeterminacy can itself be a social variable, related to particular forms of social systems and networks and to the ways that selves are socially produced. As Coser (1975) notes, social complexity may be a source of individuality and autonomy. As the networks and competing demands of social roles diversify and multiply, individual behavior becomes less specifically predictable and more "self-produced," of necessity. Granting both the importance of constraints on and of autonomy in human behavior, a concept such as self or its equivalent must enter our explanatory lexicon. Understanding this is important for the life-course theorist who seeks to come to grips with variability in the life course.

IV. The Relevance of Life Course for Self

The life course as an age-linked pattern of movement into and out of social roles must, according to identity theory, carry implications for the commitments within which personal identities are established and maintained. The role changes by which the life course is experienced often entail altering patterns of one's social relationships, entering new networks of interaction which are premised on new or changed identities, leaving existing networks of interaction that depend on a prior role. Since interactional networks shape commitments, life-course events that lead to role change or to changes in social relationships will have an effect on the salience of identities. While in principle identity theory recognizes the reciprocity over time of self and commitment, its more basic thesis is that the content of self is responsive to changes in commitments. That is, the theory gives causal priority to the impact of commitment on self-concepts, on the ground that social constraints will limit the extent to which a person can freely alter his/her social relationships. Although a theoretical presumption, there is evidence from longitudinal research that this priority is justified (Serpe, 1985). These considerations provide the propositional frame for our treatment of the relevance of life course for the self. In brief, life-course events alter commitments which in turn alter selves.

We will focus our discussion primarily on aspects of self that have entered prior statements of identity theory, but allow consideration of some additional features closely related to identity theory formulations. We will also focus on life-course transitions rather than enduring states, although clearly a life-span model must account for both change and stability to be theoretically complete; it is in the analysis of change that the causal dynamics of a phenomenon are most effectively revealed. It is transitions that provide a relatively clear window on the social production of commitments and correspondingly (according to identity theory) on the structure of salience in the self.[12] Our discussion is interested in processes that characterize the life course as a whole, or at least multiple transitions within the life course, rather than particular transitions or age periods, leaving the latter to persons with expertise in specific age-linked substantive specialities (e.g.. child development, adolescence, occupations, gerontology).

A. ASSUMPTIONS ABOUT CHANGE AND DEVELOPMENT

Any attempt to consider the self in life-span terms must begin by confronting two general issues. The first: Is there a general and universal trajectory which self-changes and "growth" follow over the course of a lifetime? Various theories have suggested life-span models depicting universal sequences of stages, crises, and forms through which all normal selves develop. Deriving primarily from (psychoanalytical) ego psychology (e.g., Erikson, 1959; Jung, 1933; Lidz, 1968), cognitive developmental theory (e.g., Edelstein & Noam, 1982; Kohlberg, 1969), or a synthesis of these (e.g., Kegan, 1982; Loevinger, 1976), such theories assert an invariant, underlying order for self-concept changes during a lifetime, that is, a natural "deep structure" of self-development. While suggestive and useful, such models presume an answer to our question a priori: The analysis of self begins with the assumption of a common underlying order; the task remaining is to fill out its details and the diverse ways it may be manifest in different contexts and cultures.

Our own presumption is that the evolution of selves through the life course is characterized by considerable variability and fluidity. In part, this presumption follows from fundamental assumptions about the relation of society to self

[12]An analogous if not identical rationale underlies Stefan Hormuth's (1984) choice of physical relocation as a paradigmatic case for examining his social ecology of self theory.

contained in the interactionist position taken in the foregoing discussion (Mead, 1934; Stryker, 1980). In part, it follows from the view of the life course we have adopted. That is, the generalized life course is taken to represent a rather idealized summary of the numerous and diverse patterns out of which individuals construct their lives. While we presume there are clear constraints—biological, cultural, structural—they are far from determinate.[13] Following Atchley (1975), we presume that:

> The life course is a heuristic and conceptual tool. . . . relat(ing) social structure and process to the life spans and unique biographies of individuals. . . . Ideas concerning what is *appropriate* for people to be and to do at various ages pervade life. These ideas are organized into rough timetables, ... alternative path(s) through the maze of prescriptive, proscriptive, and permissive norms concerning age-appropriate positions, roles groups, social situations, skills, attitudes, ambitions, and a host of other characteristics. It is because of this complexity that the life course must remain a heuristic concept. There is no one life course; there are many (p. 262).

A second, related issue concerns how much stability and change in self occur over the life span. Is the self a shifting chameleon that dramatically evinces the changing social categories and contingencies characterizing the social structures of aging and socialization, as Gergen (1977), for example, suggests? Or is the self a stable dispositional structure that provides a sense of identity, continuity, and integration across virtually all situations, as others (e.g., Block, 1971; Costa & McCrae, 1980) argue? Again, the answer is substantially determined by our definitions and initial presumptions. It depends first of all on how we conceptualize the important features of self. Defining self as a global, dispositional, or deep-structural process predisposes us to find continuity and stability, while situational variations and fluctuations are interpreted as surface noise. Defining the self in more specific, situated, behavioral terms predisposes us to look for variability and difference.[14] In addition, the answer will depend on what we take ''change'' vs. ''continuity'' to involve. As Kagan (1980) notes, the concept of change is philosophically complex and multidimensional; the same events seen by one analyst as clear indicators of discontinuity and change may be viewed by another as the orderly maintenance of essential stability. This means that the issue cannot be resolved by a simple appeal to collections of empirical data and hypothesis testing; it is fundamentally a metatheoretical issue.

[13]Within any of these categories of constraints, some are more clearly ''determinative'' than others. A rite of passage in some society may well be an absolute requirement for movement into adult status, something that is not true of a ''sweet 16'' party or attaining legal drinking age. Clearly no 3-year-old will enter college (or bear children), but of course not all 20-year-olds, and some 60-year-olds, do.

[14]An adequate discussion of the issue of change versus continuity would require too much of a digression; we defer to the incisive essay by Kagan (1980) for an explication of the issue and to an application of these ideas to the self-concept of adolescents by Mortimer, Finch, and Kumka (1982).

Our interactionist framework argues that neither an imagery of total flux nor of total stability of self is appropriate. As earlier suggested, a key to either stability or change in self will lie in structures of interaction and the larger social organizational features of society that constrain or alter structures of interaction. We expect stability in self insofar as one's relationships to and within various networks of interaction remain relatively constant; there will be change insofar as these relationships are altered. Stability will also reflect the ways in which self intrudes itself into a variety of situations, serves as the basis for the construction of interaction in that variety of situations, and is subsequently reinforced by the interaction that occurs. There will be change insofar as the interactions constructed fail to reinforce extant selves. There will be stability in self-concept that is the consequence of identities associated with master statuses that cross many situations—for example, reflecting sex, race, and even age—and underlie the organization of behavior in those many situations (Stryker, in press-a; Stryker & Statham, 1985). There will be change insofar as either new master statuses evolve in the context of life course or old master statuses take on new meanings under changing historical circumstance. There will be stability of self-concept so long as a large repertoire of available self-defense mechanisms are permitted to operate effectively, without challenge from interactional partners. There will be change when structural circumstance bring persons into contact with interactional partners who will deny the use of those self-defense mechanisms (Stryker, in press-b). What is important to recognize is that neither stability nor change in self is a given, and that life-course processes help to account for both.

Thus, there may be good reason why adulthood is treated as a largely undifferentiated period in standard life-course discussions. With marriage, having children, and settling into a job, the major outline of commitments appears to remain relatively constant through a significant portion of the life span. It must be understood, however, both that this stability will not characterize everybody. (If nothing else, the increasing frequency of divorce as a life-course event guarantees that.) What may be read as a stable situation can contain important elements of instability. Being a parent means something quite different when one is the parent of one, two, or more children; and the role of a parent vis-à-vis an infant child, a 3-year-old, a high school junior and a college student is different indeed.

The stability of self in the face of limited or even no change in commitments should not be exaggerated or regarded as an absolute. As suggested earlier, change can be self-initiated and self-produced, even while a person's social contexts and social ties remain stable. For instance, "midlife crises" and midlife career changes represent phenomena in which persons begin questioning who they really are and wish to be, precisely as a consequence of the lack of change in their lives (Farrell & Rosenberg, 1981; Levinson et al., 1978; Lowenthal, Thurnher, & Chiriboga, 1976). Such events, though probably limited in their frequency of occurrence, are nonetheless real and serve to remind that the person is actor as well as reactor. Persons as minded beings can and do initiate self-changes in the face of social circumstances that seem to dictate lack of change. It is oversimplistic to maintain that all changes in self are linked to shifts in the extent and nature of commitments, to entry into new social relationships with new and different sets of others. Some role transformations occur during periods of apparently high levels of stability in patterned social relationships and the roles involved in those relationships. Long-term roles can remain nominally the same while major transformations in the meanings of those roles take place, and this is likely to occur as a consequence of aging and the age-related expectations that help define the life course.

The expectations others have of the person who is involved with them can transform the role even as the role itself is maintained—different behaviors are expected as the student moves from freshman to senior; a college student who has not completed his undergraduate career at age 30 is faced with different responses than he was at 18; the married daughter who is childless at age 38 is likely to get a very different set of signals from her parents than she did at age 22. In such instances, commitments can be threatened to the extent that the altered expectations attached to a role are not incorporated into the form of the older identities.

We turn now to more circumscribed considerations of self in the context of life course by focusing on self as conceptualized within identity theory. Taking identity salience, the range of identities that comprise the self, the content of identities, the closure or permeability of self, and self-evaluations[15] as key aspects or dimensions of self, we ask: How may locating these in the life course enlarge our understandings of variations in them? We begin with a discussion of the content of identities, because of the absolute centrality of "meaning" in an interactionist framework. We then turn to identity salience, since that concept is central to identity theory, and follow with our consideration of the remaining dimensions.

B. CONTENT OF IDENTITIES

Age categories that reflect age grading may themselves imply and give content to an identity. To be identified as a baby, a child, a teen-ager, an adult, or an elder is to be identified specifically in age-graded terms. While generally reflecting physical states and chronological passage, age identities are thoroughly products of social definitions. Societies differ considerably in the number of age grades they recognize, the behavioral content by which these are defined, the

[15]At this point, we are not quite prepared to assert how or even if evaluations are integral to identity theory. See Stryker (in press-a) and Stryker and Statham (1985) for relevant discussions.

degree of formality and concreteness in the age-graded structure, and the social and psychological importance of the grades (e.g., Neugarten, 1979; Neugarten & Hagestad, 1976; Riley, 1976). Within our own cultural tradition, substantial change has occurred in the system of recognizable age categories moving generally toward increasing differentiation of age identities: Childhood, adolescence, senior citizen and middle age as distinctive ages represent fairly recent social inventions (Giele, 1980; Neugarten, 1968).

Age grades have identity implications because they are linked to social structures of opportunities, resources, and networks (Atchley, 1975; Neugarten, 1979). They relate to the distribution of social experiences, relationships, and interactions that people are likely to have (Elder, 1975; Riley, 1976; Neugarten & Datan, 1973). Accomplished formally (through legal age requirements and criteria) or informally (through interactional age groupings and dominance orders), age grading fundamentally reflects the operation of institutionalized practices (Neugarten & Moore, 1968). For example, the structure of activities and opportunities for teen-agers shape their social contacts and experiences, contributing to the distinctiveness of the group and criteria for its evaluation. Persons in this age grade spend most of their time in common activities with same-age peers, are constrained from legitimate participation in certain activities and from establishing independent households, are compelled to attend mass educational structures. Such constraints provide part of the meaning of age identities, and are intimately related to age-graded, differentiated social beliefs about personhood. These beliefs define the persons contained within the categories, their moral, physical, psychological, and social attributes. They shape the identity premises by which people act and interact.

Age identities can change the temporal and phenomenal content of self-concepts (Chiriboga & Gigy, 1976). To be identified as a "youth" implies a temporal framework for conceptualizing a person as an ongoing phenomenon. The youth identity has a forward tilt to it. One's self (the person one is) is *yet to come;* its substance lies primarily in the future. The youth's self is expected to change and to become something else, something more; indeed, this change is socially required to be "normal." To remain a youth would be regarded as deviant from a practical, everyday perspective. Young selves are expected to "grow up," to accept responsibility, to contribute to the larger community, to be productive as they age. Thus, the "youth" self is premised as much on what the person *will be* (e.g., on plans and aspirations) as on what the person is (Chiriboga & Gigy, 1976; Coleman, Herzberg, & Morris, 1977). To be identified as an "old person" implies a very different temporal frame for conceptualizing the person as a social and psychological phenomenon. The "old" self has a backward tilt, pointing to what one was or did. One's substantial self *has been* (in contrast to the youth's self which is yet to be). The old self is expected to hold on to what was (i.e., memories and reminiscences) rather than be based on what will be (a more limited and negative set of prospects), or even on what is (a diminished set of outcomes) (e.g., Butler, 1963; Lewis, 1971).

Age categories may be meaningful in themselves because social, intellectual, physical, and moral meanings are attached to them. However, age or life-course location may be more important for the connections it has with identities that are not in themselves age categorical. Age may function as an eligibility (or ineligibility) marker where particular identities are contingent upon the person being in a specific age category (Neugarten, 1979; Neugarten & Moore, 1968). Age may also function as a less explicit but important correlate of social identities, either because of the actual distribution of resources or opportunities to accomplish those identities (e.g., being a parent or a grandparent, being a professional athlete) or because of cultural definitions of what age means in social, physical, and psychological terms (e.g., sexual identities, political identities, religious identities) (Elder, 1975; Neugarten & Datan, 1973).

This discussion suggests that people assign age identities or age-linked identities to themselves through self-perception. However, identity theory holds that the substantial impact of social identities on individual self-concepts occurs through social networks and relationships to which persons are committed. A person comes to identify herself or himself as "middle-aged" or "old" in large part because interaction with other persons who count brings definitions, reminders, reinforcements, and validations of that identity. This may occur directly through verbal and nonverbal feedback (e.g., receiving birthday gifts appropriate to a middle-aged person, receiving comments about physical indicators of aging); or it may occur indirectly through social comparisons with interactional others. The effects here are dependent on the person's social interactional contexts. For example, older persons who primarily interact with same-age others, such as persons living in healthy retirement communities, tend to identify themselves as younger than do persons interacting in age-heterogeneous sets of others: Relative to their interactional and reference others, they are not "old" (Bengtson, 1973; Rose & Peterson, 1965; Rosow, 1974).

C. IDENTITY SALIENCE

The salience of identities is argued by identity theory to be ordered by commitments. Consequently, the major way in which life-course events can be expected to change the salience structure of identities is through altering existing patterns of commitments.[16]

[16]Obviously salience of identities is in part a reflection of situational demands (Alexander & Wiley, 1981; McCall & Simmons, 1966; McGuire & McGuire, 1982). Incorporating such demands into identity theory is a barely begun project (see Stryker, in press-a, in press-b).

Not all life-course events are likely to impact commitments seriously, but major transitions are. Movements into new levels of schooling, in particular movement which removes the person from the home community, involves considerable alternation in networks of social relationships—contact with old friends is gradually lost and new friendship relationships open, interaction with peers grows disproportionately with roughly equivalent reduction in interaction with family, and so on. Thus, identities premised on continued interaction with high school friends and with family will lose salience, identities that reflect the emergent new relationships—serious student, playboy, or artist—will gain salience.[17] Another example: Marriage creates a variety of new relationships with spouse's family and friends, or perhaps with a new circle of "young married." Doing so, new commitments are formed with subsequent impact on the salience of identities that comprise the self. However, marriage may also reinforce older commitments to one's own family and one's own friends who are married. In that way, the salience of already existing identities may be strengthened. So, too, with transitions into parenthood, entry into the world of work and other age-related alternations in the character of one's life (e.g., George, 1980, 1982; Rossi, 1980).

Further, it appears likely that there is a "novelty" effect on identity salience. That is, new relationships in which persons are feeling their way may well make them more sensitive to cues from others about the role expectations underlying the relationships, thus—and at least in the short run--increasing the salience of the related identity (e.g., McGuire & McGuire, 1982). Insofar as life course transitions open up new patterns of commitment, this novelty effect can be anticipated.

The discussion thus far has implied limited interruption or alteration of commitments as a consequence of life-course events, for example, marriage opens new relationships that may curtail older commitments in some degree. Some life-course events occasion more severe and virtually total change in commitments that can initiate radical change in the organization of self (Boyanowsky, 1984). Entry into military service, insofar as this entails enforced segregation from prior life (Dornbusch, 1955) or movement to a distant or foreign location, can end prior commitments and almost require considerable restructuring of the self. Although persons can actively seek out or produce means through which prior salient identities can be maintained under novel circumstance (Hormuth, 1984),

[17]True, relationships with older friends and with family may continue apart from face-to-face contact, via letters or phone calls with occasional reinforcement through face-to-face interaction. To some degree, absence may make the heart grow fonder. However, absence is also likely to reduce the impetus for introducing into current interactions an identity based in physcially distant and indirect relationships. In any event, our assertions should be read in ceteris paribus terms.

successful accomplishment of that end will depend on what resources (objects or persons) are available in the new environment. As with entry into the military, perhaps so too with entry into a retirement community or nursing home that increasingly represent events in the life course accompanying old age (e.g., Kosloski, Ginsburg, & Backman, 1984).

As suggested, some life-course changes may serve to reinforce or reaffirm old commitments. Such reaffirmation may, as noted, increase the salience of old identities. It may, as well, strengthen new conceptions of self. To once again choose an example from the arena of family, becoming a parent is likely to strengthen relationships to kin, who in turn are likely to behave in ways that increase the salience of the new identity as parent. And, some life events alter commitments only indirectly, by introducing changes in the premises of commitments rather than in the number of persons or the level of activities involved in networks of relationships. These changes in premises may in turn impact the salience of identities through communicated expectations from members of interactional networks, responsiveness to whom is ''enforced'' by the potential costs of failure to be responsive. To illustrate, the age identity one has as one grows older—conceptualizing oneself no longer as ''a promising young man'' but as a mature, even middle-aged, academic—is likely to derive from persons implicated in continuing commitments who respond to our physical changes, or changes in age-linked social statuses, or perhaps only to our biological age by altering their expectations of us and by supplying us with behavioral cues we are hard put to resist or avoid.

An important feature of life-course processes is the normative expectations for ''proper'' timing of entry into and egress from social roles that exist at least for some transitions (e.g., Atchley, 1975; Elder, 1975; Neugarten, Moore, & Lowe, 1965). We can be early, on time, or late in our maturational processes, our entry into and departure from the school system, marriage, parenthood and the labor force, our movement through an occupational carrer, our retirement and even our death.[18] Departure from ''normality'' in these terms is likely to increase the salience of the identities that are linked to the early off-time entry or departure. This occurs through reflected appraisals within ongoing commitments. Others with whom we interact in our out-of-step roles through their responses to us will make us more or less continuously aware of our deviance. Remarks such as ''You're too young to be married'' (or in college, or head of a firm, or retired), questions like ''What does it feel like to be a mother for the first time at 40?,'' or behaviors that are equally overt reminders of a special age-linked status force

[18]The issue of timing norms for life-course events remains a lively topic, reflecting the analytical difficulties in what seems a simple observation. Marini (1984) details some of the attendant difficulties, particularly noting an important (but often blurred) distinction between norm in a statistical sense (as modal occurrences) and in a sociocultural sense (as sanctioned expectations).

attention to it and to its identity implications. It may also involve social comparison processes with peers by which persons become aware of a distinctive age-linked status (McGuire & McGuire, 1982).

If we now consider not the location of particular identities within a hierarchical salience structure as a consequence of life-course events, but the identity salience structure itself, other kinds of linkages between life course and self can be hypothesized.[19] It seems likely, for example, that the more rapidly a sequence of events occasioning changes in patterns of commitment occur within a specified period in the life course, the greater the instability of that salience structure. It seems equally reasonable to suppose that the synchronicity of life-course changes—leaving school *and* getting married *and* taking a new job in a new location—destabilizes the salience structure to a greater degree than would be the case were these events separated by some minimal duration of time. This last assertion suggests yet another reasonable hypothesis: The longer the duration in a given life-course state prior to a transition, the more resistant will be the identities relevant to that state to dislocation in salience.

D. IDENTITY RANGE AND ACCUMULATION

For an identity salience hierarchy to exist, the self must incorporate multiple identities. Further, if identities shape behaviors at all, likely to be important in understanding why and how that effect occurs is the range of the identity system of which the particular identity is a part (as well as the substance of the particular identities included in that range). Behavior possibilities and probabilities, we are asserting, will differ in systematic ways when two persons each hold a given identity, but one has a salience hierarchy consisting of 5 identities and the other has a salience hierarchy incorporating 50 distinct identities. An early argument (Goode, 1960) growing out of role conflict theory held that the more roles and identities one had, the greater the probability of active role conflict. That position has been superseded on the basis of reasonable argument (Marks, 1977; Sieber. 1974) and evidence (Thoits, 1983) that sees role and identity accumulation as positive in consequences: Roles and identities are characterized as resources that can be called into play in a wide range of situations rather than competitors with

[19]It may be appropriate here to remind the reader that the concept of identity salience refers to the probability that given identities will come into play (i.e., affect the course of behavior) in or across situations. This is not the equivalent of the subjectively felt importance of given identities, although the literature is sometimes confusing about the relation of salience and importance. McCall and Simmons (1966) stress "importance" as a key aspect of identities. Salience is also not equivalent to "psychological centrality" as Rosenberg (1979) has explicated it. It should also be said that invocation of an identity does not in itself guarantee behavior in accord with that identity, only that the identity will be part of the "awareness context" within which the behavior takes place.

other roles and identities for scarce resources. Either way, identity range may be an important characteristic of self-structures.

How do life-course events affect identity range? It is generally, and not unreasonably, assumed that the very young have few salient identities, that the process of identity accumulation accelerates through adolescence and emergent adulthood, stabilizes in later adulthood, and decelerates in old age, with the last stages of life being characterized by the rapid loss of identities (e.g., Atchley, 1982; George, 1980; Rosow, 1974.)[20] These processes generally parallel the expansion and contraction of commitments, as one might expect from identity theory. The life-course events that underlie expansions and contractions of commitments do not space themselves evenly over the life span; consequently, identities will not be accumulated and lost in a continuous even flow. Rather, the shifts will cluster around more drastic (and dramatic) life-course transitions. Insofar as the picture of storm and stress of adolescence in our society has validity, at least for some in our society, the source of that validity may well be the uneven pace of identity accumulation and the time it takes to permit emergent new identities to ''settle'' into place in a salience structure. For many, retirement brings with it drastic reductions in commitments and thus identities.

E. IDENTITY CLOSURE AND PERMEABILITY

In the discussion above, the self would seem to be a continually open life-course project. However, there may be points in the process when the self is relatively closed to identity changes and the permeability of the self to new identity-linked inputs is reduced. A major proposition of a traditional ego-development perspective (e.g., Erikson, 1959; Hauser, 1971; Josselson, 1980; Marcia, 1980) is that the mature self has ''consolidated'' into a stable and integrated identity that has autonomy from social contingencies and continuity across time and social contexts. The life course may be divided into periods of differential permeability: growing and acquiring skills in childhood; searching and testing identities in adolescence; consolidation, continuity, and productivity in adulthood; review and evaluation in old age. At certain life stages (e.g., ''identity crises''), according to this perspective, the self will be more open to change, in other periods relatively closed and stable. Persons who do not achieve identity

[20]Accumulation of identities will reflect operation of both social and psychological processes. In the former it reflects the complexity and specificity of adult roles (e.g., Brim, 1966). In the latter, it may reflect the fact that identifications, once made, are not automatically dropped when they become socially inactive. Prior identities (e.g., star athlete, alcoholic, college professor) may continue to be salient features of a person's self-concept even when that role is no longer available or effectively enacted (e.g., Zurcher, 1979).

consolidation at appropriate times will be socially and psychologically disabled. For instance, failure to consolidate (identity diffusion) will result in unstable, vulnerable selves; consolidating too soon (identity foreclosure) will result in rigid, limited, nonadaptable selves (e.g., Hauser, 1971).

An alternative view maintains that the permeability of the self is not centered in one life-course period (such as adolescence) but recurs in smaller cycles repeatedly over the life span. Levinson (1980; Levinson et al., 1978) for example, argues that the life course is an extended succession of alternating crises and stable periods, each involving new social tasks and personal dilemmas. Openness (versus closure) varies over the life course but in short, recurrent, socially grounded patterns. Still others depict the life span as one long extended process of gradually opening (e.g., Haan, 1981) or closing (e.g., Lowenthal et al., 1976) the self.

At this point, the permeability of self-concepts to social shifts in identity and context remains a suggestive but unresolved issue; the available research provides conflicting conclusions (e.g., Haan, 1981; Lowenthal et al., 1976). However, it is useful to note that the receptivity of self-conception (to the identity implications of changing social conditions) is not necessarily constant but may be a life-course variable in itself. It is also useful to note a connection between permeability and the reciprocity of self and life course, acknowledging that the self is not automatically (and passively) open to received changes. The self is a selective, constructive process in which a person may be more or less open to new inputs and new possibilities. The person has an active hand in determining whether social opportunities will be utilized, whether commitments will be made and kept, how long identities are maintained (e.g., Mortimer, Finch, & Kumka, 1982).

F. SELF-EVALUATION AND SELF-ESTEEM

Beyond the content and structure of identity, other substantial aspects of the self may be linked to the life course. In particular, many theoretical perspectives, including symbolic interactionism, posit self-evaluation and self-esteem as basic and important components of self-conception (Gecas, 1982, Gergen, 1971; Rosenberg, 1979, 1981).

According to identity theory, life-course patterns in self-evaluations and self-esteem should be tied to the age-linked shifts (and stabilities) in identity. While not determinate, the relation between identities and evaluations is theoretically important. Identities invariably carry evaluative connotations, reflecting the social and psychological meanings by which they are culturally defined (Neugarten, 1968, 1979). Age identities are seldom evaluatively neutral, although the specific relationship of social value to age is a variable that depends on the evaluative context.[21] In general, age has a curvilinear relationship with most evaluative dimensions—such as physical attractiveness, physical skills, social competence, social dependence, productivity—where increasing age corresponds to increasing value up to some age level beyond which value decreases with increasing age. In some respects, it is good to be young, but often being young or ''new'' in some settings carries connotations of incompetence and dependence.

Identities may be evaluatively important in less direct ways. Roles invariably contain performance criteria and norms by which persons can be evaluated as good or bad at those roles (Neugarten et al., 1965; Neugarten & Datan, 1973; Rosow, 1976). This suggests several mechanisms through which age or life course influences self-evaluation. Where life-course locations mean movement into new roles (e.g., getting married, becoming a parent, going to school, entering a profession), people may be interactionally committed to identities in which they feel incompetent or ill-suited. That is, people may be pressured by family or close peers to go to college, get married, or have children because such things are expected of a person at their age. Committed to the role via important relationships, it is difficult to exit that identity; also, because they are committed to the role, the identity will be more salient and likely to impact on self-esteem. The life course may also affect self-evaluation within a role where performance is related to aging: Persons are sometimes committed to roles in which they are not yet good (apprentice) or no longer as good as they once were (''over the hill''). Roles that depend on physical criteria (e.g., attractiveness, prowess, exertion, endurance, etc.) are likely to show this curvilinear effect.

Being ''off time'' or ''on time'' in role enactments often has evaluative meaning (Bush & Simmons, 1981; Neugarten, 1968, 1979). The executive (or assistant professor) who is promoted behind or ahead of schedule will be aware of evaluative implications. Reaching puberty early or late may carry evaluative import for adolescents, although the effects seem to differ substantially between males and females (Berzonsky, 1983; Simmons et al., 1979). For boys early physical maturity enhances self-esteem; for girls, it produces at least a temporary decrease in self-esteem.

Age-linked shifts in the normative content of roles affect self-evaluations when the content becomes vague and ambiguous (Kuypers & Bengtson, 1973; Rosow, 1974). Role identities in old age may reduce self-esteem substantially

[21]The existence of negative age-stereotypes and identities paradoxically may provide enhancing reference points. Given the stereotype of old age as a period of feebleness and infirmity, elder persons may be pleasantly surprised at how healthy and capable they feel (relative to the ''norm'' for people their age), in this way enhancing their relative self-esteem. We thank Ralph Turner for contributing this point.

because their performance criteria and norms are undefined.[22] Without clear feedback about how role occupants are doing, self-esteem is disconnected from daily activities, uncertain, and vulnerable to other forms of negative feedback about the deficits of aging. Kuypers and Bengtson's (1973) "social breakdown syndrome" is an instance of this process. A similar difficulty may underlie "adolescent crisis."

It is important to not overdraw the link between age-related role identities and self-esteem. The relationship between identity and self-evaluation, while fundamental (Gecas, 1982; Rosenberg, 1981), is not determinate but fluid and variable. As research on the self-esteem of minorities shows (e.g., Rosenberg, 1979; Wylie, 1979), the relationship between social valuation of an identity and the self-evaluation of persons in that identity can be very loose. Contrary to simple predictions, persons in disvalued statuses do not necessarily have low self-esteem—a finding that is replicated by the research on aging. This reflects the fact that self-esteem will be substantially shaped by perceptions of personal attributes and abilities which cut across roles (Cooper & Goethals, 1981). Physical features and skill, intellectual abilities, social accomplishments provide the bases for self-evaluations that are not tied to specific role identities. Since these represent more generalized features of the person's self, they can have considerable impact on an overall sense of self-evaluation or self-esteem. Such features may also be age-linked in the sense that they wax and wane as people go through the life course.

The link between evaluation and identity will be moderated by social context and by the structure of the self-concept (e.g., Kaplan, 1971). While self-esteem, as a cumulative, generalized sense of competence or worth, does not depend directly on any one identity or attribute, it will be more strongly affected by identities and attributes that are personally and interpersonally salient. This suggests that interactional commitments will qualify the relationship between identity and evaluation. Where age-linked identities are rendered salient by important social ties, they will have powerful effects on self-evaluation (e.g., Stryker & Serpe, 1982). It also suggests that the range of the self-concept will be a moderator: Where the self is comprised by a large number of identities, the influence of specific identities on self-evaluation will be reduced.

The identity-evaluation relationship is not "stationary": The very process of evaluation itself evolves and changes with age. That is, the practices and opera-

[22]As analysis of the role-person merger indicates (Turner, 1978), attributes attached to roles are readily transferred to the person or self enacting them. However, the relationship also may work in the reverse direction. Brubaker and Powers (1976) find that persons with positive self-concepts tend to define the aged role (as it applied to themselves) in more positive attributes, ignoring or minimizing the negative elements of age stereotypes.

tions by which people form self-evaluations seem to shift with movement through the life course. Initially, shifts in evaluation processes may substantially reflect cognitive developmental changes in the ways that persons are able to think about themselves as abstract objects, to represent and categorize themselves, to form judgments and attributions about objects, to comprehend the viewpoints of others, etc. With increasing age, self-conceptions become increasingly differentiated and schematized so that self-evaluation is both more automatic and more discriminative (e.g., Mueller & Ross, 1984; Mullener & Laird, 1971): Self-representations evolve from dependence on concrete, physical facts to elaboration of more generalized, abstract, individuating categorizations (e.g., Lynch, 1981; Montemayor & Eisen, 1977); the use of social information in self-evaluation increases as skills in role taking and social judgment develop (Heckhausen, 1983; Ruble et al., 1980; Schoeneman, Tabor, & Nash, 1984); and the dependence on significant others for self-evaluation changes.

There are good reasons to believe that the process of change in evaluative perceptions continues over the span of a life although probably not as dramatically as in childhood, reflecting not only basic developmental change but also social context shifts tied to the life course (Back & Gergen, 1968; Cooper & Goethals, 1981). For example, according to Suls and Mullen (1982), the *modes* of self-evaluation change in a stage-orderly fashion over the life course, each stage characterized by a preferred mode of evaluation. Across the life span, persons change from dependence on direct physical feedback (in very young children) to generalized social comparisons (with "everybody") to highly differentiated social comparisons (with others similar to themselves) to generalized social comparisons (with others different from themselves) to temporal comparisons (retrospective self-comparisons) (see also Breytspraak, 1984; Chiriboga & Gigy, 1976). Continuity in self-esteem is presumably maintained over substantial shifts in social psychological contexts because the modes of evaluation adapt to fit one's life-course circumstances, reflecting both developmental and social interactional dynamics; that is, "young children do not use social comparison because of cognitive reasons, whereas the elderly show the same tendency but mainly for social reasons "(Suls & Mullen, 1982, p. 120).

Passage through the life course brings shifts in the *bases* for self-evaluation, that is, the content dimensions by which competence and value are assessed (L'Ecuyer, 1981; Mortimer et al., 1982). Shifts in social contexts across the life course may change the functional value of personality characteristics. Dispositions and attributes that may be esteemed in adolescence (e.g., recklessness, independence, impulsiveness) can be liabilities in adulthood with career and family responsibilities. While separating the "real" from "apparent" in this area is difficult, existing evidence suggests that in early adulthood, achievement and instrumentality are the dominant evaluative themes, while in later years, moral worth and integrity become more important (e.g., Chiriboga & Thurnher, 1976; Gurin, Veroff, & Feld, 1960; Riley & Foner. 1968).

Age also brings shifts in the social *sources* of evaluation, corresponding not only to developmental growth (as already suggested) but also to the organization of social networks within the life course. Adolescence initiates an important shift in the "significant others" on whom self-evaluation depends from family to peers, even as family remains influential, a shift that reflects in large part the way adolescence is institutionally structured by mass education. Research on early adulthood (e.g., Mortimer et al., 1982; Mortimer & Lorence, 1981) shows another shift in the significant others for self-evaluation, the change from a general network of age peers to smaller networks of intimate others (e.g., spouse, children). Thus, life-course transitions lead to shifts in networks of interaction which change the nature and composition of significant reference groups acting as sources of self-evaluations.

V. Conclusion

Rather than seeking to summarize the prior pages of this chapter, we conclude by drawing some very general inferences from what has been said about the fundamental question raised: What is to be gained by examining the relationship between the self and the life course?

One clear answer to this question is that the adoption of a more extended temporal frame forms a basis for connecting and integrating works on self that deal with specific and limited portions of the life course. Many of these works explicitly locate the self within life cycle and historical frames but do so by adopting a restricted temporal focus. Consequently, the research literatures on the self in childhood, in adolescence, in various spheres of adult life, and in old age exist in relative isolation from one another. The life-course perspective challenges us to explicate a framework within which this disparate collection of implicitly linked accounts can be explicitly connected and given continuity.

A. TEMPORALITY AND THE SELF

On a deeper level, articulating the life course and the self serves to expand our understanding of the self as a quintessentially human phenomenon by addressing its temporality and by providing an extended framework within which the self can be viewed as both dynamic and enduring. As Mead's analyses (1932, 1934, 1938) argue, the linkage between the experience of time and the self is fundamental. Mind, "time," and the self emerge jointly with symbol-using activity through representing distant and nontangible objects. In this sense, the self is in essence a *time-bound* process by which persons become aware of their own life spans, historical locations, and mortality. The self is also, and importantly, a *time-binding* process by which the passage and duration of time become integral features of human activity (Becker, 1962; Verhave & van Hoorn, 1984). Self-consciousness provides the mechanism by which time may be experienced and constructed, since awareness of time fundamentally involves *self*-awareness—that is, recognition of one's place within the present moment vis-à-vis one's place in other possible moments, past or future. Without self-consciousness, time as a larger field or flow does not exist; rather, the organism is stuck within a continuous "now." The emergence of self carries with it the capacity for organized personal memories (the self as the reference point for recollection) and for intentionality and planning (the self as the subject of anticipated and imagined "nows").

Correspondingly, time constitutes a fundamental part of the substance of self-conception. In one sense, the self-concept consists of a collection of memories about one's past experiences that provide a referential framework for interpreting one's own activities in the present. But the self also includes anticipations of future events and outcomes which provide motivational as well as referential structure for present activity. While behavior is always literally in the present (as a continual passage of "nows"), that present is always saturated with the past and the future. The self of this moment is heavily predicated on recollected and anticipated self-images.

B. LIFE COURSE AS "NATURAL" FRAMEWORK

Beyond acknowledgement of time as a basic variable, the life course provides a substantively useful, even "natural," framework for describing this temporal character of the self. The framework suggests that the self is a mechanism for both continuity and change—for structure as well as for adaptation. The life-course perspective deals with the self as an enduring, generally stable phenomenon; it directs us to identify and explain the regular recurrent structures of people's selves and lives. Yet it does so without reducing the self to stationary, atemporal terms as most extant sociological analyses of the self seem to do. The latter implicitly depict the self as indifferent to time (either in the sense of duration or of temporal location). The features and structures of the self implicitly seem to apply comparably to all persons, whether children, adolescents, adults, or elders. Change tends to be viewed from a homeostatic perspective as error or disturbance variation. The life-course orientation acknowledges stability and continuity while affirming that growth, adaptation, and emergence are also essential features of the process. Even while examining its enduring structures, the self must be embedded in time and an ongoing process of change.

On the other hand, the life course also provides a way of dealing with the dynamic character of the self—for depicting it as an active, constructive, negotiated process—that does not necessarily reduce it to momentary, transient impressions. This contrasts with the more "situational" or phenomenological orientation that focuses on the self as situationally accomplished in a socially precarious, moment-to-moment production (Alexander & Wiley, 1981; Goffman, 1959, 1967). While that approach clarifies situational fluctuations in the self, it is relatively indifferent to how situational processes may be substantially shaped by large sociotemporal processes. It treats the "lived present" of the self in relatively transient terms, essentially limited to the tangible here and now. It deemphasizes the behavioral reality of distant objects and goals in ongoing conduct. This implicitly defines a rather short-term view of mind as a social and psychological process, being limited to the momentary awareness of immediate events. The life-course perspective extends this view of the self as an active, creative process by emphasizing the importance of longer time frames for consciousness and intentionality. Rather than contradicting a situational approach, the life-course orientation raises different (ostensibly complementary) questions about the dynamic content of the self.

In this respect, what the life course adds to the analysis of self is an explicit recognition that the negotiation of self and identity can be a cumulative, long-term (indeed a life-span) process as well as a momentary, situational one. It does not negate the dynamic qualities of the self but views them within a more extended temporal frame. It embodies Shalin's (1984, p. 44) assertion that the self "is a process that can be understood only in its genesis and evolution," where evolution is viewed in gradual, cumulative terms. The life-course orientation encourages us to consider that self-awareness of time may be distant as well as immediate. It prompts us to consider that the self is "in time" as well as "aware of time." It is shaped by larger temporal structures, as well as by momentary exigencies. The time-binding nature of the self is not purely of conscious awareness; it has an externalized, spatialized, objective component as well which can fruitfully be viewed as part of the life course.

What has been said in this concluding section asserts the import of viewing self in a life-course frame. We close by returning to an earlier insistence. Incorporating considerations of self into the discourse of the life course enables recognition of both the extent to which human experience is the product of determinate social psychological, and biological processes *and* the extent to which such processes are themselves the product of autonomous human actors.

Acknowledgment

Preparation of this chapter was supported by a grant from the National Institute of Mental Health, PH T32 MH 14588.

References

Alexander, C. N., & Wiley, M. G. (1981). Situated activity and identity formation. In M. Rosenberg & R. Turner (Eds.), *Social psychology: Sociological perspectives* (pp. 269–290). New York: Basic Books.

Atchley, R. (1975). The life course, age grading, and age-linked demands for decision making. In N. Datan & L. Ginsberg (Eds.), *Life-span developmental psychology: Normative life crises* (pp. 261–278). New York: Academic Press.

Atchley, R. (1982). The aging self. *Psychotherapy: Theory, Research, and Practice, 19,* 388–396.

Back, K., & Gergen, K. (1968). The self through the latter span of life. In C. Gordon & K. Gergen (Eds.), *The self in social interaction* (Vol. 1, pp. 241–250). New York: John Wiley.

Ball, D. (1973). *Microecology: Social situations and intimate space.* Indianapolis, IN: Bobbs–Merrill.

Bandura, A. (1977). Self-efficacy: Toward a unifying theory of behavioral change. *Psychological Review, 84,* 191–215.

Becker, E. (1962). *The birth and death of meaning.* New York: Free Press.

Bem, D. (1972). Self-perception theory. In L. Berkowitz (Ed.), *Advances in experimental social psychology* (Vol. 6, pp. 1–62). New York: Academic Press.

Bengtson, V. L. (1973). *The social psychology of aging.* Indianapolis, IN: Bobbs-Merrill.

Berzonsky, M. (1983). Adolescent research: A life-span developmental perspective. *Human Development, 26,* 213–221.

Block, J. (1971). *Lives through time.* Berkeley, CA: Bancroft.

Boyanowsky, E. (1984). Self-identity change and the role transition process. In V. Allen & E. van de Vliert (Eds.), *Role transitions: Explorations and explanations* (pp. 53–61). New York: Plenum Press.

Brandtstädter, J. (1984). Personal and social control over development: Some implications of an action perspective in life span developmental psychology. In P. B. Baltes & O. G. Brim, Jr. (Eds.), *Life-span development and behavior* (Vol. 6, pp. 1–32). New York: Academic Press.

Breytspraak, L. (1984). *The development of self in later life.* Boston, MA: Little, Brown.

Brim, O. G., Jr. (1966). Socialization through the life cycle. In O. G. Brim, Jr. & S. Wheeler, *Socialization after childhood: Two essays* (pp. 1–50). New York: John Wiley.

Brockner, J. (1983). Low self-esteem and behavioral plasticity: Some implications. In L. Wheeler & P. Shaver (Eds.), *Review of personality and social psychology* (Vol. 4, pp. 237–271). Beverly Hills, CA: Sage.

Brubaker, T., & Powers, E. (1976). The stereotype of old: A review and alternative approach. *Journal of Gerontology, 31,* 441–447.

Bryson, C. (1945). *Man and society: The Scottish inquiry of the eighteenth century.* Princeton, NJ: Princeton University Press.

Bush, D., & Simmons, R. (1981). Socialization processes over the life course. In M. Rosenberg & R. Turner (Eds.), *Social psychology: Sociological perspectives* (pp. 133–164). New York: Basic Books.

Butler, R. (1963). The life review: An interpretation of reminiscence in the aged. *Psychiatry, 26,* 65–76.

Carver, C., & Scheier, M. (1981). *Attention and self-regulation: A control-theory approach to human behavior.* New York: Springer-Verlag.

Chiriboga, D., & Gigy, L. (1976). Perspectives on life course. In M. Fiske Lowenthal, M. Thurnher. & D. Chiriboga (Eds.), *Four stages of life* (pp. 122–145). San Francisco: Jossey–Bass.

Chiriboga, D., & Thurnher, M. (1976). Concept of self. In M. Fiske Lowenthal, M. Thurnher, & D. Chiriboga (Eds.), *Four stages of life* (pp. 62–83). San Francisco: Jossey–Bass.

Coleman, J., Herzberg, J., & Morris, M. (1977). Identity in adolescence: Present and future self-concepts. *Journal of Youth and Adolescence, 6,* 63–75.

Collins, R. (1981). On the micro-foundations of macro-sociology. *American Journal of Sociology, 83,* 984–1014.

Cooper, J., & Goethals, G. (1981). The self-concept and old age. In S. Kiesler, J. Morgan, & V. Kincade Oppenheimer (Eds.), *Aging: Social change* (pp. 431–452). New York: Academic Press.

Coser, R. L. (1975). The complexity of roles as a seedbed of individual autonomy. In Lewis A. Coser (Ed.), *The idea of social structure: Papers in honor of Robert K. Merton* (pp. 237–263). New York: Harcourt, Brace, Jovanovich.

Costa, P., & McCrae, R. (1980). Still stable after all these years: Personality as a key to some issues in adulthood and old age. In P. B. Baltes & O. G. Brim, Jr. (Eds.), *Life-span development and behavior* (Vol. 3, pp. 65–102). New York: Academic Press.

Dewey, J. (1940). *Human nature and conduct.* New York: Modern Library.

Dornbusch, S. (1955). The military academy as an assimilating institution. *Social Forces, 33,* 316–321.

Edelstein, W., & Noam, G. (1982). Regulatory structures of the self and ''postformal'' stages in adulthood. *Human Development, 23,* 407–422.

Elder, G. (1975). Age differentiation and the life course. *Annual Review of Sociology, 1,* 165–190.

Erikson, E. (1959). *Identity and the life cycle.* New York: W. W. Norton (Norton edition, 1980).

Farrell, M., & Rosenberg, S. (1981). *Men at midlife.* Boston: Auburn House.

Gecas, V. (1982). The self-concept. *Annual Review of Sociology, 8,* 1–33.

George, L. (1980). *Role transitions in later life.* Monterey, CA: Brooks/Cole.

George, L. (1982). Models of transitions in middle and later life. *Annals of American Association of Political and Social Sciences, 464,* 22–37.

Gergen, K. (1971). *The concept of self.* New York: Holt, Rinehart & Winston.

Gergen, K. (1977). Stability, change and chance in human development. In N. Datan & H. Reese (Eds.), *Life-span development psychology* (pp. 135–158). New York: Academic Press.

Giddens, A. (1984). *The constitution of society: Outline of the theory of structuration.* Berkeley, CA: University of California Press.

Giele, J. Z. (1980). Adulthood as transcendence of age and sex. In N. Smelser & E. Erikson (Eds.), *Themes of love and work in adulthood* (pp. 151–173). Cambridge, MA: Harvard University Press.

Goffman, E. (1959). *The presentation of self in everyday life.* Garden City, NY: Doubleday.

Goffman, E. (1967). *Interaction ritual: Essays on face-to-face behavior.* Garden City, NY: Doubleday.

Goode, W. J. (1960). A theory of role strain. *American Sociological Review, 25,* 483–496.

Gordon, C. (1971). Role and value development across the life cycle. In J. Jackson (Ed.), *Role* (pp. 65–105). London: Cambridge University Press.

Gordon, C. (1976). Development of evaluated role identities. *Annual Review of Sociology, 2,* 405–433.

Gurin, G., Veroff, J., & Feld, S. (1960). *Americans view their mental health: A nationwide interview study.* New York: Basic Books.

Haan, N. (1981). Common dimensions of personality development: Early adolescence to middle life. In D. Eichorn, J. Clausen, N. Haan, M. Honzik, & P. Mussen (Eds.), *Present and past in middle life* (pp. 117–151). New York: Academic Press.

Harre, R. (1982). *Personal being: A theory for individual psychology.* Cambridge, MA: Harvard University Press.

Hauser, S. (1971). *Black and white identity formation.* New York: John Wiley.

Heckhausen, H. (1983). Concern with one's competence: Developmental shifts in person–environment interaction. In D. Magnusson & V. Allen (Eds.), *Human development: An interactional perspective* (pp. 167–185). New York: Academic Press.

Hochschild, A. (1983). *The managed heart.* Berkeley, CA: University of California Press.

Hormuth, S. (1984). Transitions in commitments to roles and self-concept change: Relocation as a paradigm. In V. Allen & E. van de Vliert (Eds.), *Role transitions: Explorations and explanations* (pp. 109–124). New York: Plenum Press.

House, J. (1981). Social structure and personality. In M. Rosenberg & R. Turner (Eds.), *Social psychology: Sociological perspectives* (pp. 525–561). New York: Basic Books.

Israel, J. & Tajfel, H. (Eds.). (1972). *The context of social psychology: A critical assessment.* London: Academic Press.

James, W. (1890). *The principles of psychology.* New York: Henry Holt (reprinted Dover, 1950).

Josselson, R. (1980). Ego development in adolescence. In J. Adelson (Ed.), *Handbook of adolescent psychology* (pp. 188–210). New York: John Wiley.

Jung, C. G. (1933). *Modern man in search of a soul.* New York: Harcourt, Brace.

Kagan, J. (1980). Perspectives on continuity. In O. G. Brim, Jr., & J. Kagan (Eds.), *Constancy and change in human development* (pp. 26–74). Cambridge, MA: Harvard University Press.

Kaplan, H. (1971). Age-related correlates of self-derogation: Contemporary life space characteristics. *Aging and Human Development, 2,* 305–313.

Kaplan, H. (1980). *Deviant behavior in defense of self.* New York: Academic Press.

Kegan, R. (1982). *The evolving self.* Cambridge, MA: Harvard University Press.

Kemper, T. (1978). *A social interactional theory of emotions.* New York: John Wiley.

Kihlstrom, J., & Cantor, N. (1984). Mental representations of the self. In L. Berkowitz (Ed.), *Advances in Experimental Social Psychology* (Vol. 17, pp. 1–46). New York: Academic Press.

Kohlberg, L. (1969). Stage and sequence: The cognitive-developmental approach to socialization. In D. Goslin (Ed.), *Handbook of socialization theory and research* (pp. 347–480). Chicago: Rand-McNally.

Kosloski, K., Ginsburg, G., & Backman, C. (1984). Retirement as a process of active role transition. In V. Allen & E. van de Vliert (Eds.), *Role transitions: Explorations and explanations.* New York: Plenum Press.

Kuypers, J. A., & Bengtson, V. L. (1973). Social breakdown and competence. *Human Development, 16,* 181–201.

LaGory, M. (1982). Toward a sociology of space: The constrained choice model. *Symbolic Interaction, 5,* 65–78.

Langer, J. (1978). Rethinking the role of thought in social interaction. In J. Harvey, W. Ickes, & R. Kidd (Eds.), *New directions in attribution research* (Vol. 2). Hillsdale, NJ: Lawrence Erlbaum Associates.

Laws, J. L., & Schwartz, P. (1977). *Sexual scripts: The social construction of female sexuality.* Hinsdale, IL: Dryden Press.

Leahy, R. (1983). Development of self and the problems of social cognition: Identity formation and depression. In L. Wheeler & P. Shaver (Eds.), *Review of personality and social psychology* (Vol. 4, pp. 206–236). Beverly Hills, CA: Sage.

L'Ecuyer, R. (1981). The development of the self-concept through the life span. In M. Lynch, A. Norem–Hebeisen, & K. Gergen (Eds.), *Self-concept: Advances in theory and research* (pp. 203–218). Cambridge, MA: Ballinger.

Levinson, D. (1980). Toward a conception of the adult life course. In N. Smelser & E. Erikson (Eds.), *Themes of work and love in adulthood* (pp. 265–290). Cambridge, MA: Harvard University Press.

Levinson, D., Darrow, C., Klein, E., Levinson, M., & McKee, B. (1978). *The seasons of a man's life*. New York: Knopf.

Lewis, C. N. (1971). Reminiscing and self-concept in old age. *Journal of Gerontology, 26*, 240–243.

Lidz, T. (1968). *The person: His development throughout the life cycle*. New York: Basic Books.

Loevinger, J. (1976). *Ego development*. San Francisco: Jossey–Bass.

Lowenthal, M. F., Thurnher, M., & Chiriboga, D. (1976). *Four stages of life*. San Francisco: Jossey–Bass.

Lynch, M. (1981). Self-concept development in childhood. In M. Lynch, A. Norem–Hebeisen, & K. Gergen (Eds.), *Self concept: Advances in theory and research* (pp. 119–132). Cambridge, MA: Ballinger.

Lynch, M., Norem–Hebeisen, A., & Gergen, K. (Eds.). (1981). *Self concept: Advances in theory and research*. Cambridge, MA: Ballinger.

McCall, G., & Simmons, J. L. (1966). *Identities and interactions*. New York: Free Press.

McCrae, R. R., & Costa, P. T. (1982). *Emerging lives, enduring dispositions: Personality in adulthood*. Boston, MA: Little, Brown.

McGuire, W., & McGuire, C. (1982). Significant others in self-space: Sex differences and developmental trends in the social self. In J. Suls (Ed.), *Psychological perspectives on the self* (Vol. 1, pp. 71–96). Hillsdale, NJ: Lawrence Erlbaum Associates.

Marcia, J. (1980). Identity in adolescence. In J. Adelson (Ed.), *Handbook of adolescent psychology* (pp. 159–187). New York: John Wiley.

Marini, M. M. (1984). Age and sequencing norms in the transition to adulthood. *Social Forces, 63*, 229–244.

Marks, S. (1977). Multiple roles and role strain: Some notes on human energy, time and commitment. *American Sociological Review, 42*, 921–936.

Markus, H., & Sentis, K. (1982). The self in social information processing. In J. Suls (Ed.), *Psychological perspectives on the self* (Vol. 1, pp. 41–70). Hillsdale, NJ: Lawrence Erlbaum Associates.

Mead, G. H. (1932). *The philosophy of the present*. Chicago: University of Chicago Press.

Mead, G. H. (1934). *Mind, self, and society*. Chicago: University of Chicago Press.

Mead, G. H. (1938). *The philosophy of the act*. Chicago: University of Chicago Press.

Merton, R. K. (1957). *Social theory and social structure* (rev. ed.). New York: Free Press.

Montemayor, R., & Eisen, M. (1977). The development of self-conceptions from childhood to adolescence. *Developmental Psychology, 13*, 314–319.

Mortimer, J., Finch, M., & Kumka, D. (1982). Persistence and change in development: The multidimensional self-concept. In P. B. Baltes & O. G. Brim, Jr. (Eds.), *Life-span development and behavior* (Vol. 4, pp. 263–313). New York: Academic Press.

Mortimer, J., & Lorence, J. (1981). Self-concept stability and change from late adolescence to early adulthood. In R. Simmons (Ed.), *Research in community and mental health* (Vol. 2, pp. 5–42). Greenwich, CT: JAI Press.

Mortimer, J., & Simmons, R. (1978). Adult socialization. *Annual Review of Sociology, 4*, 421–454.

Mueller, J., & Ross, M. (1984). Uniqueness of the self-concept across the life span. *Bulletin of the Psychonomic Society, 22*, 83–86.

Mullener, N., & Laird, J. (1971). Some developmental changes in the organization of self-evaluations. *Developmental Psychology, 5*, 233–236.

Neugarten, B. (1968). The awareness of middle age. In B. Neugarten (Ed.), *Middle age and aging* (pp. 43–98). Chicago: University of Chicago Press.

Neugarten, B. (1979). Time, age and the life cycle. *American Journal of Psychiatry, 136*, 887–894.

Neugarten, B., & Datan, N. (1973). Sociological perspectives on the life cycle. In P. B. Baltes & K.

W. Schaie (Eds.), *Life-span developmental psychology* (pp. 53–69). New York: Academic Press.

Neugarten, B., & Hagestad, G. (1976). Age and the life course. In R. Binstock & E. Shanas (Eds.), *Handbook of aging and the social sciences* (pp. 35–55). New York: Van Nostrand.

Neugarten, B., & Moore, J. (1968). The changing age-status system. In B. Neugarten (Ed.), *Middle age and aging* (pp. 5–21). Chicago: University of Chicago Press.

Neugarten, B., Moore, J., & Lowe, J. (1965). Age norms, age constraints, and adult socialization. *American Journal of Sociology, 70,* 710–717.

Proshansky, H., Fabian, A., & Kaminoff, R. (1983). Place-identity: Physical world socialization of the self. *Journal of Environmental Psychology, 3,* 57–83.

Riley, M. W. (1976). Age strata in social systems. In R. Binstock & E. Shanas (Eds.), *Handbook of aging and the social sciences* (pp. 189–217). New York: Van Nostrand Reinhold.

Riley, M. W., & Foner, A. (1968). *Aging and society: Vol. 1. An inventory of research findings.* New York: Russell Sage.

Riley, M. W., Johnson, M., & Foner, A. (Eds.). (1972). *Aging and society: Vol. 3. A sociology of age stratification.* New York: Russell Sage.

Rochberg-Halton, E. (1984). Object relations, role models, and cultivation of the self. *Environment and Behavior, 16,* 335–368.

Rose, A., & Peterson, W. (Eds.). (1965). *Older people and their social world.* Philadelphia: F. A. Davis.

Rosenberg, M. (1979). *Conceiving the self.* New York: Basic Books.

Rosenberg, M. (1981). The self-concept: Social product and social force. In M. Rosenberg & R. Turner (Eds.), *Social psychology: Sociological perspectives* (pp. 593–624). New York: Basic Books.

Rosow, I. (1974). *Socialization to old age.* Berkeley, CA: University of California Press.

Rosow, I. (1976). Status and role change through the life span. In R. Binstock & E. Shanas (Eds.), *Aging and the social sciences* (pp. 457–482). New York: Van Nostrand Reinhold.

Rossi, A. (1980). Aging and parenthood in the middle years. In P. B. Baltes & O. G. Brim, Jr. (Eds.), *Life-span development and behavior* (Vol. 3, pp. 137–205). New York: Academic Press.

Rossi, A. (1985). Gender and parenthood. In A. Rossi (Ed.), *Gender and the life course* (pp. 161–191). Chicago: Aldine.

Rowles, G., & Ohta, R. (Eds.). (1983). *Aging and milieu: Environmental perspectives on growing old.* New York: Academic Press.

Ruble, D., Boggiano, A., Feldman, N., & Loebl, J. (1980). Developmental analysis of the role of social comparison in self-evaluation. *Developmental Psychology, 16,* 105–115.

Runyan, W. M. (1978). The life course as a theoretical orientation: Sequences of person-situation interaction. *Journal of Personality, 46,* 569–593.

Runyan, W. M. (1984). Diverging life paths: Their probabilistic and causal structure. In K. Gergen & M. Gergen (Eds.), *Historical social psychology* (pp. 191–210). Hillsdale, NJ: Lawrence Erlbaum Associates.

Schoeneman, T., Tabor, L., & Nash, D. (1984). Children's reports of the sources of self-knowledge. *Journal of Personality, 52,* 124–137.

Secord, P. F. (Ed.). (1982). *Explaining human behavior: Consciousness, human action and social structure.* Beverly Hills, CA: Sage.

Serpe, R. T.(1985). *Commitment: Measurement and longitudinal analysis.* Unpublished doctoral dissertation, Indiana University, Bloomington, IN.

Shalin, D. (1984). The romantic antecedents of Meadian social psychology. *Symbolic Interaction, 7,* 43–65.

Sieber, S. (1974). Toward a theory of role accumulation. *American Sociological Review, 39,* 567–578.

Simmons, R., Blyth, D., Van Cleave, E., & Bush, D. (1979). Entry into early adolescence: The impact of school structure, puberty, and early dating on self-esteem. *American Sociological Review, 44,* 948–967.

Stokes, R., & Hewitt, J. P. (1976). Aligning actions. *American Sociological Review, 41,* 838–849.

Strauss, A. (1978). *Negotiations.* San Francisco: Jossey–Bass.

Stryker, S. (1968). Identity salience and role performance: The relevance of symbolic interaction theory for family research. *Journal of Marriage and the Family, 30,* 558–564.

Stryker, S. (1980). *Symbolic interactionism: A social structural version.* Menlo Park, CA: Benjamin/Cummings.

Stryker, S. (1981). Symbolic interactionism: Themes and variations. In M. Rosenberg & R. Turner (Eds.), *Social psychology: Sociological perspectives* (pp. 3–29). New York: Basic Books.

Stryker, S. (1983). Social psychology from the standpoint of a structural symbolic interactionism: Toward an interdisciplinary social psychology. In L. Berkowitz (Ed.), *Advances in experimental social psychology* (Vol. 16, pp. 181–318). New York: Academic Press.

Stryker, S. (in press-a). Identity theory: Developments and extensions. In T. Honess & K. Yardley (Eds.), *Self and Identity: Psychosocial Perspectives.* London: Wiley.

Stryker, S. (in press-b). Status inconsistency from an interactionist perspective: A theoretical elaboration. In H. Strasser & R. W. Hodge (Eds.), *Status inconsistency in modern society.*

Stryker, S., & Serpe, R. (1982). Commitment, identity salience, and role behavior. In W. Ickes & E. Knowles (Eds.), *Personality, roles, and social behavior* (pp. 199–218). New York: Springer–Verlag.

Stryker, S., & Statham, A. (1985). Symbolic interactionism and role theory. In G. Linzey & E. Aronson (Eds.), *Handbook of social psychology* (3rd ed.). New York: Random House.

Suls, J. (Ed.). (1982). *Psychological perspectives on the self* (Vol. 1). Hillsdale, NJ: Lawernce Erlbaum Associates.

Suls, J., & Greenwald, A. (Eds.). (1983). *Psychological perspectives on the self* (Vol. 2). Hillsdale, NJ: Lawrence Erlbaum Associates.

Suls, J., & Mullen, B. (1982). From the cradle to the grave: Comparison and self-evaluation across the life span. In J. Suls (Ed.), *Psychological perspectives on the self* (Vol. 1, pp. 97–125). Hillsdale, NJ: Lawrence Erlbaum Associates.

Thoits, P. (1983). Multiple identities and psychological well-being. *American Sociological Review, 48,* 174–187.

Tuan, Y. (1982). *Segmented worlds of self.* Minneapolis: University of Minnesota.

Turner, R. (1978). The role and the person. *American Journal of Sociology, 84,* 1–23.

Verhave, T., & van Hoorn, W. (1984). The temporalization of the self. In K. Gergen & M. Gergen (Eds.), *Historical social psychology* (pp. 325–345). Hillsdale, NJ: Lawrence Erlbaum Associates.

Victor, J. (1978). The social psychology of sexual arousal: A symbolic interactionist interpretation. *Studies in Symbolic Interaction, 1,* 147–180.

Wegner, D., & Vallacher, R. (Eds.). (1980). *The self in social psychology.* New York: Oxford University Press.

Wicklund, R., & Gollwitzer, P. (1982). *Symbolic self-completion.* Hillsdale, NJ: Lawrence Erlbaum Associates.

Wylie, R. (1979). *The self concept: Theory and research on selected topics, Vol. 2* (rev. ed.). Lincoln, NB: University of Nebraska Press.

Zurcher, L. (1979). Role selection: The influence of internalized vocabularies of motive. *Symbolic Interaction, 2,* 45–62.

The Role of Family Experience in Career Exploration: A Life-Span Perspective

Harold D. Grotevant and Catherine R. Cooper
UNIVERSITY OF TEXAS AT AUSTIN

Abstract

This chapter presents a dynamic interactional perspective on the family's role in the career exploration of its adolescents and young adults. The nature of career exploration is first addressed, reviewing the changing meaning of the construct from a stage of development to a life-span process. The family's role in career exploration is then considered. Whereas much of the career development literature has viewed the family in terms of unilateral influence from parents to children, the purpose of this section is to conceptualize the role of relationships in development. The authors' model of individuation as a key quality of relationships, including those between adolescents and their parents, is presented with supportive evidence from recent research. Second, three aspects of individual competence and personality orientations that are mediated by the family and serve as resources for the adolescent's exploration are discussed: self-esteem, ego control and ego resiliency, and intellectual ability. Third, the cultural and societal contexts in which career exploration takes place are addressed. Special attention is devoted to issues of ethnicity, socioeconomic status, and gender and the ways in which they might facilitate or inhibit the expression of career exploration by adolescents. Finally, issues for future research involving the dynamic interactions among the family, the individual's personality and intellectual resources, and the cultural and societal context are identified and discussed.

I. Introduction

Contemporary psychological theories of career development and identity formation have been based on the assumption that adolescent competence is evaluated in terms of the success with which the young person has been launched into worlds beyond the family, especially the world of work. A second assumption of these theories is that adolescents have choices available to them as they go about forming their sense of identity or selecting a career.

Although most theoretical and empirical work in the area has been based on these two assumptions, there are many adolescents for whom the assumptions are not valid. The first assumption is based on notions of autonomy that view the adolescent as necessarily leaving the family in order to become established in work and in intimate relationships (see Hill & Holmbeck, 1986, for discussion). Current research on the relational contexts of development (e.g., Cooper & Ayers-Lopez, 1985; Grotevant & Cooper, 1986; White, Speisman, & Costos, 1983; Youniss & Smollar, 1985), however, has shown that the family continues to be an important context for development throughout adolescence and at least into young adulthood. The second assumption, that adolescents have unlimited choices from which to form their career identities, is valid for some American adolescents. However, when choices are ascribed on the basis of ethnicity, socioeconomic status, or gender, different models of career development and identity formation must be invoked.

Most scholars of adolescence would agree with Erikson (1968) that the development of an occupational identity is a central challenge for adolescents and young adults. However, few developmental psychologists have devoted research attention to this domain. Much of the research in this area has been undertaken by counseling psychologists or industrial/organizational psychologists; therefore, much of it is oriented toward adult clients and does not highlight developmental issues. Although the important role of the family in such development is recognized, there are many domains for which our understanding of the family's role in the development of competence is inadequate.

Conceptualizations that do address developmental issues (e.g., Jordaan, 1963; Super, 1981) have pointed to the centrality of career exploration as a key developmental construct. This emphasis dovetails well with the emphasis on exploration in the identity formation literature (e.g., Grotevant, Thorbecke, & Meyer, 1982; Marcia, 1980; Waterman, 1982). To the degree that choices are available to the adolescent, exploration is an important process because of the role that it potentially plays in contributing to congruence between the qualities of the individual and the environment in which the individual functions (e.g., Grotevant, Cooper, & Kramer, 1986; Holland, 1985; Jordaan, 1963). When there is a good "match" between individual and work environment, both job satisfaction (Mount & Muchinsky, 1978) and longevity in the career (Vaitenas & Wiener, 1977) are enhanced.

This chapter presents a perspective on the family's role in the career exploration of its adolescents and young adults, drawing primarily upon the career development, identity formation, and socialization literatures. Although the importance of career exploration has been acknowledged in the past, empirical work concerning this process has been limited. Thus, the discussion that follows will be somewhat speculative, aimed at encouraging model building and further research in this area.

This chapter will begin with a discussion of the changing position of the career exploration construct from referring to a stage of development to an ongoing life-span process. Second, discussion of the family's role in career exploration will be presented. The discussion will focus upon ways in which the expression of career exploration on the part of the adolescent or young adult is mediated by the dynamic interaction between his or her individual personality and intellectual resources, the quality of the relationships experienced within the family, and the societal and historical contexts in which the developing individual is embedded. Finally, it will be argued that the life-span perspective is a useful framework in which to consider the development of career exploration, given the weight of empirical evidence demonstrating the ongoing interaction between developing individuals and their changing contexts.

II. Career Exploration: Stage or Process?

Although the concept of career exploration has been discussed for a number of years, its meaning has shifted as different theories have waxed and waned in popularity. In early formulations, exploration was viewed as a stage of development. For example, Ginzberg et al. (1951) viewed career development as an irreversible process consisting of three stages: fantasy, tentative, and realistic. Exploration was the first step in the realistic stage, and it presumably occurred around age 18. The exploration stage was marked by a gradual narrowing of goals until a specific choice is made. In the original formulation of Super's theory (1953), career development was again seen in terms of movement through a sequence of stages, including growth, exploration, establishment, maintenance, and decline. Tiedeman and O'Hara (1963) viewed career development as a decision-making process, but again, exploration was considered a phase of the anticipation stage of development.

In these three conceptualizations, several commonalities which have been refined in current theory may be noted. First, all three assumed that exploration has a relatively late onset; the exploration that may begin in childhood or early adolescence was discounted. Second, all three theories viewed career development as a linear process and did not adequately take into account those cases in which individuals reconsider commitments or make false starts. Third, none of these theories considered career development as a life-span process.

A major advance in conceptualizing career exploration was made in Jordaan's (1963) seminal paper on the role of exploratory behavior in the formation of self and occupational concepts. In this paper, the multidimensional nature of exploration was explicitly recognized, and hypothesized antecedents and consequences of exploration were discussed. Behavior was considered to be exploratory only if it involved experimentation, investigation, trial, search, or hypothesis testing. Exploration, therefore, was seen as problem-solving behavior aimed at eliciting information about oneself or one's environment in order to choose, prepare for, enter, adjust to, or progress in an occupation (Jordaan, 1963).

More current views of career exploration have attempted to describe the process of exploration in more detail and to consider that this process may extend across the life span. However, it should be noted that most research in this area has investigated the outcomes of exploration (such as job satisfaction or employee turnover) rather than the antecedents of exploration or the process itself. Therefore, the following account of the process of career exploration is based on limited theoretical and empirical work.

The most differentiated account of career exploration as a component of the decision-making process has been presented by Harren (1979a,b; Pitz & Harren, 1980). Although the model is intended to apply to college undergraduate students, some of its principles appear applicable to younger and older individuals as well and fit with the available empirical data.

In Harren's model, exploration is viewed as a process that takes place primarily during the *planning* stage of career development (following *awareness* and preceding *commitment* and *implementation*). It involves searching for information about career options and considering it in relation to one's self-concept. The individual experiences cycles of exploration (expanding) and crystallization (narrowing of focus) as movement is made toward a career choice. This cyclical process involves (a) information search, (b) information processing (in which the individual considers the information in terms of his or her self-concept and applies personal meaning to it), (c) evaluation of deficits blocking commitment, (d) further information search and information processing, and (e) successive reductions of alternatives to one choice (Harren, 1979a).

Other contemporary decision-making models (e.g., Janis & Mann, 1977) and process models (e.g., Stumpf, Colarelli, & Hartman, 1983) view exploration as an ongoing consideration in career development across the life span. In addition, the recent formulation of Super's theory (1981) acknowledges that career development may be a lifelong cyclical process rather than a time-restricted stage. Recycling back into a period of exploration may occur in the transition from one stage to the next or whenever a career path is unstabilized.

During the past 20 years, personality and developmental researchers from the Eriksonian tradition independently became interested in career development as an aspect of adolescent identity formation. Building in large part on Marcia's identity status work first published in 1966, a cohort of researchers have refined both the conceptual and methodological issues in this area (e.g., Adams & Montemayor, 1983; Bourne, 1978; Grotevant, Thorbecke, & Meyer, 1982; Marcia, 1980; Matteson, 1977; Waterman, 1982). Although Erikson discussed the necessity of a period of "crisis" in formation of adult identity, research has found that the majority of adolescents do not experience this phase of life as a crisis (e.g., Offer, Ostrov, & Howard, 1981). In an effort to acknowledge this reality and yet consider the ways in which adolescence is a time of search and uncertainty, Matteson (1977) proposed that *exploration* be viewed as a defining feature of identity achievement rather than crisis. This terminology has largely persisted, and current methods of assessing identity development (e.g., Grotevant, 1986; Grotevant & Adams, 1984; Grotevant & Cooper, 1981) look for evidence of both exploration and commitment. Even though career development has been assessed as one domain of identity formation since Marcia's original identity status interview was published, no one has adequately exploited the potentially rich links between the career development and identity formation literatures.

Empirical evidence to support a life-span, process view of career exploration is less abundant than might be desired because of the dearth of longitudinal studies. However, insight may be gained into the life-span nature of the exploration process by considering together evidence from several separate studies each of which concerns narrower age bands, but together cover a much broader age span. For example, in a study concerning the identity formation of high school students, Grotevant and Thorbecke (1982) found that 42% of a sample of high school juniors and seniors were rated as identity achieved (showing both exploration as well as commitment) in the area of career identity. In studies of college students, however, the proportion of freshmen rated as identity achieved is usually substantially less (e.g., Waterman, Geary, & Waterman, 1974). At first glance, these two sets of findings seem difficult to reconcile. When one adds studies of adult development to this set, the findings initially appear inconsistent, but then make sense when one takes a life-span view of career exploration.

In studies of adult career development (e.g., Levinson, 1978), one sees cycles of alternation between periods of relative stability of choices and relative instability or exploration of alternative possibilities. In Levinson's sample of middle-aged men, periods of relative instability and reconsideration of possibilities were most common around age 30, again in the early 40s and again around the time of retirement. When the high school, college, and adult studies are examined together, a pattern of development emerges that suggests a spiral: The high school years may be a time for the first "round" of mature career development, since it is first based on mature cognitive and social cognitive abilities. However, further "rounds" of exploration and stability occur during college and, potentially, several times in adulthood. This interpretation is consistent with Harren's (1979a) and Super's (1981) discussions of the alternating cycles of expanding and narrowing choices.

The view that exploration is not a one-time, linear process leading directly to career commitment was also supported in two studies using longitudinal data from the Career Pattern Study. One study (Phillips, 1982a) tested this view by hypothesizing that exploratory decision modes should generally precede "terminal" decisions (those that result in the implementation of a choice). Although approximately one-half of the 95 male subjects followed the predicted pattern of exploratory behavior followed by terminal decisions, the other half followed different patterns. For example, 13.7% of the subjects cycled from exploratory to terminal and back to exploratory behavior or from terminal to exploratory to terminal behavior over the three ages studied (21, 25, and 36). Another 32.6% showed stable exploratory or terminal behavior across the three ages. Finally, 5.3% showed terminal behavior preceding subsequent exploratory behavior. In a second report (Phillips, 1982b), hypotheses that increasing exploration followed by commitment would lead to significantly higher levels of desirable career outcomes than other patterns were generally not upheld. In interpreting these results, Phillips concluded that different occupational paths may make different demands on exploration and commitment.

Most accounts of career development appear to assume that the process of exploration is experienced by all adolescents. However, it must be emphasized that the potential to explore is directly related to the availability of choices. When economic necessities force an adolescent to earn a living, exploration is a luxury that cannot be afforded. In addition, societal or familial values about decision making may constrain or facilitate the exploration process.

Even when exploration is valued and choices are available, there are certain conditions under which the exploration process is more likely to be initiated: (a) when the individual receives negative evaluation relevant to a task being implemented, (b) when the individual experiences consistently low levels of success and satisfaction relative to the levels anticipated, and (c) when *task immanence* increases (e.g., an approaching deadline for a decision such as high school or college graduation). Exploration, or the search for alternatives, is seen as worthwhile to the individual only if the expected gain exceeds the expected cost. Thus, motivation to explore will depend on one's current level of satisfaction and perceived press to make a decision (Pitz & Harren, 1980). Further theoretical consideration of the factors influencing the orientation to explore is strongly needed.

Neither career development theories nor identity theories have placed great emphasis on the contexts in which development occurs, as both are focused more clearly on the outcomes of development. A danger inherent in this lack of attention to context is that research will be conducted under the premise that career development and identity formation proceed in a uniform manner for all adolescents regardless of context, career interests, or their individual psychological resources.

Relevant contexts for career development certainly include society, the school, the peer group, work experience, and the family. In much of the traditional theorizing and research about adolescence, the emphasis has been placed on the time period as one during which the adolescent moves away from the family and toward the worlds of peers and work. However, recent research focusing on relational contexts of adolescent development (e.g., Cooper, Grotevant, & Condon, 1983; Grotevant & Cooper, 1985, 1986; White et al. 1983; Youniss & Smollar, 1985) has shown that the family continues to serve as a context for individual development throughout adolescence and into young adulthood.

III. The Family's Role in Career Exploration

In the following section, the various contributions of family experience to the career exploration process will be examined. First, conclusions emerging from the traditional socialization literature will be reviewed. Although these findings are informative, the argument will be advanced that relational models of development may provide additional insight into those factors that contribute to career exploration. Second, the family's contribution to the general intellectual and personality resources that the individual adolescent brings to the exploration process will be discussed. These resources are viewed as adaptive skills, developed at least in part within the family, that have special implications for career development. Finally, the cultural and societal contexts in which the adolescent develops will be considered. Any discussion of the process of exploration is based on the premise that choices are available to individuals. Therefore, cultural and societal factors such as ethnicity, social class, and gender will be discussed insofar as they mediate the availability of choices.

Three points must be made with respect to the following presentation. First, although family, individual, and societal factors are discussed in three separate sections, it should be clear that they affect each other in ongoing ways throughout the life span. This view is consistent with the dynamic interactional perspective (e.g., Hartup, 1978; Lerner & Shea, 1982; Lerner & Spanier, 1978), which holds that individual development may only be understood in terms of the constant interactions between the developing person and the changing environment. Second, the primary focus of this chapter is to contribute to the understanding of career exploration. Many other career constructs (such as career maturity and career aspirations) undoubtedly have roots in societal and family factors; but development of an all-encompassing framework for career constructs in general is beyond the scope of this chapter. Career constructs other than exploration will be invoked only insofar as they clarify issues concerning exploration itself. Finally, the focus of the approach taken here concerns the origins of individual differences in career exploration. Although statement of a causal model is premature at this point, a long-range goal of this work is to clarify causal mechanisms in the development of career exploration.

A. FAMILY CONTEXTS OF CAREER EXPLORATION

Much evidence exists that parents influence their children's career development, although the processes by which this occurs are not well specified. As general models of parent–child relationships have become more sophisticated (Grotevant & Cooper, 1983; Hartup & Rubin, 1986; Hinde, 1979; Hinde, Perret–Clermont, & Stevenson–Hinde, in press; Maccoby & Martin, 1983; Youniss, 1983), models for the role of family experience in career development will also benefit. In this section, two general approaches to the role of the family will be examined. The first set of studies includes those in the "social mold" tradition (see Hartup, 1978, for an extended discussion). Despite repeated calls for more relational models of family influence (e.g., Bell, 1968; Lerner & Spanier, 1978), much of the current literature still views the family's influence as unilateral, from parent to child. Next, a newer model which focuses on relationships as contexts for development will be considered as a framework for understanding career exploration. Although parental modeling, attitudes, and behaviors do provide inputs to the child's career development process, our interest is in exploring the degree to which qualities of the relationships within the family predict additional variance.

Unilateral Parental Processes

Parents as Models. In a recent youth poll (Hedin et al., 1985), adolescents named their parents as the most important influence on their thinking about careers, although many named no one. It is notable that although most high school students reported talking to their school counselors, few adolescents named counselors or other professionals as influences on their plans (Tittle, 1981).

Mothers' and fathers' educational levels have been found to be associated with daughters' career aspirations (Fitzgerald & Betz, 1983), and mothers' working status has also been found to be related to their children's career exploration. Kindergarten and first-grade children whose mothers were currently employed chose a greater number of occupations and more masculine-oriented occupations than did children of nonemployed mothers (Selkow, 1984). Girls whose mothers had selected nontraditional fields also tended to aspire to less sex-traditional careers. Significant differences were found between girls and boys for types of occupations selected, but (unlike Riley, 1981) not for numbers of vocational choices (Selkow, 1984). Among a sample largely composed of adolescents with mothers in low-status jobs or homemaking roles, mothers were not viewed as occupational role models (Hedin et al., 1985).

Most studies viewing the mother's function as a role model have concluded that the college-student daughters of working mothers are more career-oriented and are more likely to explore less traditional careers than the children of non-working mothers (Marini, 1978; Reid & Stephens, 1985; Rollins & White, 1982; Shapiro & Crowley, 1982). An interesting within-family dynamic is suggested by the finding that girls' preference for pursuing nontraditional careers was associated with their perceptions of maternal power in their families (Lavine, 1982). Burlin (1976), however, working with 11th-grade females, discovered another possible explanation. Daughters who aspired to careers in which half or more of the workers were men had mothers who not only worked, but worked in male-dominated careers themselves. In general, teen-age sons and daughters of working mothers were less stereotyped in their conception of both provider and care-giver roles, anticipating that fathers and mothers will have responsibilities in both areas (L. W. Hoffman, 1979).

Parental Attitudes. The independent contribution of parental attitudes in addition to parental modeling of career achievement is indicated by the findings that homemaker mothers' positive attitudes were positively related to daughters' attitudes toward careers (Altman & Grossman, 1977), whereas working mothers' negative attitudes were predictive of daughters' ambivalence toward careers (Baruch, 1972). In addition, Oliver (1975) found that career-oriented college women perceived their fathers as less accepting (than did homemaking oriented students) and were more highly father-identified.

Parental Behavior. Several studies suggest that enriching experiences may lead young women in particular to broaden their conceptions of the female role and of their own potential achievement, thereby stimulating increased career exploration. For example, fathers' encouragement was predictive of daughters' choosing pioneering (nontraditional) occupations in several studies (Fitzgerald & Betz, 1983). Lemkau (1979) found that career-oriented women were more likely to have highly educated parents, working mothers, more work experience in high school and college, and to come from home environments fostering achievement, independence, and active exploration of the environment. A lack of pressure on women to choose traditional female roles (including dating, marrying, and having children), was likewise predictive of their making pioneer career choices (Matthews & Tiedeman, 1964). In a similar vein, voluntary childlessness, singlehood, and smaller number of children were also associated with professional aspirations (Helmreich et al., 1980).

Competence, self-directedness, assertiveness, and self-sufficiency could broaden women's perceived and actual career options and lead to knowledgeable choosing rather than choosing by default. Parents as well as teachers, the media, and peers socialize boys to be competent, instrumental, curious, daring, and achievement-oriented and to anticipate the adult role of worker and provider, whereas these agents more typically socialize girls to value warmth, expressiveness, conforming to the expectations and rules of others, and to anticipate the adult roles of wife and mother (Block, 1984; Shaffer, 1980).

Although parental support and encouragement have been cited as predictors of high career aspirations and the choice of pioneer occupations among women, one might ask to what extent support is offered for genuine exploration and choice (for example, of a low status occupation); or, on the other hand, the degree that support may be construed by the adolescent as pressure to achieve within a circumscribed range. Future research should examine the boundary between encouragement and pressure and the range in which encouragement supports exploration.

Limitations of the Unilateral Model. The unilateral parent-to-child influence posited in most of the studies cited in this section is informative but also limited in being able to account for career exploration for at least two reasons. First, since our society is undergoing such rapid change, it is not sufficient for parents to socialize their children through modeling and encouragement alone (Conger, 1971). Their children will be facing different demands and opportunities in the world of work: young women whose mothers were full-time homemakers may well find that such an option is not viable for them; young adults of both sexes will have opportunities to participate in technological occupations that did not even exist 20 years ago. The second limitation of this literature concerns its theoretical foundation, in that unilateral models of socialization themselves are inadequate for explaining the development of adult competence. Recent trends in conceptualizing the role of relationships in individual development will be presented in the next section.

Relational Models of Development

In the research reviewed above, the limitations of unilateral models of socialization in accounting for career exploration have been noted. Variables such as warmth and modeling are too general, unidirectional, and conformity-oriented, whereas career exploration involves the necessity of more specific and initiative-engendering family variables. As Hartup (1986) has noted, relationships constitute bases that enable the child to function in the wider world: "They are gateways or channels to an ever-widening range of experiences" (p. 2).

According to this relationship perspective, parent–child influence is reciprocal and transactional rather than unidirectional; thus, relationships between parents and children are mutually transforming over time. The parent–child relationship is seen as an enduring bond that continues throughout the life span but undergoes significant transformations in adolescence (Hill & Holmbeck, 1986) and young adulthood (White et al. 1983).

Developmental Perspectives on Attachment and Exploration. Recent developmental work consistent with this relational perspective suggests that the origins of individual differences in children may be traced by understanding continuities and changes in parent–child relationships from infancy through middle childhood and into adolescence. The greatest quantity of such work to date has focused on mappings from infancy to early childhood. Ainsworth (1979), Sroufe (1979, 1983), and others have documented the contribution of the quality of parent–child attachment to the development of exploration and autonomy in infancy and early childhood. The security of the mother–infant attachment has been found to be predictive of the child's ego resiliency (Arend, Gove, & Sroufe, 1979) and of the child's later effectiveness in problem solving (Matas, Arend, & Sroufe, 1978); in peer relations (Lieberman, 1977; Waters, Wippman, & Sroufe, 1979); and in independent exploration of spatial environments (Hazen & Durrett, 1982).

The proposition that security of attachment promotes exploration by infants and young children has been extended by Hartup (1979), who proposed that security in family relationships can promote competence by freeing the child to become engaged with worlds outside the family, including the domains of peer relationships and career choices. This argument has been extended more directly to adolescence by Hill (1980), who suggested that authoritative parents (e.g., Baumrind, 1982) provide a secure base both for the development of social competence in peer relations and for the exploration needed for identity achievement. It is important to note that authoritative parenting, as defined by Baumrind, is not a unilateral strategy but includes ongoing give-and-take and negotiation between parents and children.

However, although attachment permits exploration to occur, it is not sufficient in itself to bring about exploration. There must at least also be an interesting environment to explore (Hartup, in press). In addition, limitations imposed by ethnicity, social class, or gender may override the potential developed in the family.

The Individuation Model. For the past several years, we have been engaged in a program of research whose goal it is to develop and test a model of individuation in relationships (Cooper, Grotevant, & Condon, 1983; Grotevant & Cooper, 1985, 1986). The model is based on the premise that important skills in areas that involve both agency and communality develop in the context of relationships. In particular, the literature on the consequences of attachment for later development suggests the value of examining a similar process in adolescence:

that qualities of relationships within the family are related to the adolescent's ability to explore domains outside the family. Although the focus of this chapter concerns exploration of career identity, other work in our project concerns the adolescents' exploration of relationships outside the family with peers (e.g., Cooper & Grotevant, 1986; Cooper, Grotevant, & Ayers-Lopez, 1986).

The relational context of development is particularly important because of the qualities that all participants in the relationship bring to the situation. As the literature on exploration cited earlier suggests, the ability to "leave home" and explore the outside world depends not only on the individual's resources but also on the security of the "home base" (e.g., Ainsworth, 1979) from which the adolescent is to venture out. Neither of these qualities develops as a function of unilateral parent-to-child socialization.

The individuation model is based on developmental and clinical conceptualizations of the family that emphasize the importance of both individuality and connectedness within family relationships for the well-being of its members (Beavers, 1976; Grotevant & Cooper, 1986; Karpel, 1976; Minuchin, 1974; Sroufe, 1983). Of course, the cultural values implicit in this model must be noted. This view of family health is most prevalent in societies in which high value is placed on individuals' opportunities to have control over choices that affect their lives. Individuality is indicated in expressions of *separateness,* in which the distinctiveness of self from other is expressed; as well as in *self-assertion,* in which individuals express their own points of view clearly. For the adolescent, separateness and self-assertion in family interaction have been regarded as qualities of healthy family process because they concern the ability of each family member to possess a point of view and to have opinions that may differ from those of other family members (Beavers, 1976; Minuchin, 1974).

Connectedness is seen in expressions of *mutuality,* in which the individual shows sensitivity to the viewpoints of others by taking their needs into account in the interaction; and of *permeability,* or openness and responsiveness to the views of others. Mutuality expressed to the adolescent can be a source of support and respect for developing his or her own beliefs; on the other hand, mutuality expressed by the adolescent is an indicator of his or her ability to coordinate individual needs with the needs of larger groups, such as the family and society. Permeability involves the management of boundaries between self and others, and may be of special significance during the process of identity formation (Carter & McGoldrick, 1980). According to this model of relationships, evidence of both individuality and connectedness (i.e., an individuated relationship) would be predicted to provide for its members the context for exploring and clarifying individual points of view.

In our research program, empirical evidence for the validity of the conceptual model and support for predictions concerning the links between qualities of relationships and identity exploration have been obtained. These findings have emerged from a study that involved 121 two-parent families with adolescent children, one of whom was a high school senior. The families participating were both white and middle class, in order to examine the links between relational qualities and exploration when ethnicity and social class were held constant. Each family was observed in a situation designed to elicit the expression and coordination of a variety of points of view (Condon, Cooper, & Grotevant, 1984); in addition, the target adolescent in each family was administered an interview to assess identity exploration and commitment (Grotevant & Cooper, 1981). Each family's interaction was coded according to 14 communication behaviors hypothesized to reflect the four dimensions of self-assertion, separateness, mutuality, and permeability. Factor analysis performed on the intercorrelation matrix of these behaviors confirmed the distinctiveness and integrity of the dimensions derived from theory.

Subsequent analyses have established links between patterns of relationships within the family and adolescents' identity exploration, role-taking skill, and peer interaction behavior (Cooper, Grotevant, & Ayers–Lopez, 1986; Cooper, Grotevant, & Condon, 1983; Grotevant & Cooper, 1985). When a subset of 84 families in which the parents and two children had participated in the family interaction task was considered, communication patterns related to identity exploration were found to differ for male and female adolescents. For boys, only father–son interaction patterns were related to exploration ratings. A distinctive pattern of father–son communication predictive of high identity exploration involved sons' expressions of disagreements to their fathers as well as sons' direct statements of their own suggestions, while fathers expressed mutuality to their sons and were less likely to express their own suggestions, perhaps to allow their sons the opportunity to contribute to the family interaction. For girls, communication patterns in all three relationships in which they participated (mother–daughter, father–daughter, adolescent–sibling) as well as in the marital relationship that they observed were predictive of identity exploration ratings. Consistent with other literature cited in this chapter, these findings suggest that sources of family influence on identity exploration may be more diverse for female adolescents than for males.

Further work on the individuation model is in progress. However, findings to date suggest the usefulness of examining relational contexts of development, especially for predicting adolescent outcomes such as career exploration and peer relational competence that involve both individual agency as well as the ability to coordinate individual views with those of others.

Further Perspectives on Mutuality. Distinctive roles of fathers and mothers in their adolescents' development were suggested by Youniss and Smollar (1985). Interviews with 15- and 18-year-olds indicated that, as a group, adolescents viewed their fathers as providers and as advisers about the world beyond the family. However, fathers' interests and involvements were seen as restricted to concerns about academic performance and future plans. In contrast, both male and female adolescents viewed their mothers more as confidantes concerning personal and relational issues.

Although both parents were seen as holding expectations about behavior and achievement, most adolescents did not report feeling able to discuss doubts about their abilities with their fathers. This sense of distance was especially true for daughters, few of whom named their father as the person with whom they were most likely to discuss careers, self-doubts, or hopes and plans for the future. The picture emerging from these data is that adolescents often view their fathers as sources of information and expectations, but not as partners for candid self-exploration or consideration of their vulnerabilities. In Youniss and Smollar's words, "the fathers' expectations of adolescents—what they want their sons or daughters to be—serves as a filter that bars coming face-to-face with another personality" (1985, p. 90). Thus, although fathers were acknowledged as having expertise about the outside world, their effectiveness in sharing this information was reduced because they were not seen as sources of guidance that could help coordinate this expertise with knowledge about their adolescents as persons.

Much further work concerning the role of relationships in development remains to be undertaken. Important steps in this area include understanding the ongoing interplay between individual and relational development (Hartup, in press) and understanding relational development itself (Wynne, 1984). For example, just as individuated family relationships may facilitate the adolescent's exploration of career choices and other identity issues, the new perspectives gained by the adolescent may provoke greater mutuality in those family relationships. How are these new contributions handled within the family? How does individuation look in families with children of different ages? What are the differences between overt behavior and attributions in the complex process of coordinating individuality and connectedness in relationships?

B. INDIVIDUAL RESOURCES

This section will consider the family's role in key aspects of individual competence that mediate the capacity of adolescents to engage in exploration. These resources are not applied only to career issues; in fact, they are skills or orientations that affect individual functioning in many domains of daily living. Although they are not sufficient to motivate or produce career exploration (because they interact with the other contextual or familial factors discussed in this chapter), we view them as necessary conditions for enabling exploration to occur. Development of these aspects of competence accrues throughout childhood as a function of the dynamic interaction between the child and his or her context (Lerner & Spanier, 1978). Although many aspects of competence could have been discussed here, we have identified three that have direct bearing on adolescent's ability to explore career possibilities: self-esteem, ego control and ego resilience, and intellectual ability. For each area, the family's role in its development will be considered.

Self-Esteem

Self-esteem, the individual's evaluation of his or her worth, is an important prerequisite to exploration insofar as it frees the person psychologically to take risks and consider opportunities and options. This link was recently confirmed in a study that used path analysis to test alternative causal models concerning relations between self-worth, affect, and motivation. Harter and Hogan (1985; Harter, 1985) found that feelings of global self-worth contributed to motivation both directly and through the mediating construct of affect. Thus, the energy and interest to become engaged in new situations was found to have causal antecedents in feelings of self-esteem.

In the career area, women with positive evaluations of themselves were more likely to be career-oriented and innovative in their choices, and they were also more likely to make actual choices consistent with their early aspirations and leading to consistent life-styles (Fitzgerald & Betz, 1983).

The developmental roots of self-esteem may be found in childhood and are importantly grounded in the child's experience within his or her family. According to Coopersmith's (1967) study of self-esteem in school-age boys, parents of high self-esteem males encouraged their sons to express their opinions, permitted their sons to disagree with them, provided clear limits for their sons' behavior, frequently showed them affection, and generally took an interest in their lives. These parenting styles have been linked in other research to the development of instrumental competence (e.g., Baumrind, 1975), which involves the child's active engagement with the world, and to identity exploration and achievement in adolescence (e.g., Adams & Jones, 1983; Cooper, Grotevant, & Condon, 1983; Cushing, 1971; Grotevant & Cooper, 1985).

Ego Control and Ego Resiliency

Ego control, as formulated in the work of Jack and Jeanne Block (1980), refers to the degree of permeability of an individual's psychological boundaries (cf. Lewin, 1936). When placed on a single dimension, overcontrol refers to "excessive boundary impermeability resulting in the containment of impulse, delay of gratification, inhibition of action and affect, and insulation from environmental distractors" (Block & Block, 1980, p. 43). The opposite end of the dimension, ego undercontrol, implies "insufficient modulation of impulse, the inability to delay gratification. . . . and vulnerability to environmental distractors" (p. 43).

Ego resiliency, a companion construct of ego control (Block & Block, 1980), refers to the individual's flexibility in confronting new and potentially challenging situations. When dimensionalized, ego resiliency is defined "at one extreme by resourceful adaptation to changing circumstances and environmental contingencies, analysis of the 'goodness of fit' between situational demands and behavioral possibility, and flexible invocation of the available repertoire of problem-solving strategies'' and at the other extreme by ''little adaptive flexibility, an inability to respond to the dynamic requirements of the situation, [and] a tendency to perseverate or to become disorganized when encountering changed circumstances or when under stress . . .'' (1980, p. 48).

In the Blocks' longitudinal study (Block, 1971; Block & Block, 1980), the dimension of ego control was shown to be associated with children's active engagement with experimental tasks, with inquisitive exploration of a curiosity box, and with active efforts directed at overcoming barriers. Of specific relevance to this discussion was the finding that overcontrol was correlated with inhibition and lack of exploration. The family antecedents of overcontrol were clearer for males than for females. Parents of overcontrolled males tended to be conservative, to emphasize structure and order, to enforce demands for compliance, and mothers tended to use guilt induction as a means of punishment. In addition, mothers tended to discourage their sons' steps toward independence.

In a finding that contributes to a life-span perspective on the family's role in exploration, the tendency toward overcontrol was found to be relatively stable from the junior high school years through young adulthood. In adulthood, overcontrolled men were found to be anxious, detached, distorting, unhappy, and disengaged (Block, 1971). Although the developmental continuity of these behaviors with career exploration in adolescence remains to be established, it seems plausible to hypothesize that such a link might exist for many individuals.

Ego-resilient individuals tended to have loving, competent mothers who encouraged free discussion of feelings and problems. Individuals at the brittle end of the resiliency dimension tended to come from conflictual and discordant families (Block & Block, 1980). In an independent longitudinal study, continuity of development was found to exist between patterns of attachment at 18 months of age and ego resiliency at age 4–5 (Arend, Gove, & Sroufe, 1979). Children who had been securely attached as infants were found to score higher on three measures of curiosity and to achieve higher ratings of ego resiliency than did children who had been anxiously attached as infants. From these descriptions, it seems likely that career exploration would be greatly facilitated by an ego-resilient personality orientation. The identification of the roots of ego resiliency in early family relationships (Arend, Gove, & Sroufe, 1979) is significant and supports the importance of taking a life-span view of family contexts of career exploration.

Intellectual Ability

Although direct empirical links between career exploration and intellectual ability remain to be established, Jordaan's (1963) discussion of factors that facilitate exploration suggests that intellectual ability merits consideration as a resource. However, understanding the contribution of intelligence to exploration is difficult because the processes mediating the relationship between the two are not specified.

The family's role in intellectual development has been documented both from the perspective of behavior genetics (e.g., Scarr & Kidd, 1983) and environmental stimulation (e.g., Bradley & Caldwell, 1976; Elardo, Bradley, & Caldwell, 1975). However, general intelligence as an outcome variable is too global to be informative about career exploration at the process level.

A more direct link between intellectual ability and exploration is suggested when one considers both the exploration literature (e.g., Jordaan, 1963) and the social cognitive literature (e.g., Flavell, 1974; Hill & Palmquist, 1978). It seems reasonable to propose that, in order for individuals to benefit from exploration, they must be able to evaluate information and draw inferences both about the self and the environment. Once such inferences are drawn, the process requires integration of the products of exploration with the developing self-concept as well as with the reality constraints of society, the labor market, and family values.

The ability to coordinate multiple perspectives in this manner is a social cognitive achievement of adolescence (Hill & Palmquist, 1978). In data from the Family Process Project (Cooper, Grotevant, & Condon, 1983), the ability to coordinate multiple perspectives (as measured by Feffer's Role Taking Task) was significantly correlated with identity exploration. The same data set points to the importance of specifying the processes underlying exploration in that verbal ability (which is often considered to be a strong indicator of general intelligence) was not significantly correlated with identity exploration.

C. CULTURAL AND SOCIETAL CONTEXTS OF CAREER DEVELOPMENT

Significant numbers of American children are growing up in contexts in which their ultimate status, including occupational status, may be ascribed or at least seriously constrained as a function of their ethnicity, socioeconomic status (SES), or gender. Ethnicity, SES, and gender may function as stimulus variables that act as elicitors of how others treat children, and may thus override the impact of their distinctive individual characteristics such as ability, motivation, or potential (Fitzgerald & Betz, 1983).

There are several general ways in which exploration may vary as a function of these contexts of development. First, not all adolescents have equal access to opportunities to explore. In certain respects, exploration is a luxury of being a member of the middle class. Lower socioeconomic class adolescents and their families often have pressing economic needs to meet which preclude an extensive moratorium during which they can explore potential futures. Second, lower-class adolescents, especially minority youths, have less access to options than their middle-class peers because of discrimination and alienation from mainstream society. Third, lower-class adolescents often have less information about career possibilities (Smith, 1983).

The purpose of this section is to highlight ways in which these cultural and societal factors mediate the availability of choices in the career exploration process, both in adolescence and adulthood. Detailed information on the broader role of ethnicity, social class, and gender in career development may be found elsewhere (e.g., Walsh & Osipow, 1983).

Ethnicity

Although the experience of ethnic minorities in the United States is diverse, societal conditions, including the openness of the employment opportunity structure and the existence of racism, as well as institutions, such as schools and employers, constrain the degree of choice in the progress of career exploration. Families serve as mediators of this process, interpreting the world in ways that might caution or encourage their members. Although higher levels of occupational achievement and increased range of occupational choice for significant numbers of minority Americans will not be attained without changes in the opportunity structure, the family's interpretation of the meaning of ethnicity remains an important mediator of the child's approach to the world beyond it and may influence how the child reacts to variations in opportunities (Reiss, 1981).

Socioeconomic Status

Differences in social class have been linked to different socialization patterns in the family concerning orientation toward rules. Because of their experiences in the social system, lower-class parents are more likely to be involved in following policy than in making it. Thus, their orientation is more likely toward conformity than toward self-directedness (e.g., Kohn, 1977). To the degree that the exploration process requires initiative and proactive problem finding, adolescents from lower-class family backgrounds may not have the orientation necessary to support extensive exploration. These issues would be exacerbated in minority youths from lower-SES backgrounds, who would likely have had little opportunity or encouragement from society to exhibit initiative.

In addition, social class differences have been identified in child-rearing techniques (L.W. Hoffman, 1984). Lower-class parents tend to rely on power-assertive techniques more heavily than do middle-class parents; and middle-class parents tend to use inductive techniques more extensively than do lower-class parents (e.g., M. L. Hoffman, 1960). The consequence of this difference for career exploration is that, in general, children raised in lower-class families are socialized into obedience and conformity, whereas children from middle-class families, especially boys, are encouraged to display initiative and self-motivation.

Gender

Gender differences also have pervasive implications for the career development process (Fitzgerald & Betz, 1983; Huston–Stein & Higgins–Trenk, 1978; Reid & Stephens, 1985). Patterns of socialization experienced both at school and in the family produce vastly different career expectations and aspirations in young men and women. Because the most fully articulated theories of career development and identity formation are based on the assumption that choices are available to the adolescent, they have poor explanatory power for many young women who have been socialized into a restricted set of choices. Consequently, issues concerning gender differences in this area must be addressed.

Evidence is accumulating that occupational stereotypes associated with gender are learned early by children in the United States. Preschool children are able to identify and agree with adult job stereotypes (Tremaine & Schau, 1979). In a study with particular relevance to career exploration, kindergarten children were asked to draw a picture of what they would like to be when they grew up (Riley, 1981). Boys displayed a significantly greater variety of occupations than did girls.

Differential Treatment of Males and Females. Another key gender difference relevant to exploration concerns girls' and boys' differential treatment by their parents with regard to the world beyond the family. Studies of young children have found differential parental encouragement of boys' exploratory behavior (Block, 1984). Observational studies have documented girls' physical restriction to indoor and relatively secure environments (Medrich et al., 1982). Peer relations offer similar lessons, with girls' activities more likely to be focused on social skills and boys' play more likely to enhance exploration and independence (Brooks–Gunn & Matthews, 1979; Nicholson, 1985).

During adolescence, both girls and boys see girls as being sheltered and protected by their parents yet also restricted to the home, to stereotyped occupations, and to family roles (Hedin et al., 1985). Not surprisingly, girls report feelings of resentment for what they regard as parents' and teachers' overprotectiveness, which both boys and girls feel could erode girls' confidence and competence in challenging work settings (Nicholson, 1985).

Considerable evidence is available concerning the restricted range of occupations chosen by women, and of the concentration of their choices in the lower levels of occupational status. Their career aspirations are still generally restricted to predominantly female occupations, which creates a disadvantaged position for them in the labor market with regard to salary, mobility, and advancement

(Fitzgerald & Betz, 1983). When aspirations are thus circumscribed, exploration will be limited. Recent data are indicating some secular changes in gender-specific occupational choices, with adolescent girls expressing choices from among both male and female gender-typed jobs, and boys still restricting their choices to male gender-typed roles (Hedin et al., 1985).

Career/Family Integration. The typical white male adolescent from a middle-class family in the United States has no choice about whether work will be the primary force of his life, whereas the female's issue is whether or not to pursue work as a primary focus. Thus, for middle-class adolescents, career is typically defined in different forms for boys and girls. Girls expect that work and family roles will need to be combined, so that although they are serious about their career plans, they express concern about how to integrate family and work roles (Archer, 1985).

Children may hear adults verbalize that men and women have equal status, yet they observe mothers and fathers behaving differently (e.g., working mothers still have major responsibility for child care and housework in the family; Peplau, 1983). Thus, gender-typed family roles are continuing (Copeland & Grossman, 1984), and girls develop the expectations that although they can have career goals, they must somehow combine them with primary responsibility for home and family. When the tasks of career development are defined so differently for males and females, it stands to reason that exploration will be experienced differently as well.

Gender-related career issues also interact with ethnicity and social class to influence career exploration. Whereas white males expect to work during their adult lives, the roles may be reversed for disadvantaged black adolescents. Black women expect to work part of their lives, but the incidence of unemployment among black men and teen-age boys is so chronically high that it may take unusual circumstances for a black male adolescent to aspire to be employed at all during his lifetime (Fitzgerald & Betz, 1983; Smith, 1983). Black girls have been found to have higher career aspirations than white girls, Hispanic girls, and black boys (Leifer & Lesser, 1976). In addition, Kerckhoff (1972) noted that white girls from middle-class backgrounds had more flexibility in choosing and exploring career options than did their lower-class peers, who tended to be more traditionally feminine and were more likely to become housewives.

To describe differences in career exploration based either on ethnicity, SES, or gender is not to explain the causes of those differences, however. Process-oriented research will be necessary to enable us to move beyond status variables in understanding mechanisms of development in a causal rather than only a predictive sense. For example, such research could usefully be conducted to understand the origins of individual differences in career exploration within groups such as black males, in order to identify experiences which may counteract the impact of stereotype.

IV. Dynamic Interaction and Career Exploration

Despite the psychological focus of much of the career development literature, it seems clear that career exploration cannot be understood without reference to the context in which it is occurring (Vondracek, Lerner, & Schulenberg, 1983, 1986). The life-span developmental framework, with its emphasis on the dynamic interaction between person and context over time, appears to provide a rich vantage point for pursuing an understanding of career exploration. The issues raised in this concluding section point to ways in which this framework expands our perspective on career development and suggest specific issues worthy of further research attention.

The usefulness of the interactional point of view is supported by studies that show ways in which the application of individual resources may be inhibited or facilitated by contextual factors. For example, Bem and Bem (1970) have referred to the ''homogenization'' of American women, meaning that the role of ability in career development is less important than gender itself. Evidence for this point of view was cited in the Terman study of the gifted (cited in Fitzgerald & Betz, 1983), in which career aspirations of gifted women were found to be uniformly lower than those of men of comparable ability. Of course, this interaction of individual resources and contextual factors concerning sex roles occurred during a particular point in historical time. Further research will be necessary in order to assess whether this interaction will result in different outcomes in the future. Nevertheless, this observation underscores the importance of considering the contributions of individual resources within the context of the pertinent societal and historical issues.

The historical context also influences the nature of skills or resources that are valued at any particular time. For example, ''high-tech'' skills are currently providing avenues to rewarding careers for many young adults. However, the family's role in encouraging such skill development merits examination. In this area, parental attitudes have been found to be important predictors of children's performance. Boys report that their parents have more positive attitudes toward them as math learners than do girls (Fennema & Sherman, 1977). Thus, although aptitudes are important in career development, societal attitudes and stereotypes transmitted within the family may lead many women not to develop or utilize fully their potential capabilities in these traditionally male-dominated areas (Fitzgerald & Betz, 1983).

The life-span perspective also points to the need for a more realistic view of career exploration. Although it seems clear that career development is not a linear, time-limited process, models of career development that provide the necessary explanatory power have not emerged. The career exploration literature might benefit from consideration of the ''new look'' in mate selection research (e.g., Huston & Ashmore, 1986; Levinger, 1983). Although career exploration and mate selection involve different goals, they both involve decision making. In the traditional mate selection literature, the emphasis was placed on reviewing the field of possible partners, testing the compatibility of partners, and choosing the best one from that field. Recent work has disconfirmed this view of the mate selection process (Robins, 1985) and suggests instead that researchers examine the construction of relationships and the processes through which commitment gradually builds through subjective processes, the accumulation of rewarding interaction over time, the interconnectedness of daily routines, and the definition of the couple as a pair in the eyes of outsiders. From a career exploration point of view, attention might profitably be turned to cognitions that individuals construct about potential career paths, to the investments of time and energy that are placed into certain paths and the perceived need to reap a return on those investments, to the inertia against exploring further, and to the perceptions of the views of the individual's significant others. Such a reconceptualization would take into account the ongoing interaction between the individual's goals and resources, on the one hand, and their perceived feedback from the environment, on the other.

Finally, the dynamic interactional perspective points to the importance of understanding and considering the nature of the relationships in which individuals are embedded as they pursue processes such as career exploration. Because exploration involves both the ability of the individual to move away from one's close relationships into the larger world and the ability to coordinate individual needs with those of others, relational models must take into account aspects of both individuality and connectedness. Thus, the individuation model is offered as a potentially useful framework in which career exploration could be better understood. The research cited earlier in this chapter has shown that these relational qualities do account for variance in career exploration. A critical next step in this field is to understand how those relationships themselves develop over the life span, and how changes in the relationships may be associated with changes in the individual's exploration process.

In general, better understanding is needed of the career development process as a whole and of how career exploration fits in specifically. The integration of the literatures in identity formation and career development would assist in this regard. However, in order for the identity literature to become truly developmental, further attention must be paid to the contexts of development and to conceptualizing identity formation as a life-span process. It is hoped that the perspective offered in this chapter will be a beginning step in achieving this goal.

Acknowledgments

During the preparation of this manuscript, the research conducted by the authors was supported by Grant No. HD–17983 from the National Institute of Child Health and Human Development. The constructive comments of Gerald Adams, Richard Lerner, Alan Waterman, and three anonymous reviewers are gratefully acknowledged. We also thank Heather Johnston Nicholson for her suggestions of resources used in the preparation of this chapter.

References

Adams, G. R., & Jones, R. M. (1983). Female adolescents' identity development: Age comparisons and perceived child-rearing experience. *Developmental Psychology, 19,* 249–256.

Adams, G. R., & Montemayor, R. (Eds.). (1983). Identity formation in early adolescence (Special Issue). *Journal of Early Adolescence, 3*(3).

Ainsworth, M. D. S. (1979). Infant–mother attachment. *American Psychologist, 34,* 932–937.

Altman, S. L., & Grossman, F. K. (1977). Women's career plans and maternal employment. *Psychology of Women Quarterly, 1,* 365–376.

Archer, S. L. (1985). Career and/or family: The identity process for adolescent girls. *Youth and Society, 16,* 289–314.

Arend, R., Gove, F. L., & Sroufe, L. A. (1979). Continuity of individual adaptation from infancy to kindergarten: A predictive study of ego resiliency and curiosity in preschoolers. *Child Development, 50,* 950–959.

Baruch, G. K. (1972). Maternal influences upon college women's attitudes toward women and work. *Developmental Psychology, 6,* 32–37.

Baumrind, D. (1975). The contributions of the family to the development of competence in children. *Schizophrenia Bulletin, 14,* 12–37.

Baumrind, D. (1982). Are androgynous individuals more effective as persons and parents? *Child Development, 53,* 44–75.

Beavers, W. R. (1976). A theoretical basis for family evaluation. In J. M. Lewis, W. R. Beavers, J. T. Gossett, and V. A. Phillips, *No single thread: Psychological health in family systems* (pp. 46–82). New York: Brunner/Mazel.

Bell, R. Q. (1968). A reinterpretation of the direction of effects in studies of socialization. *Psychological Review, 75,* 81–95.

Bem, S. L., & Bem, D. J. (1970). Case study of a nonconscious ideology: Training the woman to know her place. In D. J. Bem (Ed.), *Beliefs, attitudes, and human affairs* (pp. 89–99) Monterey, CA: Brooks/Cole.

Block, J. (1971). *Lives through time.* Berkeley, CA: Bancroft Books.

Block, J. H. (1984). *Sex role identity and ego development.* San Francisco: Jossey–Bass.

Block, J. H., & Block, J. (1980). The role of ego-control and ego-resiliency in the organization of behavior. In W. A. Collins (Ed.), *Minnesota symposia on child psychology. Vol. 13: Development of cognition, affect, and social relations* (pp. 39–101). Hillsdale, NJ: Lawrence Erlbaum Associates.

Bourne, E. (1978). The state of research on ego identity: A review and appraisal. *Journal of Youth and Adolescence, 7,* 223–251.

Bradley, R. H., & Caldwell, B. M. (1976). Early home environment and changes in mental test performance in children from 6 to 36 months. *Developmental Psychology, 12,* 93–97.

Brooks–Gunn, J., & Matthews, W. S. (1979). *He and she: How children develop their sex-role identity.* Englewood Cliffs, NJ: Prentice–Hall.

Burlin, F. (1976). The relationship of parental education and maternal work and occupational status to occupational aspiration in adolescent females. *Journal of Vocational Behavior, 9,* 99–104.

Carter, E. A., & McGoldrick, M. (1980). *The family life cycle: A framework for family therapy.* New York: Gardner Press.

Condon, S. L., Cooper, C. R., & Grotevant, H. D. (1984). Manual for the analysis of family discourse. *Psychological Documents, 14,* 8 (Manuscript No. 2616).

Conger, J. J. (1971). A world they never knew: The family and social change. *Daedalus,* Fall, 1105–1138.

Cooper, C. R., & Ayers-Lopez, S. (1985). Family and peer systems in early adolescence: New models of the role of relationships in development. *Journal of Early Adolescence, 3,* 9–21.

Cooper, C. R., & Grotevant, H. D. (1986). *Gender issues in the interface of family experience and adolescent peer relational identity.* Manuscript submitted for publication.

Cooper, C. R., Grotevant, H. D., & Ayers-Lopez, S. (1986). *Links between patterns of negotiation in adolescents' family and peer interaction.* Manuscript submitted for publication.

Cooper, C. R., Grotevant, H. D., & Condon, S. M. (1983). Individuality and connectedness: Both foster adolescent identity formation and role taking skill. In H. D. Grotevant & C. R. Cooper (Eds.), *Adolescent development in the family. New directions for child development* (pp. 43–59). San Francisco: Jossey–Bass.

Coopersmith, S. (1967). *The antecedents of self-esteem.* San Francisco: W. H. Freeman.

Copeland, A. P., & Grossman, F. K. (1984, October). *Gender effects in parenting.* Paper presented at the meeting of the National Council on Family Relations, San Francisco.

Cushing, D. C. (1971). *Identity status: A developmental model as related to parental behaviors.* Unpublished doctoral dissertation, State University of New York at Buffalo.

Elardo, R., Bradley, R., & Caldwell, B. M. (1975). The relation of infants' home environments to mental test performance from six to thirty-six months: A longitudinal analysis. *Child Development, 46,* 71–76.

Erikson, E. H. (1968). *Identity: Youth and crisis.* New York: Norton.

Fennema, E., & Sherman, J. (1977). Sex-related differences in mathematics achievement, spatial visualization, and affective factors. *American Educational Research Association Journal, 14,* 51–71.

Fitzgerald, L. F., & Betz, N. E. (1983). Issues in the vocational psychology of women. In W. B. Walsh & S. H. Osipow (Eds.), *Handbook of vocational psychology, Vol. 1: Foundations* (pp. 83–159). Hillsdale, NJ: Lawrence Erlbaum Associates.

Flavell, J. H. (1974). The development of inferences about others. In T. Mischel (Ed.), *Understanding other persons* (pp. 66–116). Oxford: England, Blackwell: Mott.

Ginzberg, E., Ginsburg, S. W., Axelrad, S., & Herma, J. L. (1951). *Occupational choice.* New York: Columbia University Press.

Grotevant, H. D. (1986). Assessment of identity development: Current issues and future directions. *Journal of Adolescent Research, 1,* 175–182.

Grotevant, H. D., & Adams, G. R. (1984). Development of an objective measure to assess ego identity in adolescence: Validation and replication. *Journal of Youth and Adolescence, 13,* 419–438.

Grotevant, H. D., & Cooper, C. R. (1981). Assessing adolescent identity in the areas of occupation, religion, politics, friendship, dating, and sex roles: Manual for administration and coding of the interview. *JSAS Catalog of Selected Documents in Psychology, 11,* 52 (Manuscript No. 2295)

Grotevant, H. D., & Cooper, C. R. (Eds.). (1983). *Adolescent development in the family. New directions for child development.* San Francisco: Jossey–Bass.

Grotevant, H. D., & Cooper, C. R. (1985). Patterns of interaction in family relationships and the development of identity exploration in adolescence. *Child Development, 56,* 415–428.

Grotevant, H. D., & Cooper, C. R. (1986). Individuation in family relationships: A perspective on individual differences in the development of identity and role taking skills in adolescence. *Human Development, 29,* 82–100.

Grotevant, H. D., Cooper, C. R., & Kramer, K. (1986). Exploration as a predictor of congruence between adolescents and their career choices. *Journal of Vocational Behavior, 29,* 201–215.

Grotevant, H. D., & Thorbecke, W. L. (1982). Sex differences in styles of occupational identity formation in late adolescence. *Developmental Psychology, 18,* 396–405.

Grotevant, H. D., Thorbecke, W. L., & Meyer, M. L. (1982). An extension of Marcia's identity status interview into the interpersonal domain. *Journal of Youth and Adolescence, 11,* 33–47.

Harren, V. A. (1979a, August). *Decision-making styles and progress in the decision-making process.* Paper presented at the meeting of the American Psychological Association, New York.

Harren, V. A. (1979b). A model of career decision-making for college students. *Journal of Vocational Behavior, 14,* 119–133.

Harter, S. (1985). Processes underlying the construction, maintenance and enhancement of the self-concept in children. In J. Suls & A. Greenwald (Eds.), *Psychological perspectives on the self* (Vol. 3). Hillsdale, NJ: Lawrence Erlbaum Associates.

Harter, S., & Hogan, A. (1985, April). *A causal model of the determinants of self-worth and the affective and motivational systems which it mediates.* Paper presented at the meeting of the Society for Research in Child Development, Toronto.

Hartup, W. W. (1978). Perspectives on child and family interactions: Past, present, and future. In R. M. Lerner & G. B. Spanier (Eds.), *Child influences on marital and family interaction* (pp. 23–46). New York: Academic Press.

Hartup, W. W. (1979). The social worlds of childhood. *American Psychologist, 34,* 944–950.

Hartup, W. W. (1986). On relationships and development. In W. W. Hartup & Z. Rubin (Eds.), *Relationships and development* (pp. 3–20). Hillsdale, NJ: Lawrence Erlbaum Associates.

Hartup, W. W. (in press). Relationships and their significance in cognitive development. In R. A. Hinde, A. N. Perret–Clermont, & J. Stevenson–Hinde (Eds.), *Relationships and cognitive development.* Oxford, England: Oxford University Press.

Hartup, W. W., & Rubin, Z. (1986). *Relationships and development.* Hillsdale, NJ: Lawrence Erlbaum Associates.

Hazen, N. L., & Durrett, M. E. (1982). Relationship of security of attachment to exploration and cognitive mapping abilities in 2-year-olds. *Developmental Psychology, 18,* 751–759.

Hedin, D., Erickson, J., Simon, P., & Walker, J. (1985). *Minnesota youth poll: Aspirations, future plans, and expectations of young people in Minnesota.* St. Paul: University of Minnesota, Report AD–MR–2512, Center for Youth Development and Research.

Helmreich, R. L., Spence, J. T., Beane, W. E., Luker, G. W., & Matthews, K. A. (1980). Making it in academic psychology: Demographic and personality correlates of attainment. *Journal of Personality and Social Psychology, 39,* 896–908.

Hill, J. P. (1980). The early adolescent and the family. In M. Johnson (Ed.), *The seventy-ninth yearbook of the National Society for the Study of Education* (pp. 32–55). Chicago: University of Chicago Press.

Hill, J. P., & Holmbeck, G. N. (1986). Attachment and autonomy during adolescence. In G. Whitehurst (Ed.), *Annals of child development* (Vol. 3, pp. 145–189). Greenwich, CT: JAI Press.

Hill, J. P., & Palmquist, W. J. (1978). Social cognition and social relation in early adolescence. *International Journal of Behavioral Development, 1,* 1–36.

Hinde, R. A. (1979). *Towards understanding relationships.* New York: Academic Press.

Hinde, R. A., Perret–Clermont, A. N., & Stevenson–Hinde, J. (Eds.). (in press). *Relationships and cognitive development.* Oxford, England: Oxford University Press.

Hoffman, L. W. (1979). Maternal employment: 1979. *American Psychologist, 34,* 859–865.

Hoffman, L. W. (1984). Work, family and the socialization of the child. In R. D. Parke (Ed.), *Review of child development research, Vol. 7: The family*. Chicago: University of Chicago Press.

Hoffman, M. L. (1960). Power assertion by the parent and its impact on the child. *Child Development, 31,* 129–143.

Holland, J. L. (1985). *Making vocational choices: A theory of vocational personalities and work environments* (2nd ed.). Englewood Cliffs, NJ: Prentice–Hall.

Huston, T. L., & Ashmore, R. D. (1986). Women and men in personal relationships. In R. D. Ashmore & F. K. Del Boca (Eds.), *The social psychology of female–male relations: A critical analysis of central concepts* (pp. 167–210). New York: Academic Press.

Huston–Stein, A., & Higgins–Trenk, A. (1978). Development of females from childhood through adulthood: Career and feminine role orientations. In P. B. Baltes (Ed.), *Life-span development and behavior* (Vol. 1., pp. 257–296). New York: Academic Press.

Janis, I. L., & Mann, L. (1977). *Decision-making: A psychological analysis of conflict, choice, and commitment.* New York: Free Press.

Jordaan, J. P. (1963). Exploratory behavior: The formation of self and occupational concepts. In D. E. Super, R. Starishevsky, N. Matlin, & J. P. Jordaan, *Career development: Self-concept theory* (pp. 42–78). Princeton, NJ: College Entrance Examination Board.

Karpel, M. (1976). Individuation: From fusion to dialogue. *Family Process, 15,* 65–82.

Kerckhoff, A. C. (1972). *Socialization and social class.* Englewood Cliffs, NJ: Prentice–Hall.

Kohn, M. L. (1977). *Class and conformity,* (2nd Ed.). Chicago: University of Chicago Press.

Lavine, L. A. (1982). Parental power as a potential influence on girls' career choice. *Child Development, 53,* 658–663.

Leifer, A. D., & Lesser, G. S. (1976). *The development of career awareness in young children.* NIE Papers in Education and Work: No. 1. Washington, DC: National Institute of Education.

Lemkau, J. P. (1979). Personality and background characteristics of women in male-dominated occupations: A review. *Psychology of Women Quarterly, 4,* 221–240.

Lerner, R. M., & Shea, J. A. (1982). Social behavior in adolescence. In B. Wolman (Ed.), *Handbook for developmental psychology* (pp. 503–525). Englewood Cliffs, NJ: Prentice–Hall.

Lerner, R. M., & Spanier, G. B. (Eds.). (1978). *Child influences on marital and family interaction: A life-span perspective.* New York: Academic Press.

Levinger, G. (1983). Development and change. In H. H. Kelley, E. Berscheid, A. Christensen, J. H. Harvey, T. L. Huston, G. Levinger, E. McClintock, L. A. Peplau, & D. R. Peterson (Eds.), *Close relationships* (pp. 315–359). New York: W. H. Freeman.

Levinson, D. J. (1978). *The seasons of a man's life.* New York: Ballantine Books.

Lewin, K. (1936). *Principles of topological psychology.* New York: McGraw–Hill.

Lieberman, A. F. (1977). Preschoolers' competence with a peer: Relations with attachment and peer experience. *Child Development, 48,* 1277, 1287.

Maccoby, E. E., & Martin, J. A. (1983). Socialization in the context of the family: Parent-child interaction. In E. M. Hetherington (Ed.), P. H. Mussen (Series Ed.), *Handbook of child psychology: Vol. 4. Socialization, personality, and social development* (pp. 1–101). New York: Wiley.

Marcia, J. E. (1966). Development and validation of ego identity status. *Journal of Personality and Social Psychology, 3,* 551–558.

Marcia, J. E. (1980). Identity in adolescence. In J. Adelson (Ed.), *Handbook of adolescent psychology* (pp. 159–187). New York: John Wiley.

Marini, M. M. (1978). Sex differences in the determination of adolescent aspirations: A review of research. *Sex Roles, 4,* 723–753.

Matas, L., Arend, R. A., & Sroufe, L. A. (1978). Continuity of adaptation in the second year: The relationship between quality of attachment and later competence. *Child Development, 49,* 547–556.

Matteson, D. R. (1977). Exploration and commitment: Sex differences and methodological problems in the use of identity status categories. *Journal of Youth and Adolescence, 6,* 349–370.

Matthews, E., & Tiedeman, D. V. (1964). Attitudes toward career and marriage and the development of lifestyle in young women. *Journal of Counseling Psychology, 11,* 374–383.

Medrich, E. A., Roizen, J. A., Rubin, V., & Buckley, S. (1982). *The serious business of growing up: A study of children's lives outside school.* Berkeley, CA: University of California Press.

Minuchin, S. (1974). *Families and family therapy.* Cambridge, MA: Harvard University Press.

Mount, M. K., & Muchinsky, P. M. (1978). Person-environment congruence and employee job satisfaction: A test of Holland's theory. *Journal of Vocational Behavior, 13,* 84–100.

Nicholson, H. J. (1985). *Facts and reflections on careers for today's girls.* New York: Girls Clubs of America.

Offer, D., Ostrov, E., & Howard, K. I. (1981). *The adolescent: A psychological self-portrait.* New York: Basic Books.

Oliver, L. W. (1975). The relationship of parental attitudes and parent identification to career and homemaking orientation in college women. *Journal of Vocational Behavior, 7,* 1–12.

Peplau, L. A. (1983). Roles and gender. In H. H. Kelley, E. Berscheid, A. Christensen, J. H. Harvey, T. L. Huston, G. Levinger, E. McClintock, L. A. Peplau, & D. R. Peterson (Eds.), *Close relationships* (pp. 220–264). New York: W. H. Freeman.

Phillips, S. D. (1982a). Career exploration in adulthood. *Journal of Vocational Behavior, 20,* 129–140.

Phillips, S. D. (1982b). The development of career choices: The relationship between patterns of commitment and career outcome in adulthood. *Journal of Vocational Behavior, 20,* 141–152.

Pitz, G. F., & Harren, V. A. (1980). An analysis of career decision making from the point of view of information processing and decision theory. *Journal of Vocational Behavior, 16,* 320–346.

Reid, P. T., & Stephens, D. S. (1985). The roots of future occupations in childhood: A review of the literature on girls and careers. *Youth and Society, 16,* 267–288.

Reiss, D. (1981). *The family's construction of reality.* Cambridge, MA: Harvard University Press.

Riley, P. J. (1981). The influence of gender on occupational aspirations of kindergarten children. *Journal of Vocational Behavior, 19,* 244–250.

Robins, E. J. (1985). *A theoretical and empirical investigation of compatibility testing in marital choice.* Unpublished doctoral dissertation, Pennsylvania State University.

Rollins, J., & White, P. N. (1982). The relationship between mothers' and daughters' sex-role attitudes and self-concepts in three types of family environment. *Sex Roles, 8,* 1141–1155.

Scarr, S., & Kidd, K. K. (1983). Developmental behavior genetics. In M. Haith & J. Campos (Eds.), *Handbook of child psychology (4th Ed.), Vol. 2: Infancy and developmental psychobiology* (pp. 345–433). New York: John Wiley.

Selkow, P. (1984). Effects of maternal employment on kindergarten and first-grade children's vocational aspirations. *Sex Roles, 11,* 677–690.

Shaffer, K. F. (1980). *Sex-role issues in mental health.* Reading, MA: Addison–Wesley.

Shapiro, D., & Crowley, J. E. (1982). Aspirations and expectations of youth in the United States, P. 2: Employment activity. *Youth and Society, 14,* 33–58.

Smith, E. J. (1983). Issues in racial minorities' career behavior. In W. B. Walsh & S. H. Osipow (Eds.), *Handbook of vocational psychology, Vol. 1: Foundations* (pp. 161–222). Hillsdale, NJ: Lawrence Erlbaum Associates.

Sroufe, L. A. (1979). The coherence of individual development. *American Psychologist, 34,* 834–841.

Sroufe, L. A. (1983). Infant–caregiver attachment and patterns of adaptation in preschool: The roots of maladaptation and competence. In M. Perlmutter (Ed.), *Minnesota Symposia on Child Psychology* (Vol. 16, pp. 41–83) Hillsdale, NJ: Lawrence Erlbaum Associates.

Stumpf, S. A., Colarelli, S. M., & Hartman, K. (1983). Development of the career exploration survey (CES). *Journal of Vocational Behavior, 22,* 191–226.

Super, D. E. (1953). A theory of vocational development. *American Psychologist, 8,* 185–190.

Super, D. E. (1981). A developmental theory: Implementing a self-concept. In D. H. Montross & C. J. Shinkman (Eds.), *Career development in the 1980's: Theory and practice.* (pp. 28–42) Springfield, IL: Charles C. Thomas.

Tiedeman, D. V., & O'Hara, R. P. (1963). *Career development: Choice and adjustment.* New York: College Entrance Examination Board.

Tittle, C. K. (1981). *Careers and family: Sex roles and adolescent life plans.* Beverly Hills, CA: Sage.

Tremaine, L. S., & Schau, C. G. (1979). Sex-role aspects in the development of children's vocational knowledge. *Journal of Vocational Behavior, 14,* 317–328.

Vaitenas, R., & Wiener, Y. (1977). Developmental, emotional, and interest factors in voluntary mid-career change. *Journal of Vocational Behavior, 11,* 291–304.

Vondracek, F. W., Lerner, R. M., & Schulenberg, J. E. (1983). The concept of development in vocational theory and intervention. *Journal of Vocational Behavior, 23,* 179–202.

Vondracek, F. W., Lerner, R. M., & Schulenberg, J. E. (1986). *Career development: A life-span developmental approach.* Hillsdale, NJ: Lawrence Erlbaum Associates.

Walsh, W. B., & Osipow, S. H. (1983). *Handbook of vocational psychology, Vol. 1: Foundations.* Hillsdale, NJ: Lawrence Erlbaum Associates.

Waterman, A. S. (1982). Identity development from adolescence to adulthood: An extension of theory and a review of research. *Developmental Psychology, 18,* 341–358.

Waterman, A. S., Geary, P. S., & Waterman, C. K. (1974). A longitudinal study of changes in ego identity status from the freshman to the senior year at college. *Developmental Psychology, 10,* 387–392.

Waters, E., Wippman, J., & Sroufe, L. A. (1979). Attachment, positive affect, and competence in the peer group: Two studies in construct validation. *Child Development, 50,* 821–829.

White, K. M., Speisman, J. C., & Costos, D. (1983). Young adults and their parents: Individuation to mutuality. In H. D. Grotevant & C. R. Cooper (Eds.), *Adolescent development in the family. New Directions for Child Development* (pp. 61–76). San Francisco: Jossey–Bass.

Wynne, L. C. (1984). The epigenesis of relational systems: A model for understanding family development. *Family Processes, 23,* 297–318.

Youniss, J. (1983). Social construction of adolescence by adolescents and parents. In H. D. Grotevant & C. R. Cooper (Eds.), *Adolescent development in the family. New directions for child development* (pp. 93–109) San Francisco, CA: Jossey-Bass.

Youniss, J., & Smollar, J. (1985). *Adolescent relations with mothers, fathers, and friends.* Chicago: University of Chicago Press.

The Demography of Kinship and the Life Course

Susan De Vos
CENTER FOR DEMOGRAPHY AND ECOLOGY,
UNIVERSITY OF WISCONSIN-MADISON
Steven Ruggles
DEPARTMENT OF HISTORY,
UNIVERSITY OF MINNESOTA

Abstract

This chapter explores theoretical and methodological issues related to the demography of kinship and the life course. We examine two contrasts in particular, the general set of kin during the life course of males, compared with females, and of two historical periods corresponding to different demographic regimes. Since data requirements are rigorous, we are persuaded that microsimulation is the most promising tool currently available for the life-course analysis of kinship. For expositive purposes, we simulate possible situations for the West before the twentieth century.

I. Introduction

A particular demographic regime will produce regular distributions of individuals who have few and many kin. These distributions are characteristics of individuals, influencing their life chances and their social position, just as characteristics such as personality and skill do. Individuals have very little control over their position in the kinship group. (Howell, 1979, p. 329)

This chapter explores theoretical and methodological issues relating to the demography of kinship and the life course. The kin context of human aging is crucial because the kin group is the primary social unit mediating an individual's position vis-à-vis larger social, economic, and political institutions. This pertains to the individual throughout the life span, not just during infancy or old age. Demographic factors, such as marriage, fertility and mortality, work within limits set down by culture to produce kinship ties among individuals.[1] Demographers have begun to explore the implications of this fact for kinship, but have not yet developed a demography of kinship that explicitly includes consideration of the life course.

The life-course perspective opens a wide array of possible approaches to the demographic study of kinship. We demonstrate one, with microsimulation. We focus on sex and historical differences in the kin context of human aging, because important demographic factors are known to vary by sex and time period, but we do not know how important they are. For instance, mortality tends to be higher for males than for females, while females tend to start childbearing and grandparenthood at a younger age. Historically in the West, there has been a marked decline in mortality, fertility and age at marriage. Here, we simulate a Western preindustrial population, and one with the demographic rates for the United States in 1900. Mortality and the median age at first marriage had fallen during this time, while the level of fertility had remained about the same (see Table I).[2]

We use the term *kin group* instead of *family* because the family has been defined as members of a household who are related through marriage, blood or adoption (United Nations, 1980) whereas we do not wish to be confined by coresidence. We wish to consider such distant kin as aunts, uncles, nieces, and nephews, in addition to more immediate kin, such as parents, children, siblings, grandparents, and grandchildren.[3]

The rest of the chapter is organized into two major sections. The first section motivates our study by (a) reviewing past research relevant to the topic, (b) discussing sex and historical differences in demographic characteristics that

[1]Although anthropologists have well documented the fact that people can and do use fictive kin ties for various purposes, this is slight in most societies, compared with those ties created through demographic processes.

[2]For exploration of the effect of post-1900 changes in the demographic regime of the United States on the kin availability of the elderly, see Hammel, Wachter, and McDaniel (1981). A minor problem with this study, acknowledged by the authors, is that it does not consider divorce. Our model does not consider divorce either, but this is not a problem for the period before 1900. For an exploration of the effect of mortality decline after 1900, see Uhlenberg, 1980.

[3]In its present form, our model only tabulates three generations of kin. Although the existence of four generations is becoming more common in the United States, this was not the case before 1900. The model does not consider the siblings of grandparents.

could affect kinship, and (c) treating general issues of data and method. The second section presents an exploration of kinship and the life course in the West prior to the twentieth century.

II. Background

A. Past Studies

Despite the importance of the kin group for human development, there has been surprisingly little study of the relationship between human development and the kin group from a life-course perspective (see e.g., Ruth Monroe et al., 1981). Life-span psychologists generally have not researched in the area of family or kinship (see e.g., Baltes, Reese, & Lipsitt, 1980). A life-course perspective is also rare in kin studies. Kinship studies typically map out relationships in an attempt to identify kinship rules; also, to describe ethnic or social status variation in kinship or kinship networks (see e.g., Lee, 1980), but from a static perspective. Anthropologists have studied the age stratification of various societies, and have noted its relationship to kinship (Maybury–Lewis, 1984), but have usually ignored the demographic component of this kinship. Finally, demographers have considered kinship at different ages and life stages.[4] However, life-course analysis extends beyond examining the probability of having kin at different ages because it adds the dimension of personal time.

Family studies typically focus on the development of an individual at only one stage of family life or address a time-limited family relationship, such as that between young children and their parents, parents and adult children, siblings, and recently, between grandchildren and grandparents (see e.g., Olson & Miller, 1984; but see also Dunn, 1984). Social demographers have applied a concept of *family life cycle* to add a dynamic quality to family studies, but this is very different from the idea of individual aging within a family or kin context. Instead of tracing an individual from birth to death, the family life-cycle approach traces a family from when it is formed by a marriage until it ends through the maturation of children and the death of a spouse (Glick, 1947; Young, 1977). The family life-cycle approach fails to address the lives of children, older people, or

[4]For more general theory see Goodman, Keyfitz, & Pullum (1974, 1975). More specific issues have been the probability of orphanhood under different demographic regimes (LeBras, 1973/1978; Lotka, 1931; Uhlenberg, 1980) and the probability of attaining old age without a surviving child (or son), (e.g., Heer & Smith, 1968, 1969; Immerwahr, 1967; Krishnamoorthy, 1980). Hammel, Wachter, and McDaniel (1981) addressed the issue of kin among the elderly more broadly, projecting demographic rates and their implication into the future. A study by the Cambridge Group has looked into the implications of China's one-child policy (''News from the ESRC,'' 1985.)

people who deviate from the expected life path through divorce, sterility, or the early death of a spouse (Uhlenberg, 1969, 1974) and it has been most successfully applied to the special case of the nuclear family (Collver, 1963; Santini, 1977).

An important exception to the relative neglect of a life-course perspective in family studies is the work of Glen Elder (1974, 1978) and such family historians as Tamara Hareven (1977, 1978). They have insisted on the need for "models that represent processes of family adaptation and change over time; the timing, arrangement, and duration of events in the life course; the ever-changing pattern of interdependence and synchronization among the life histories of family members; and the cycle of generational exchange and succession" (Elder, 1978, pp. 17–18). This ambitious call for individual-level models of kinship and the life course has not yet been effectively answered. The most promising avenue for investigations of this kind is suggested by Peter Uhlenberg's demographic analyses of "typical" life paths (1969, 1974, 1978, 1980).

Uhlenberg challenged the usefulness of the family life-cycle concept for understanding an individual's family life course. According to Paul Glick and others, the typical family life cycle involves marriage, childbearing, the "empty nest," and widowhood, in that order (see, e.g., Glick, 1947). Focusing on the immediate family, and on females only, but looking at historical change, Uhlenberg estimated the extent to which women deviated from the typical family life cycle. Such deviations could arise from early death, spinsterhood, childlessness, death in middle age or early widowhood. According to his calculations, only a fifth of native-born Massachusetts females born into the 1830 cohort followed the typical life path. This more than doubled for the 1920 cohort, but still only 57% of the cohort could be expected to follow the typical life path. Most of the deviation from the "typical" life path was caused by involuntary demographic factors such as mortality (Uhlenberg, 1969, 1974). One of our aims is to expand on this idea of a life path by considering a wider kin group beyond the immediate family of procreation, and by considering males as well as females.

The only demographic analysis of which we are aware that has looked at the kin universe of individuals throughout the life course has been the work of Nancy Howell on the Dobe !Kung or Bushmen of Southern Africa (1979). Using microsimulation, she traced ties between individuals that were implied in the mortality, fertility, and nuptiality patterns of the population, given what she knew about the culture's definition of kinship (bilineal, etc.). Howell derived the proportion of individuals of any given age who would have kin of a particular kind (e.g., living father, living aunt, living grandparent, etc.). Then she reported the distribution of the total number of kin of individuals in different age groups. This captured a sense of distribution around the expected mean of 16 kinsmen, there being few people without any kin or more than 40 kin. This was not compared with other societies. Kinsmen of varying "distances" from the individual (relative to an immediate family) were summed without regard to potentially important differences, and Howell did not try to describe a number of common life paths with respect to the kinship universe.

Although there was no historical or comparative depth to the study, Howell did note an interesting sex differential in kinship during the life course. She noted that women tended to have more kin earlier in life whereas the opposite became true later in life. Thus "women tend to be socially more important than men earlier in life, particularly during their childbearing years, whereas men take a more dominant position in the social structure of kinship later in life, especially after age 50" (Howell, 1979, p. 330). We aim to build on some of the basic ideas in Howell's study.

B. SOME SEX AND HISTORICAL DIFFERENCES

Sex. The demographic experiences of males and females differ throughout the life course, and this can be expected to lead to differences in their kinship arena at comparable ages. But how sizable are these differences? Most obvious perhaps is that there are usually significant sex differentials in mortality, making it more likely for individuals of a given sex to survive through certain ages. This situation is most obvious where preferential infanticide or neglect is practiced (see Clark, 1983), but occurs "naturally" as well. In the U.S. in 1900 for example, the female expectation of life was an average of 2.4 years higher than the expectation for males. The sex differential in death rates was highest at the young ages, particularly under 1 year old, but they remained throughout life (U.S. Bureau of the Census, 1975). This would imply then, holding other things constant, that males would have a greater chance of *not* participating in a "normal" life course at any given age. They would have a lesser chance of reaching marriage age, a lesser chance of having children, a lesser chance of having grandchildren, and a lesser chance of outliving a spouse. It would also imply that females would have a greater chance of being widowed before their children had reached adulthood. There would be many more women eligible to remarry than men of comparable ages, and a lower remarriage rate among women.

Less obvious is the impact of a later average age at first marriage for men than for women. Although the average gap between males and females can be as high as 9 years (Dixon, 1971), it has been much narrower in Western countries. In the United States in 1900 for instance, the mean age interval between spouses was 3.7 years. Holding other things constant, this would imply that on the average men would be older when they had children or grandchildren, and would be less likely to survive to see the fertility of their offspring. It also implies that men would be older when they acquired a second set of kin through marriage.

Yet whereas the marriage of younger men to older women is unheard of in many societies, it has been much more common in the West. For instance, Peter

Laslett (1972) reports that in his historical samples of English and French households, between 21% and 27% of the couples had wives who were older than their husbands.[5] In the U.S. in 1900 the proportion was 13%. This implies that there are countervailing forces at work here that might minimize the sex difference in Western populations.

History. The historical dimension of most interest to demographers has been the demographic transition that occurred in most societies that now have low fertility and low mortality. Although there are important exceptions to the general experience, mortality tended to decline first. There was then a "transition" period in which mortality was low but fertility remained fairly high. The third stage has low fertility and low mortality. This study explores the impact of the first step in the West's transition on kinship during the life course. Between preindustrial times and 1900, mortality had fallen but fertility had remained about the same, actually increasing slightly.[6] The expectation of life at birth increased roughly 13 years while the total fertility rate differed by only about 0.3 of a child (see Table I).

Mortality decline has an important effect on the number of kin during childhood, young adulthood, middle age, and old age (Uhlenberg, 1980). For instance, it affects the likelihood of orphanhood, of having a live sibling or of having a grandparent during childhood (see LeBras, 1978; Lotka, 1931). It affects the chance of completing the childbearing years with a spouse and of entering the "empty nest" stage of having grown children. It affects the chance of having a surviving child or grandchild during old age (see Bongaarts & Menken, 1983; Heer & Smith, 1968, 1969; Immerwahr, 1967; Krishnamoorthy, 1980). In all cases, holding other things constant, lower mortality is associated with a greater likelihood of having kin throughout the life course, but by how much? What are the combined effects of these likelihoods? Such questions can be answered with a simulation such as ours.

C. SOME ISSUES OF DATA AND METHOD

Data requirements for life-course analysis are rigorous. Ideally, we should observe the same individuals over a span of time. If we wish to understand how the kin universe would be affected by demographic change, we would want to gather kinship data for samples of a number of cohorts from their birth to death. Even if possible, this would be very expensive, and we would still face the problem of attrition in the sample. Likewise, it is possible to gather life histories, but one is plagued by the accuracy of recall and by the inability of nonsurvivors

[5]The proportion was only 0.5% in the Serbian sample and 1.9% in the Japanese sample.
[6]See footnote 2.

to enter the sample. For historical investigations there is no chance of gathering either prospective or retrospective data that do not already exist. As the purpose of many investigations is to explore patterns and associations between characteristics rather than to describe those characteristics in precise terms, we may employ models of kinship that allow us to examine implications of demographic forces that might not be intuitively obvious.

Demographic models of kinship have been of three types: analytical, macrosimulation, and microsimulation. Analytical models are mathematical expressions in which the dependent variables are characteristics of the kin group and the independent variables represent demographic factors, principally fertility, mortality, and nuptiality. Several examples of a general analytical approach include Lotka's investigation of orphanhood (1931) and a more general study by Goodman, Keyfitz, and Pullum (1974, 1975). While elegant, analytical models tend not to be well adapted to assessing the life course of kinship. To avoid unmanageable complexity, such models generally include more assumptions about the homogeneity of a population than are assumed by other approaches. The point is well illustrated by a comment in a recent analytical study of kinship by Thomas Pullum. That study derived the probability distribution of kin of the 1948–1953 birth cohort of American women, but not by age. Pullum states: "It is possible that one could extend the use of probability generating functions, by incorporating an age index in the [fx] distribution. However, a major virtue of the approach given here is the simplicity of formulas and computations . . ." (1982, p. 564). There is thus an important tradeoff made between generating means of expected kin for different ages, and generating distributions for a group without further differentiating by age. Finally, since the general analytical models are concerned with the aggregate behavior of a population, they are not well suited to the estimation of the frequencies of particular kinship histories over the life course.[7]

On a less abstract level, Peter Uhlenberg (1969, 1974) used census and vital registration data for different time periods and applied related probabilities of experiencing different events to different cohorts as they were expected to pass through time. The model adheres closely to real estimated occurrences but is also limited by the availability of data for this very reason. That is, Uhlenberg did not address the fertility-related experiences of males because fertility is usually only reported in terms of females. Since census and vital registration data are reported in terms of the immediate family of origin or procreation, his approach kept him from analyzing the situation of grandparents, grandchildren, or more distant kin. Finally, Uhlenberg's analyses have been limited by the time span of available data, generally no earlier than 1870 for the U.S. or 1830 for Massachusetts. Thus

[7]For discussion of the limitations of analytical models, see Barrett (1977), De Vos and Palloni (1984), Ruggles (in press), and Sheps (1969).

the generality of his findings beyond the particular populations and time periods is questionable.

Demographic simulations provide an alternative to the analytical approach. There are two general types of demographic simulation: *macro*simulation, which operates at the level of groups and is determinate, and *micro*simulation which operates at the level of individuals and is stochastic. In macrosimulation, a population is broken into subgroups based on such characteristics as age, sex, and marital status. Over a given time period, a portion of the members of each subgroup may die, give birth, or marry. Death results in removal from the population; other demographic events result in shifting individuals between groups. As time passes, all individuals are shifted into older subgroups, and the youngest subgroups are filled with newborn babies. Thus, the population is projected over time.

The most promising macrosimulation model of the family devised to date was developed by John Bongaarts (1981). This model can generate distributions of nuclear family size and children surviving over the course of a woman's reproductive years, but it has not been employed for the study of extended kin relationships.

Microsimulation has much more flexibility than either of the approaches mentioned before because the number of characteristics taken into account may be increased dramatically without greatly altering the structure or complexity of the model. Demographic events are assigned to individuals to construct life histories. For instance, the probability of an individual's death is based on the individual's characteristics (e.g., age and sex). Suppose it is determined to be 4 chances in 1000. A random number from 1 to 1000 is generated, and if this happens to be 4 or less, a death takes place. By applying this method for the different demographic events considered, a complete life-process model can be simulated for each hypothetical individual in the sample (Ruggles & Ruggles, 1970). When enough individuals have been created, a microsimulation model generates summary statistics. The output resembles a complete set of data from an ideal survey.[8]

[8]A discussion of the relative merits of microsimulation compared to other models and methods for studying kinship can be found in De Vos and Palloni (1984), Hammel, Wachter, and Pullum (1981), and Ruggles (in press). Unlike microsimulations, macrosimulation models provide determinate solutions; there is no random element. For example, suppose that according to a predetermined probability, we know that 10% of the population with a given set of characteristics will die. In a macrosimulation model, we can simply select the subgroup which shares the appropriate characteristics and reduce its size by 10%. There is no need to determine *which* members will die. The main advantage of macrosimulation relative to microsimulation is that by providing determinate solutions it avoids numerous iterations and offers savings of computer time. But there are profound disadvantages. If a large number of characteristics must be taken into account—such as interrelationships with extended kin—then the number of subgroups required by macrosimulation multiplies rapidly and the

An example of a microsimulation model of kinship is the already-mentioned study of the Dobe !Kung by Nancy Howell (1979). Howell fit her field data to curves estimated by stable population theory and then used microsimulation to introduce a sense of randomness to the allocation of event probabilities (see Howell & Lehotay, 1978). We are persuaded also that microsimulation is the most promising tool currently available for the life-course analysis of kinship.

However, our model differs from that of Howell in an important respect: It is "open" rather than "closed." Closed models such as Howell's assume perfect endogamy—marriage partners must be found within the hypothetical population. The assumption is probably realistic when studying populations like the Dobe !Kung. However, in order to find a spouse, the population of eligible mates must be searched. The decision about which spouse is best suited for the marriage is based upon a set of marriage rules. All of this is rather complex, and it tends to be expensive in terms of computer time. If the hypothetical population is small, it may be impossible to find an appropriate spouse, even if the random number generator has decreed that a marriage should take place. On the other hand, the complexity of the task multiplies rapidly with the size of the population; for this reason, closed models have generally assumed a small population. In any case, the marriage rules are by necessity somewhat arbitrary, and may yield unrealistic characteristics of spouses. Our model simply creates a spouse with the appropriate characteristics when an individual is supposed to marry. Large, closed models in which the marriage rules are empirically determined may ultimately prove to be the most useful means of analyzing the life course of kinship, especially in view of the declining cost of computing power. However, bearing in mind issues of efficiency, simplicity, and the accuracy of spouses' characteristics, we find an open microsimulation model preferable for our purposes at the present time.

III. The Study

A. METHOD

We employ an open microsimulation to mimic the kinship ties that could have occurred in historical populations if certain demographic rates had persisted over a long period of time. In this chapter, we omit discussion of affines (in-laws), concentrating on people's "blood" relations only, and omit consideration of relatives' age, sex, and marital status. We will forgo a description of the mechanics of the model; it is quite complex, and our main purpose here is to provide

model becomes unwieldy. While it is likely that more sophisticated macrosimulation models will be developed in the future, the technique will never be as powerful or flexible as the microsimulation approach.

TABLE I

Basic Demographic Parameters for Preindustrial and 1900 Simulation Runs

	Preindustrial	1900
Total fertility rate	4.62	4.92
Expectation of life at birth—females	34.8	48.4
Expectation of life at birth—males	32.5	46.0
Percentage of women never married at age 40	14.1	8.6
Percentage of women surviving to age 50 with no children ever born	18.4	13.4
Median age at first marriage—females	26.2	22.2
Median age at first marriage—males	27.2	25.0
Mean age interval between spouses	2.12	3.72
Mean age of mothers over age 44 at:		
Birth of first child	31.2	26.2
Birth of last child	41.4	38.6
Birth of all children	34.7	30.7

examples of the kinds of analysis possible with these techniques.[9] Briefly, we use parameters derived from the U.S. Census of 1900, the U.S. life table for 1900–1902, and Wrigley and Schofield's *Population History* (1981) pertaining to the first half of the eighteenth century in England.[10] Various demographic parameters used for a "preindustrial" and 1900 run are shown in Table I. As can be seen from such parameters as the median age at first marriage, both populations but especially the preindustrial one, have very late ages at marriage. This pattern was identified as peculiarly "Western" by John Hajnal in his classic work on European marriage patterns in comparative perspective (1965).

Perhaps even more startling are the models' estimated mean ages of first birth among mothers who survived to age 44 and above: 31 years in the preindustrial run and 26 years in the 1900 simulation. This is approximately 5 and 4 years later than the median ages at marriage respectively. This can be explained by two factors. First, the second figures are the *mean* instead of the median. They are skewed upward by women who married much later than the median. Second,

[9]Detail regarding Ruggles's microsimulation model of kinship are contained in Ruggles (forthcoming.) Here, we describe the model's use for the present exploration. The types of kin which can be analyzed by the model include maternal and paternal grandparents, parents, parents-in-law, aunts, uncles, aunts-in-law, uncles-in-law, spouses, siblings, siblings-in-law, half-siblings, cousins, children, children-in-law, stepchildren, nieces, nephews, nieces-in-law, nephews-in-law, and grandchildren. Furthermore, each of these relatives has an age, sex, and marital status at any point in time, as does the referent. Most important, one can analyze the history of individuals' kin relationships, as well as take cross-sectional measurements.

[10]The preindustrial parameters are only rough approximations, but they serve to illustrate the magnitude of effects of demographic changes on kinship. For discussion, see Ruggles (in press).

women who began their childbearing later had a lower risk of dying before they reached age 44; they could have an unexpected influence on the figure. The overall distribution of mother's ages at the birth of all children is essentially the same in the simulation as is calculated from the Census.

The model assumes a cognatic (bilineal) kinship structure in which females as well as males are recognized as kin, and kinship occurs through both lines. Females retain membership in their kin group after marriage, and children become members of the kin groups of both parents.[11] Since cognatic kinship rules potentially create an overwhelmingly large and complex kin group, Americans tend to prioritize kin relations in terms of distance from a family of origin or of procreation. It might be assumed that American kinship patterns follow a homogeneous set of rules, at least among those with a Judeo-Christian heritage, but Bernard Farber (1977) has outlined four common models that Americans use for allocating distance among kin: the Canon Law model, the Genetic model, the Civil Code model, and the Parentela Orders model. Each model has a different historical root, is related to religious and socioeconomic factors, and may express different cognitive styles.[12] We use the Civil Code model because of its widespread use. An individual's parent or child is equally close to *ego* in terms of kinship. Grandparents, siblings and grandchildren all have equal closeness, and are a step farther removed than parents or children. A next step removed are aunts, uncles, nieces, and nephews. A fourth step removed are great aunts, great uncles, first cousins, grandnieces, and grandnephews. This scheme regards the parent–child relationship as the core of kinship, and the genealogical distance of a relative to be a function of his nearness to this relationship.

Our strategy is to start with a relatively simple description of the availability of kin, adding to it the issue of variation and then end by estimating the proportion of individuals who are expected to experience a "preferred" kinship path. Throughout, we maintain a focus on differences by age, sex, and time period. To

[11]It should be pointed out though, that the current model assumes: (a) a socially homogeneous population—we do not consider potential class or ethnic differences; (b) static demographic rates—demographic rates are allowed to run for a long period of time instead of changing every 5 or 10 years; (c) independence of many demographic phenomena; for example, the model does not increase an individual's probability of dying if a spouse or sibling dies. Relaxing each of these assumptions would require considerably more information than is presently used (or available) and more complex modeling. While increased complexity might bring us closer to realism, we do not as yet know what the benefit might be. Such complexity is not necessary for our present illustration.

[12]"According to the Canon Law model, members of one's family of procreation and of orientation constitute the core of kinship; all other relatives are placed in successive layers in accordance with their distances from the individual's nuclear family" (Farber, 1977 p. 229). According to the Genetic model, distance is calculated in terms of shared chromosomes. The Civil Code model allocates distance by distance from a common ancestor. There is a hierarchy of groups in the Parentela model in which the most important is the lineal one of an ego, his/her children, and then grandchildren.

simplify the present exposition we limit our discussion to three categories of kin—near, intermediate, and distant—omitting discussion of the fourth group of great aunts, great uncles, first cousins, grandnieces and grandnephews, and omitting discussion of affines (in-laws). The first three categories involve seven sets of kin.[13] Detailed tables referring to each type of kin separately can be obtained from the first author.

B. RESULTS

Expected Number of Kin. Our first set of results, in Table II, are the (mean) expected number of kin of a certain kind by age. Since the model assumes stability in the demographic parameters, it is possible to consider differences by age group in the population as true differences according to age, there being no difference between periods (within the same run) or between cohorts. This is only a first step because individual heterogeneity tends to be smoothed out in the average. We use the greater flexibility of our model to calculate the expected values for men as well as for women, and aggregate different kinds of kin into the three categories discussed above. Each category is addressed in a separate panel of Table II. The fourth panel contains sums of all three categories of kin. Table II contains both the estimated values, and differences therein between males and females and between time periods.

Age Differences. In general, in the two demographic regimes, the average number of kin is smallest at the youngest ages and increases into middle age. The overall age pattern is similar for both males and females although there are some noticeable differences, to be mentioned subsequently. A major difference in the age pattern of overall kin between demographic regimes is that the average number of kin declines slightly from middle to old age in the preindustrial population, but stays at about the same level in the 1900 population (Table II, panel 4). This general pattern occurs within the different kinds of kin.

Sex Differences. Under both demographic regimes, we expected to find females to have more children than men during the childbearing years of 15 to 49, and more grandchildren between 50 and 65, because they were on average younger than males when they had children. Since the existence of parents should be the same for both sexes of the same age, we expected a difference in average number of children to come through as the difference in the expected number of ''near'' kin. Similarly, since the existence of siblings or grandparents should be the same for both sexes of the same age, we expected a difference in

[13](a) parents, (b) children, (c) siblings, (d) grandparents, (e) grandchildren, (f) aunts and uncles, (g) nieces and nephews.

TABLE II

Expected (Mean) Number of Living Kin of Males and Females under Simulated Preindustrial and 1900 Demographic Conditions and Differences between Sexes and Demographic Regimes

	Preindustrial			1900			1900–Preindustrial		
Age	Male	Female	Diff.	Male	Female	Diff.	Male	Female	Total
Near Kin									
0–4	1.9	1.9	0.0	2.0	2.0	0.0	0.0	0.0	0.0
5–9	1.8	1.8	0.0	1.9	1.9	0.0	0.1	0.1	0.1
10–14	1.6	1.6	0.0	1.8	1.8	0.0	0.1	0.2	0.2
15–19	1.5	1.5	0.0	1.7	1.7	0.0	0.2	0.2	0.2
20–24	1.4	1.4	0.0	1.6	2.0	−0.4	0.3	0.6	0.4
25–29	1.5	1.5	0.0	1.9	2.4	−0.5	0.4	0.9	0.7
30–34	1.9	1.8	0.0	2.4	3.0	−0.6	0.6	1.2	0.9
35–39	2.2	2.2	0.0	2.9	3.5	−0.6	0.8	1.3	1.0
40–44	2.4	2.3	0.1	3.3	3.9	−0.6	0.9	1.6	1.2
45–49	2.4	2.3	0.1	3.6	3.8	−0.2	1.2	1.5	1.4
50–54	2.8	2.5	0.3	3.7	3.8	−0.1	0.9	1.3	1.1
55–59	2.6	2.2	0.4	3.7	3.5	0.2	1.1	1.3	1.2
60–64	2.5	2.0	0.5	3.4	3.3	0.1	0.9	1.3	1.1
65–69	2.7	1.9	0.8	3.6	3.1	0.5	0.9	1.2	1.1
70–74	2.2	1.8	0.4	3.3	2.9	0.4	1.1	1.2	1.2
Intermediate Kin									
0–4	4.5	4.4	0.1	5.2	5.4	−0.2	0.7	1.0	0.8
5–9	5.0	4.9	0.0	5.8	5.7	0.1	0.8	0.8	0.8
10–14	5.3	5.3	−0.1	6.4	6.5	0.0	1.1	1.1	1.1
15–19	5.6	5.5	0.1	6.7	6.6	0.1	1.1	1.0	1.1
20–24	5.7	5.7	0.0	6.7	6.7	0.1	1.1	1.0	1.0
25–29	5.7	5.4	0.2	6.5	6.7	−0.2	0.9	1.3	1.1
30–34	5.4	5.3	0.1	6.5	6.6	−0.1	1.1	1.2	1.2
35–39	5.5	5.5	0.0	6.4	6.4	−0.1	0.8	0.9	0.9
40–44	5.6	5.6	0.0	6.5	6.5	0.0	0.8	0.9	0.9
45–49	5.8	5.6	0.2	6.7	7.1	−0.4	1.0	1.5	1.2
50–54	5.9	6.2	−0.3	7.5	8.6	−1.1	1.6	2.4	2.0
55–59	6.4	6.0	0.3	8.6	10.5	−1.8	2.3	4.4	3.4
60–64	6.9	7.3	−0.4	10.3	11.3	−0.9	3.4	4.0	3.7
65–69	8.0	7.8	0.2	12.3	13.1	−0.8	4.3	5.3	4.9
70–74	8.6	8.4	0.2	14.7	14.6	0.1	6.1	6.2	6.1
Distant Kin									
0–4	9.7	9.7	0.1	11.7	11.7	0.0	2.0	2.0	2.0
5–9	9.8	9.6	0.1	11.9	12.0	−0.2	2.1	2.4	2.3
10–14	9.9	9.7	0.2	12.6	12.3	0.2	2.7	2.7	2.7
15–19	9.6	9.6	0.0	13.0	13.0	0.0	3.4	3.4	3.4
20–24	9.8	9.9	−0.1	14.1	14.0	0.1	4.4	4.2	4.3

(continued)

TABLE II (*Cont.*)

	Preindustrial			1900			1900–Preindustrial		
Age	Male	Female	Diff.	Male	Female	Diff.	Male	Female	Total
25–29	10.2	10.0	0.2	15.5	15.9	−0.4	5.3	5.8	5.5
30–34	10.4	10.7	−0.3	17.9	18.3	−0.4	7.4	7.6	7.5
35–39	10.8	10.4	0.4	19.4	19.8	−0.4	8.6	9.4	9.0
40–44	10.5	10.3	0.3	21.0	21.0	0.0	10.5	10.7	10.6
45–49	10.7	10.0	0.7	21.8	21.2	0.6	11.1	11.1	11.1
50–54	9.5	9.8	−0.3	20.7	20.5	0.2	11.2	10.7	11.0
55–59	8.9	8.4	0.5	19.6	19.2	0.4	10.7	10.8	10.8
60–64	7.9	7.8	0.1	17.4	18.1	−0.8	9.5	10.3	9.9
65–69	7.1	6.9	0.2	17.4	16.0	1.4	10.2	9.1	9.7
70–74	5.8	6.5	−0.6	15.7	15.3	0.4	9.9	8.9	9.4
Total Kin									
0–4	16.1	16.0	0.2	18.9	19.0	−0.1	2.7	3.0	2.9
5–9	16.5	16.3	0.2	19.5	19.6	−0.1	3.0	3.3	3.2
10–14	16.8	16.6	0.2	20.8	20.6	0.2	4.0	4.0	4.0
15–19	16.7	16.6	0.1	21.4	21.3	0.1	4.6	4.7	4.7
20–24	16.8	16.9	−0.1	22.5	22.6	−0.2	5.7	5.7	5.7
25–29	17.4	16.9	0.5	24.0	25.0	−1.0	6.5	8.1	7.3
30–34	17.7	17.9	−0.1	26.8	27.9	−1.1	9.1	10.0	9.5
35–39	18.5	18.1	0.3	28.7	29.7	−1.0	10.2	11.6	10.9
40–44	18.5	18.1	0.4	30.8	31.3	−0.6	12.2	13.2	12.7
45–49	18.8	17.9	1.0	32.1	32.1	0.0	13.3	14.2	13.8
50–54	18.1	18.4	−0.3	31.8	32.9	−1.0	13.7	14.4	14.1
55–59	17.9	16.7	1.2	31.9	33.2	−1.3	14.1	16.6	15.4
60–64	17.3	17.1	0.2	31.1	32.6	−1.5	13.8	15.5	14.7
65–69	17.8	16.5	1.2	33.3	32.2	1.1	15.5	15.6	15.6
70–74	16.5	16.6	−0.1	33.7	32.8	0.9	17.2	16.2	16.6

Note: Near kin are parents and children; intermediate kin are siblings, grandparents, and grandchildren; distant kin are aunts, uncles, nieces, and nephews.

average number of grandchildren to come through as a difference in expected number of ''intermediate'' kin.

Expectations of differences by sex were only partly supported by the simulation. Figures in the first two panels of Table II indicate that there was a difference in 1900, but not in preindustrial times. Regarding near kin, females 20–24 years of age in 1900 had on average 0.4 more kin than males. This difference grew to 0.6 among individuals aged 30–34, and stayed this large until age 45–49.[14]

[14]After age 55 it actually appears from both the 1900 and preindustrial runs that males had a slightly higher average number of near-kin than did females. This would be understandable for the 1900 run since males would be older than females when children were born and before such children would be exposed to the risk of mortality over a long period of time.

Regarding intermediate kin, females had an average of 0.4 more kin among the 45- to 49-year-olds. The difference grew to 1.8 more kin among the 55- to 59-year-olds.[15] In contrast, the preindustrial figures show no advantage for females.

Fluctuations such as the ones in the second panel of Table II, in which preindustrial males 45 to 49 are expected to have 0.2 *more* intermediate kin but males 50 to 54 are expected to have 0.4 *less* intermediate kin, are probably best interpreted as the cause of random variation in our estimates. Such random variation is both the advantage and disadvantage of microsimulation as opposed to deterministic estimation procedures. The random variation could be decreased if we were willing to generate a larger sample size.

Time Differences. Overall, the demographic parameters of the preindustrial population compared with the 1900 population shown in Table 9.1 led us to expect that the expected number of kin in 1900 would be greater than in preindustrial times. This was found to be the case, as shown in the last column of the four panels of Table II. There was a small difference in the number of near kin, of between 0.1 and 1.6 persons among the age and sex groups 5 to 69. There was a modest difference in the number of intermediate kin, between 0.8 and 5.3; and there was a larger difference in the expected number of distant kin, between 2.0 and 11.2

In most cases, the difference between the 1900 and preindustrial populations is the same for both sexes. There is however, one interesting and unexpected exception. Since there was little gender difference in the expected number of near kin in the preindustrial population but a noticeable gender difference in the 1900 population, there is a greater difference in expected near kin among females than among males in the two time periods. For instance, among females 40 to 44, there is a difference of 1.6 in expected near kin. Among males, the difference is 0.9, or nearly half as much.

C. VARIATION IN THE EXPECTED VALUE

Individual variation around an average is commonly expressed in terms of a variance, or standard deviation. We choose to report variation in terms of the population proportion without *any* kin of the specified kind because this is conceptually more interesting when considering kin to be a "backup net" in case of need. The proportion of the population without any kin is shown in Table III in the same format as the previous table. Since the population percentage without any distant kin (aunts, uncles, nieces, or nephews) is near zero among both sexes

[15]Among the 70- to 74-year-olds, in fact, one might be seeing the beginning of a slight advantage for males, but the number of cases used to estimate these means is not sufficient for confident interpretation.

TABLE III

Percentage of Age and Sex Groups without Any Living Kin of Specified Kind Simulated under Preindustrial and 1900 Demographic Conditions in the West, and Differences in Percentage between Sexes and Demographic Situations

	Preindustrial			1900			1900–Preindustrial		
Age	Male	Female	Diff.	Male	Female	Diff.	Male	Female	Total
Near Kin									
0–4	0.4	0.2	0.2	0.0	0.1	−0.1	−0.4	−0.1	−0.2
5–9	2.2	1.3	0.9	0.3	0.3	0.0	−1.9	−1.0	−1.4
10–14	4.2	4.1	0.1	1.5	1.4	0.1	−2.7	−2.7	−2.7
15–19	7.8	7.5	0.3	4.5	4.0	0.5	−3.4	−3.5	−3.5
20–24	15.2	14.6	0.6	7.0	5.5	1.5	−8.2	−9.1	−8.8
25–29	17.6	19.7	−2.1	8.2	6.9	1.3	−9.4	−12.8	−11.2
30–34	18.6	19.3	−0.7	8.6	6.6	2.0	−10.0	−12.7	−11.5
35–39	19.7	21.0	−1.3	11.2	7.9	3.3	−8.5	−13.1	−11.1
40–44	20.7	22.8	−2.1	12.9	9.1	3.8	−7.7	−13.6	−11.0
45–49	24.6	26.3	−1.7	12.8	11.4	1.3	−11.9	−14.9	−13.5
50–54	21.1	23.8	−2.6	15.6	13.0	2.6	−5.5	−10.7	−8.4
55–59	24.4	28.8	−4.4	16.4	15.6	0.8	−8.0	−13.2	−10.9
60–64	26.4	30.5	−4.1	19.5	18.9	0.6	−6.9	−11.5	−9.4
65–69	24.1	33.0	−8.8	19.4	17.9	1.5	−4.7	−15.1	−10.7
70–74	26.9	30.7	−3.8	19.9	18.5	1.4	−7.0	−12.2	−10.0
Intermediate Kin									
0–4	0.0	0.0	0.0	0.0	0.0	0.0	0.0	0.0	0.0
5–9	0.0	0.0	0.0	0.0	0.0	0.0	0.0	0.0	0.0
10–14	2.5	2.5	0.0	0.6	0.7	−0.1	−1.9	−1.8	−1.8
15–19	2.0	2.5	−0.5	0.7	0.9	−0.2	−1.3	−1.7	−1.5
20–24	2.7	2.6	0.1	1.0	1.3	−0.2	−1.7	−1.3	−1.5
25–29	3.7	3.7	0.0	1.6	1.6	0.0	−2.1	−2.1	−2.1
30–34	3.9	4.2	−0.3	2.1	1.5	0.6	−1.8	−2.7	−2.3
35–39	3.3	4.1	−0.8	2.8	2.4	0.4	−0.5	−1.6	−1.0
40–44	4.7	4.1	0.6	1.7	2.3	−0.5	−3.0	−1.8	−2.4
45–49	4.0	3.4	0.6	1.6	1.7	−0.1	−2.4	−1.7	−2.0
50–54	3.4	3.1	0.3	1.7	1.6	0.1	−1.7	−1.5	−1.6
55–59	2.8	3.1	−0.3	1.1	1.0	0.1	−1.7	−2.0	−1.9
60–64	2.7	1.9	0.8	1.4	1.1	0.3	−1.3	−0.8	−1.0
65–69	1.7	2.1	−0.4	0.5	0.9	−0.4	−1.1	−1.2	−1.2
70–74	1.5	2.2	−0.7	1.0	0.7	0.3	−0.6	−1.5	−1.1
Distant Kin									
0–4	0.0	0.0	0.0	0.0	0.0	0.0	0.0	0.0	0.0
5–9	0.0	0.0	0.0	0.0	0.0	0.0	0.0	0.0	0.0
10–14	0.0	0.0	0.0	0.0	0.0	0.0	0.0	0.0	0.0
15–19	0.0	0.0	0.0	0.0	0.0	0.0	0.0	0.0	0.0
20–24	0.0	0.0	0.0	0.0	0.0	0.0	0.0	0.0	0.0

TABLE III (*Cont.*)

Age	Preindustrial			1900			1900–Preindustrial		
	Male/Female		Diff.	Male/Female		Diff.	Male/Female		Total
25–29	0.0	0.0	0.0	0.0	0.0	0.0	0.0	0.0	0.0
30–34	0.0	0.0	0.0	0.0	0.0	0.0	0.0	0.0	0.0
35–39	0.0	0.0	0.0	0.0	0.0	0.0	0.0	0.0	0.0
40–44	0.1	0.1	0.0	0.0	0.0	0.0	0.0	0.0	0.0
45–49	0.1	0.1	0.0	0.0	0.0	0.0	0.0	0.0	0.0
50–54	0.1	0.1	0.0	0.0	0.0	0.0	−0.1	−0.1	−0.1
55–59	0.1	0.1	0.0	0.0	0.0	0.0	−0.1	−0.1	−0.1
60–64	0.1	0.1	0.0	0.0	0.0	0.0	−0.1	−0.1	−0.1
65–69	0.1	0.1	0.0	0.0	0.0	0.0	−0.1	−0.1	−0.1
70–74	0.1	0.1	0.0	0.0	0.0	0.0	−0.1	−0.1	−0.1

Note: Near kin are parents and children; Intermediate kin are siblings, grandparents, and grandchildren; Distant kin are aunts, uncles, nieces, and nephews.

at all ages for both demographic regimes, our discussion will be limited to the near and intermediate kin.

Age Differences. The general age pattern in both periods is for the proportion of individuals without any near or intermediate kin to increase with age from a low of near zero at ages 0 through 4. The proportion of individuals without any near kin (parents or children) at any age is greater than the proportion without any intermediate kin (siblings, grandparents or grandchildren). For instance, whereas around a quarter of both males and females 45–49 years of age had no near kin in the preindustrial population, only between 3 to 4% of the same age group had no intermediate kin (and only 0.1% had no distant kin).

Sex Differences. There are sex differences in the proportion without any near kin in both the preindustrial and 1900 populations, but contrary to expectation, there is no consistent sex difference in the proportion without any intermediate kin. Even more interesting, the sex difference for near kin is opposite for the two demographic regimes. In the preindustrial population after age 24, males are *less* likely to be without any near kin than are females. The high mortality of the preindustrial period means that remarriage was an important determinant of surviving children, and men were much more likely to remarry than women. In the 1900 population after age 20, in contrast, males are *more* likely to be without any near kin. The sex contrast is greatest between 20 and 54 years of age.

Time Difference. As was expected from the higher mortality pattern of the preindustrial demographic regime, the proportion of males and females without any near kin or without any intermediate kin is much higher in the preindustrial population than in the 1900 population. In the age groups 15 through 49, the proportion in 1900 is half or less as much as in the preindustrial population. For people 50 years and over, the proportion of the preindustrial population without near kin rises above one quarter whereas it does not reach a fifth in the 1900 population. The pattern for individuals without any intermediate kin is similar.

As a result of the opposite gender difference in the proportion without any near kin between periods, the period contrast is higher for females than males. The difference in contrasts is largest for the 40–44-year-old group, where it is 13.6% for females but only 7.7% for males.

D. THE KINSHIP LIFE PATH

An individual's kinship life path, in which his or her state at any given age depends on previous states, is very complicated because of the multitude of possible paths, even if one categorizes a number of different kin—such as aunts, uncles, nieces, and nephews—into the same category, that is, as "distant" kin. The finding of the previous analysis, that practically no one is without at least a distant relative, prompted us to hypothesize about a life path of kinship that refers specifically to the existence of near and intermediate kin only. We conceived a preferable life path to be one in which (a) both parents live during childhood (until age 18), (b) at least one grandparent is alive at birth, (c) one is married by age 49, (d) one has an adult (age 18 or older) child living at death, (e) one has one or more grandchildren alive at death, and (f) one's spouse lives at least until the children are grown (to age 18). We calculate this path in two ways. First, we calculate it for all individuals born. Second, we calculate it for individuals who survive to age 49. The choice of the pathway was arbitrary; we could have calculated many variations on the basic theme. The major purpose is to illustrate that such paths can be estimated with our model.

Table IV contains estimates of the proportion of males and females who encounter one of the life events mentioned heretofore, and the proportion who experience all of them. The results are predictable in direction but not in magnitude. There is no sex difference in the proportion not experiencing orphanhood and/or having at least one grandparent alive at birth, but more women than men tend to experience marriage by age 49, have an 18-year-old child at death and have a grandchild at death. Females were also more likely to become widowed before their children were grown. These differences are greater in the 1900 run than in the preindustrial run, and they are greater for everyone than when the analysis is limited to individuals surviving to age 49. The fact that women are more likely to experience early widowhood counteracts their greater tendency to experience other, preferred, events in the life course. In the net, the proportion of males and females who experience all the life events is virtually the same.

In contrast, the difference between demographic periods is huge. Whereas roughly a fifth of all individuals are expected to have experienced a preferred

TABLE IV

Percentage of Males and Females Born or Surviving to Age 49 Who Experience a Preferred Life Path of Kinship—Preindustrial West and 1900

	Preindustrial		1900	
	Male	Female	Male	Female
	Everyone Born			
Not orphaned by age 18	89.3	89.3	96.8	96.8
A grandparent alive at birth	85.2	85.2	95.6	95.6
Married by age 49	45.9	48.4	58.9	67.9
Child(ren) over 18 years at death	23.7	25.4	40.3	45.5
Grandchild(ren) alive at death	15.2	17.3	34.1	40.2
Single parent of a child under 18	9.3	11.4	11.5	16.0
Follow preferred life path	2.7	3.5	21.3	22.5
	Surviving to Age 49			
Not orphaned by age 18	89.3	89.3	96.8	96.8
A grandparent alive at birth	85.2	85.2	95.6	95.6
Married by age 49	87.8	89.4	86.7	92.2
Child(ren) over 18 years at death	61.0	60.3	71.3	74.2
Grandchild(ren) alive at death	41.8	44.3	61.9	68.4
Single parent of a child under 18	22.7	25.7	19.3	26.2
Follow preferred life path	19.6	19.7	41.5	40.3

kinship life path in 1900, only 4% did so in preindustrial times. Of those surviving to age 49, 43% of the males and females experienced the preferred kinship life path in the 1900 run, compared with about 22% in the preindustrial run.

Summary and Discussion

The purpose of this chapter has been to explore the application of life-course analysis to the demography of kinship. Demographic analyses of kinship inquire into the impact of macrolevel demographic processes (e.g., mortality or fertility decline) on the microlevel situation of individuals. This can be important insofar as kin often serve as an individual's first line of defense against economic and emotional destitution. Life-course analysis involves the consideration of individual states as dependent on past states. It acknowledges individual variation in experience. Whereas certain modeling techniques are not amenable to such analysis, microsimulation proves to be a flexible modeling procedure that can perform such analysis for males as well as for females.

The number of topics that can be addressed by a demographic analysis of kinship over the life course is vast. We chose to examine two contrasts: the general kin context of males and females during the life course, and the general kin context of human aging under the demographic regimes of two historical periods in the Western Hemisphere. We chose to extend previous studies in one or another way by (a) incorporating a life-course perspective, (b) considering males as well as females, (c) examining kin ties beyond the immediate family, and (d) comparing different demographic regimes.

A major finding was that differences between demographic regimes were much greater than differences between the sexes. As expected, given the lower mortality of 1900 compared with earlier times, the number of kin of different kinds tended to be larger, and the proportion of males and females without any kin of a given kind tended to be much lower in the 1900 run compared with the preindustrial run. A second noteworthy finding was that sex differences tended to be greater in the 1900 run than in the preindustrial run.

We conceived a ''preferred'' life path of kinship to include (a) having both parents at least until age 18 (adulthood), (b) having at least one grandparent alive at birth, (c) marrying and having at least one child, (d) having at least one adult (18 or more years) child alive at death, (e) having at least one grandchild alive at death, and (f) not being widowed until the children grow to adulthood. Whereas over a fifth of both males and females experienced all these events in the 1900 population, only about 4% did so in the preindustrial population. Among those surviving to age 49, the figures were 43% and 22% respectively. Although women were much more likely to experience the preferred events of having at least one child, having at least one adult child alive at death, and having at least one grandchild alive at death, this was countered by their greater likelihood of being widowed before their children had grown to adulthood.

Our discussion is only a beginning. We considered sex and period differences in the availability of kin in the West's past, under rules of kinship thought to have been common in the United States. It is our hope that future studies consider specific kinship relations in more detail, (e.g., parents and children only, siblings only, or the marital status of certain kin), consider kinship more broadly (e.g., include consideration of cousins, siblings of grandparents, or a fourth generation), and compare various patterns under different kinship systems (e.g., unilineal vs. cognatic).

Acknowledgments

The chapter was written with the assistance of NICHD Postdoctoral Grant HD 5 T32 HD07014 and Grant HD18788. The authors thank Shirley Mellema and Valerie Kelley for help in manuscript preparation and the helpful comments of several reviewers. Facilities of the Institute on Aging, and the Center for Demography and Ecology of the University of Wisconsin–Madison funded by NICHD Center Grant HD05876, are also gratefully acknowledged.

References

Baltes, P. B., Reese, H. W., & Lipsitt, L. P. (1980). Life-span developmental psychology. *Annual Review of Psychology, 31,* 65–110.

Barrett, J. C. (1977). Criteria for choosing between analytic methods and simulation. *International Population Conference Mexico, 1977* (Vol. 1, pp. 243–252). International Union for the Scientific Study of Population.

Bongaarts, J. (1981). Simulation of the family life cycle. In *IUSSP International Population Conference Manila, 1981* (pp. 399–415). International Union for the Scientific Study of Population: Liege, Belgium.

Bongaarts, J., & Menken, J. (1983). The supply of children: A critical essay. In R. A. Bulatao & R. D. Lee, with P. E. Hollerbach & J. Bongaarts (Eds.), *Determinants of fertility in developing countries* (pp. 27–60). New York: Academic Press.

Clark, A. W. (1983). Limitations on female life chances in rural central Gujarat. *Indian Economic and Social History Review, 20*(1), 1–29.

Collver, A. (1963). The family life cycle in India and the United States. *American Sociological Review, 28*(1), 86–96.

De Vos, S., & Palloni, A. (1984). Formal methods and models for analyzing kinship and household organization. *CDE Working Paper,* No. 84–30 (Center for Demography and Ecology, University of Wisconsin–Madison).

Dixon, R. (1971). Explaining cross-cultural variations in age at marriage and proportions never marrying. *Population Studies, 25*(2), 215–233.

Dunn, J. (1984). Sibling studies and the developmental impact of critical incidents. In P. B. Baltes & O. G. Brim, Jr. (Eds.), *Life-Span Development and Behavior* (Vol. 6, pp. 335–353). New York: Academic Press.

Elder, G. (1974). *Children of the Great Depression.* University of Chicago Press: Chicago.

Elder, G. (1978). Family history and the life course. In T. Hareven (Ed.), *Transitions in the family and the life course in historical perspective* (Chap. 1, pp. 17–64). New York: Academic Press.

Farber, B. (1977). Social context, kinship mapping, and family norms. *Journal of Marriage and the Family, 39,* 227–240.

Glick, P. C. (1947). The family cycle. *American Sociological Review, 12,* 164–174.

Goodman, L. A., Keyfitz, N., & Pullum, T. W. (1974). Family formation and the frequency of various kinship relations. *Theoretical Population Biology, 5,* 1–27.

Goodman, L. A., Keyfitz, N., & Pullum, T. W. (1975). Addendum: Family formation and the frequency of various kinship relations. *Theoretical Population Biology, 8,* 376–381.

Hajnal, J. (1965). European marriage patterns in perspective. In D. V. Glass & D. E. C. Eversley (Eds.), *Population in history* (pp. 101–143). Chicago: Aldine.

Hammel, E. A., Wachter, K. W., & McDaniel, C. K. (1981). The kin of the aged in A.D. 2000: The chickens come home to roost. In S. B. Kiesler, J. N. Morgan, & V. K. Oppenheimer (Eds.), *Aging: Social change* (pp. 11–39). New York: Academic Press.

Hareven, T. (1977). Family time and historical time. *Daedalus, 106,* 57–70.

Hareven, T. (Ed.). (1978). *Transitions: The family and the life course in historical perspective.* New York: Academic Press.

Heer, D. M., & Smith, D. D. (1968). Mortality level, desired family size, and population increase. *Demography, 5,*(1), 104–121.

Heer, D. M., Smith, D. D. (1969). Mortality level, desired family size and population increase: Further variations on a basic model. *Demography, 6*(2), 141–149.

Howell, N. (1979). Social structural implications of demographic parameters: Kinship ties and kinship groups. In N. Howell (Ed.), *Demography of the Dobe !Kung* (pp. 306–332). New York: Academic Press.

Howell, N., & Lehotay, V. A. (1978). AMBUSH: A computer program for stochastic microsimulation of small human populations. *American Anthropologist, 80,* 905–922.

Immerwahr, G. E. (1967). Survivorship of sons under conditions of improving mortality. *Demography, 4,* 710–720.

Krishnamoorthy, S. (1980). Effects of fertility and mortality on estimation of family and number of living children. *Social Biology, 27*(1), 62–69.

Laslett, P. (1972). Introduction. In P. Laslett (Ed.), *Household and family in past time* (pp. 1–90). Cambridge, England: Cambridge University Press.

LeBras, H. (1978). Parents, grandparents, bisaieux. In K. Wachter (Ed. and Trans.), *Statistical studies of historical social structure* (pp. 163–188). New York: Academic Press. (Original work published in 1973).

Lee, G. R. (1980). Kinship in the seventies: A decade review of research and theory. *Journal of Marriage and the Family, 42*(4), 923–934.

News from the ESRC Cambridge group for the history of population and social structure. (1985). *Local Population Studies, 34,* 8–11.

Lotka, A. J. (1931). Orphanhood in relation to demographic factors: A study in population analysis. *Metron, 9,* 37–109.

Maybury–Lewis, D. (1984). Age and kinship: A structural view. In D. I. Kertzer & J. Keith (Eds.), *Age and anthropological theory* (pp. 123–140). Ithaca, NY: Cornell University Press.

Monroe, R., Monroe, R. L., & Whiting, B. B. (1981). *Handbook of cross-cultural human development.* New York: Garland Press.

Olson, D. H., & Miller, B. C. (Eds.). (1984). *Family studies: Review yearbook.* Beverly Hills, CA: Sage.

Pullum, T. W. (1982). The eventual frequencies of kin in a stable population. *Demography, 19*(4), 549–565.

Ruggles, N., & Ruggles, R. (1970). *The design of economic accounts.* New York.

Ruggles, S. (in press). *Prolonged connections: Demographic change and the rise of the extended family in nineteenth century England & America.* Madison, WI: University of Wisconsin Press.

Santini, A. (1977). The family life cycle as a context for the measurement of nuptiality and fertility. *International Population Conference Mexico, 1977* (Vol. 1, pp. 371–387). International Union for the Scientific Study of Population, Liege, Belgium.

Sheps, M. (1969). Simulation methods and the use of models in fertility analysis. *International Population Conference, London* (Vol. 1, pp. 53–64). The Hague, Netherlands: International Union for the Scientific Study of Population.

Uhlenberg, P. (1969). A study of cohort life cycles: Cohorts of native born Massachusetts women, 1830–1920. *Population Studies, 23*(3), 407–420.

Uhlenberg, P. (1974). Cohort variations in family life cycle experiences of U.S. females. *Journal of Marriage and the Family, 36*(2), 284–292.

Uhlenberg, P. (1978). Changing configurations of the life course. In T. Hareven (Ed.), *Transitions: The family and the life course in historical perspective* (pp. 65–98). New York: Academic Press.

Uhlenberg, P. (1980). Death and the family. *Journal of Family History, 5*(3), 313–320.

United Nations. (1980). Principles and recommendations for population and housing censuses. *Statistical Papers Series M, No. 67.* New York: Department of International Economic and Social Affairs United Nations.

United States Bureau of the Census. (1975). *Historical statistics of the United States: Colonial times to 1970.* Washington, DC: Government Printing Office.

United States Bureau of the Census. (1900–31). *United States life tables.* Washington, DC: Government Printing Office.

United States Bureau of the Census. (1905). *Special Reports. Mortality statistics, 1900–1904*. Washington, DC: Government Printing Office.

Wrigley, E. A., & Schofield, R. S. (1981). *The population history of England, 1541–1871: A reconstruction*. Boston: Harvard University Press.

Young, C. M. (1977). The family life cycle: Literature review and studies of families in Melbourne, Australia. *Family Formation Project Monograph No. 6*. Canberra, Australia: Australian National University Press.

Reconstruction in Cognitive Development: A Post-Structuralist Agenda

Daniel P. Keating and Darla J. MacLean
UNIVERSITY OF MARYLAND
BALTIMORE COUNTY

Abstract

Much recent work in cognitive development has highlighted the problems of universal structural models, especially the problems of external validity and cross-domain reliability. We argue that this reflects a central weakness of structural models of cognitive development—in fact, a "cognitive problematic." To move beyond this dilemma, we propose a "reconstructive" project for the study of cognitive development. Within this reconstructive project, the phenomenological perspective (as in Gibsonian direct perception) and hermeneutic accounts (involving reinterpretation of existing developmental findings as well as cognitive socialization research) are integrated with more traditional schema-based models of cognitive development. Several examples from our own and others' research provides an initial introduction for this agenda.

The expansion of research in human development over the past several decades has been extraordinary. In this context, the increasing predominance of cognitive models is significant. Cognitive explanations of a wide range of developmental phenomena are proposed with increasing frequency, and the centrality of cognitive activity to much of contemporary psychological theorizing is apparent.

In this regard, an interesting paradox emerges. As cognitive accounts of development have increased in influence, there has been a concomitant decline in the cohesiveness of what is understood by "cognitive development." The range of possible answers to Siegler's question—"What develops?"—most resembles an ever-expanding universe. Even a cursory review of current theoretical and empirical work in cognitive development indicates the extraordinary diversity of approaches which have been generated in the recent past. The advantage of such diversity is self-evident: Given that we know relatively little about the origins, sources, and dynamics of cognitive development, we need to entertain many possibilities and to avoid closing promising avenues prematurely. The disadvantage is less obvious but equally important: As each possibility is pursued, it tends to establish its own isolated paradigm, and the opportunity for integrating the findings into a coherent account which addresses the initial question in a theoretically or practically significant way diminishes.

Indeed, many contemporary critiques of cognitive developmental research and theory focus precisely on this lack of meaningful synthesis, pointing out the inadequacies of a fragmented approach. In contrast, this chapter focuses primarily on a positive agenda, the eventual goal of which is just such a synthesis. We therefore draw on the analyses which have already been advanced, although space constraints do not permit a full examination of all these critiques. A selective review, however, highlights some key points in the current problematic of cognitive development.

I. The Current Problematic

The *external validity* of many theoretical accounts of cognitive development has been challenged from several perspectives. Two versions of this critique can be noted. Morrison, Lord, and Keating (1984) review the difficulties which have emerged in attempts to apply developmental psychology to the solution of real-world problems. It is of course possible to dismiss the Morrison et al. critique as arising from the inadequacies of the application process itself. That is, the failure of the research to generalize may be due to inappropriately conceived field research. For example, using cognitive developmental findings to write an educational curriculum may fail even though the findings are valid, if the translation into a curriculum is done poorly. Morrison et al. argue, however, that such an application failure may equally (or even primarily) reflect more fundamental problems with the generalizability of isolated laboratory findings. Such isolation is, of course, a problem for cognitive research in general, as numerous reviews have suggested (e.g., Neisser, 1976).

A similar validity critique has been advanced from the perspective of cross-cultural research (Cole & Means, 1981; Laboratory of Comparative Human Cognition, 1983; Luria, 1979). If our cognitive developmental accounts are intended to be universal, then an obvious test is the cross-cultural one. As is now well known through these and other reviews, such tests have proved difficult for universalist theories. Two rather extreme inferences from these validity difficulties have been entertained, and we will argue against both of them. The first suggests that structural or schema-based accounts of cognitive development should be abandoned. While universal, content-free schemas may be difficult to specify, we believe that knowledge-based schemas incorporating the cognitive socialization experiences occurring throughout ontogenetic development are likely to be important. The second inference proposes that there are *no* universals of the human experience. Clearly, this cannot be the case: The self-evident universality of human culture and human language are sufficient argument against this.

Partly in response to the difficulties faced by universalist accounts of cognitive development, and partly due to the failure of cognitive structural accounts to generalize *reliably across domains,* a number of proposals have been advanced to move beyond cognitive universals in the traditional—especially Piagetian—sense (Commons, Armon, & Richards, 1984; Feldman, 1980; Fischer, 1980). Though a variety of approaches have been proposed, several common themes emerge from this work (Keating, 1985). The notion of broad, universal stages which characterize children's developing cognitive structures—the traditional structural approach—is explicitly rejected. Specifically, the cross-domain generalizability of such Piagetian stage notions is found wanting, and different structural accounts are substituted. These newer accounts tend to focus either on within-domain stage models (e.g., Feldman, 1980; Fischer, 1980), or on more general mechanisms which "generate" stages, but perhaps do so differentially across content domains (e.g., Commons et al., 1984). These more "local" structural approaches do, however, tend to anticipate the possibility of more generalized accounts in the future, arising either from cross-domain similarities, once a sufficient number of different domains has been correctly modeled, or from the demonstration that a small number of structure-generating mechanisms perform adequately across different domains.

It remains an open question whether such generalization will be possible within specifically *structural* accounts. It may be the case that even for within-domain models, explanations which analyze competence at the level of the *individual actor's* developing cognitive structures omit some crucial factors. The attempt to abstract structural models of competence out of the variety of cognitive performances may require that we inappropriately ignore some crucial content and context factors. If so, then analyses of the social transmission process (which we will label "cognitive socialization") and the social nature of the content or skill (which we will call "hermeneutics") must of necessity be included in structural or schema-based analyses. Note, however, that in either case—revised structural models, or cognitive socialization and hermeneutic accounts—the work of modeling the nature and development of schemas within specific domains of knowledge and skill remains a necessary intermediate step.

Perhaps the structural organization of cognitive activity is not the best place to seek the universals of cognitive development. If we explore a more elementary level, that of cognitive processing, it may be the case that cognitive developmental universals can be identified. Further, it may be possible to arrange these processing components into a coherent model of cognitive activity at a more general level. Such "componential" models have been studied developmentally, both as "top–down" decompositions of complex tasks (Sternberg, 1977) and as "bottom–up" correlational analyses of parameters of processing with variance in complex task performance (Keating & Bobbitt, 1978). Both attempts (cognitive components and cognitive correlates) to construct "purer" psychological models of cognitive development have encountered significant problems (see reviews by Sternberg, 1984, and Keating, 1984). Sternberg has argued the necessity of incorporating social factors into an expanded "triarchic" theory, at least partly because the psychological accounts are empirically inadequate: They account for too little of the interesting variance, and it is difficult to ascertain that the components are content-free. The cognitive correlates approach has similar empirical weaknesses (Keating, List, & Merriman, 1985), and it may be that the weaknesses arise directly from the attempt to abstract "pure" processing (Keating, 1984; List, Keating, & Merriman, 1985).

We argue that a common problematic unites these concerns—external validity, cross-domain reliability, and the difficulties uncovered in attempting to construct a "pure" psychological processing model rigorously—and that we can best make use of the existing work in cognitive development by exploring that common theme in order to go beyond the problematic. It is in this sense that we have intentionally borrowed the philosopher's term, "problematic." Having encountered converging difficulties at the limits of our current attempts, we can use the central tendency within the set of problems to define our task. This set, then, is that to which the "cognitive problematic" refers.

The common theme which emerges is the recurring tendency to root cognitive developmental accounts *within* the individual, and to do so by modeling the individual as a closed, well-ordered system. Thus, such models tend to focus on *structure* as opposed to function (an alternative explored below, e.g., Dixon & Nesselroade, 1983; E. J. Gibson, 1982), and to emphasize the internal, subjective aspects of cognitive activity rather than its social components. Though we are in accord with the broad-based move toward "systems" accounts (e.g., Sameroff, 1983), the tendency to "enclose" the cognitive system prematurely in terms of purely psychological order needs to be guarded against. While an open-systems notion is complex, it may be necessary, in that the interactions of a variety of closely related systems need to be incorporated into a meaningful understanding of human cognitive development in actual human environments.

Similar arguments have been made from other perspectives, two of which will be briefly noted here. First, Neisser (1976) has questioned the necessity of positing an internal information-processing system through which all knowledge of reality is mediated. Hypothesizing such mediating processes and structures as necessary to the processing of all knowledge encounters both epistemological and empirical problems. Instead, he argues (following J. J. Gibson, 1966) that at least some aspects of the world are *directly* perceived. As we will argue, the Gibsonian perspective suggests that *some* content knowledge is always present, and thus the attempt to abstract "pure" processes or structures which mediate knowledge is an endless search. Specifically, the assertion that a hypothesized aspect of cognitive processing can be identified rests on the ceteris paribus assumption, which, for human cognitive activity, may be difficult (if not impossible) to assure in practice (Dreyfus & Rabinow, 1982; Trabasso & Foellinger, 1978). We argue further, however, that while direct perception of some aspects of reality is likely, it is *unlikely* that all cognitive activity is unmediated by schemas. Over the course of development, individuals surely construct anticipatory schemas to guide "information pick-up" (Neisser, 1976).

The second arena in which similar arguments have been advanced is contemporary epistemology (Dreyfus & Rabinow, 1982; Norris, 1982, 1984). In its most general form, postmodern epistemology concludes that arguments regarding the "truth" of our knowledge about the world, when pushed to their limits, cannot be adequately defended. Traditionally, post-Kantian epistemology has explored three "bases" from which truth claims can be advanced. First, the subjective basis asserts that we come to know the world that our *internal mental structures* allow us to know. Examples of this approach range from Platonic idealism, through Kantian categorical imperatives, to Piagetian logical structures (Keating, 1986). Indeed, most "cognitive psychological" approaches have argued from such a basis. Second, the objective basis asserts that the truth is "in" the social and physical world, and it imprints its truth on us (*tabula rasa*). Truth thus arises from a better understanding of the objective world; the subjective knower is secondary. *Hermeneutic, or interpretive,* approaches tend to assume this basis (as have behavioral approaches, though they have been less concerned with explaining "knowledge"). Third, one can assert that the subjective knower and the objective world are intimately "attuned to" each other, such that we perceive what is real, and what is real is perceived. This *phenomenological approach* (e.g., Merleau–Ponty, 1962) is explored developmentally in the Gibsonian model. Within epistemological investigations, each of these bases is viewed as asserting some "privileged" relationship to truth: the a priori knower; the "objective" world; or their inseparability. But these privileged assertions can each be undermined from the arguments of the alternative positions.

Such undermining can also be accomplished in a literary analysis of the assertions of "truth," as has been pursued in "deconstruction" (Norris, 1982, 1984). One common problem of deconstruction and the postmodern epistemological critique is that they share a tendency toward nihilism: If nothing can be truthfully asserted, then perhaps nothing is, or can be, real or serious. Our common human experience is, however, that there *is* a shared reality, both physical and social (which may itself be an outworn dichotomy). Understanding that reality, and how we come to know it, is a desirable goal for both theory and practice. This attempt to reconstruct human development is the goal of the positive agenda we outline here.

II. The Reconstructive Agenda

Indeed, an outline of this agenda is all that is possible here, for several reasons. In addition to the standard concern about constraints of space, it is the case that the agenda we propose is one that is to be defined as it is done, rather than a priori. That this is necessarily so will become clearer following the analyses to be presented.

By reconstruction, we mean both a goal for the study of human development, and a process by which we might move toward that goal. The aim is the integration of theory and practice in the study of development. As a number of commentators have noted (e.g., Morrison, Lord, & Keating, 1984), the distancing of theory from practice tends to be unproductive for both. As we will argue, it is precisely the success of practice which ought to be the criterion for theoretical "truth"—as is historically the case in mathematics (Kline, 1984) and physics (Feyerabend, 1975)—but this has been more difficult in the human sciences, given the problems of defining "success." Whether the airplane flies or falls is an obvious test of the theories by which it was built, but whether a particular child-rearing practice is "successful" is never so clear, depending as it does on the values and belief systems of those who judge its outcome. The construction of those values and belief systems is in turn a developmental process—both in terms of social and ontogenetic history—and thus *requires* us to understand development at several levels simultaneously, and ultimately to integrate these analyses.

Fortunately, we have a variety of relevant methodologies available, and useful empirical information which they have generated. In this chapter, we will briefly illustrate some examples of how the desired integration might be approached. With respect to evolutionary history, it is clear that humans do not enter the world as *tabulae rasae*. Here, the functional phenomenology of J. J. Gibson (1966, 1977, 1979) and his collaborators and followers is likely to be most relevant. The accumulating evidence suggests strongly that some aspects of reality are directly perceived. In the first section, we briefly review some of these arguments and evidence. But it will be clear from that review that phenomenology cannot address all the important questions. In particular, our understanding of and ability to interpret the world is based both on perception *and* knowledge; phenomenological approaches have not successfully addressed the connection between them (except to assert their unity). Thus, the radical phenomenological approach described by Giorgi (1985), although a telling critique of typical inferences from experimental psychology, does not readily explain how alternative accounts can be validated. As we will point out, this becomes most apparent in considering the problems of "misperception" (J. J. Gibson, 1977; Shaw & Bransford, 1977).

As noted, most cognitive developmental theories have presumed that internal structures or schemas of some kind guide or constrain knowledge and its acquisition. The agenda of these theories has typically been to specify the essence or nature of cognitive structures. No doubt much of the future work in cognitive development will involve the further elaboration and specification of such schema-based models of knowledge and knowledge acquisition. But such schema-based models will not be adequately built as purely internal structures—thus, our perspective is "poststructuralist." Rather, they will need to draw in the perspectives of both phenomenology and hermeneutics.

Why are both perspectives necessary additions? If the schemas are constructed to guide exploration in circumstances where direct perception is an inadequate guide to action, then they are likely to be sensitive to a wide range of ontogenetically specific environmental contingencies. Developmentalists have largely focused on what is "universal" about schema-construction, and have thus tended to ignore the investigation of how *specific* environments participate in that construction at virtually any level of analysis (Bronfenbrenner & Crouter, 1983; Laboratory of Comparative Human Cognition, 1983). Such a perspective—which we will refer to as "cognitive socialization"—requires an analysis of the social practices at many levels (in the home, in the school, in the culture at large) before we can hope to connect cognitive development with its socialization in any meaningful way.

Dannefer (1984) has contended that developmental psychology, especially life-span psychology, displays an "ontogenetic bias," that is, that models of development tend to ignore the contribution of socialization factors. That this is not *necessarily* the case has been argued persuasively in the rejoinder by Baltes & Nesselroade (1984): Their general model can accommodate explanations at the social level as easily as explanations at the individual or psychological level. But it is nonetheless true, as Bronfenbrenner and Crouter (1983) illustrate in a historical review of the available environmental models in developmental theory and research, that the connection between social practices and human development is woefully underspecified. To move this part of the agenda forward, we pursue two strategies in sections 4 and 5 below (on hermeneutics and reconstruction). First, we review several important previous approaches to the critical analysis of social practices, which might usefully serve as underpinnings for hermeneutic approaches to human cognitive development. At the same time, we briefly note some of their limitations as isolated analyses. Second, we illustrate with two kinds of empirical examples the form such analyses might take when applied to current work in cognitive development. The first involves the method of *reinterpreting* existing empirical work from alternative, social critical perspectives. The second offers several examples of the type of research which has been (and might be) conducted from the perspective of "cognitive socialization."

As will become apparent, we have selected analyses and examples broadly. We focus on describing phenomenological and hermeneutic approaches, rather than structural or schema-based approaches, because the former are largely underrepresented in cognitive developmental theory and practice. We use examples from developmental research on infancy and on aging to illustrate, we hope, the potential life-span generalizability of a "reconstructive" approach to cognitive development. We view reconstruction, then, as an ongoing activity which makes extensive use of existing developmental methodologies and data-bases, but is not restricted to them.

III. Phenomenological Priors

In the Gibsonian model we encounter a theoretical perspective which is the strongest break with structuralist epistemology to be found in contemporary empirical research. From this perspective, we need not posit a system which in some complex, analytic–synthetic fashion "extracts" knowledge from the incoming sensory information (Neisser, 1976). The preconstituted cognitive processing system implicit in nearly all structuralist accounts has no place here; instead, for the example of visual perception, the structure *in* the ambient light (the invariants) specifies to the animal what the environment "affords" (Mace, 1977, p. 50): "The optic array is taken as structure *surrounding* a point of observation." J. J. Gibson's (1979) theory of perception, captured best in the notion of "ecological optics," stresses the immediacy of the perception of reality. The organism is largely preadapted through evolutionary history to recognize directly the significance to the self of objects and events in a world which "affords" their meaning. Gibson (1979) defined these environmental "affordances" in this way: "The *affordances* of the environment are what it *offers* the animal, what it *provides* or *furnishes,* either for good or ill. The verb *to afford* is found in the dictionary, but the noun *affordance* is not. I have made it up. I mean by it something that refers to both the environment and the animal in a way that no existing term does" (p. 127).

If indeed it is the case that much of the world, particularly the physical world, is thus understandable to the organism directly and immediately, then it should be the case that even young infants will behave appropriately relative to the *meaning* of objects and events, rather than to their constituent parts: They should reach for desired but not-yet-grasped objects; they should avert their gaze or turn away from looming objects; they should perceive the unity of objects which behave appropriately, even if those objects are partly occluded in the visual field; they should avoid crawling on surfaces which do not "afford" support. Indeed, according to the extensive research reviewed by E. J. Gibson and Spelke (1983), this is what they do. Knowledge of such affordances, if evidenced early and consistently in an infant's behavior, would seem to argue against the Piagetian model of a "reflexive" infant. For these objects, no prior or concurrent action on the part of the infant seems to be required to elicit their meaning.

The contrasting notion that infants have ". . . an extremely limited and chaotic awareness of self and the physical or social environment" (Butterworth, 1983, pp. 1–2), was a popular belief for much of this century, reinforced by the dominance of associationist learning theories, within which the notion of cognitive activity was largely absent. A resurgent interest in specifically cognitive questions in the mid-1960s, spawned by the work in information processing on the one hand (Neisser, 1967), and by Piagetian theory on the other (Piaget, 1954), reopened the issue of cognition, its development, and hence the origin of mind. In this wave of infant research, largely influenced by the work of Piaget and his colleagues, the theme remained one of an initially *reflexive* infant developing through his/her action on the world into a toddler capable of *mental representation*. To the infant, according to Piaget: "[t]he world is a world of pictures, lacking in depth or constancy, permanence or identity, which disappear and reappear capriciously, in which the subject's activity is conceived as being the sole motive power" (1954, p. 3).

In recent years, however. accumulating evidence has raised serious questions about this view of young infants as egocentrically incapable of perceiving the world as the objective reality we, as adults, know it to be (Brainerd, 1978; Butterworth, 1983; A. J. Caron & R. F. Caron, 1982; E. J. Gibson & Spelke, 1983; Harris, 1983; Spelke, 1985b). Instead, an emerging picture of the young infant, and even the newborn, is that of an organism which, in many ways, is competent to experience its world directly and meaningfully.

A basic assumption of Piaget's theory is that "object perception is mediated; . . . there is no *direct* perception of the invariant properties of objects such as their permanence and spatiotemporal identity" (Butterworth, Jarrett, & Hicks, 1982, p. 435). Most of the early studies which investigated Piaget's claims about sequencing of the infant's behavior in search tasks in fact replicated his observations (Harris, 1983). More recent empirical reviews, however, focus on alternative ways of testing Piaget's competence inference, and make a compelling case that Piaget's strong claims about infant's naïveté are in error (Butterworth, 1983; A. J. Caron & R. F. Caron, 1982; E. J. Gibson & Spelke, 1983; Harris, 1983; Spelke, 1985a,b). Among the numerous studies demonstrating the infant's *direct* perception of many invariants of the object, two will be selected for more detailed description in order to illustrate the key points of this section.

Both studies focus on the basic object concept, that is, the infant's understanding of the permanence, identity, or constancy of objects in the world, *independent* of the infant's own actions. There are several reasons for the concentration of research effort on this question. First, the claim that infants lack a notion of the permanence of objects is, to adults, strikingly counterintuitive; Harris (1983) describes these as Piaget's "startlingly radical conclusions" (p. 715). Second, the object concept in Piaget's theory occupies a central theoretical place, in that it requires the increasing coordination of several developing schemas. This sets up a dramatic contrast to the Gibsonian claim that "[a]n infant's looking and listening and to some extent her feeling, smelling, and tasting are inherently coordinated for obtaining information. Furthermore, coordinated multimodal exploration, such as auditory-visual coordination, is functional very early and does not appear to depend on learning" (E. J. Gibson & Spelke, 1983, p. 4).

Because the infant may not be capable of demonstrating the most appropriate behavior—for example, reaching for a hidden object—how can we determine what an infant perceives or knows? It is necessary to employ more "indirect methods" (A. J. Caron, R. F. Caron, & Antell, 1984). Two features of infant activity are of special value in this regard: "[I]nfants are apt to show two patterns of visual exploration. They tend to look at events that are relatively novel and perhaps unexpected, and they tend to look at events that they also hear" (Spelke, 1985b, p. 358). This does not completely solve the interpretive problem of infant's visual preferences, of course; for example, when shown several novel objects, infants do not necessarily choose the most novel among them (McCall, Kennedy, & Applebaum, 1977). But indirect methods which make use of these tendencies in infant visual exploration can substantially enhance our understanding of information apprehended by the young infant.

Because of the difficulties with search tasks, Baillargeon, Spelke, and Wasserman (in press) used an indirect method to explore infants' understanding of object permanence. They examined infants' understanding of a "solidity principle": that an object cannot move through the space occupied by another solid object. In this study, 5-month-old infants were habituated to a screen moving through a 180-degree arc about its base. Each habituation trial was defined as the amount of time the infant spent looking at the stimulus, until a 2-second look-away was recorded by an observer, or until the infant had looked at the stimulus for 120 seconds. In this "infant-controlled" habituation paradigm, infants were considered to be habituated to the display when there was a 50% or greater decrease in the infant's looking time on three consecutive trials relative to the mean looking time on the first three trials for that infant.

Following habituation to the 180-degree rotation, infants were presented with two contrasting displays, one of which is labeled "possible" and the other "impossible," conforming to *adults'* perception. In both cases, a box was placed behind the screen, such that to adult observers, the box would be expected to stop the rotations of the screen. In the "possible" case, the screen rotated to a 120-degree position, where it then stopped and returned to its original position. This is of course what adults would predict as the screen reached the obstructing object. In the "impossible" case, the screen continues through the location of the solid object—the box—and then returns, completing the full 180-degree rotation, just as in the habituation trials. If infants have no recognition that the box has solidity, continuity, or permanence, then the "impossible" event should be *less* novel and therefore less attended to. In contrast, the "possible" event will be novel, because it is a rotation of only 120 degrees, which they have not seen previously. On the other hand, if they do have a sense of object permanence, that is, the "solidity principle," then the surprise of seeing the screen rotate "through" a solid object should result in longer looking by the infants, even though it is visually similar to the habituation display. The results are clear-cut: Infants significantly preferred looking at the impossible event, with recovery from habituation of about 15 seconds for the impossible event, compared with about 3 seconds for the "possible" event. Thus, Baillargeon et al. (1985) conclude that these infants, who have just entered Piaget's stage 3, are already beginning to attribute permanence to objects. It is difficult to account for their visual preference for the *habituated* (i.e., 180-degree) rotation, except to infer that they realize that the box continues to exist in its same location. Otherwise, they should prefer the new (i.e., 120-degree) rotation as presenting a novel visual stimulus. Second, they must attribute solidity as well as three-dimensionality to the box.

In another study examining infants' knowledge of the invariant properties of objects, Kellman and Spelke (1983) investigated infants' responses to partly occluded objects. At issue here is what expectation infants have about the nature of the partly occluded object, after having been familiarized with some of its properties, specifically motion. Infants were habituated to a "rod" moving in a coherent fashion, but which was occluded by a box in the foreground; the habituation criterion was again a 50% decrement in looking time from the first three trials. Having met this criterion, 4-month-old infants were presented with test displays in which either the connected rod or a broken rod were alternately shown (in counterbalanced order across infants). In prior experiments, the investigators ruled out simple preference for either the connected or the broken rod. In the principal experiment, adults would expect that the rod behind the partly occluding block is in fact connected: "Surfaces that move together rigidly are perceived to be connected in the places where they are hidden" (Spelke, 1985b, p. 331). Again, infants preferred to look at the object which is "novel" or surprising relative to the belief that the rod seen only partly during habituation is in fact unitary. That is, they looked longer at the broken rod, compared with the connected rod, even though the visual properties of the broken rod were more similar to what they had actually seen in habituation. Thus again, infants' perceptions seem to be guided by the invariant properties which specify objects, rather than by the superficial visual surfaces.

The two studies described cannot fairly be said to have established a full-fledged concept of the object within the infant. Taken together with much of the recent work in infant perception, however, a consistent picture emerges. The infant does not begin perceptual experiences with a wholly disorganized or confusing stream of incoming stimuli, which await the construction of an interpretive system to sort out.

But equally clearly, our mature understanding of the nature of reality goes beyond these "simple" affordances. As E. J. Gibson (1982) has noted, in reviewing much of the "Gibsonian" work in infant perception: "The affordances I have considered are quite primitive ones, such as a surface of support, graspability of something, substances of things, and the contrasting affordances of barriers and passageways. But affordances of things and events can be much more complicated" (p. 77).

What might some of these "much more complicated affordances" be? As well as knowledge about the permanence and unity of objects, we develop understandings of the functional properties of objects, and of means of grouping objects (that is, according to their function and to their semantic categories). Spelke (1985b) describes this move to more complex aspects of understanding in these terms: "Once we can recognize what kind of thing a particular object is, our knowledge about things of its kind allows us to apprehend aspects of the object that would otherwise be obscure" (p. 325).

As an attempt to discover the possibility of real knowledge in its phenomenological origin, though, some familiar problems surface. In particular, the attempt to identify in some final way the actual "invariants", or what is really an "affordance," results in a tautological oscillation: What reality affords is defined by what is perceived, and vice versa. The absence of an independent criterion for invariants is less obvious with "self-evident" aspects of the external world (objects, motion, and so on), but infants quickly move into "meaningful" exchanges with their physical and social environment. At that point, separation into phenomenological givens and constructed schemas becomes difficult.

The difficulty is highlighted in the problem of "misperception," or, as Shaw and Bransford (1977) term it, "the possibility of error" (p. 16). Misjudgments may occur, they argue, if the individual "elects to go beyond the information given.'' Such situations can ultimately be ''corrected,'' so that ''true perceptual experience'' is possible. This suggests a line between perception and knowledge that may be useful; indeed, ''cognitive judgments are parasitical on perceptual experiences'' (p. 17). Still unresolved, however, and yet necessary for an integrated, reconstructive analysis, is the problem of understanding developmentally the connection between the phenomenological priors of perception and the constructed schemas of knowledge.

We begin as infants ''to go beyond the information given.'' Consider two phenomena of infant development which seem at first widely disparate. Cohen and Younger (1983) and Younger (1985) provide evidence suggesting that as early as 10 months of age, infants begin to extract categorical inferences even from imperfectly correlated instances. At about the same period of development, infants look toward a parent in a strange situation or at the approach of a strange adult, seemingly referencing the parent to understand the significance of the situation (i.e., ''safe'' or ''unsafe''). The recognition that the situation or the adult is ''strange'' may be a perception, but the extraction of ''meaning'' goes beyond this perception. We would further argue, though not in any detail here, that there is common thread here: Infants begin to construct interpretive schemas about their world from a very early age, both in relatively more ''abstract'' categorical inferences and in the interpersonal domain.

This is why it is so difficult to draw any clear empirical distinction between Gibsonian affordances and schema-based accounts, except by appeal to an ever-earlier origin. Even this is not always decisive: Attempts to uncover more complex invariants in human neonates (e.g., ''numerosity'' in Antell & Keating, 1983) are themselves open to a range of interpretations which invoke more primitive processes (spatial spectral frequency, density, and so on). The performance of infants beyond the neonatal period poses even more difficult problems; the possible role of differential experience for schema construction has not been much explored. This tendency threatens to miss the critical Gibsonian insight, by merging the phenomenological necessity of an organism shaped by evolution with the assumption that this evolutionary adaptation yields a preconstituted subject, ''prewired'' with a richly structured and sophisticated knowledge apparatus, merely waiting to unfold.

Integrating this insight into a reconstructive agenda thus involves some modifications. These can be conveniently grouped as restrictions, on the one hand, and additions, on the other. The key restriction is to recognize that the Gibsonian invariants and affordances are really the ''phenomenological priors'' of human knowledge and cognitive activity, not cognition per se. Thus, the notions of neonatal or infant ''cognition'' (e.g., Mehler & Fox, 1985; Spelke, 1985b) may be somewhat misleading.

This recognition is evident in Neisser's (1976) notion of a perceptual cycle. The necessity of this cyclical aspect (exploratory activity samples objects in the world, feedback about those objects modifies schemas, schemas direct exploration) is even more apparent when we consider more complex cognitive activity than perception of the physical world. If schemas allow the formation of anticipatory outcomes of exploration, then it is also possible to have anticipations increasingly disconnected from actual objects—that is, images of things never personally experienced. These images, connected to schemas but historically beholden to the phenomenological priors (e.g., the affordance of graspability), are the "stuff" of cognitive activity. Further, these images can be "spoken." Discourse is then the attempt to share socially these images, whether "real" (as in the phenomenological priors) or "only" imagined (as in schema-generated but not immediately "real" images). Cognitive socialization may proceed quite rapidly, and hence the difficulty of separating direct perception from schema-based accounts of performance.

The implied research agenda for infant perception is thus straightforward, at least conceptually. It is of interest to specify more precisely the range of such phenomenological priors, both because they "ground" the perceptual/cognitive system and because they constrain future developments. Specifically, characterizing the systematic response patterns of infants as young as possible is important (Antell & Keating, 1983). When working with older infants, the possibility of constructed schemas being involved in perception cannot be overlooked. Thus, observations of differences in cognitive socialization (i.e., experience) before inferring invariants or affordances are also desirable. Intervention studies may be of great value, even at this early developmental period (MacLean, 1986). Such studies also highlight the crucial importance of understanding the early transition from phenomenological priors to schema construction, for which clearer understanding of the infant's environment and the infant's activity are central. We know relatively little about this crucial transition, especially given the difficulties of the Piagetian model (Harris, 1983). As with embryological systems, it will likely to prove necessary to integrate the structural and functional aspects of development (Sameroff, 1983).

The additions are as important as the restrictions. First, cognitive activity has until recently been investigated with the implicit assumption that socioemotional factors and motivational factors can be generally ignored; this assumption of "all else being equal" is, as noted above, in need of more serious attention. We simply do not know how deeply such factors penetrate even the most "neutral" cognitive activity. A resurgent interest in infant socioemotional development (Campos, Barrett, Lamb, Goldsmith, & Sternberg, 1983; Gelman & Spelke, 1981) suggests that the interpersonal interactions of infants are quite complex from a very early point. There is thus a strong likelihood that, from its earliest developmental instantiation, cognitive activity is thoroughly intertwined with socioemotional and motivational fundamentals. These socioemotional aspects are equally important phenomenological priors, and they surely contribute substantially to the quality of cognitive activity.

Consider only exploratory activity: It is reasonable to assume that it is a phenomenological given, to try to make sense of the world; but exploratory activity is likely to be met in a variety of ways, depending on the nature of the parent/child interaction. Thus, such exploratory activity may, through socialization, become more closed off in the child, in a defensive attempt to look for a secure base; or these activities may be rewarded as a laudable characteristic to develop (such as "curiosity for its own sake"). The quality of the interactions, and thus the affective tone associated with cognitive exploration, may thus become intimately involved in the kind and extent of generated cognitive schemas. Nurturance is thus an essential feature of knowledge, but we can understand this only by understanding its developmental history.

A second important addition to the phenomenological priors is what may be called the "sense" of one's body. Cognitivists (and to a large extent other psychologists) have often shied away from extensive discussions of the body (perhaps an internal or mentalist model has little use for the body, except its brain), but in many ways, the body is the ultimate self-referent phenomenologically (Foucault, 1979; Merleau–Ponty, 1962). One key exception is Piaget (1954), who nevertheless argues that truly operative cognition hinges precisely on moving *away from* the body, that is, from reflex to mental representation.

Included within this set of phenomenological priors is a hedonistic reality: We are capable under any cognitive or social regimen of registering pleasure and pain. Objective determinations of the specific features of this is less relevant; what we have in mind is that individuals are able to determine and to express what they regard as pleasurable or not.

Taken together, these phenomenological priors (of perception, of nurturance and interpersonal connection, and of the body) establish a developmental origin or grounding for the individual. They do not establish or validate any specific form or content of knowledge, but they do provide the starting point for its construction as well as constraints on its expression.

IV. Hermeneutic Accounts

The "cognitive problematic" (see section 1) has been critiqued historically from a variety of perspectives. One group of such critiques focuses on the analysis of social practices; in this tradition, the clearly relative nature of knowledge (across history, between cultures, between different intellectual traditions) emerges from a more careful consideration of the ways in which social practices serve to construct knowledge. This alternative perspective has been described recently in terms such as sociogenesis, as opposed to ontogenesis (Dannefer, 1984), or exogenic, as opposed to endogenic (Gergen, 1985). Though the role of social practices in the constitution of cognitive activity is clearly evident at a conceptual level among theorists of cognitive development (Baltes & Nesselroade, 1984), there has historically been less rigorous investigation of such factors (Bronfenbrenner & Crouter, 1983). Consequently, recognition of the importance of such factors, which has a long history within developmental psychology (Dixon & Nesselroade, 1983), has not much penetrated psychological models of cognitive development.

A key component of the proposed reconstructive project is precisely the role of cognitive socialization in the individual's construction of a cognitive schema. Thus, a brief review of perspectives which argue for the richness and diversity of such socialization is needed. Further, such a review connects these more familiar critiques to a reconstructive agenda for development. Specifically, they introduce the necessity of hermeneutic or interpretive readings of social practices as an essential element in understanding cognitive development and activity. Finally, the review attempts to suggest some of the pitfalls of an uncritical analysis of social practices, particularly those in which the "hidden" establishment of a privileged access to "truth" arises.

A. PRAGMATIC PLURALISM

In an important historical analysis, Dixon and Nesselroade (1983) describe the early emergence within psychology of the philosophy of pluralism, most clearly articulated by William James. The undercurrent of this perspective has continued within the discipline, bringing together what they refer to as a "tacit triumvirate": pluralism, contextual-developmental psychology, and multivariate-correlational analytical techniques. In many ways, this tradition, whose practitioners have implicitly eschewed epistemological claims, has been an alternative from the beginning of scientific psychology. The reasons for its historically lower visibility are likely to be complex, but among them would be psychology's preference for physicalist explanations (Keating, 1984).

Dixon and Nesselroade (1983) make a strong case for pluralism as the most theoretically advanced position within cognitive or developmental psychology. Its association with a contextual-developmental position, which requires careful historical analysis of both social practices and ontogenesis, reflects the interactive nature of schema construction. And the development of multivariate techniques, with the goal of providing rigorous tests of competing explanatory models while recognizing their inability to *establish* causal chains, is a significant methodological advance.

Within this valuable perspective, there is one problematic which, however, remains largely hidden: social power (Foucault, 1984). The pragmatic view hopes to examine the competing versions of human development, and choose those which are most adaptive or useful. This presents both a criterion problem, and a problem of who is empowered to participate in this social choosing.

''Adaptive'' and ''useful'' are empty terms until they are filled in with a specific content, but are often used socially without the specification of that content. The American educational system, for example, has been analyzed as being well adapted to the reproduction of a society hierarchically organized by social class, but poorly adapted to the fulfillment of individual developmental needs (Bowles & Gintis, 1976; Rubin, 1976; Sennett & Cobb, 1976).

Second, the contests between competing explanations of development must be presumed to operate in an open and free ''arena'': ''All such [interpretive] schemes must be allowed an opportunity to demonstrate their worth in the arena of intellectual inquiry'' (Dixon & Nesselroade, 1983, p. 139). The ethical necessity of this can easily be defended (e.g., Feyerabend, 1978; Habermas, 1975). But in practice, social power substantially invalidates its possibility. Even conceiving such an unconstrained discourse is difficult, in that experts are likely to claim the arena for their own, disallowing as irrelevant or irrational those ''voices'' which have historically been excluded from the definition of the arena.

It is in this practice that the radical possibilities of the pluralist, contextualist position arc historically lost. Restricting the arena, by excluding ''different voices,'' defuses the need to consider how social power operates in the very definition of the criteria for what is socially adaptive or useful. Opening the arena to different and perhaps less ordered world-views—which is admittedly not without risk—goes against the grain of social power. A careful analysis of power as it ''sets'' the pluralist agenda is thus a necessity.

B. VYGOTSKY'S DIALECTIC

The contextualist, developmentalist strain grew stronger and more influential elsewhere. A unifying and founding theorist for this tradition, recently rediscovered in American developmental psychology (e.g., Brown, Bransford, Ferrara, & Campione, 1983; Chapman et al., 1984), is L. S. Vygotsky (1962, 1978). Vygotsky proceeded from the assumption that knowledge is socially constructed, principally though not exclusively through discourse. Cognitive activity was thus conceptualized as ''inner spcech,'' the internalization of discourse—the interpsychic becomes intrapsychic. A full understanding of cognitive activity thus involves four levels of historical analysis: evolutionary, social/cultural, ontogenetic, and microgenetic (Wertsch, 1981). The last involves internalizations occurring over a short term, the cumulative and dialectical interplay of which become ontogenesis, in concert with the other historical forces. They also permit empirical investigation of the social construction of internal schemas.

Besides the useful importation of tools and methods (Brown et al., 1983), Vygotsky's influence is increasingly felt in the work and insights of his early (Luria, 1979) and later (Sharp, Cole, & Lave, 1979) followers. The central thrust of his contribution is similar in many respects to the American tradition of contextualism described by Dixon and Nesselroade (1983). Taken together, these two traditions provide many of the key methods and insights for a reconstructive project, particularly for a concerted effort to study cognitive socialization.

There is one key difference between them worthy of note. Vygotsky's (1978) model, in contrast to pluralism, does incorporate a hidden, hermeneutically derived epistemology. This is most evident in his central notion that human cognition is historically defined by the unification of tool use and sign or symbol systems (Vygotsky, 1978):

> [W]e believe that these sign operations are the product of specific conditions of *social* development (p. 39). A most essential difference between sign and tool . . . is the different ways that they orient human behavior. The tool's function is to serve as the conductor of human influence on the object of activity; it is *externally* oriented. . . . The sign . . . changes nothing in the object of a psychological operation. It is a means of internal activity aimed at mastering oneself; the sign is *internally* oriented. [T]he real tie between these activities and phylo- and ontogenesis [is that] the mastering of nature and . . . behavior are mutually linked . . . . (p. 55)

This internalization of sign systems so as to master one's own behavior thus reflects the social historical unification of sign systems with tool use or practical applications. In this sense, the origin of human intelligence is discovered in the social organization of production. Vygotsky (1978) is adept at generating fascinating insights and methods while submerging this "discovery of the origin." (This may have been a "socially necessary" claim; the historical context in which he worked, the late 1920s and early 1930s, in the Soviet Union, should be kept in mind.)

But two types of "privileged" access to truth inherent in the claim should be made explicit. First, Vygotsky's claim—that mind arises historically out of the social organization of production—may restrict the possible directions of cognitive activity, and in the final analysis may render such activity to be a subsidiary of social development. The reality of knowledge is ultimately in the social object—the forces and mode of economic production—and thus leaves Vygotsky's model of development open to exploitation from a perspective which would attempt to "direct" human development in such a way as to make it conform better to a "correct" analysis of economic forces. Human ontogenesis then plays second fiddle to technological reproduction.

Second, in linking sign use to tool use as the origin of human intelligence, it eliminates or attenuates the contributions to intelligence from the linking of sign use with affective and emotional aspects of development. It thus elevates an instrumental intelligence to a privileged position (as would be assumed from its role in the social organization of production), relegating to second place (or lower), or as outside intelligence, the development through nurturance and desire. Though the sign/tool linkage is an important insight for understanding human development, its elevation as the essence of human intelligence reveals the hidden hermeneutic that the origin is to be historically "captured" in the forces of production.

C. SOCIAL CRITICAL THEORY

A third trend related to both of the foregoing is the social critical theory approach most closely associated with the "Frankfurt School" (Buck–Morss, 1977). The work of two theorists within this perspective—Adorno and Habermas—is relevant to the reconstructive agenda. The first, Adorno's "negative dialectic," is accessibly described by Buck–Morss (1977). Adorno was suspicious of all attempts to establish privileged claims, whether rooted in an idealism of the subject or of the object, thus questioning both "structuralist" (especially Kantian) claims as well as the "positive" dialectic associated with Marxist analysis (and as hidden in the Vygotskyian sign/tool linkage). The method of negative dialectics, then, is to undermine critically all such claims by arguing its opposite: Subjective claims are confronted with examples and arguments of knowledge as being socially constituted; claims that the social object "produces" knowledge are confronted with a recognition of the inherently valid, personal claim to reality permitted to individual subjects.

It is unclear how this critical analysis (a negative dialectic) can move toward a positive description of development. While defending and maintaining the social role and activity of the critical theorist, it ultimately makes it unsafe to "speak" any version of reality. Buck–Morss (1977) argues that the transition from a negative dialectic to a positive agenda is left unresolved in Adorno's work. In conclusion, she implicitly answers negatively her own question: "Did the perpetual motion of Adorno's arguments go anywhere? [p. 190]"

The problem of ever again articulating a positive meaning in the face of such negativity is identical to the apparent endpoint of deconstructive criticism. On the other hand, the critical techniques, especially the close scrutiny of social practices, both discursive and nondiscursive, as a means of spotting hidden claims to truth, are valuable. As we turn to a more rigorous study of cognitive socialization, such techniques take on added importance.

Is there a safe ground to speak of rationality and meaning, given negative dialectics and deconstructive criticism? One possible solution is that advanced by Habermas (1975). From his perspective, the pluralism of perspectives is taken for granted, but the establishment of validity claims is not against an underlying metaphysical reality, but is judged historically against the practical value of any given perspective. This cumulative historical process may subserve an "emerging" universalism of perspectives, if a given perspective can prove its practical worth across many situations.

For this analysis, it is important to separate instrumental rationality, which applies principally to the ability to master the external, physical world, and "practical" rationality, which deals with social arrangements, as in ethics, politics, and morality. In the former case, there is typically a clearer criterion of success: As already noted, the plane flies or falls, the bridge stands or collapses, and so on. The validity of systems which permit accurate control (mathematics and physics are key examples) is *defined* by their successful practice—a case that Kline (1984) makes quite clear in the history of mathematics. For social arrangements, however, the task is more difficult. How do we recognize a successful solution? (This is the question that pragmatism avoids, by references to "adaptive" or "useful" solutions: By what criteria?) If they cannot be identified by a claim to metaphysical validity, nor to the application of correct methods, are we left totally adrift, with an ultimately empty relativist ethics?

Habermas (1975) argues that we are not: We can imagine a universalist linguistic ethic. Social arrangements agreed to as a consensus after unconstrained discourse in which all individuals are able to speak freely their own desires, are by definition "ethical." Thus, the validation of social claims is always against this (imagined) universal discourse. Further, Habermas (1975) argues that some such principles of thinking about social organization have emerged historically, and he uses as an example the developmental validation of Kohlberg's (1971) stages of moral judgment (Habermas, 1975, p. 73ff.). He rereads these developments in terms of social role theory rather than as the unfolding of an internal logic, and adds an historically emerging stage beyond Kohlberg's stage 6, in which he locates the criterion of practice for social arrangements in the unconstrained discourse of individuals capable of expressing their "true" needs and desires in a meaningful way (p. 102).

For the proposed reconstructive project, this embodies several crucial insights. The historical emergence of epistemologies is carefully argued, making new "idealist" claims hard to justify. It emphasizes the role of practice as crucial to the development of valid theories, and notes the similarity of this criterion for both instrumental and practical rationality.

Like its pluralist cousin, however, it does leave largely unmentioned the question of social power. This is evident in two aspects of the project. First, Habermas's too-easy acceptance of moral principles, such as Kohlberg's stages, as having historically emerged from a (quasi-) universal discourse, is unsettling. If these historically developed principles of moral action have emerged during the *actual* exclusion of "different voices" (such as those of women; Gilligan, 1982; Hartsock, 1983) from the discourse, then the acceptance of its "universality" is premature. Second, Habermas has not described how we are to arrive at a universal discourse in which "different voices," especially those of the less powerful, are to be represented. The constraints of social power would seem, at least superficially, to make such discourse improbable. Our fear is that the real and substantial difficulties of achieving this open discourse can be used to justify the substitution of a discourse among "experts," within which the voices of the socially dominated can all too easily be repressed.

D. THE FEMINIST CRITIQUE

A specific contemporary example of the "reconstruction," and an important emerging critique of cognitive developmental theories, is to be found in the "feminist" psychological analyses of Gilligan (1982) and Chodorow (1978). Gilligan (1982) seeks to: "[H]ighlight a distinction between two modes of thought and to focus a problem of interpretation rather than to represent a generalization about either sex. . . . My interest lies in the interaction of experience and thought, in different voices and the dialogues to which they give rise, in the way we listen to ourselves and to others, in the stories we tell about our lives [p. 2]." Gilligan's method is to re-examine the responses that girls and women give to the hypothetical dilemmas used in Kohlberg's (1971) research on the development of moral judgment. The empirical confrontation of Gilligan and Kohlberg is less important at this point than the conceptual distinction. She argues that the models of "ideal" developmental outcomes, specifically those which emphasize autonomy and independent judgment, represent predominantly masculine images of what is "desirable" for the mature adult. In contrast to this ideal, the "feminine" ideals of community, nurturance, and the maintenance of the social network, are viewed as developmentally less mature. Gilligan argues that these represent a priori rather than scientifically validated claims about developmental universals, and in so doing raises precisely the issue of how we are to decide in practice upon the criteria of developmental maturity.

Gilligan also draws on Chodorow's feminist critique of psychoanalytic interpretations. Chodorow (1978) argues that the presumption that girls, as a result of different early experiences with individuation, are less "mature" is a biased perspective. Instead, Chodorow argues (1978):

> [G]irls emerge from this period [of early development] with a basis for "empathy" built into their primary definition of self in a way that boys do not. . . . From very early, then, because they are parented by a person of the same gender . . . girls come to experience themselves as less differentiated than boys, as more continuous with and related to the external object-world, and as differently oriented to their inner object-world as well. (pp. 166–167)

The critiques by Gilligan, Chodorow, and others writing from a feminist perspective, can be understood in several ways. At a minimum, they raise the issues of content and context in cognitive development in a different light. If questions must be raised about the very *definition* of mature cognitive activity, then substantial reinterpretations of existing empirical evidence might be necessary. In a reconstructive approach, then, two complementary methods—reinterpretation on the one hand, and cognitive socialization research, on the other—can be used. In the final section, we briefly explore other examples to illustrate this approach.

E. SUMMARY

We argue that the constellation of social practices—whether regarded as the criterion for successful models of cognition; as the formative aspect of cognitive socialization; or, in the guise of social power, as the obstacle to discovering what may be "desirable"—requires far more careful attention that we have given it. This hermeneutic enterprise is the most demanding and least developed within the reconstructive project (cf. Bronfenbrenner & Crouter, 1983; Gergen, 1985), but, without it, our ability to understand anything about human cognitive activity is compromised. If cognitive activity is fully embedded within the larger social system, as these "hermeneutic" critiques as well as our own reconstructive perspective would contend, then such analyses of social practices are central to understanding cognitive activity and cognitive development.

V. Reconstruction: Some Examples

There are several levels of analysis at which what we term "reconstruction" might occur. One example is Gilligan's (1982) reevaluation of a self-contained developmental theory of moral judgment. She executes that analysis through the reinterpretation of empirical data. Our first example is a similar but less comprehensive analysis of a key issue in the study of cognitive aging. Subsequently, we will briefly consider some examples of research in "cognitive socialization," that is, the attempt to link analyses of specific socialization experiences to specific cognitive developments.

Are older adults' performance decrements on some intellectual tasks indicative of an underlying deficit in intellectual capacity? One claim that such decrements represent real cognitive losses is that advanced by Horn (1982). A crucial aspect of this claim is the distinction between crystallized intelligence and fluid intelligence. How sound is this distinction? And are the data possibly open to reinterpretation, and reconstruction?

In a lengthy series of studies, Horn and his colleagues have extended the Cattell model to examine the pattern of changes in adult intellectual functioning (Horn, 1979, 1980, 1982; Horn & Cattell, 1967; Horn & Donaldson, 1976). It is important to note that the distinctions between Gc (crystallized intelligence) and

Gf (fluid intelligence) represent constructs which continue to change with time and additional research. This necessitates a brief description of the current conceptualization of the distinction.

Excerpts drawn from Horn (1980) will perhaps best illustrate the difficulty of defining the Gf/Gc distinction with precision:

> The Gc dimension represents a concept that pertains to the universe of abilities that are most valued in a culture believed to be most essential. . . . [S]ystematic efforts are developed within a culture to impart these abilities to the members of the culture. [T]he Gc dimension is only a rough, fallible indicator of a complex latent attribute of intelligence. . . . The Gf dimension is no less fallible as an indicator of the latent attribute referred to as fluid intelligence. . . . The abilities that indicate the factor depend on learning, but this is not clearly a part of the systematic processes of acculturation. (pp. 294–295)

The key evidence for validation of the distinction involves two claims: (a) the factor-analytic pattern for a variety of tasks across different samples; and (b) the construct validity of the factors, in that they relate differently, and in conceptually meaningful ways, to other variables. A major variable which appears to be differentially related to Gf/Gc is, in fact, age, and thus age-change data are used both to explain developmental differences in intellectual functioning *and* to establish the validity of the theory used as explanation. The success of this bootstrapping strategy will be considered.

The first issue, factor-analytical validity, can be addressed briefly by reference to other recent reviews. Sternberg (1977), for example, argued cogently that factor analysis cannot, standing alone, be the final arbiter of theoretical issues about the structure of human abilities: It is both ambiguous and arbitrary. It is arbitrary in that the selection of tasks, samples, and analytical strategy can dramatically change the obtained factor structures. As one example, the exchange between Guilford (1980) and Horn and Cattell (1982) is illustrative. Guilford argued against the Gf/Gc notion, and for his 120-factor structure of intellect, through the use of narrow age ranges, with highly homogeneous samples, in order to obtain more finely differentiated, ''purer'' ability factors. Horn and Cattell (1982) countered with a claim that uncovering the structure of the broad range of human abilities required the use of a wider age range with greater heterogeneity. Not surprisingly, these analytical strategies yielded factor structures consistent with each theorist's a priori model. Similarly, Horn (1984) has vigorously attacked ''g'' (general intelligence), single-factor models (such as Jensen's 1984), on the basis that it simply reads the first principal component as meaningful, without any further analysis. In this way, he contends, one obtains nothing more than a miscellaneous collection of tasks with no real theory.

Factor-analytic evidence is ambiguous in the sense that the interpretation of the factor structure is not ''given'' in the pattern of factor loadings, but is rather derived from the theorist's inferences about what is being tapped by the tasks or tests which enter into it. The standard assumption about what Gf and Gc represent are indicated in the foregoing quotation; in the arguments herein, it will become clear that these are not the only possible, not perhaps the best, interpretations.

Before turning to the specific critiques, it is helpful to consider briefly the age-decline claims advanced by Horn (1982, p. 267). He estimates decline in fluid intellectual abilities at about 3.75 IQ-units per decade of adult development (from the 20s through the 60s). In contrast, per decade *increases* across the same age range in crystallized intellectual abilities—about 3.64 IQ-units—are similar in magnitude. Since these abilities are not considered to be entirely independent—indeed, they correlate at about .50 across several studies (Horn, 1980)—then the decline in Gf may be "masked" to some extent by the rise in Gc, and the increase in Gc may also be attenuated by the fall in Gf. Using a part-correlation analysis, Horn (1982) estimates the actual changes when statistically controlling for these effects. These suggest that the maximum "independent" change is about 6 "IQ-units" per decade, as a decline in Gf and an increase in Gc.

This same part-correlation strategy can be used to isolate statistically some of the key tasks, and hence inferred intellectual processes, which contribute to these changes over the adult years. This strategy is analogous to the componential approach of Sternberg (1977) or the cognitive correlates approach of Keating (1984), except that in this case the inferences are based on the *reduction* of the construct-validity correlations. That is, when intellectual "process" factors are partialed out of the age-Gf or the age-Gc correlations, the magnitude of the correlations is presumably reduced in proportional degree that these factors (i.e., "process" marker tasks) are accounting for the age changes in the Gf or Gc dimensions. The key process variables identified (and therefore those variables most responsible for Gc increases with age) are the factors: TSR (tertiary storage and retrieval) which is defined by tasks such as the *number* of associations generated by subjects in response to a target word; and USES, defined by the *number* of uses for common objects generated by subjects. Horn (1982) interprets this factor pattern as indicating more flexible access to a greater store of information in long-term memory, for older as compared with younger adults.

In contrast, the Gf decline is best initially explained by four factors: EOG—organization at the stage of encoding in memory (which accounts for much of the short-term memory involvement in Gf decline); COS—concentration-attentiveness, as in trying to trace very slowly; EIR—eliminating irrelevancies in concept attainment (which accounts for much of the incidental memory involvement in Gf decline); HYP—hypothesis formation in the 20-questions game. Partialing out any three of these four factors accounts for about half of the Gf decline.

The strongest version, then, of Horn's claim is that Gf (fluid intellectual abilities) shows substantial decline through the adult years, that these declines are real (Horn & Donaldson, 1976), and that they are largely but not wholly accounted for by declines in specific cognitive processes characterized as involving primarily attentiveness, incidental learning, alertness, and organization in short-term memory.

A. THE CRITERION PROBLEM

A thorough critique of specific tasks and their interpretations is beyond the scope of this review; nevertheless, an important general question is whether a consistent and meaningful alternative interpretation can be advanced for the factor patterns described heretofore. In other words, is the inferred criterion of what is considered "fluid" intelligence in the Cattell–Horn model the only reasonable way of interpreting this evidence? Horn himself seems to back off from such a strong claim; indeed, he has described fluid intelligence as being defined by tasks "readily accepted as indicating intelligence but are not so clearly indicative of sophistication as are the abilities of Gc" (1982, p. 243). The point here is not to belabor semantics, but rather to attempt to grasp the essence of the distinction in terms of some independent criteria.

The distinction clearly hinges on the role of "systematic acculturation": those skills thought to be subject to that process are defined as crystallized; those abilities thought to be less subject to such acculturation are viewed as fluid—in other words, "incidentally acquired," purportedly through greater alertness and more effective initial encoding. Both the tasks which are used to define the Gf factor—such as Raven's Progressive Matrices—and the process factors which account for its decline, are presumsed to be "less acculturated" than Gc tasks such as vocabulary or "esoteric" verbal analogies.

Is this view of the role of acculturation in distinguishing between Gf and Gc the only reasonable one, consistent with the accumulated evidence? Recent work by Scribner and Cole (1981), Olson (1984), and Johnson–Laird (1983) suggests another possible approach. Instead of being the most "culture-free," such tasks may instead represent the epitome of acculturation through formal education. What they have in common is the requirement that the test-taker be able to deploy resources to deal with decontextualized rules or "text" which have meaning *only* in themselves. Accumulating cross-cultural research (e.g., Sharp, Cole, & Lave, 1979) suggests further that the role of schooling in the development of such skills is central and perhaps necessary.

If this is so, how does this impact on the interpretation of the age-change data? "Fluid" abilities—which in this alternative view, are understood as the systematic acquisition of and acculturation into the schooled ability to abstract and deal with test as an object unto itself—would show decline because older adults are further removed from active involvement with such cognitive demands. Two expectations would follow from such a reconsideration. First, there should be as much or more *cohort* change as age change, given that the length of time in formal education has substantially increased in this society in the past century. Data reviewed by Baltes and Schaie (1976) suggest that this is clearly the case. Second, modest efforts at training such "fluid" skills should have relatively large effects. Training research programs by Baltes and his colleagues (Baltes, Dittman–Kohli, & Kliegl, in press; Baltes & Willis, 1979, 1982) suggest that such effects, even with modest interventions, are readily obtained.

Note, however, that these lines of evidence do not "prove" the alternative interpretation, nor disprove Horn's claims. Instead, they raise to a level of plausibility an alternative account, namely that "fluid" skills, as the fruit of formal education, can be expected to show the greatest decline merely as a function of "time since education." (The implications for other aspects of intelligence theory are also major, but beyond the scope of this chapter; see, e.g., Keating, 1984.)

In terms of overall construct validity, it is not clear that *which* of these interpretations is more accurate can be decided on the basis of the psychological performance data alone. Horn's (1980) reference to other types of data to address questions of construct validity is a clear recognition of this requirement. He supports the claim to different forms of intelligence not only through the use of factor analyses ". . . but also in the sense that they have quite different relationships to other variables that can help indicate construct validity" (p. 295). Given that the distinction focuses centrally on the role of acculturation, we contend that understanding the cognitive socialization expectations for *both* older and younger adults is crucial to theoretical progress in understanding changes in intellectual functioning during the adult years.

Further, the meaning of the task, and thus the performance-based inferences about competence, may themselves vary with age. As one specific example, the 20-questions game, the key task for HYP (see p. 306 above), may rest upon a different set of cognitive schemas for the 20-year-old science major as compared with the elderly retiree—and not merely as a "poorer" set of schemas for the latter. For example, given the older adults' generally broader knowledge base, they may form substantive hypotheses earlier in the questioning. Although this is not as useful a strategy in the constraints of this artificial task as highly abstract categorical narrowing would be, it is likely to be a highly efficient strategy in analogous real-world tasks. Indeed, Chi and Rees (1983) review a substantial amount of the expert/novice literature, and conclude that experts do in fact move to substantive hypothesis formation in an earlier point than do novices.

Older adults, then, may not be employing less efficient strategies or have deficient processing in general, but are inappropriately applying highly effective strategies from their own experience. College students, in contrast, may be characterized as in a "learning" phase, in which being an "expert at being a novice" is at a premium in their cognitive activity.

Such "reinterpretations," attempting as they do to link the specific experiences of individuals with their cognitive development, are both necessary and difficult. In addition, however, to this reexamination of existing developmental data from a perspective which emphasizes the role of cognitive socialization, it is important to suggest how original research examining cognitive socialization might be carried out. We first present two brief empirical examples, and then specify several general methodological guidelines.

The first (MacLean & Keating, 1986) relates specifically to the frequently reported age decrements in intellectual performance, specifically memory. In many studies comparing younger and older adults, lists of common words are frequently used in an incidental memory task. Such word lists, generated by the experimenters, may unintentionally incorporate age differences in experiences with the words. Differential ability to recall or recognize these words later may reflect different opportunities by the subjects to have used them, and thus to assist their recall. Worden and Sherman–Brown (1983) examined this possibility using general word norms from the 1920s and 1960s to construct their list of to-be-remembered words. The historical period in which words showed high frequency did interact with age groups, though the form of the interaction was complex. Overall, younger adults recalled more words, but older adults recalled more of the "dated" words—the words that had been high-frequency in the early historical period, and low-frequency more recently.

We followed a similar logic (MacLean & Keating, 1986), but sought to explore some additional features not examined by Worden and Sherman–Brown (1983). First, it is possible that differential norms of word frequency (derived from word counts in newspapers, magazines, and so on) might not be a sufficiently sensitive index of familiarity with the words. We thus used direct ratings by different age groups of the familiarity of words to derive our list of to-be-remembered words, selecting items which were highly familiar to both groups (older and younger adults), highly unfamiliar to both, and those which were differentially familiar to young adults and to old adults, respectively. Second, we wanted to contrast the typically examined age effect to a more directly specified "expertise" effect. Thus, we selected all the words from a defined field—business—and all the initial raters, both young and old, had either educational or occupational experience in business. In the memory study, we selected subjects at both ages who either had or did not have a background in business, using either educational or occupational criteria. These subjects then participated in an incidental memory task, in which they first rated the (shorter) list of preselected words, and then were unexpectedly asked first to recall them and then to pick them out of a much longer list of similar words.

The main results were quite straightforward. On recall, the "expertise" factor—a background in business—was strongly related to performance. In contrast to many studies of memory aging, however, there was no age effect, and age did not interact with background. On recognition, those with a business background were slightly but not significantly better than the "nonexperts," probably due to a ceiling effect. Again, however, there was no age effect, nor an interaction of age and background. When presented with a list of words *balanced* across age for familiarity and unfamiliarity (with "new" business words such as *arbitrage* and *modem,* and "old" words such as *celluloid* and *linotype* occurring in equal proportion), the generic age effect does not emerge. In contrast, the "expertise" effect is quite evident.

We do not argue on the basis of these findings, of course, that all age effects in adult cognitive performance are necessarily artifactual. We do suggest, however, that a more careful analysis of the possible impact of differential background and socialization experiences is *necessary* before seemingly straightforward "age" effects are interpreted. Reducing (or eliminating) such confounds for "pure" developmental inferences may prove to be quite difficult; even in highly controlled, "engineered" cognitive tasks such as those reported by Kliegl, Smith, and Baltes (in press), differential knowledge bases and experiences may well "creep in" unexpectedly. Age differences in image-generating ability, for example, may reflect true "process" differences, or differences in the range of relevant, usable images which can be drawn upon, or some combination of the two.

If *how* a cognitive system operates is difficult to separate from *what* it is operating upon within the mature cognitive actor, then perhaps it would be productive to study the cognitive system as it is *acquiring* some of those complex skills. The investigation of information processing might usefully turn its attention to a study of "processes in formation" (Keating, 1984). This is an admittedly difficult task, especially if our goal is to integrate the understanding of that cognitive processing development with a study of the social practices—especially discourse (Vygotsky, 1978)—within which it is embedded and from which it arises.

A meaningful context in which this might be pursued is the early acquisition of academic skills in a classroom setting. Not only are the cognitive skills of obvious importance, but there exist both models of the cognitive processing (especially for the central skill of reading) and the means to capture a significant portion of the "social practices" within the setting, especially the discourse between the "expert" (the teacher) and the "novices" (the students). Fox and Keating (1984) have reported a preliminary attempt to set the stage for such investigations.

The research design was an example of a "microgenetic" study (Wertsch, 1981): An initial assessment of developmental level with respect to the target skill (in this case, reading) was followed by an observation of a naturally occurring instructional session in the classroom. Following the instruction, a second assessment of the relevant skills was carried out. Of greatest interest were any specific changes in performance (on the rather carefully defined cognitive tasks, such as speed of decoding, literal versus inferential comprehension, and so on), and particularly any connection between such "microgenetic" or short-term developments and the coding of the instructional session. In this study (Fox & Keating, 1984), two second-grade (mostly 7-year-olds) reading groups were studied, one of which was high-functioning, while the other was a little below average.

The key results from this preliminary research are intriguing, though far from conclusive, for important reasons to be noted later. The instructional discourse in the two reading groups was quite different. The discussion in the low reading group is almost entirely about decoding the written symbols—the "meaning" of the text, either as literal or inferential comprehension, almost never arises. The reverse pattern is true in the high reading group. Even though these "good" readers do make decoding errors, these are rarely the focus of instructional discourse. Instead, these seem to be regarded as of minor significance for them (in contrast to the low group, where such issues are focal), whereas grasping the "meaning" of the text, and relating that meaning to the students' everyday experiences, occupies the instructional discourse. This is not surprising, of course, given that the current American reading curricula tend to be "bottom–up": decoding is seen as a preliminary basis for comprehension, so students who have not mastered this step are not exposed to the next task in the sequence, that is, comprehension.

What is interesting, however, is that the "instructional focus" is systematically related to microgenetic changes in cognitive processing. In a series of regression equations relating the before-and-after instruction cognitive assessments to the instructional discourse codes, it was clear that what changed cognitively was precisely what was focused on during the instructional session. The low-group showed significant gains in decoding speed and accuracy, but not in comprehension. The high-group showed the reverse pattern: little or no growth in decoding speed and accuracy, but substantial gains in both literal and inferential comprehension. If such clear relationships emerge even in a small-scale study, the possibility exists that much more of what we have considered as "fundamental" cognitive development might be better understood in the connections between cognitive change and the specific social practices within which it is embedded.

It is readily apparent that such an implicit causal connection is premature. The instructional focus of the classroom discourse is perhaps wholly confounded with the students' readiness. That is, the poorer readers may not yet be "ready" for comprehension, because their decoding skills are not adequate. An obvious and desirable experimental intervention study would be to reverse the instructional focus to see if there is a concomitant shift in the pattern of microgenetic changes. At the same time, however, we would need to examine the prevailing school practices in considerable detail. The confounding of presumed learner readiness and instructional focus may exist either because the curriculum is well grounded developmentally (though this seems unlikely, given the history of research on similar questions, as described for example by Farnham–Diggory & Nelson, 1984) *or* for a host of more complex reasons embedded in the larger social practices (e.g., Bowles & Gintis, 1976; Sennett & Cobb, 1976). What is required, then, for a reconstructive agenda in cognitive development is the simultaneous and serious pursuit of several questions: What is the developmentally most effective route (or routes) for knowledge and skill acquisition? What are the prevailing social practices with respect to these developmental processes? And, what is the relationship between these functions?

It is useful methodologically to note some additional constraints on the findings. Not all aspects of the social interactions could be coded, of course, and thus a priori theoretical judgments enter into what will be examined. The content of the teacher–student discourse was the focus here, although other aspects were coded. Also, the methods to examine possible effects are not at all straightforward: In some cases, the individual is the appropriate level of analysis; in other cases it is the group; and in yet other *both* are conceptually appropriate. One suspects that it is just such difficulties which have limited research attempts to link cognitive development to detailed analyses of the social situations in which it occurs. Specifying the relevant features of the latter and analyzing the connections are formidable tasks (Bronfenbrenner & Crouter, 1983), in which the elegant controls of laboratory experimentation can only be approximated at best. As we have noted above, however, the external validity threats to experimental methods are conceptually comparable with the internal validity threats (from lack of experimental control) to these methodologies (Morrison, Lord, & Keating, 1984).

B. SUMMARY

The "reconstructive" project for cognitive development which we have attempted to illustrate here with a few widely disparate examples is thus likely to be conceptually straightforward but challenging in practice. We have described two general methods of proceeding. The first is a "reinterpretive" strategy. Much of the existing research in development has proceeded from an explicit or implicit assumption that development could be viewed internally, largely apart from its social context. As Gilligan (1982) has argued with respect to the moral judgment literature, and as we have illustrated here with respect to the cognitive aging literature, such findings may take on a quite different aspect if viewed in their social context. The second strategy is to look directly for effects of "cognitive socialization" in the performance of individuals on cognitive tasks. Again, we have illustrated this with two examples, one from cognitive aging and the other from the early acquisition of skill in reading.

We recognize the difficulty of this inherently interdisciplinary agenda. Yet contemporary cognitive developmental research has successfully begun to tackle some of these important questions. As cognitive developmental theory moves further away from universal structural models, a "reconstructive" perspective which seeks to integrate phenomenological/organismic accounts, schema-based models, and hermeneutic/cognitive socialization investigations will prove increasingly valuable, especially for life-span developmental psychologists.

Acknowledgments

We thank Albert Caron, Kenneth Maton, and an anonymous reviewer for helpful comments on an earlier draft of this manuscript. The first author also thanks Paul Baltes for a kind invitation for an extended visit at the Max Planck Institute for Human Development and Education in Berlin, and for the opportunity this provided to think about and to engage in vigorous discussion regarding some of the ideas contained in this chapter.

References

Antell, S. E., & Keating, D. P. (1983). Perception of numerical invariance in human neonates. *Child Development, 54,* 695–701.

Baillargeon, R., Spelke, E., & Wasserman, S. (1985). Object permanence in five-month-old infants. *Cognition, 20,* 191–208.

Baltes, P. B., Dittmann-Kohli, F., & Kliegl, R. (in press). Reserve capacity of the elderly in aging-sensitive tasks of fluid intelligence. *Psychology and Aging, 1.*

Baltes, P. B., & Nesselroade, J. R. (1984). Paradigm lost and paradigm regained: Critique of Dannefer's portrayal of life-span developmental psychology. *American Sociological Review, 49,* 841–846.

Baltes, P. B., & Shaie, K. W. (1976). On the plasticity of intelligence in adulthood and old age: Where Horn and Donaldson fail. *American Psychologist, 31,* 720–725.

Baltes, P. B., & Willis, S. L. (1979). The critical importance of appropriate methodology in the study of aging: The sample case of psychometric intelligence. In F. Hoffmeister & C. Muller (Eds.), *Brain function in old age* (pp. 164–187). Heidelberg, Germany: Springer.

Baltes, P. B., & Willis, S. L. (1982). Plasticity and enhancement of intellectual functioning in old age. In F. I. M. Craik & S. E. Trehub (Eds.), *Aging and cognitive processes* (pp. 353–389). New York: Plenum Press.

Bowles, S., & Gintis, H. (1976). *Schooling in capitalist America.* New York: Basic Books.

Brainerd, C. J. (1978). *Piaget's theory of intelligence.* Englewood Cliffs, NJ: Prentice–Hall.

Bronfenbrenner, U., & Crouter, A. C. (1983). The evolution of environmental models in developmental research. In P. Mussen (Ed.), *Handbook of child psychology* (Vol. 1, pp. 357–414). New York: Wiley.

Brown, A. L., Bransford, J. D., Ferrara, R. A., & Campione, J. C. (1983). Learning, remembering, and understanding. In P. Mussen (Ed.), *Handbook of child psychology* (Vol. 3, pp. 77–166). New York: John Wiley.

Buck–Morss, S. (1977). *The origin of negative dialectics.* Sussex, England: Harvester.

Butterworth, G. (1983). Structure of the mind in human infancy. In L. P. Lipsitt (Ed.), *Advances in infancy research* (Vol. 2, pp. 1–29). Norwood, NJ: Ablex.

Butterworth, G., Jarrett, N., & Hicks, L. (1982). Spatiotemporal identity in infancy: Perceptual competence or conceptual deficit? *Developmental Psychology, 18,* 435–449.

Campos, J. J., Barrett, K. C., Lamb, M. E., Goldsmith, H. H., & Sternberg, C. (1983). Socioemotional development. In P. Mussen (Ed.), *Handbook of child psychology* (Vol. 2, pp. 783–915). New York: Wiley.

Caron, A.J., & Caron, R. F. (1982). Cognitive development in early infancy. In T. M. Field, A. Huston, H. C. Quay, L. Troll, & G. Finley (Eds.), *Review of human development* (pp. 107–147). New York: John Wiley.

Caron, A. J., Caron, R. F., & Antell, S. E. (1984, April). *Infant perception of a complex affordance.* Paper presented at the biennial meeting of the International Conference on Infant Studies, New York.

Chapman, M., Brandtstädter, J., Meacham, J. A., Mischel, H. N., Skinner, E. A., Youniss, J., & Baltes, P. B. (1984). Intentional action as a paradigm for developmental psychology: A symposium. *Human Development, 27,* 113–144.

Chi, M. T. H., & Rees, E. (1983). A learning framework for development. *Contributions to Human Development, 9,* 71–107.

Chodorow, N. (1978). *The reproduction of mothering.* Berkeley, CA: University of California Press.

Cohen, L. B., & Younger, B. A. (1983). Perceptual categorization in the infant. In E. Scholnick (Ed.), *New trends in conceptual representation: Challenges to Piaget's theory?* (pp. 211–247). Hillsdale, NJ: Lawrence Erlbaum Associates.

Cole, M., & Means, B. (1981). *Comparative studies of how people think.* Cambridge, MA: Harvard University Press.

Commons, M., Armon, C., & Richards, F. (1984). *Beyond formal operations.* New York: Praeger.

Dannefer, D. (1984). Adult development and social theory: A paradigmatic reappraisal. *American Sociological Review, 49,* 100–116.

Dixon, R. A., & Nesselroade, J. R. (1983). Pluralism and correlational analysis in developmental psychology: Historical commonalities. In R. M. Lerner (Ed.), *Developmental psychology: Historical and philosophical perspectives* (pp. 113–145). Hillsdale, NJ: Lawrence Erlbaum Associates.

Dreyfus, H. L., & Rabinow, P. (1982). *Michel Foucault: Beyond structuralism and hermeneutics.* Chicago: University of Chicago Press.

Farnham–Diggory, S., & Nelson, B. (1984). Cognitive analyses of basic school tasks. In F. J. Morrison, C. Lord, & D. P. Keating (Eds.), *Applied developmental psychology.* (Vol. 1, pp. 21–74). Orlando. FL: Academic Press.

Feldman, D. (1980). *Beyond universals in cognitive development.* Norwood, NJ: Ablex.

Feyerabend, P. (1975). *Against method.* London, England: NLB.

Feyerabend, P. (1978). *Science in a free society.* London: NLB.

Fischer, K. W. (1980). A theory of cognitive development: The control and construction of hierarchies of skills. *Psychological Review, 87,* 477–531.

Foucault, M. (1979). *Discipline and punish: The birth of the prison,* A. Sheridan (Trans.). New York: Vintage.

Foucault, M. (1984). Truth and power. In P. Rabinow (Ed.), *The Foucault reader* (pp. 51–75). New York: Pantheon.

Fox, M. H., & Keating, D. P. (1984, April). *Socialization factors in cognitive development: When context becomes content.* Paper presented at the biennial meeting of the Southeastern Conference on Human Development, Athens, GA.

Gelman, R., & Spelke, E. S. (1981). The development of thoughts about animate and inanimate objects: Implications for research on social cognition. In J. H. Flavell & L. Ross (Eds.), *Social cognitive development* (pp. 43–66). Cambridge, England: Cambridge University Press.

Gergen, K. J. (1985). The social constructionist movement in modern psychology. *American Psychologist, 40,* 266–275.

Gibson, E. J. (1969). *Principles of perceptual learning and development.* New York: Appleton–Century–Crofts.

Gibson, E. J. (1982). The concept of affordances in development: The renascence of functionalism. In W. A. Collins (Ed.), *Minnesota symposium on child psychology* (Vol. 15, pp. 55–81). Hillsdale, NJ: Lawrence Erlbaum Associates.

Gibson, E. J., & Spelke, E. (1983). The development of perception. In P. Mussen (Ed.), *Handbook of child psychology* (Vol. 3, pp. 1–76). New York: Wiley.

Gibson, J. J. (1966). *The senses considered as perceptual systems.* Boston, MA: Houghton-Mifflin.

Gibson, J. J. (1977). The theory of affordances. In R. Shaw & J. Bransford (Eds.), *Perceiving, acting, and knowing* (pp. 67–82). Hillsdale, NJ: Lawrence Erlbaum Associates.

Gibson, J. J. (1979). *The perception of the visual world.* Boston, MA: Houghton-Mifflin.

Gilligan, C. (1982). *In a different voice.* Cambridge, MA: Harvard University Press.

Giorgi, A. (1985). *Phenomenology and psychological research.* Pittsburgh, PA: Duquesne University Press.

Guilford, J. P. (1980). Fluid and crystallized intelligences: Two fanciful concepts. *Psychological Bulletin, 88,* 406–412.

Habermas, J. (1975). *Legitimation crisis.* T. McCarthy (Trans.). Boston, MA: Beacon Press.

Harris, P. L. (1983). Infant cognition. In P. Mussen (Ed.), *Handbook of child psychology* (Vol. 2, pp. 689–782). New York: John Wiley.

Hartsock, N. (1983). *Money, sex, and power.* New York: Longman.

Horn, J. L. (1979). The rise and fall of human abilities. *Journal of Research and Development in Education, 12,* 59–78.

Horn, J. L. (1980). Concepts of intellect in relation to learning and adult development. *Intelligence, 4,* 285–317.

Horn, J. L. (1982). The theory of fluid and crystallized intelligence in relation to concepts of cognitive psychology and aging in adulthood. In F. I. M. Craik & S. E. Trehub (Eds.), *Aging and cognitive processes* (pp. 237–282). Boston: Plenum.

Horn, J. L. (1984, March). *Remodeling models of intelligence.* Paper presented at the Gatlinburg Conference on Theory and Research in Mental Retardation, Gatlinburg, TN.

Horn, J. L., & Cattell, R. B. (1967). Age differences in fluid and crystallized intelligence. *Acta Psychologica, 26,* 107–129.

Horn, J. L., & Cattell, R. B. (1982). Whimsy and misunderstandings of Gf/Gc theory: A comment on Guilford. *Psychological Bulletin, 91,* 623–633.

Horn, J. L., & Donaldson, G. (1976). On the myth of intellectual decline in adulthood. *American Psychologist, 31,* 701–719.

Jensen, A. R. (1984). Mental speed and levels of analysis. *Behavioral and Brain Sciences, 7,* 295–296.

Johnson–Laird, P. N. (1983). *Mental models: Towards a cognitive science of language, inference, and consciousness.* Cambridge, MA: Harvard University Press.

Keating, D. P. (1984). The emperor's new clothes: The "new look" in intelligence research. In R. J. Sternberg (Ed.), *Advances in the psychology of human intelligence* (Vol. 2, pp. 1–35). Hillsdale, NJ: Lawrence Erlbaum Associates.

Keating, D. P. (1985). Beyond Piaget: The evolving debate. Review of *Beyond formal operations*. *Contemporary Psychology, 30,* 449–450.

Keating, D. P. (1986, May). *Structuralism, deconstruction, reconstruction: The limits of reasoning.* Paper presented at the annual meeting of the Jean Piaget Society, Philadelphia.

Keating, D. P., & Bobbitt, B. L. (1978). Individual and developmental differences in cognitive-processing components of mental ability. *Child Development, 49,* 155–167.

Keating, D. P., List, J. A., & Merriman, W. E. (1985). Cognitive processing and cognitive ability: A multivariate validity investigation. *Intelligence, 9,* 149–170.

Kellman, P. J., & Spelke, E. S. (1983). Perception of partly occluded objects in infancy. *Cognitive Psychology, 15,* 483–524.

Kliegl, R., Smith, J., & Baltes, P. B. (1986). Testing-the-limits, expertise, and memory in adulthood and old age. In F. Klix & H. Hagendorf (Eds.), *Proceedings of a symposium in memoriam Hermann Ebbinghaus* (pp. 395–407). Amsterdam: North Holland.

Kline, M. (1984). *Mathematics: The loss of certainty.* New York: Oxford University Press.

Kohlberg, L. (1971). From is to ought. In T. Mischel (Eds.), *Cognitive development and epistemology* (pp. 151–235). New York: Academic Press.

Laboratory of Comparative Human Cognition. (1983). Culture in cognitive development. In P. Mussen (Ed.), *Handbook of child psychology* (Vol. 1, pp. 295–356). New York: Wiley.

Luria, A. (1979). *Cognitive development: Its cultural and social foundations.* Cambridge, MA: Harvard University Press.

MacLean, D. J. (1986). *Infants' understanding of containment: Development within an object concept.* Doctoral dissertation, University of Maryland Baltimore County, Catonsville, MD.

MacLean, D. J., & Keating, D. P. (1986, April). *Adult recall and recognition performance: Knowledge vs. age.* Paper presented at the biennial Conference on Human Development, Nashville, TN.

Mace, W. M. (1977). James J. Gibson's strategy for perceiving, Ask not what's inside your head, but what your head's inside of. In R. Shaw & J. Bransford (Eds.), *Perceiving, acting, and knowing* (pp. 43–65). Hillsdale, NJ: Lawrence Erlbaum Associates.

McCall, R. B., Kennedy, C. B., & Applebaum, M. I. (1977). Magnitude of discrepancy of the distribution of attention in infants. *Child Development, 48,* 772–785.

Mehler, J., & Fox, R. (1985). *Neonate cognition.* Hillsdale, NJ: Lawrence Erlbaum Associates.

Merleau-Ponty, M. (1962). *The phenomenology of perception.* London, England: Routledge & Kegan Paul.

Morrison, F. J., Lord, C., & Keating, D. P. (Eds.). (1984). *Applied developmental psychology* (Vol. 1, pp. 4–20). New York: Academic Press.

Neisser, U. (1967). *Cognitive psychology.* New York: Appleton–Century–Crofts.

Neisser, U. (1976). *Cognition and reality.* San Francisco, CA: Freeman.

Norris, C. (1982). *Deconstruction: Theory and practice.* London: Methuen.

Norris, C. (1984). *The deconstructive turn.* London: Methuen.

Olson, D. (1984). *Intelligence and literacy: On the relations between intelligence and the technologies of representation and communication.* Unpublished manuscript, Ontario Institute for Studies in Education, Toronto, Ontario.

Piaget, J. (1954). *The construction of reality in the child.* New York: Basic Books.

Rubin, L. (1976). *Worlds of pain.* New York: Basic Books.

Sameroff, A. (1983). Developmental systems: Contexts and evolution. In P. Mussen (Ed.), *Handbook of child psychology* (Vol. 1, pp. 237–294). New York: Wiley.

Scribner, S., & Cole, M. (1981). *The psychology of literacy.* Cambridge, MA: Harvard University Press.

Sennett, R., & Cobb, J. (1976). *Hidden injuries of class.* New York: Random House.

Sharp, D. W., Cole, M., & Lave, C. (1979). Education and cognitive development: The evidence from experimental research. *Monographs of the Society for Research in Child Development, 44,* (Serial No. 178).

Shaw, R., & Bransford, J. (1977). Introduction: Psychological approaches to the problem of knowledge: In R. Shaw & J. Bransford (Eds.), *Perceiving, acting, and knowing* (pp. 1–39). Hillsdale, NJ: Lawrence Erlbaum Associates.

Siegler, R. S. (1978). *Children's thinking: What develops?* Hillsdale, NJ: Lawrence Erlbaum Associates.

Spelke, E. S. (1985a). Perception of unity, persistence, and identity: Thoughts on infants' conceptions of objects. In J. Mehler & R. Fox (Eds.), *Neonate cognition* (pp. 89–114). Hillsdale, NJ: Lawrence Erlbaum Associates.

Spelke, E. S. (1985b). Preferential-looking methods as tools for the study of cognition in infancy. In G. Gottlieb & N. Krasnegor (Eds.), *Measurement of audition and vision in the first year of postnatal life* (pp. 323–363). Norwood, NJ: Ablex.

Sternberg, R. J. (1977). *Intelligence, information processing. and analogical reasoning: The componential analysis of human abilities.* Hillsdale, NJ: Lawrence Erlbaum Associates.

Sternberg, R. J. (1984). Toward a triarchic theory of human intelligence. *Behavioral and Brain Sciences, 7,* 269–315.

Trabasso, T., & Foellinger, D. B. (1978). Information processing capacity in children: A test of Pascual–Leone's model. *Journal of Experimental Child Psychology, 26,* 1–17.

Vygotsky, L. S. (1962). *Thought and language.* Cambridge, MA: MIT Press.

Vygotsky, L. S. (1978). *Mind in society.* Cambridge, MA: Harvard University Press.

Wertsch, J. (1981). *The concept of activity in Soviet psychology.* Armonk, NY: Sharpe.

Worden, P. E., & Sherman–Brown, S. (1983). A word-frequency cohort effect in young versus elderly adults' memory for words. *Developmental Psychology, 19,* 521–530.

Younger, B. A. (1985). The segregation of items into categories by ten-month-old infants. *Child Development, 56,* 1574–1583.

Author Index

Numbers in *italics* indicate pages with complete bibliographic information.

C

L

M

Y,Z

Subject Index

Page numbers followed by n indicate footnotes.

C

D

E

I

J

K

L

Q

R

S

T